Developing Innovation Systems

Science, Technology and the International Political Economy

Series Editor: John de la Mothe

The upheavals of the international political economy during recent decades have fundamentally altered the relationships between firms and states, citizenship and management, social institutions and economic growth. The changing pace of competition, firm performance and geo-economics is shifting the pressures on public policy and corporate strategy alike. As a result, our conceptual frameworks for analysing key events, emerging trends and driving forces are being challenged. As unclear as the future is, what remains certain is that science, technology and innovation will occupy a central place. By looking at a wide array of issues – ranging from security and foreign affairs, the environment, international institutions, corporate strategy and regional development to research policy, innovation gaps, intellectual property, ethics and law – this series will critically examine how science and technology are shaping the emerging international political economy.

Published titles in the series:

The Complexity Challenge by Robert W. Rycroft and Don E. Kash

Evolutionary Economics and the New International Political Economy edited by John de la Mothe and Gilles Paquet

Global Change and Intellectual Property Agencies by G. Bruce Doern

The Governance of Innovation in Europe by Philip Cooke, Patries Boekholt and Franz Tödtling

Regional Innovation, Knowledge and Global Change edited by Zoltan Acs

Services and the Knowledge-Based Economy edited by Ian Miles and Mark Boden

Systems of Innovation edited by Charles Edquist

Universities and the Global Knowledge Economy edited by Henry Etzkowitz and Loet Leydesdorff

Forthcoming titles in the series:

Innovation Strategies in Middle Power Countries edited by John de la Mothe and Gilles Paquet

Science Technology and Governance edited by John de la Mothe

Proposals for books can be sent directly to the series editor:
  John de la Mothe
  Program of Research on International Management and Economy (PRIME)
  Faculty of Administration
  University of Ottawa
  275 Nicholas Street
  Ottawa, Canada K1N 6N5

Developing Innovation Systems

Mexico in a Global Context

Edited by
M. Cimoli

CONTINUUM

London and New York

Science, Technology and the International Political Economy Series
Series Editor: John de la Mothe

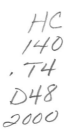
Continuum
The Tower Building, 11 York Road, London SE1 7NX
370 Lexington Avenue, New York, NY 10017–6503

First published 2000

© M. Cimoli and contributors 2000

British Library Cataloguing-in-Publication Data
A catalogue record for this book is available from the British Library.

ISBN 0-8264-4768-6

Library of Congress Cataloging-in-Publication Data
Developing innovation systems: Mexico in a global context/edited by M. Cimoli.
    p. cm. – (Science, technology and international political economy series)
    ISBN 0-8264-4768-6
    1. Industries–Technological innovations–Mexico. 2. Industrial policy–Mexico. 3. Technological innovations–Economic aspects–Mexico. 4. Technological innovations–Government policy–Mexico.
I. Cimoli, Mario. II. Science, technology, and the international political economy series.

HC140.T4 D48 2000
338.972–DC21   00-035835

Typeset by YHT, London

Printed and bound in Great Britain by TJ International, Padstow

Contents

List of Figures   ix
List of Tables   x
List of Contributors   xii
Acknowledgements   xiv

1. Developing Innovation Systems   1
    M. Cimoli
    Introduction   1
    Technological capabilities and development process   2
    National innovation systems: main building blocks and linkages   7
    A model of integration for the Mexican innovation system   12

**Part I: Macroeconomic Setting, Production System and
           Globalization of Technology**

2. Macroeconomic Setting and Production System   23
    M. Cimoli
    Productivity, investment and sectoral patterns   23
    The Mexican economy: a new scenario and performances   26

3. The Macroeconomic Setting for Innovation   32
    J. Fernandez
    Introduction   32
    Import substitution industrialization (ISI) period   33
    Transition period and abandonment of the ISI pattern   37
    New regulatory framework: deregulation and trade reform   41
    Conclusions   52

4. Production System and Technological Patterns   57
    M. Capdevielle, J. M. Corona and C. Hernandez
    Introduction   57
    The structure of the production system and its performance   58
    Sectoral technological patterns of efforts and competencies   70
    Conclusions   75

5. Globalization of Production and Technology   81
    K. Unger and M. Oloriz
    Introduction   81

FF and NF: their international and domestic linkages   83
The importance of foreign firms and foreign investments   86
Foreign technological sources   88
Fixed capital investment   89
R&D activities and technology transfer   91
Technology embodied in equipment and intermediates   94
Conclusions: a sectoral cluster analysis of global and localized
   technological flows   95

Part II: Institutional Infrastructure and Networks

6.   Institutions and the National Innovation System: an Introduction   103
     M. Cimoli
     The concept of institutions and their role in the NIS   103
     Institutions in the Mexican innovation system   105

7.   The Institutional Matrix and Its Main Functional Activities
         Supporting Innovation   109
     M. Casalet
     Introduction   109
     Historical path of the Mexican institutions   110
     Institutions and modernization: a new interactive pattern   111
     Functional matrix of Mexican institutions   114
     The SEP-CONACYT system centres   120
     Conclusions   122
     Appendix: a note on intellectual property rights (*J. Aboites and
        M. Soria*)   134

8.   Human Resources and Competencies   137
     G. Valenti, G. Varela and G. del Castillo
     Introduction   137
     HRST and their linkages with the NIS   138
     Governmental policies   139
     Government expenditure on education   140
     Human resources in science and technology   142
     Primary, lower secondary level and enrolment in HEIs   142
     Flows in the HEIs by field of knowledge   144
     Interplay with the production system   147
     Conclusions   149

9.   University, Knowledge Production and Collaborative Patterns
         with Industry   154
     R. Casas, R. de Gortari and M. Luna
     Introduction   154
     Evolution and current trends of science competencies   155
     The magnitude of university–industry collaboration: some
        indicators   159

The dynamics of university–industry collaboration   163
Taxonomy of university–industry collaboration   166
Conclusions   169

Part III: Sectoral and Regional Innovation Systems

10. Co-evolution and Innovation Systems   175
    M. Cimoli
    Introduction   175
    Production system and institutions: a co-evolutionary path   175
    The sectoral system of innovation: a clustering approach   185

11. Learning and Innovation in the Chemical Industry   189
    R. Arvanitis and D. Villavicencio
    Introduction   189
    Overview of the chemical innovation system worldwide   190
    Some general characteristics of the chemical industry   192
    The learning capabilities in chemical firms   195
    Clusters of companies in the chemical industry   198
    Conclusions   204

12. The Pharmaceutical Industry   206
    R. Gonsen and J. Jasso
    Introduction: characteristics and performance   206
    The pharmaceutical innovation system   209
    Conclusions: technological regime   214

13. The Case of Biotechnology   218
    R. Gonsen
    Introduction   218
    Institutional framework and technological capabilities   218
    Technological regime of biotechnology   222

14. Strategies and Technological Capabilities in a Multinational
    Mexican Firm   226
    G. Dutrénit
    Introduction   226
    The industry   227
    Profile of the case study   231
    The capability building process and the dual and unstable
      technology strategy   232
    Conclusions   239

15. The Automobile Sector   243
    R. Constantino and A. Lara
    Introduction   243
    The path of the Mexican automobile sector   245

Cumulativeness and improving performance	246
The automobile innovation system	248
Conclusions	258

16. Regional and Local Systems of Innovation in Aguascalientes — 262
    G. Abdel Musik

Introduction	262
Framework: regional clusters in the national system	263
ISI period: creation of basic infrastructure	265
Transition period: close contact between large firms	268
New regulatory framework: upgrading of technological capabilities	270
Conclusions	274

17. Conclusions: an Appreciative Pattern of the Mexican Innovation
    System — 278
    M. Cimoli

Stylized fact: towards a modernized assembly plant	278
The Mexican NIS: consequences of forging ahead, catching up and falling behind	287
Final remarks	290

Bibliography	293
Index	313

Figures

1.1   The Integrative Model for the Mexican Innovation System   15

1.2   Levels of Analysis and the Main Building Blocks in the Mexican Innovation System   18

4.1   Distribution of Added Value in Terms of Technological Sectors for the Mexican and US Manufacturing Industries, 1970–1994   61

4.2   Average Labour Productivity (a) and Average Total Factor Productivity (b) for Each Technological Sector, 1970–1994   63

4.3   Description of the Production System: Technological Effort, Performance and Gaps   76

5.1   Globalization of the Mexican NIS, Technological Flows and Sectors   98

7.1   Evolutionary Path of the Mexican Institutions Supporting Innovation   110

7.2   Mexican Institutions: a Non-articulated Network   124

10.1   Co-evolution of Production System and Institutions   177

11.1   Internal Technological Learning Activities   195

11.2   External Technological Linkages of Companies   198

15.1   User–Producer Linkages in the Mexican Automobile Cluster   248

15.2   Institutional Cluster: Automobile Industry and Auto Parts   256

16.1   Technological Capabilities and Degree of Internationalization   264

16.2   Summary of the Situation at the End of the ISI Period   267

16.3   Summary of the Situation at the End of the Transition Period   269

16.4   Summary of the Situation after the NAFTA   273

17.1   Mexican Technological Capabilities   286

17.2   NIS, Trade Growth Performance and Catching Up   288

Tables

2.1	Macroeconomic Indicators	27
4.1	Added Value Shares in the Mexican and US Manufacturing Industries, 1970–1994	59
4.2	International Trade, 1990–1998	69
4.3	R&D Shares in Mexican and US Manufacturing Industries, 1989–1991	72
4.4	Sectoral R&D Shares in Terms of Mexican and US Manufacturing GDP, 1989–1991	73
4.5	Matrix of Knowledge Flows from User to Producer	75
5.1	Economic and Technological Indicators	83
5.2	Manufactures Output of Foreign Firms, Exports and Imports, 1988–1993	84
5.3	Imports, Exports, R&D and Technology Transfer According to Market Orientation, 1991	85
5.4	Investment, Capital Intensity and Labour Productivity in Foreign and National Firms, Proportional Variation, 1993–1998	90
7.1	Functional Matrix of Mexican Institutions Supporting Innovation	115
7.2	Programmes Oriented to Supporting Industrialization and Technology	125
7.3	Specialized Research Institutions	128
7.4	General Information on the SEP-CONACYT System Centres	130
7.5	Institutions Providing Information and Reducing Uncertainty	131
8.1	Major Expenditure Indicators on Education and R&D	141
8.2	Indicators of Human Resources	143
9.1	Taxonomy of Science-based University–Industry Collaborations	168
10.1	The Main Characteristics of Modernization Processes in Mexico, 1989–1991	181
11.1	Comparison of General Characteristics of the Chemical Industry in Industrialized Countries and Mexico	192
11.2	Firms, Markets and Technological Regimes of the Clusters in the Chemical Industry	200
12.1	Linkages and Institutional Framework in the Pharmaceutical Industry	211
12.2	Technological Regime: a Cluster of the Pharmaceutical Industry	215
13.1	Technological Regime: Biotechnology	222
13.2	Inventors' Certificates in Biotechnology, Mexico, 1980–1988	224

15.1   Composition of the Mexican Automobile Sector   244
15.2   Sources of Knowledge in the Automobile Sector   251
15.3   Technological Regime: a Cluster of the Automobile Sector   259

Contributors

Jaime Aboites is Professor in the Economics Department of the Metropolitan Autonomous University–Xochimilco (UAM–X), Mexico City.

Rigas Arvanitis is researcher at the Institut de Recherche pour le Développement (IRD), Paris.

Mario Capdevielle is Professor of Economics at the Metropolitan Autonomous University–Xochimilco (UAM–X), Mexico City.

Mónica Casalet is Professor of Sociology at the Facultad Latinoamericana de Ciencias Sociales (FLACSO), Mexico City.

Rosalba Casas is currently senior researcher at the Social Research Institute, National Autonomous University of Mexico (UNAM), Mexico City.

Gloria del Castillo is a PhD student at the Facultad Latinoamericana de Ciencias Sociales (FLACSO), Mexico City.

Mario Cimoli has been Professor of Economics at the University of Venice Ca' Foscari) since 1990 and is currently Economic Affairs Officer at ECLAC (Economic Commission for Latin America and the Caribbean), United Nations, Santiago.

Roberto Constantino is Associate Professor in the Economics Department of the Metropolitan Autonomous University (UAM–X), Mexico City.

J. M. Corona is Professor of Economics at the Metropolitan Autonomous University–Xochimilco (UAM–X), Mexico City.

Gabriela Dutrénit is Professor in the Economics Department of the Metropolitan Autonomous University (UAM–X), Mexico City.

Jorge Fernandez is Associate Professor of Economics at El Colegio de Mexico, Mexico City.

Ruby Gonsen is a freelance consultant and has been doing research into technological capabilities and technology policy issues.

Rebeca de Gortari is researcher in Science and Education Area at the Social Research Institute, National Autonomous University of Mexico (UNAM), Mexico City.

C. Hernandez is Professor of Economics at the Metropolitan Autonomous University–Xochimilco (UAM–X), Mexico City.

Javier Jasso is researcher at the Centre of Research and Teaching in Economics (CIDE), Mexico City.

Arturo Lara is Professor in the Economical Production Department of the Metropolitan Autonomous University–Xochimilco (UAM–X), Mexico City.

Matilde Luna is researcher at the Institute of Social Research, National Autonomous University of Mexico (UNAM), Mexico City.

Kurt Unger is Professor at the Centre of Research and Teaching in Economics (CIDE), Mexico City.

M. Oloriz is researcher at the Centre of Research and Teaching in Economics (CIDE), Mexico City.

Manuel Soria is Professor in the Economics Department of the Metropolitan Autonomous University–Xochimilco (UAM–X), Mexico City.

Guillermo Abdel Musik is Professor of Operations Management and e-business at ITAM, Mexico City.

Giovanna Valenti is Professor of Public Policy at the Metropolitan Autonomous University–Xochimilco (UAM–X), Mexico City.

Gonzalo Varela is Professor of Sociology at the Metropolitan Autonomous University–Xochimilco (UAM–X), Mexico City.

Daniel Villavicencio is Professor at the Department of Politics and Culture at the Metropolitan Autonomous University–Xochimilco (UAM–X), Mexico City.

Acknowledgements

This book is the result of two projects. The first project, on the Mexican Innovation System, was made in Mexico with the financial support from CONACYT. The second was a UE DGXII project on Science and Technology Policies in Developing and Transition Countries. Without the support from these two sources it would have been impossible to write this book.

I am especially indebted to the people who made comments and gave advice when parts of this book were presented in different seminars around the world, particularly M. Hobday, G. Dosi, P. Guerrieri, S. Lall, J. de la Mothe, J. Katz, F. Malerba and S. Winter. I would also like to give special thanks to one person, S. Naranjo, because she gave her continued support to this project, as well as translating a significant portion of the chapters included here.

However, the ideas, contents, opinions and data used in this book are exclusively the responsibility of the researchers who participated in the two projects mentioned above.

M. Cimoli

CHAPTER ONE

Developing Innovation Systems

M. Cimoli

Introduction

Since it was recognized as an engine for economic growth in the 1940s, Mexican manufacturing industry has been growing under a regime of intensive protection. The orientation maintained a strong inward bias, at least until the 1982 financial crisis. In contrast, the more recent period has undergone a major shift in its orientation: the nation faced a 'radical shock' involving new economic reforms, in which the primary objective was to generate the conditions for faster economic growth and a new pattern of economic development. This 'radical shock' should provide an effective way to retool economic activities, by combining a favourable environment in terms of relative prices with an improvement in the incentives for technology upgrades. Since the beginning of this liberalization period, and combined with the further privatization of services, Mexican industry has experienced a profound structural transformation, and one of the major consequences has been a steady internationalization process that is based on an external performance which the nation had never experienced before.

At the present time, it is particularly difficult to evaluate the long-term effect of these policy instruments, since they were only created in recent years and were designed to influence phenomena of an inherently long-term nature. This situation is a sharp contrast with the sometimes very brief horizon for most macropolicies. Furthermore, the country's geographical position and its participation in the North American Free Trade Agreement (NAFTA) are extremely influential factors.

However, under these circumstances, the modes to adopt and diffuse innovation processes are causing a transformation towards a new pattern. Specifically, our aim is to understand whether the set of incentives that are responsible for Mexican exports' increase in competitiveness has upgraded or, rather, downgraded local efforts in endogenous innovation. We are interested in the different modes of technological efforts and the learning capabilities in the manufacturing firms, as defined by research and development (R&D) efforts, linkages within the local productive and institutional networks, and the firms' ability to solve both technical and organizational problems.

Today it is generally accepted that a society's economic development is based on its capacity to generate and absorb innovation processes. New approaches assert that innovation has to be considered and defined as an interactive process in which firms almost never innovate in isolation. In this context, strategic alliances and interactions between firms, research institutes, universities and other institutions are at the heart of this analysis. In fact, innovation is seen as a social process that evolves most successfully in a network in which there is intensive interaction between the suppliers and buyers of goods, services, knowledge and technology, including the public sector organizations that promote knowledge infrastructure, such as universities and government agencies that produce knowledge. A great deal of empirical research supporting this view has developed since the 1980s.

The steps leading from innovation towards a more aggregate analysis are numerous and complex. The concept of a national innovation system (NIS), as explained by Nelson (1993), consists of a set of institutions whose interactions determine the innovative performance of national firms (whereby innovative activity is broadly understood as inclusive of all the processes by which firms master and put into practice product designs and manufacturing processes that are new to them). In order to capture differences in development between countries, a schematic representation of the NIS and its interplay with economic performances is introduced here (de la Mothe and Paquet, 1996; Cimoli and della Giusta, 2000). The purpose is to carry out a comparative analysis of the 'goodness' or 'badness' of the NIS in terms of the main implications involved in specialization and economic performances, as shown through different scenarios characterized by perspectives dealing with catching up, falling behind and forging ahead (Cimoli and de la Mothe, 2000).

The systematization of the NIS presented in the following pages allows us to pursue two different directions. On the one hand, we can identify a representation in which the main threads that link technology, institutions and economic performances may be organized and described. On the other hand, and in relation to a broader set of approaches that search for a framework in which the mechanisms that support technical change and innovation can be understood, there exists the possibility for governments to form and implement policies in order to influence the innovation process. By analysing the linkages from micro studies on innovation to a broad aggregate system, we propose a concept and representation of innovation systems – (macro, regional, sectoral and micro levels) – with a view to empirically capturing some components of the Mexican innovation system. In this introductory chapter, the first section describes technological capabilities and production capacity in the development process. The next section reviews the theme of the national innovation system in the context of developing economies. The final section provides a model of integration for the Mexican innovation system through four different dimensions: temporal, technological, institutional and different aggregation levels. As part of this section, the organization of the book is described.

Technological capabilities and development process

During the past three decades, developing countries have displayed increased technological dynamism, which is associated with the subsequent development of their industrial structures; thus, some significant technological progress did indeed occur in the new industrialized economies (NIEs). The evolutionary path of technological learning is related to both the capacity to acquire technologies (capital goods, know-how, etc.) and the capability to absorb these technologies and adapt them to local conditions. In this respect, we now have a good deal of micro-technological evidence highlighting the mechanisms that stimulate and limit endogenous learning in the NIEs. A number of empirical studies describe the increased technological accumulation which has matured in some NIEs during the past three decades; in fact, some of them even have become exporters of technology (see Katz, 1984, 2000; Teitel, 1984; Teubal, 1984; Lall, 1987; Kim, 1999).

In order to understand the steps by which development process takes place, a distinction between production capacity and the accumulation of technological capabilities has to be made. Production capacity is associated with the development of the industry and its sectoral composition in terms of GDP participation, specialization and employment in manufacturing activities. Technological capabilities are the resources needed for the generation and management of technological change, the acquisition of embodied technology and labour skills, the management of organization and the assimilation of knowledge.

Analysis of the increase in the NIEs' technological capabilities has revealed the crucial role of certain 'core technologies' (in the past, electricity and electrical devices; nowadays, also information technologies) which play an essential role as sources of technological skills, problem-solving opportunities and improvements in productivity. These core technologies determine the overall absolute advantages or disadvantages of each country, in that they also imply infrastructures and networks common in a wide range of activities (electricity grid, highway system, telecommunications and, more recently, the information network). Moreover, some patterns appear to have formed, albeit rather loosely, in the industrialization process and in the development of a national production capacity, and these patterns explain how technological capabilities are acquired and upgraded. For example, practically every country starts with the manufacturing of clothing and textiles, and possibly natural resource processing; and, in turn, the nation moves on – if it does – to more complex and knowledge-intensive activities. A recent statement of that rationale is as follows:

> Even at today's advanced stage, the competitive advantage of East Asia's latecomers is low-cost, high-quality production engineering, rather than software or R&D. Although the NIEs are increasing their investments in science and advanced technology, they remain conspicuously weak compared with Japan and other OECD countries.
>
> Also in contrast with leapfrogging, much latecomer learning took place in a field which could be described as pre-electronic: mechanical, electromechanical and precision engineering activities, for example. Competencies tended to build upon each other incrementally, leading to advanced engineering and software. Firms tended to enter at the mature, well-established phase of the product life cycle, rather than at the early stage, again contrary to the leapfrogging idea.
>
> The policy implication of this finding is that to build an electronics industry, local firms require human resources trained in a range of basic craft, technician, engineering and industrial skills, rather than the software and computer-based skills normally associated with information technology. Like the NIEs, other developing countries should take very seriously the low-technology side of so-called high-technology industries. Only by developing capabilities in fields such as plastics, mouldings, machinery, assembly and electromechanical interfacing, did East Asia emerge as the leading export region for electronics. (Hobday, 1995: 200).

Thus, in general, it is possible to identify a pattern of development that evolves as sectors emerge, according to the technological complexity and direct investment requested. We do not at all suggest that there is any invariant sequence of industrial sectors which account for the upgrading of national technological capabilities. However, one might still be able to identify some rough sequences in the predominant modes of technological learning. In this respect, the taxonomy of the sectoral patterns for the acquisition of innovative knowledge suggested by Pavitt (1984) is a good – albeit somewhat theoretically fuzzy – point of departure. Pavitt identifies five sectoral patterns which allow the derivation of industry-specific models for technological change:[1] the supplier-dominated sector (agriculture and traditional manufacture), the scale-intensive sector (consumer durables, automobiles, civil engineering and bulk materials), the information-intensive sector (finance, retail, publishing and travel), the science-based sector (electronics and chemicals) and the specialized suppliers (machinery, instruments and software). In the supplier-dominated and information-intensive sectors, the main sources of technical knowledge are located outside the firm. In the science-based sectors, the main sources of technical advance are in-house R&D and basic science; in terms of the discussion presented in this section, the science-based sector can be characterized as being of the late Schumpeter-type (science-push and anticipated demand). The scale-intensive sector, which is characterized by continuous processes, finds its main sources of technology in production engineering, production learning, suppliers and design offices, whereas design and advanced users are the sources for specialized suppliers; both sectors are characterized by conservative and very incremental processes and can be described as being closer to the Schmookler-type (demand-driven).

In the broadest sense, it is important to bear in mind that it is not possible to formulate a general theory for technical change based exclusively on the technology-push or demand-pull models. From this brief summary of the main characteristics of innovation it is perhaps already possible to understand how certain components of technology do not make it feasible to apply definitions that would be appropriate in all sectors, industries and firms. The demand-pull and technology-push explanations include elements which permit the description of specificities of innovative processes in certain sectors, or during certain periods in the historical dynamics of technology. In these cases, one model prevails over the other, depending on the circumstances (Cimoli and della Giusta, 2000.) For example, Walsh's (1984) analysis on the changes in innovation during the developmental stages for two chemical industry subsectors confirms the general sectoral characteristics included in Pavitt's taxonomy, as well as the specificities of the subsectors' evolution. Plastics seem to have, at first, followed an early-Schumpeterian pattern, in that the first goods primarily were developed through inventors' entrepreneurial activity; later on, however, science and anticipated demand in large corporations played a major role, following the late-Schumpeterian model. Analysis of patents in dyestuffs, on the contrary, produces conflicting results if either a solely quantitative, or a qualitative analysis is performed. When only quantitative analysis is carried out, a demand-pull model seems to emerge; in contrast, when a qualitative analysis is conducted, an early-Schumpeterian pattern is evident again.

More generally, despite the difficulties in describing the intermediate steps that relate to industrialization, production capacity and technological capability, a comprehensive pattern can be traced. The initial stage in the development of a manufacturing sector is led by the supplier-dominated and specialized supplier sectors, since activity is related to the transfer of foreign technology and various forms of incremental learning take place (use of equipment, development of engineering skills in machine and product adaptation and manufacturing). A second stage is related to the emergence of scale-intensive industries, which have new technological efforts focused on creating a technological synergism between production and use of sets of innovations (which gives rise to horizontal and vertical integration); the adoption of technologies is associated with the exploitation of static and dynamic economies to scale; and, finally, the development of formal R&D occurs and is a complement to informal learning. The final stage is that in which a science-based sector is created, and the knowledge base is exploited economically through formalized research efforts; R&D is the typical learning mechanism.

Among these sectors, input–output linkages and knowledge flows give rise to a wide set of externalities and interdependencies that are based upon common knowledge bases, complementarities and technological spillovers. Such non-negotiable or non-tradable technological flows are essential not only for the technological development of the enterprises involved, but also for the nation's entire industrial development in general. Specialized suppliers produce product innovation and capital inputs for the other sectors, whereas through the production of components and materials the science-based sector generates positive effects which are propagated throughout the whole system. All these linkages are fundamental for industrialization, in particular those which establish themselves between the most innovative and the traditional and natural resources-based sectors. Applications of this type of taxonomic dynamic analysis to the cases of some Latin American and Southeast Asian countries can be found in Katz (1984), Cimoli (1988) and Bell and Pavitt (1993a).

The firms and sectoral learning patterns, however, clearly form part of broader ('macro') conditions that exist at the regional and national level, such as those defining the educational system (Cimoli and Dosi, 1995; Hobday, 1995). For example, in 'supplier-dominated' and 'specialized supplier' sectors, a significant role is played by the levels of the labour forces' literacy and skills, as well as the skills and technical competence of engineers and designers in the mechanical and (increasingly) electronics fields. In scale-intensive sectors, the existence of managers capable of efficiently running complex organizations is also likely to be important. In science-based sectors, the quality of higher education and research capabilities is obviously relevant. In particular, the role of technology transfer as a source for the local technological accumulation has been extensively investigated: increasing technology flows towards developing economies have taken place, with a special emphasis on Asian countries. The development of technological capabilities, which is at the centre of the industrialization processes, is related to both the capacity to acquire technology and the ability to absorb and adapt it to the local environment. By looking at the nature and direction of learning at the level of companies, it is possible to identify a few major activities through which such learning takes place. In particular, the modification of an adopted technology entails learning how to develop an adequate production capacity and how to adapt it to the local specificities; through these processes, incremental innovation takes place, and, moreover, a specific pattern of technical change begins to take shape.

Knowledge accessibility and local absorption

The perception that the patterns of technological accumulation described above are assuming a new path emerges fundamentally from the changing nature of the world economy. In order to begin to understand the complex nature of innovative activity, it is useful first to summarize some stylized facts concerning innovative activity. Scientific inputs have become increasingly important in the innovative process, and R&D activities have become more complex; therefore, it is necessary to adopt a long-term perspective in planning innovative activities within firms. Likewise, there are a number of studies that correlate such R&D efforts with innovative output, for various industrial sectors (in which market and demand changes do not exhibit significant correlation). Another stylized fact that has emerged is the importance of innovation generated through learning-by-doing, as embodied by people and organizations. In terms of the nature of the innovation process, an intrinsically uncertain vision prevails over the assumption of known *ex ante* fixed sets of choices. However, this does not imply that technical change occurs randomly: the direction of technological change is determined by the state-of-the-art technologies and, at the level of firms, by the technology that they possess. Indeed, it is possible to identify patterns of change, which are defined in terms of the technological and economic characteristics of the products and processes.

Since the world economy is becoming more interdependent this phenomena is adding a new dimension to analysis of technological asymmetries. The growing interdependence between all the economies and regions, through increased commercial and financial flows and combined with domestic institutional constraints, is affecting the traditional path of knowledge production and innovation process. Today, policies oriented towards increasing local investment in technological variables and linkages (that essentially refers to improvement in the local functionality of the system) are not enough. In fact, with the growing internationalization of technology and production, the improvement in capabilities has to be related to the ability to access international networks, which is where knowledge and technology are produced.

The international economy has been transformed from a model of multiple limited commercial trade-offs, to a model of international scale production and increasing knowledge flows. At the level of sectoral patterns, those changes – also called 'new complexity' – appear as a shift in the productive and organizational behaviour of economic agents: from physical skill-extensive production to knowledge-intensive production. Therefore, the process of globalization is a key issue in the explanation of the ascent of knowledge-based economies. Likewise, knowledge-based economies are characterized by the intensification of innovative actions as the basis for successful integration in the world economy and increasing capabilities to capture and develop locally the benefit of knowledge.

The term 'knowledge-based economy' is a result of the recognition that knowledge, as embodied in human beings (as 'human capital') and in technology, has always been central to economic development. But only over the last few years has the importance of knowledge production been recognized, and furthermore, this recognition is growing. Today, the world economy is more strongly dependent on the production, distribution and use of knowledge than ever before. Output and employment are expanding most rapidly in the high technology industries, such as computers, electronics and aerospace. In the past decade, high technology's share of manufacturing production and exports has more than doubled. Likewise, knowledge-intensive activities are becoming increasingly important from an economic point of view.

In fact, today, firms and countries have significant opportunities to access knowledge and technology at the international level. The globalization of industrial research – traditionally a function carried out at the company headquarters – is also increasing in the 1990s, and this will continue into the twenty-first century. The factors that are the driving force in this situation are becoming more complicated and diverse as firms join university-based, private–public research consortia and cross-industry strategic alliances. Traditionally, the industrial propensity to invest in research abroad was highly correlated with the internationalization of the firm's functions, such as production and marketing. In an economic sense, market access still is an important factor in the globalization of research, particularly in those sectors that have high levels of foreign manufacturing. As product cycles shorten and technology becomes increasingly complex and specific, more R&D facilities are created near foreign plants; in addition, shared R&D activities are developed to reduce the time for knowledge transfer. In recent years, access to personnel and knowledge have become the more significant factors in the globalization of research. Research has shown, for example, that personal contacts and proximity are a *sine qua non* in the formation of networks and in research productivity. Cyber-networks, without loyalty and interpersonal relations, are not sustainable (de la Mothe and Paquet, 1998).

In this context, it is possible to infer that an economy's technological performance is mainly determined by the composition, size, flexibility and international accessibility of the NIS. It is possible to find quite successful economies in terms of developing local abilities through strong linkages between different parts of the NIS. In addition, it is possible to find prosperous economies that have intensive connections with international technological knowledge. At the heart of the latest inquiry there is an irrefutable fact: a society's economic success relies upon the local abilities that have been developed to generate and incorporate the knowledge produced in other economies (Cimoli and de la Mothe, 2000).

National innovation systems: main building blocks and linkages

Government intervention in the Latin American and Pacific Rim NIEs played an essential role in these countries' industrialization processes, but they took opposite directions in terms of market orientation and specialization. The Latin American NIEs have been characterized by production for their domestic markets; whereas the Southeast Asian NIEs have been oriented towards exports and specialization in manufactured commodities. In the Southeast Asian economies, a particular emphasis has been placed on the promotion of linkages between enterprises, often involving multinational enterprises' (MNEs') subsidiaries, with the intention of promoting stable access to technology transfer and a fruitful mode of diffusion throughout the whole economy. Another essential aspect in the development of these countries has been that of human capital formation; in particular, the role of the scientific and educational system in industry has been repeatedly underlined in the technical literature on the Asian NIEs, where it has often been considered as a fundamental precondition to their success. On the whole, the general pattern of incentives as defined by the existing institutions has accounted for the type of response to internal and external stimuli, which in turn has determined the NIEs' relative successes and failures.

There is a significant body of literature that explains the importance of institutions and their role in economic and industrial development. In particular, regarding the Pacific Rim NIEs, the works by Amsden (1989) and Wade (1990) and many others help us to understand how there is not only institutional success, but institutional failure as well. Bardhan (1996) analyses this issue as one of coordination, which has to be seen in terms of the interaction of conflicts in distribution with state capacity and governance structure. The author suggests that the success of institutions in some NIEs (namely South Korea and Taiwan) has to be understood in terms of the capacity to establish and apply rules of performance criteria, so that, for example, government credit allocation was closely related to export performance; thus, international competition was used to foster internal learning. Most of these approaches point out that growth is not automatic. Growth needs a 'social capability' which can be viewed as a 'rubric that covers countries' levels of general education and technical competence, the commercial, industrial, and financial institutions that bear on their ability to finance and operate modern, large-scale business and the political and social characteristics that influence the risks, the incentives and the personal rewards of economic activity, thus including those rewards in social esteem that goes beyond money and wealth' (Abramovitz, 1994).

In modern innovation theory, the firms' strategic behaviour and alliances, as well as the interactions between firms, research institutes, universities and other institutions, are at the heart of analysis of the innovation process. More specifically, in the concept of a national innovation system, as introduced by Freeman (1987) in the mid-1980s and as further developed by Nelson (1993), Lundvall (1993), Metcalfe (1995), Edquist (1997), de la Mothe and Paquet (1998) and Cimoli and della Giusta (2000), innovation is considered an interactive process in which the above-mentioned features are captured. In general terms, most of the contributions cited above support the idea that the main building blocks in NIS are articulated by a collection of different agents and their interaction.

Following the concepts introduced in Freeman (1987) and Nelson (1993), and within national boundaries, analysis is carried out on a set of actors (firms and, particularly, other institutions, such as universities, research organizations), as well as on the links between these actors in the innovation and diffusion processes. Metcalfe (1995) provides the following policy-oriented definition of NIS: a 'set of institutions which jointly and individually contribute to the development and diffusion of new technologies and which provide the framework within which governments form and implement policies to influence the innovation process' (pp. 462–3). He argues that the nature of each NIS is fundamentally shaped by the division of labour and the peculiarities of information, which cause non-market means to predominate in the coordination process. The institutions that form this group (private firms, universities, other educational institutions, public research labs, private consultants, professional societies and industrial research associations) 'make complementary contributions, but they differ significantly with respect to motivation and in commitment to the dissemination of the knowledge they create'. A more recent analysis referring specifically to the NIS approach in the NIEs can be found in the works by Katz (1997a), Kim (1997a) and Lall (1997). The argument here emphasizes the 'message' that growth and catch-up potentiality are clearly related to a country's historical path and to the development of a local NIS. Institutions and industrial and science and technology policies (those that support science, human capital, competencies and learning capabilities) are the main variables introduced to explain the differences between the NIS developed in Latin American and Asian NIEs.

In Cimoli and Dosi (1995) it is suggested that the specificities concerning national systems of production and innovation are seen as the joint outcome of the three levels of analysis presented in the present work:

- *The national level*: the set of social relationships, rules and political constraints into which microeconomic behaviours are embedded (which has been extensively studied, together with the first level, in evolutionary/institutional analysis).
- *The mesoeconomic* level of networks of linkages between firms and other organizations, both within and outside their primary sectors of activity, which enhances each firm's opportunities to improve its problem-solving capabilities (and, inasmuch as it can be interpreted as an externality or an economy-wide mechanism for the generation of knowledge, the mesoeconomic level has been at the centre of new growth theories).
- *The firm level*: in which companies are seen as the repositories of the knowledge embodied in their operational routines, which is modified over time by their higher level rules of behaviours and strategies.

The evolutionary foundations which account for the characteristics of national systems of production and innovation develop through to the ideas that firms are repositories of knowledge, that they are nested in networks of linkages with other firms and also with other non-profit organizations (networks which enhance the opportunities facing each firm to improve their problem-solving capabilities), and finally that there exists a broader notion (at a wider level of aggregation) of embeddedness of microeconomic behaviours into a set of social relationships, rules and political constraints (Granovetter, 1985; Coriat and Dosi, 1998; Dosi, Nelson and Winter 2000). Thus, in general, nations are represented as *containers of microeconomic behaviours* characterized by particular modes of institutional governance that, to a certain extent, make them diverse self-reproducing entities. Indeed, there is an element of nationality which is provided by shared language and culture, as well as by the national focus of other policies, laws and regulations, which condition the innovative environment (Metcalfe, 1995). Together they contribute to the shaping of the organizational and technological context within which each economic activity takes place. In a sense, they set the opportunities and constraints facing each individual process of production and innovation – including the availability of complementary skills, information on intermediate inputs and capital goods and demand stimuli to improve particular products. Institutional and technological diversities are seen in this context as the true determinants of development.

The processes described here are, in fact, inherently co-evolutionary in nature and therefore are characterized by constant feedback mechanisms (Nelson, 1994).

Even at a micro-level, the momentum associated with single technological trajectories is itself a largely social concept: 'it points to the organizations and people committed by various interests to the system, to manufacturing corporations, research and development laboratories, investment banking houses, educational institutions and regulatory bodies' (Misa, 1991, p. 15). And, in turn, these interests and institutions are sustained by the increasing return and local nature of most learning activities. Even more so, at a system level, the interpretation presented here is consistent with, and indeed is a complement to, institutional approaches that build on the observation that markets do not operate apart from the rules and institutions that establish them and that 'the institutional structure of the economy creates a distinct pattern of constraints and incentives', which defines the interests of the actors, as well as shaping and channelling their behaviour (Zysman, 1994, pp. 1–2).

Technological capabilities and performances

The hypothesis here is that differences in technological capabilities are a fruitful starting point for a theory showing how technological gaps and national institutional diversities can jointly reproduce themselves over rather long spans of time in ways that are easily compatible with the patterns of incentives and opportunities faced by individual agents, even when they turn out to be profoundly suboptimal from a collective point of view. Conversely, in other circumstances, it might be precisely this institutional and technological diversity among countries that fosters catching-up (and rarely, leapfrogging) in innovative capabilities and per capita incomes. A definition of national technological capabilities which captures the ideas and approaches described in the above sections, at the firm level and within a given institutional setting, is associated with a

> complex of skills, experience and conscious effort that enables a country's enterprises to efficiently buy, use, adapt, improve and create technologies. The individual enterprise is the fundamental unit of technological activity, but national capability is larger than the sum of the individual firms' capabilities. It comprises the non-market system of linkages, business culture and institutions that enables firms to interact with each other, exchanging the information needed to coordinate their activities and to undertake what effectively amounts to collective learning. (Lall, 1997, p. 1)

Rigorous demonstrations of these propositions would indeed require many intermediate steps, linking externalities and positive feedback mechanisms, based on technological learning, with the institutional context in which microeconomic agents are embedded, taking into consideration the economic signals they face as well. Let us just emphasize that systematically different rates of learning might have very little to do with 'how well markets work'. Rather, incentives and opportunities, as perceived by agents in a particular context, are themselves the result of particular histories of technologies and institutions. In this framework, the possibility of institutional failures becomes incorporated into a broad structure that accounts for the interactions among the principal agents in the development process.

It is necessary to assemble the components that deal with technological capabilities and the NIS which have been developed so far and to try to provide a further step in understanding the technological change process at institutional levels. We now propose the idea of national technological capabilities (evolving in both time and space); they are defined by effort and competence that essentially refers to a firm's, organization's and country's abilities to solve both technical and organizational problems. Effort and competencies are a complex set of elements which are not easily identified and measured. However, in a broader sense, we can find an approximation for these elements through a set of indicators. For example, at the firm level, effort and competencies reflect educational skills, R&D expenditures and propensity for technology transfer. At the national level, the relevant effort and competencies can be identified as those which pertain to the following groups: educational competencies (literacy rate, secondary and tertiary level enrolment ratios, advanced students in maths, science and engineering), R&D capabilities (scientists and engineers in R&D, R&D as a percentage of GNP and the ratio of private vs. public R&D) and technology transfer related capabilities (direct foreign investment and capital goods imports) (Cimoli and della Giusta, 2000).

Moreover, firm efforts and competencies are supported and shaped by a system that is formed by a collection of institutions. As Nelson has pointed out:

> Of course, what firms do, and the technologies they employ and develop, are influenced to a considerable extent by the environment they are in. Economists are inclined to define the environment in terms of markets. In turn, behind markets are demanders of products and suppliers if inputs (who may be individuals or organisations like other firms), and their preferences, and the constraints which they face.
>
> However, in recent years at least some economists have become cognisant of aspects of the environment not really considered in the simple treatment. (In a way the new awareness of institutions represents a renaissance of earlier thinking. For a discussion, see Hodgson, 1988.) There is increasing recognition among economists that there are entities out there like universities that do research that feed into technical advance in industry, and whose teaching programmes affect the supply of scientists and engineers; government agencies financing certain kinds of R&D, and others setting standards; banks and banking systems; and a variety of organisations and laws which affect labour supply and demand. Patent, regulatory, and liability law are part of the environment. And so also are a variety of widely shared beliefs and values and customs that affect common expectations about what should be done, and what will be done, in a particular context . . .
>
> Thus historians like Landes (1970) have argued that an important reason why British industry did poorly in the new chemical products industries, was the failure of British universities to develop strength in the teaching of science and engineering. A recent study (see Nelson, 1993) compares the institutional structures supporting industrial technical advance in a number of different countries, and argues that differences in the systems explain a great deal about differences in national economic performance. As noted earlier, Perez (1983) has argued that, for rapid growth to proceed, a nation's institutions must be tuned to the dominant technologies of the era. (Nelson, 1998: 512–13)

The description above captures both the notion of technological capabilities and the fundamental element of a NIS. Thus, by systematizing the difference between technological capabilities (effort and competence) and economic performance (GDP growth, international competitiveness etc.), it is also possible to come up with a measurement of the 'goodness' or 'badness' of the NIS. Through the representation introduced above, it is possible to explain why technological gaps among countries reproduce themselves over time, due to the fact that individual behaviours (in response to the existing patterns of incentives and opportunities) produce suboptimal collective outcomes. In other words, the existence of diverse institutions and organizations and their modes of interaction determine specific national systems of innovation, which over time present certain invariable characteristics that account for their phases of relative 'technological success and failure' (Cimoli and Dosi, 1995). When organized appropriately, the NIS is a powerful engine that stimulates progress; poorly organized and connected, the NIS may seriously inhibit the process of innovation (Metcalfe, 1995; de la Mothe and Paquet, 1996).

A model of integration for the Mexican innovation system

The major points mentioned above link production capacity and technological capabilities within the broader institutional framework of each country's political economy. The interplay and linkages between these pieces of the NIS will be analysed through the main historical changes faced by the Mexican economy. Moreover, this analysis will be carried out through different aggregate levels. The national unit is too large to understand the effects on the innovative process in a particular area; it therefore becomes important to focus on the appropriate unit of analysis, and thus on the distinct systems that are geographically and institutionally localized. In a broad sense, the idea proposed here is aimed at maintaining the concept of the NIS anchored in an institutional specific container that permits a description of the historical path of each country, region or industry. Upon macro, meso and micro levels, we will analyse the effects of the above-mentioned dimensions: first, the main changes in the technological and economic variables (efforts, competencies and performances); second, the changes in the institutional framework. In Figure 1.1, we introduce a representation of the above proposed approach.

It is important to bear in mind that within this context the representation proposed here can be considered an experimental approach in which certain relationships between technical change and economic performance are being analysed from a different perspective. First, it is very important to stress our other interests concerning the functional role that networks play and the functional relationships among the different agents incorporated in the NIS. It is essential to concentrate on the evaluation and description of the co-evolving process that relates the different part of the system. Second, we will more extensively investigate the intuitive hypothesis that improvements in products or in the efficiency of production performances techniques may be a determinant, or at least a binding precondition, for growth in per capita income and consumption. We will debate, from a dynamic perspective, the issue of whether institutions supporting technological capabilities are sufficiently adaptive to be able to adjust to whatever underlying economic change emerges from market interactions, or, conversely, whether they are inertial enough to shape the rate and direction of innovation and economic performance. Third, we will focus on the role played by multinational enterprises (MNEs) and foreign direct investment (FDI), in performing local technological capabilities, efforts and competencies. Today, there is the perception that the globalization of production and knowledge is assuming an increasing role in the development of technological capabilities. In fact, trade policies and MNEs strategies provide an international dimension which means that the effects of technology policy in one nation affect policy in other nations. In this context, increasing the mobility of firms' resources (FDI, strategic alliances, etc.) has a very influential effect on trade and growth performance, as well as on the main variables that explain a nation's technological capability.

Temporal dimension and phases of history

Mexico is a nation that after the 'radical and selective shocks' that characterized the 1980s has increased its participation in the world arena, in terms of exports as well as imports. Most of the surviving and efficient firms (MNCs and large domestic firms) have increased their exports of final commodities, components for automobiles, chemicals, plastic products, glass, beer, electronics, steel, cement, etc. According to recent analysis of Mexican competitiveness, the country's external performance should be considered one of the main fields in which we can appreciate the positive results of the major structural changes induced in the economy since the 1982 crisis. Data on the overall volume and composition of exports during the 1980s and early 1990s are interpreted as an unprecedented success: there was a remarkable improvement in Mexico's strategic position and the nation experienced an overall increase in competitiveness. A great deal of emphasis has been placed on the fact that within the overall increase in Mexican participation in the world market (Mexico's share in exports grew from 1.49 to 2.0 per cent between 1986 and 1994), manufacturing industry gained a new leading role. During the 1980s, the rate of growth for exports averaged 15.3 per cent, while the world market increased by 7.5 per cent per year.[2] Although different studies on these data have different time frames and samples, most of them seem to agree in detecting not only a growing participation of Mexican production in the world market, but also an increasing orientation towards those markets in which growth is higher than the average international level.[3]

The heterogeneity of manufactures' structural change as they faced this phase of the liberalisation process has been emphasized by various authors: Casar (1993, 1994, 1996) stresses a growing specialization in automobiles and chemicals, while traditional manufactures such as textiles, metal products, machinery and wood have lost importance within the manufacturing sector. At a more detailed level of analysis, Dussel (1996) shows how the group of industries with the highest levels of growth, and which accounts for 41 per cent of the sector's export performance in 1988–92, has been the most dynamic since the 1970s, and is characterized by being MNEs (automobiles, electrical equipment), monopolies (basic petrochemicals) or national oligopolies (glass and beer). In fact, the development and diffusion of technological learning seem at present to have a higher integration in the world economy: the import of capital goods and intermediates, motivated by the trend of relative prices, remains the main source of technology, and in most sectors, activities are concentrated in efforts to improve personnel training and organizational efficiency. In contrast, local R&D and production engineering efforts seem to have been reoriented, and firms concentrate on short-term problem-solving and quality control activities (as in the glass and beer industries) (Cimoli *et al.*, 1998).

In fact, from the beginning of this period of liberalization and structural reforms, Mexican industry has experienced an in-depth structural transformation; one of the major consequences of which has been a steady process of globalization from a previously inexperienced external performance. An attempt will be made to understand to what extent the Mexican NIS has influenced recent trends in the performance of industry, trade and competitiveness, as well as how this is actually configured. In addition, this analysis will determine the direction of the technological capabilities within manufacturing, in that these capabilities are thought of as endogenous processes and determinants for economic performances. The underlying presumption is that the present situation is the result of subsequent phases that have characterized the NIS configuration; each of these is distinguished by a specific industrial structure and institutional framework, which all have concurred to explain what we observe today. Furthermore, we also wish to describe the feedback mechanism by which the strategies and performance of Mexican firms across different sectors, and in particular those of the multinational enterprises located in Mexican territory, have contributed to the determination of the present innovation system. Thus, the relationship between the innovation system and industrial performance will be seen as conducive to the ways in which innovation processes are carried out.

It is presently uncertain whether the pattern of policies accompanying liberalization and structural reforms is a successful one. In particular, it seems necessary to understand whether the liberalization process provided a favourable environment for both innovative activities and learning processes within Mexican firms and whether there is presently an innovation system capable of adopting, capturing and supporting technology flows from the international arena.

In-depth relationships of some sort between economic performance and the innovation system are now generally acknowledged. Still, the nature of these relationships is a matter of debate, as far as the precise current links are concerned. For example, experts have recognized that Mexico has achieved improvements in production efficiency or organization techniques. More experts indicate the need for debate concerning 'how the Mexican NIS has supported it' and 'whether or not the actual production system still offers new technological opportunities'. More specifically, will new technological opportunities emerge from the competitive environment attained so far, an environment that appears to be exclusively driven by market and price incentives? Or does effort to increase competition have to be channelled through support for institutions, competencies, flows and networks? Are foreign direct investment (FDI) and specialization in assembly plants a vehicle through which local technological capabilities, R&D efforts and local networks could be upgraded? Are technological efforts supported by a pre-competitive framework (in terms of institutional support, increasing knowledge flows, improving networks, etc.) as the driving force for new opportunities? Is it possible to assume that the Mexican system supporting innovation was sufficiently adaptive to adjust to the innovative opportunities in firms and industry? Or, conversely, is additional effort necessary to shape the rates and direction of the diffusion of innovation and local capacity to capture benefits?

The temporal dimension and historical phases can be followed through the three parts developed in this book. A pattern for the evolution of the Mexican NIS can be postulated by the analysis proposed through the different chapters and figures. For example, Part I describes the macroeconomic setting, the structure of production system and its technological globalization across the three phases of Mexican

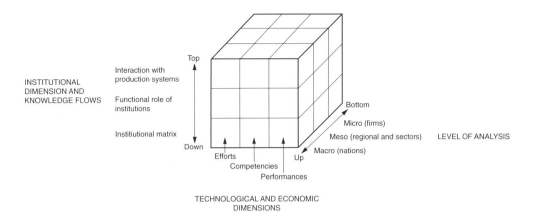

Figure 1.1 The Integrative Model for the Mexican Innovation System.

industrialization; the historical changes of institutions supporting innovation, education policies and knowledge production are deeply analysed in Part II; and the
co-evolution of production system and institutional patterns is described in Part
III.

Technological capabilities: efforts, competencies and performances

In Figure 1.1, on the *x*-axis the technological dimension should be considered, and
the processes that explain the efforts and the competencies created can be associated
with performances. Economic performance depends on how each country imple-
ments policies (to stabilize the macroeconomic setting, to promote the industrial
sectors, etc.) and organizes its institutional matrix and competencies. The relevant
variables which can be considered as an approximation for the scope of catch-up and
improved performance are: rate of GDP growth, exports as a percentage of the
GDP, productivity growth, technological sectorial distribution for the GDP, exports
in terms of technological classification (using Pavitt's taxonomy or others), international market share of exports and imports and employment in manufacturing
sectors. In Part I, economic performances are obtained and analysed at the industrial
level, as well as the sectors that mostly explain the globalization process in the
Mexican system (e.g. foreign and domestic firms). In contrast, in Part III economic
performances are more specifically considered to evaluate the gaps and role of
sectoral clusters in the Mexican innovation system.

Throughout this discussion we will establish that the interplay between the NIS
and performances is not linear and, hence, a deterministic conclusion cannot be
drawn. In Part I, we will particularly stress too that the nature of the interplay
between the NIS and economic performances is shaped, among other things, by the
historical events related to industrial and technological strategies, the specialization
pattern, the constraints imposed by balance of trade conditions, the policies related

to the macroeconomic setting and exchange rate stabilization. At a system level, there are some macro indicators of policy that, in our opinion, have to be viewed as both conditioning elements and results of the system's performance (macroeconomic and regulatory settings, industrial and trade policies). For example, an aspect which could clearly neutralize the effects of innovative efforts is related to the cases where the macroeconomic setting is characterized by high instability, frequently emerging in the vicious circle of the depreciation–appreciation of the exchange rate. This scenario is characteristic of most of the semi-industrialized economies in Latin America (Argentina, Brazil and Mexico). Under such scenarios, the main economic actors involved in the process of the acquisition of knowledge and diffusion of innovation do not make decisions involving a long-term perspective because their strategies are 'take care, wait and see how the exchange rate will move'. Efforts oriented towards increasing NIS competencies can easily be neutralized by a macro-setting characterized by high instability.

At a national level, efforts and competencies are clearly very difficult to estimate and quantify. Efforts and competencies are not incorporated in a single institution, organization, sector or firm; both are also inherent in a collection of agents which has to be mapped and differentiated according to their functional role in the system. Thus, efforts and competencies are analysed through the three parts of the present book: production system (Part I), institutional framework (Part II) and the sectoral clusters (Part III).

National efforts could be considered as an approximation of the main competencies available in each economy.[4] Through this book, competencies can be identified as pertaining to the following groups: educational (literacy rate, secondary and tertiary level enrolment ratios, third level students in mathematics, science and engineering), R&D efforts (scientists and engineers in R&D, R&D as a percentage of GNP, ratio of private and public R&D), technology transfer efforts (direct FDI stock, capital goods imports). An essential aspect of competencies deals with the interplay and the catch-up argument. In particular, when a country that is behind the world innovation frontier is considered, most of the competency variables could be conceived of as a support for imitation. Thus, through the representation introduced above, a catch-up process based on appropriation, imitation and adaptation of established technologies from more advanced countries is captured (Gomulka, 1971; Abramovitz, 1989; Maddison, 1991; Fagerberg, 1995).

Institutional dimension

In Figure 1.1, the institutional dimension is represented on the *y*-axis. The institutional matrix with the different institutions and their functional role can be viewed as the agents that produce efforts and competencies according to their particular roles. The matrix of the NIS is akin to the concept of an 'institutional matrix which supports and sustains the activities of innovating firms' proposed by Metcalfe (1995). As is suggested in Chapter 6, the possibility of institutional failures is incorporated within a broad structure which is able to account for the interactions among the main agents in the development process. The essential feature of this process is the interface between efforts, competences and performance and the role that the NIS plays as the wider representative of institutions (both public and private).

Most countries are characterized by different types of institutions, which, however, can be distinguished by how they contribute to the development of
technologies and the role they play in the whole system. Thus, one can think of the
following institutions as a sort of representative sample of those actually existing in
Mexico: higher education institutions, research and technological development
organizations, industrial research laboratories, government research institutes,
agencies for education and training programmes, certificate research and technology
organizations, technological information centres and technology transfer-
institutions. Over the past fifty years, institutions have changed a great deal in terms
of their competencies and function within the Mexican NIS. From the early years of
the import substitution phase up to nowadays, organizations have been continuously
evolving: some have been created; some have endured significant changes; yet others
have disappeared. Hence, throughout this chapter, an effort is made to describe and
analyse a process where change is constant. In Part II, the specific institutional
matrix of Mexico is provided. The institutional networks around specific sectors and
regions are analysed in Part III.

Levels of analysis and main building blocks in the Mexican innovation system

In Figure 1.1, the aggregation levels are depicted on the z axis. For our purposes, let
us just mention again that the analytical dimensions – technological capabilities and
institutional framework – outlined above are identified along the main threads that
link different aggregation levels. In fact, there seems to be a larger domain which the
link between aggregation levels provides a firmer ground where innovation and
institutional studies could develop a fruitful dialogue. In this respect, to induce this
dialogue further, an analysis of the different levels of innovations system is pursued
in this study. Such a study could be applied at different levels of analysis: macro,
regional and sectorial systems (see Figure 1.2).[5]

In Parts I and II, the macro system will be analysed. A *macro* system containing
industry and institutions is studied at the national level where the analysis is
principally based on industrial technological specificities, the institutional matrix,
efforts, competencies, knowledge diffusion process, macroeconomic setting, and
their interplay with economic performance at the national and international levels.

Chapter 2 provides a description of the main pieces that link studies on the
macroeconomic setting, the technological pattern and the globalization of the
production system. Chapter 3 refers to the periods into which we have chosen to
divide the experience of Mexico's industrialization. Each of these three periods
contains a brief description of the main policies undertaken during the period, and
then it analyses the interaction between macro and micro policies and their effects on
incentives to innovate. The focus here is mainly related to the behaviour of productivity and investment after trade reform. In Chapter 4, the analysis is carried out in two
directions: the performance of the production system in terms of sectoral technological patterns and the system's efforts to upgrade its technological capabilities.
Chapter 5 is dedicated to new globalization processes in the Mexican production
system. Modes and intensity of Mexican globalization are analysed, focusing on

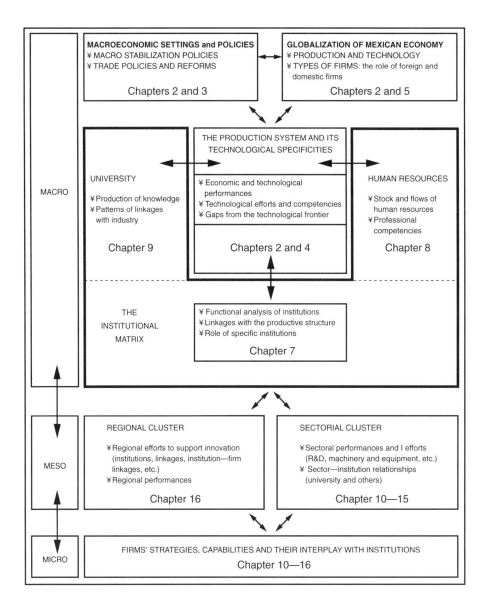

Figure 1.2 Levels of Analysis and the Main Building Blocks in the Mexican Innovation System.

sectoral production lines and the main channels for technological flows. These involve foreign sources of technology related to FDI, technology transfer and technology incorporated into capital goods imports, intermediate inputs and components.

Chapter 6 introduces the institutional framework and the main building blocks in the Mexican system. Chapter 7 and its appendix deal with the Mexican institutional matrix; we identify the competencies and functions, in which different types of organizations are distinguished and analysed. Chapter 8 is focused on the educational system; we discuss competencies in terms of the human resources produced, together with their linkages – or the lack thereof – to the production system. Chapter 9 deals with the portion of the institutional system that specializes in producing knowledge as well as differences regarding other developed countries. Furthermore, in this chapter, a great deal of attention is given to the linkages and networks between universities and production system.

The *meso* and *micro* systems are described and analysed in Part 3. In this context, performance can be viewed as an effort dominated by local institutions and competencies, which are found at a regional level or, conversely, by the sector's technologies (Cimoli and della Giusta 2000). A sectoral innovation system (SIS) could be identified as a 'system [group] of firms active in developing and making a sector's products and in generating and utilising a particular sector's technology; such a system of firms is interrelated in two different ways: through the processes of interaction and cooperation in artefact-technology development and through processes of competition and selection in innovative [activities] and market activities' (Breschi and Malerba, 1997). This system here is based on surveys and *micro* studies which could be defined as where the firms and the interplay among them are considered at a more disaggregated level of analysis. Thus, both aspects of the firm's learning processes and technological competencies can be studied. First, we discuss the internal efforts related to R&D activities, in which improvements in production processes and organizations are considered the main assets. Second is the external linkage associated with the main agents 'institutions and/or organizations' which interchange knowledge and technological flows with firms. Moreover, the interplay between firms in their competitive relationships comprehends these two linkages.

The regional boundary aims at the identification of an area where the specific institutional matrix and competencies, and their interaction with the industry, can be related to the generation of local economic performances (de la Mothe and Paquet, 1998). In this context, the main emphasis is placed on institutions and competencies identified in a specific area. However, it is more frequent to identify performance as a result of the overlap at both regional and sectoral levels (for example, the automobile industry). An interdependent system could result from the interaction between the regional and sectoral systems. From this perspective, the empirical and theoretical domain to which this system can be applied is related to interaction, cooperation and competition in firms' activities, developed in a specific region or area. It follows that such a system is not necessarily related to a specific sector's product, and the system could be characterized by different firms located at different points on the 'value added chain'.

Chapter 10 introduces a relationship between the way production systems have evolved over time and the institutions in the different historical phases of the Mexican economy. Chapters 11, 12, 13, 14 and 15 are devoted to specific case studies in the chemical, pharmaceutical, biotechnological, glass and automobile industries. The rationale behind the selection of the three specific sectors of the Mexican economy dealt with throughout this part was not only because they are important in economic activities, but also principally because they illustrate three important issues within Mexican industry: historical evolution and importance (chemical industry), institutional changes that favoured or discouraged the development of a science-based sector in Mexico (pharmaceutics and biotechnology), technological strategies and capabilities of a large domestic firm (glass) and competitiveness (automobile). The objective of Chapter 16 is to analyse how one particular regional system, the state of Aguascalientes, has been able to upgrade its industrial and technological capabilities in a relatively short time. In order to describe this evolution properly, the analysis builds on two critical concepts: the relationships with clusters inside/outside the region and the interdependence of markets and institutions in providing a virtuous circle for technological upgrading to take place. Chapter 17 is dedicated to conclusions.

Notes

1. As we have repeatedly underlined, one of the building blocks for evolutionary thinking is the recognition of the specificities of technical change; according to Dosi (1988a) it is simply not possible to propose one model of technical change which would adequately describe the characteristics of all sectors. Indeed, the peculiar characteristics of innovative processes historically observed in empirical studies of different sectors have brought Pavitt (1984) to the formulation of a taxonomy describing industry-specific models of technical change.
2. See Mattar (1996) and Casar (1994).
3. This result is confirmed in Mattar (1996), where particular emphasis is also placed on the fact that overall exports increased their weight on GDP by more than 30 per cent (with the share of manufactures progressively substituting oil in importance), and in the analyses of Casar (1994, 1996). This author adds strong support to the thesis of a repositioning of Mexican economy in the international arena through the analysis of the revealed comparative advantages (RCA) and external performance indexes in the period 1980–90.
4. 'Competencies' here are used in a specific sense, capturing those that are developed in the industrial sector (firms, institutions, etc.), incorporated in the human capital and specific institution dedicated to support innovative activities. The definition utilized here includes only the efforts addressed to the innovative activities, while performances, in terms of export activities and growth, are viewed as the outcome of the above representation (Cimoli and della Giusta, 2000).
5. According to Carlsson and Stankiewicz (1995) and Edquist (1997), the systems of innovation 'may be supranational, national or subnational (regional and local) – and at the same time they may be sectoral within any of these geographical demarcations'.

PART I

Macroeconomic Setting, Production System and Globalization of Technology

CHAPTER TWO

Macroeconomic Setting and Production System

M. Cimoli

Productivity, investment and sectoral patterns

From Solow's treatment of technical change as an unexplained residual to the concept of national innovation system, as it has been briefly introduced in Chapter 1, there has been an enormous amount of literature covering many different facets of the innovation process. In an early classic study, Solow (1956) addressed the issue of what determines growth. He set out to study what fraction of the growth of output could be attributed to growth of accumulated capital and what fraction to the increase in the labour employed. Perhaps the most surprising fact was that a great deal of growth remained unexplained by the supply of these inputs (the so-called 'Solow residual'). Technicalities aside, this essentially meant that a change occurred which allowed the creation of more value from a given set of resources. This change was in fact a series of changes, of discoveries of better ways to produce; it was a process of learning how to do things differently, which was the result of searching, questioning and probing. In turn, these activities were the result of 'a complicated set of market and non-market institutions that constitute what has been called a National Innovation System' (Romer, 1993, p. 345).

But, of course, the analysis of the specific configuration of an NIS and its performance require three important suppositions. The first supposition deals with the idea that the basic source of productivity growth is a learning experience which takes time and evolves along different historical phases. This is precisely what innovation is all about. As Dosi (1988b, p. 222) points out, innovation concerns the 'search for, and the discovery, experimentation, development, imitation and adoption of new products, new production processes and new organizational set-ups'. This process is not a linear one, and there is no single acceptable indicator that could, in and of itself, capture the complexity of this phenomenon. None the less, to be specific, we have chosen to make ample use of two indicators for this complex process of searching, questioning and probing new ways of performing production and, more generally, economic activities. One is productivity growth, which, as was pointed out above, is a major, tangible result of the process, as well as an essential ingredient in economic progress. Indeed, as the new literature on endogenous growth points out, 'no sustained economic growth can be achieved without the countless discoveries required to create more value from a fixed set of natural resources' (Romer, 1993, p. 345). We are quite aware that the link between innovation and productivity is not a simple one. Two features of the innovation process contribute to the complexity of this linkage. First, only when innovations are diffused through industry does measured productivity increase and, second, innovations in one industry may have a more significant impact on productivity in other industries; this fact is especially clear when a supplier's innovation causes an increase in productivity in the user industry. The other indicator is investment, which embodies a great deal of new technology and for which there is a large series of reliable data.

The second supposition is supported by a good deal of circumstantial evidence from contemporary as well as recently industrialized countries, which shows that production capacity is a prerequisite for developing technological capabilities (such as, in their days, the United States, Germany, the Scandinavian countries, Japan). There seem to be some patterns, albeit rather loose, in the development of a national production capacity. For example, practically every country starts manufacturing clothing and textiles and possibly natural resource processing, and moves on – if it does – to more complex and knowledge-intensive activities. However, the crucial and tricky question is whether there are some activities that hold a special status in the construction of a national system of production that is able, other things being equal, to develop technological capabilities. This supposition is quite old (and goes back at least to List, Ferrier and Hamilton), and it is present in contemporary notions such as those of filire or Dahmen's 'development blocks' (Dahmen, 1989), but this supposition might gain strength on the grounds of the interplay between production capacity and technological capability outlined in Chapter 1. The pattern of each country's production capacity does not average out with the technological efforts and competencies in production activities; instead, it is a complement to them. Empirical evidence strongly conveys the idea that the proper development of technological capabilities in newly industrialized countries is impossible without major structural changes and a sequential construction which expands the manufacturing sector and also involves indigenous skills in a set of 'core' technologies.

Our starting point is simple: an analysis of technological capabilities in the production system and specific sectors requires an understanding of the process by which industrialization takes place (Chapters 3, 4 and 5). The dynamics of production capacity is also based on major structural transformations, which involve a modification in the importance of the different branches of economic activity as sources of both technological/organizational innovations and demand impulses. Sectoral learning patterns and overall national capabilities are dynamically coupled through input and output flows, spillovers of knowledge, complementarities and context specific externalities. Together, they contribute to shape the organizational and technological context within which each economic activity takes place. In a sense, they set the opportunities and constraints facing each individual process of production and innovation, including the availability of complementary skills, information on intermediate-stage inputs and capital goods and demand stimuli to improve particular products.

The third supposition is based on the need for an accountable approach for the description and understanding of technological capabilities in the production system. We do not intend to suggest that there is an invariant sequence of industrial sectors which accounts for the upgrading of technological capabilities; nevertheless, it may still be feasible to identify some sort of growth sequence within the predominant mode of sectoral technological patterns. Different productive sectors have distinct ways of carrying out innovation, which is precisely the central idea underlying different approaches (Pavitt taxonomy, Ferraz taxonomy and Cimoli–Katz on the sectoral historical paths; see Pavitt, 1984; Katz, 1984; Cimoli, 1988; Ferraz *et al.*, 1996) that consider, among other things, the origin of the implicit information embedded in technology, the capacity to diffuse knowledge among productive agents and the extraordinary profits derived from the utilization of technology. For example, the taxonomy of the sectoral pattern for the acquisition of knowledge leading to innovation, together with the efforts to upgrade it, as suggested by Pavitt, is a good point of departure. Pavitt distinguishes four groups of industrial sectors, namely: (a) supplier dominated (SD), in which innovations mainly occur through exogenous changes in capital and intermediate goods, and in which learning is primarily associated with adoption (adaptation) and production skills; (b) specialized suppliers (SS), which provide equipment and instruments for the industrial system – here innovative activities are founded on both formal (more or less scientific) and tacit knowledge, and they are often based on user-producer relationships; (d) scale-intensive sectors (SI), in which innovative abilities reside in a combination of developing or adapting innovative equipment, designing complex products, taking advantage of economies to scale and mastering complex organizations; and (d) science-based sectors (SB), in which innovative opportunities are more directly linked to advances in basic research (see Chapter 1).

The emergence of SI industries entails further forms of learning related to the development and utilization of capital equipment. Moreover, unlike the SD sectors, technological efforts are also focused on: (a) the development of technological synergy between the production and utilization of innovations, often internalized via horizontal and vertical integration; (b) the exploitation of static and dynamic economies to scale; and (c) the establishment of formal institutions carrying out research (typically corporate R&D laboratories), as a complement to informal learning and diffusion of technological knowledge. Furthermore, sectoral learning patterns and overall national capabilities are dynamically coupled through input–output flows, spillover of knowledge, complementarity and context-specific externalities (external factors). Together they contribute to shaping the organizational and technological context within which all economic activity takes place. It can be said that they establish the opportunities and constraints facing every process involving production and innovation – including the availability of complementary skills, information on intermediate inputs and capital goods and demand stimuli to improve particular products.

The flows of knowledge and skills between technological sectors, which are incorporated in human capital and organizational culture, are essential to enhancing the economy's technological capability. Technological information which is not transmitted via price – since it requires multiple and diverse linkages among productive agents where proximity (central idea of regional economies: de la Mothe and Paquet, 1998) and direct relationship are key elements, or, in order to master it, several idiosyncratic modifications should be made – can only be gained within a context of proximity and interaction. In order for this transfer of information to be efficient, a critical sectoral mass which allows for these types of relationships is essential. Externalities such as agglomeration and linkages, which may reduce costs and generate technological capabilities, rely on the existence of this sectoral critical mass and on strong linkages with its interior. Other important elements are externalities which are generated outside the productive sector, the existing social, educational and legal infrastructure, etc.

The Mexican economy: a new scenario and performances

Around the mid 1980s, the set of rules under which the Mexican economy operated changed dramatically. The new set of rules included a different trade regime – without many of the barriers that had been established during the previous decades and with a more limited role for the government in the development process – which implied a modification in the management of the nation's macroeconomic variables. It was an institutional change that brought about a whole new environment in which the firms would operate, and there were important implications for these firms' innovative performance. In this chapter, we put these changes into perspective by examining: the evolution of the broad lines that have guided macroeconomic policy, the changes in the trade policy regime and the interaction of the two. This scenario defines a 'macro' setting that greatly influences the environment in which firms innovate. The need to consider the macroeconomic environment is especially clear in the case of Mexico, as an examination of almost any macroeconomic indicator would suggest. The Mexican economy is highly unstable, compared to other OECD countries. GDP growth is more variable; the real exchange rate is more volatile and inflation is higher (Table 2.1). This instability spreads to almost all key variables affecting the innovation process. Furthermore, the modification in Mexico's trade regime has had significant implications in the way domestic firms function. Trade policy is especially important in developing economies, where the industrialization process relies heavily on borrowing and adapting foreign technology (Cimoli and Dosi, 1995), and thus depends crucially on the relationship with foreign actors, as moulded by the trade regime. These two dimensions define a 'macro' environment that shapes the way in which agents participating in the innovation process interact, as well as the way technological progress occurs. For example, in this circumstance of high instability, most small and medium firms assume a defensive behaviour with regard to their investment in innovative activities. In fact, local financial investments are a better long-term alternative. Large firms and MNEs take a lower risk for investment in capital goods and innovative projects; in particular, they interact with the international financial markets through their financial divisions and controlled banks.

Mexico's production structure has gone through significant changes, from the import substitution period to the new scenario characterized by stabilizing macro policies and a growing effort to open the economy to increased foreign competition. In recent years, a new pattern of sectors and production lines has been created, in that economic activities are coordinated and integrated across geographic borders. In fact, production activities are now widely recognized to be the centre of gravity for larger participation of the newly industrialized economies in the new 'world specialization'. These new globalized scenarios increasingly modify a nation's com-

Table 2.1 Macroeconomic Indicators

Years	GDP[a]	Inflation rate[b]	Real exchange rate[c]	Trade balance[d]
1980	–	–	100	−254.8
1981	8.5	28.70	87	−323.1
1982	−0.5	98.87	251	587.2
1983	−3.5	80.80	150	1175.3
1984	3.4	59.17	122	1098.7
1985	2.2	63.74	160	699.8
1986	−3.1	105.75	111	418.3
1987	1.7	159.17	94	732.3
1988	1.3	51.66	93	217.5
1989	4.1	19.70	92	33.8
1990	5.2	29.93	80	−73.5
1991	4.2	18.79	72	−606.6
1992	3.5	11.94	67	−1482.8
1993	1.9	8.01	64	−1127.9
1994	4.5	7.05	63	−1566.0
1995	−6.2	51.97	80	500.9
1996	5.1	27.70	72	527.1
1997	6.8	15.72	66	52.0
1998	4.8	18.61	64	−714.1

Notes: [a]Average annual growth rate, [b]Consumer prices index, [c]Index (1980 = 100), [d]Average monthly balance (current millions of US dollars).
Source: Indicadores Económicos de Coyuntura, INEGI, Mexico.

petitiveness, as well as integration in terms of production capacities among firms, industries and nations. For example, Capdevielle *et al.* (1997) argue that the firms exclusively related to assembly activities within what is called *maquiladora* (or 'screw-driver') industry are the central actor in the new Mexican competitiveness. In fact, from 1988 the importance of the *maquiladora* industries increased steadily: in terms of number of plants and workers employed and value added. The *maquiladora* phenomenon poses a problem in the present perspective, considering the effects of their presence on the dynamics of local industry. As far as the creation of backward linkages is concerned, it can be observed that there is a lack of local sourcing by *maquiladoras*, which make very limited purchases of Mexican material inputs. There appear to be several reasons for this, among which the authors include: (a) the characteristic inward orientation before liberalization, which hampered their development in terms of both scale of operations and quality of products; (b) inadequate access to credit and financial capital for medium and small firms during the economic crisis of the 1980s and mid 1990s; (c) the lack of a skilled human capital base, coupled with the tendency for the existing human resources to move within *maquiladoras* rather than set up their own companies or enter Mexican firms; (d) materials shortages; and (e) an insufficient number of national independent consulting firms. Another relevant issue regards the role played by large domestic firms and the subsidiaries of MNEs, which together have incorporated the pattern of international integration in terms of product specialization and technology absorbed from foreign economies.

It is of considerable interest to note that the 'inward' oriented pattern that supported industrialization and local technological capabilities has been increasingly eroded. Industries and firms now are integrated in an international network, according to the different types of linkages designed as networks of contractors or more coordinated, integrated and organized production lines in different sites around the world (Brainard, 1997).

Moreover, with different timing, one can infer an 'optimal cycle' of globalization, which relates increasing production capacities with dynamic and higher technological efforts and competencies. In the beginning, foreign firms start their production activities in a domestic location and adapt organization equipment around the main home-based business. Manufacturing activities are mainly located on the basis of labour costs and local markets that have specific regulatory frameworks (think, at the NAFTA level, of introducing a new regulatory framework). For some authors, local technological competences become an early ingredient for the attraction of MNEs in a large range of industries (Eaton *et al.*, 1994). In the following steps, subsidiaries of MNEs should develop their own technological competencies by adapting the production organization/processes and product designs. In the last step, one can suppose that R&D moves on, establishing research centres and linkages with local centres dedicated to the production of applied research and the formation of human capital.

This last step, associated with the new phenomenon of the globalization of industrial research activities, as more multinationals invest in research abroad and the acquisition of laboratories, has generally occurred in the most industrialized economies in the OECD, area (OECD, 1996b, 1997d). Nevertheless, recent evidence on the contribution of the large multinational firms to the world's technology shows that, despite increasing talk about the globalization of large firms' technological activities, they remain remarkably domestic. For foreign firms, in global terms, the evidence seems to point to the opposite of the expected convergence between the globalization of production and research activities. Technical literature cites international evidence which shows that the large MNEs keep most of their technological activity at home (Patel and Pavitt, 1995a). Or, in other words, the MNEs prefer to keep research activities at home, rather than their production activities (Cantwell, 1992).

The Mexican system is thus facing challenges that require an analysis of the following significant points: (a) the effect of the macro-setting and structural reforms on the manufacturing industry's performance; (b) the changes of production system in terms of both technological efforts and economic performances; and (c) the nature of the globalization process taking place in production and technological activities.

The macro-setting: productivity and investment

In Chapter 3, to assess the extent of innovation by the Mexican production system and this interplay with the macro-setting, we rely on several indicators, especially on productivity and investment. At first sight, we now justify this approach. As described in Chapter 1, we want to stress that at the heart of innovation processes are firms' efforts to search and learn, their willingness to question, probe and experiment with new ways of doing things. Firms' efforts can take on a wide variety of forms, and we do not have long established statistical records for many of these forms – including the time spent searching and testing new technologies and the willingness to experiment with new organizational set-ups. These innovation efforts are manifest in many different ways. None the less, it is important to bear in mind that an ideal measure should capture this drive which moves firms to exert these efforts. The reason is that knowledge is not some public good which can be freely accessed by anyone. Instead, it is embodied in firms, and predominantly so in a tacit form. Thus, firms are the repositories for knowledge (Cimoli and Dosi, 1995), and they are the central actors in the innovation process. Their active role is essential because it is mainly on these firms' accumulated knowledge that new knowledge is built, and for this building process to happen, there is no substitute for a firms' own efforts. Moreover, innovations often occur as a natural result of the production process: 'a significant amount of innovations and improvements are originated through "learning by doing" and "learning by using" ' (Dosi, 1988b, p. 223).

Process innovations which improve quality, as well as product innovations, find their way into increased productivity in a more tortuous manner. If the new products are used as inputs, productivity in the user industry will increase, such as when new equipment ups the productivity in the industry using it. Baily and Chakrabarti (1985) note that during the 1970s, the machinery industry introduced new textile equipment, replacing the mechanical shuttle with air or water jets, an innovation which produced enormous gains in productivity in the textile industry. If the supplier and user industries happen to be the same, the increase in productivity will be clear-cut. Otherwise, productivity gains resulting from the supplier's innovation will be shared between the supplier and the user, with the distribution of the gains in productivity depending on many features, including market structures (OECD, 1996a). New final products also increase productivity, since the enhanced quality translates into higher added value (Chakrabarti, 1990), though in this case the technicalities in the measurement of productivity are likely to understate this increase 'relative to a true economic measure of productivity' (Baily and Chakrabarti, 1985). A detailed analysis of productivity trends is presented in Chapters 3 and 4.

Another indicator we rely on heavily is investment, in part because of the availability of data over a long period. In addition, existing studies on the determinants for investment show it to be very valuable information, because investment is a major component of innovation. By now it is widely accepted, as an OECD study points out, that 'much new technology is embodied in the capital goods (machinery and structures) that industries purchase to expand and improve production' (OECD, 1996a). According to this study, the share of technology obtained through investment in capital goods ranges from one-quarter to almost half of all the technology that the private sector acquired in the ten countries analysed. This study states that the methodology used – which only considered investment, rather than the R&D embodied in the whole capital stock – probably underestimated the role of capital as a means of appropriating technology. Thus, one can be confident that investment in capital goods is, indeed, a very important element in the innovation process. Fernandez (Chapter 3) provides an analysis of investment behaviour along the different historical phases: import substitution, transition and deregulation periods.

The production system: sectoral efforts and performances

In Chapter 4, Capdevielle, Corona and Hernandez describe Mexico's production system according to the main development paths followed by the various industrial sectors, in terms of their technological patterns. As part of this, we explain these patterns considering both effort and performance. It should be stressed that in this chapter we attempt to come up with an accountable exercise for the classification of industrial activities according to the ISIC-industrial groups, the STAN-OECD sectors and the technological classification developed in Pavitt's taxonomy. These classifications provide an excellent basis for the illustration and measurement of the gaps between Mexico and other developed economies.

An important concern is associated with whether Pavitt's taxonomy may or may not be used to detect patterns in Mexico's development of technological capabilities. The advent of manufacturing industry generally is considered to have an initial stage in which SD sectors predominate, accompanied by an emergent SS sector. The process of technical change in these sectors is characterized by the subsequent development of various forms of tacit, incremental learning, which are related to the transfer and acquisition of foreign technology, mainly through the utilization of equipment, the development of engineering skills in machine-transformation and the adaptation of existing machines and final products to specific environmental conditions.

Although we have duly acknowledged that Pavitt's taxonomy was developed for the purpose of explaining technological patterns in more advanced economies, it is none the less quite useful for a better understanding of the main features and specifications of the economies that present lesser degrees of development. In fact, from the accountable aggregation of sectors into a broader technological taxonomy, we can detect those distinctive features which are responsible for the differences in the modes of acquisition of knowledge and the efforts devoted to innovative activities. Consider, for instance, and this point is further elaborated in Chapter 4, the case of the SB sector, which has increased its participation in world trade and exports and has demonstrated a good performance in terms of escalating production capacities. However, upon consideration of the SB sector's main modes of acquiring knowledge and its innovative efforts in Mexico, it can readily be seen that the patterns differ a great deal from those followed in more developed economies, particularly in terms of the linkages with advanced research centres, universities, R&D expenditure and so forth.

In other words, taking into consideration that the accountable aggregation in this taxonomy is fixed, we can identify the differences in terms of efforts and performances, which could also be seen as an exercise to establish a *benchmark* in sectoral patterns. However, it should be borne in mind that unequal efforts and levels of outcome imply that production in Mexico differs not only regarding the integration of production lines but also in the type of productive activities carried out. It is a well-known fact that Mexican plants and factories are not remotely as productive as those in the United States and that their production activities vary a great deal, even in those cases in which the final generic good thus produced may be the same. As described earlier in this work, different modes of utilization of knowledge and sources of technology are associated with dissimilar types of production, as are the variations in the appropriation of technology and the relationships between production and the chains of technology that span various sectors.

Moreover, in the case of Mexico, it must be stressed that neither the industrialization pattern nor the technological trajectories have necessarily coincided with those followed by the industrialized world. Nevertheless, this intuitive exercise, which establishes a benchmark, is helpful in that it can provide a way to approach the distance to be covered in order to attain the specialization and technological levels that are located at the technological front line.

The globalization of production systems and technological linkages

Mexico is a nation which, after trade reforms, has increased its participation in the world arena, in terms of exports as well as imports. Most of the surviving and efficient firms (MNEs and large domestic firms) have increased their exports of final commodities and components for automobiles, chemicals, plastic products, glass, beer, electronics, steel, cement, etc.; on the other hand, imports of intermediate goods, machinery and equipment have also grown. The image that we have is that Mexico is a country in which production activities are highly globalized and that a new Mexican specialization in the global chain of production is emerging.

Adjustments must be made to apply the basic NIS scheme, which was devised for the other OECD countries, to the case of Mexico, in order to capture the specific dynamics of the interactions among the actors in the Mexican NIS. Globalization processes also have to be analysed regarding the ways in which the innovation system, particularly associated with both foreign and domestic firms, interacts with the rest of the world. The methods and intensity of Mexico's globalization will be analysed, focusing on both the sectoral chains of production and the main channels for technological flows. These involve foreign sources of technology, which are related to foreign direct investment, technology transfer and the technology that is incorporated into capital goods imports, intermediate inputs and components.

In Chapter 5, the globalization process is analysed, observing the existing interaction between sectoral production capacities, technological channel flows and the localization of industrial R&D. In the search for a pattern of globalization, it is of considerable interest to establish a number of critical questions about the ways in which this pattern is evolving. How is the actual pattern evolving in the light of its capability to change from a globalized assembly pattern to a more domestically integrated one, in terms of flows of technology and local capacity to adapt technology? Is Mexico developing a production pattern that is capable of integrating domestic production capacities and technological capabilities? How is this pattern evolving, when the globalization of production is compared to the globalization of industrial R&D activities? Which are the principal channels through which technology is globalized for the Mexican economy? These issues are addressed below through the use of several of the indicators listed by Unger and Oloriz in Chapter 5.

CHAPTER THREE

The Macroeconomic Setting for Innovation

J. Fernandez

Introduction

This chapter is organized in four sections. The following sections refer to the periods into which we have chosen to divide the experience of Mexico's industrialization. The import substitution industrialization (ISI) period is characterized by external protection and an active role of the state in promoting an inward-oriented industrialization pattern (i.e. mainly addressed to domestic demand). The economic environment (exchange rate, inflation, fiscal deficit) was relatively stable in this phase, and particularly in the second half of the period, and the aim was to provide a favourable set of incentives to industry: in a sense macroeconomics seems to have been modelled in order to favour local industry growth. The transition period, was characterized by macroeconomic turbulence, rising inflation and massive capital outflow, particularly after the debt crisis of 1982. In this phase the necessity to restore stability represented a major constraint and the set of incentives to manufacture, combining trade liberalization, large devaluations, protected export promotion and sharp reductions of domestic demand, seems to have been the result of a lack of coordination between industrial and macroeconomic policies. The new regulatory period is, in this sense, less problematic because industrial policy was subordinated to macroeconomic priorities. Trade policies, capital liberalization, deregulation of the economy and privatization of public assets accelerated in the pursuit of deeper market driven incentives.

Each of these three sections contains a brief description of the main policies undertaken during the period, and an analysis of the effects of the interaction of macro and micro policies on the incentives to innovate. We recognize the difficulty of measuring the process of searching and learning at the core of the innovation activity, and the fact that we will have to rely on evidence that measures only some facets of this complex phenomenon. Among this evidence, two types of measures deserve special mention: productivity measures, which we use because, as was pointed out above (Chapters 1 and 2), increased productivity is a natural manifestation of the 'search and learn' process of innovation, albeit only one of them; and measures on investment in capital goods, because investment is a well documented, amply studied element in which innovation materializes. The final section is dedicated to conclusions.

Import substitution industrialization (ISI) period

From the mid-1950s to the early 1970s the Mexican economy experienced sustained growth amid low inflation and a fixed exchange rate. Output per capita grew above 3 per cent annually, real wages above 6 per cent and inflation was kept at an average of 3.8 per cent, and was never above 6 per cent. Compared to Mexico's later performance, and to other Latin American countries – where high inflation was chronic – these results were remarkable.

Macroeconomic policy was characterized by low government deficits. This feature was the result of both low public expenditure and low fiscal pressure – even by Latin American standards. Fiscal deficits were easily financed with moderate seignorage, limited external debt and compulsory lending by the banking sector through reserve requirements. The whole macroeconomic scheme was consistent. A prudent monetary policy was allowed by the small need for deficit financing. This resulted in low inflation, which was consistent with a fixed exchange rate and growing financial intermediation. This growth in financial intermediation, in turn, provided reliable financing to the government through reserve requirements.

The stable macroeconomic setting was accompanied by an attempt to foster industrialization by creating an environment protected from external competition with trade barriers. Trade barriers were a combination of tariffs and permits, and were complemented with a wide variety of government policies aimed at promoting industrialization. Industry did grow in this environment, raising its participation in output from 21.5 per cent in 1950 to 29.4 per cent in 1970.

We now turn to a brief description of the specific instruments on which the government relied to promote industrialization. Trade policy made use of tariffs and permits. Tariff rates had an escalated structure. They were in the range of 5–15 per cent for raw materials and intermediate products, 20–25 per cent for machinery, 25–35 per cent for other manufactured products and 100 per cent for automobiles (Solis, 1981). Yet tariffs continually lost importance as a means to protect domestic industries from foreign competition and foster their growth as compared to quantitative restrictions, to the point that the requirement of obtaining licences to be able to import goods from abroad became the main instrument of protection. Moreover, according to some authors (Ten Kate and Wallace, 1980, p. 43), the system of licences became the 'most important instrument not only of commercial policy but also of the general industrialization policy'. In 1957, 35 per cent of imports (in value terms) were subject to licence, a percentage that rose to 68 per cent by 1970. When deciding whether to grant permission for importing a good, there was a large set of criteria that would officially guide the authorities, including the consideration of whether the good was produced in the country, and, if so, in sufficient amounts, at good quality and at reasonable price and terms of delivery. The impact on the balance of payments and whether the product was 'luxury consumption' or not would ideally be considered. Yet several authors (e. g. Ten Kate and Wallace, 1980) point out that, in practice, the decisive consideration was whether the good was produced in the country. Only when there was no domestic production and no sufficiently close substitute would an import licence be granted. The fact that this was the overriding criterion is illustrated by the allowance of price differences even greater than 100 per cent.

The system of licences was complemented by other instruments to promote the development of domestic industries. Lists of industrial products with the potential for import substitution were published annually. Besides new products, the government included products whose domestic production was considered insufficient. Through these lists, the government guided investments in its preferred directions. Local content requirements were established in the automobile industry, and several 'fabrication programmes' were issued. The aim of these programmes was to promote local vertical integration in the production of heavy intermediaries, and to rely on a variety of incentives, including import licences and fiscal incentives. For instance, the government would allow imports of components only if the importing firms committed themselves to raising the fraction of local contents. An Interministerial Committee for Public Sector Imports was established with the aim of rationalizing public-sector imports, thus helping import substitution by promoting the use of domestic suppliers.

There were two legal dispositions which granted fiscal incentives to industry, and merit special mention: the Law of Promotion of New and Necessary Industries, and Rule XIV of the General Import Tariff. The Law of Promotion of New and Necessary Industries established tax exemptions on industries belonging to one of its categories. The definition of a new industry was simply one that produced a good not previously produced in Mexico. The concept of necessary referred to an industry where domestic production was low relative to domestic demand (less than 80 per cent), but in the mid-1950s several other types – including export firms and assembly plants – were added. Several authors have argued that, in practice, the conditions to qualify for the benefits of this law were very restrictive. They included the requirement that at least 60 per cent of the direct costs be of domestic origin, and that at least 10 per cent of 'the degree of elaboration originated in the enterprise itself'. The taxes subject to exemptions were (a) the import tax on inputs, equipment and capital goods; (b) a reduction of up to 40 per cent on the tax on profits; (c) federal receipts due to its participation in the excise tax; and (d) the general export tax (Ten Kate and Wallace, 1980). The duration of exemptions was of ten years for the so-called basic activities (machinery and equipment and raw materials), seven years for semi-basic activities (tools, scientific equipment, 'vital' consumer goods) and five years for secondary activities, defined as those not included in the previous two categories.

Rule XIV of the General Import Tariff promoted imports of machinery and equipment. It granted fiscal exemptions on these imports, and on accessories, parts and replacements necessary for their installation. As opposed to the Law of Industries, firms did not need to be new or necessary to qualify for these exemptions. Its application was very liberal, in the sense that it was very easy to obtain the exemptions it granted. The constrast with the greater difficulties associated with the Law of New and Necessary industries made Rule XIV more important in its impact on the modernization of plants. Firms that wanted to import machinery could seek tax exemptions through Rule XIV rather than trying to qualify as new or necessary.

Other features of fiscal policy that raised the returns on domestic investment were the amendment, in 1961, of the corporate income tax, establishing accelerated depreciation allowances, and the complete exception from taxation, from 1965, of capital gains and retained profits – to simulate reinvestment of profits. The government also intervened directly in many industrial firms, and made a very important contribution to industrialization through public investment complementary to private. According to Ramírez (1994), public investment reached more than half of total investment during some years in the 1960s. Government production took the form mainly of the provision of inputs for the private sector. These inputs were sold at low prices, a feature that accentuated as public sector prices increased at a lower rate than inflation. According to Clavijo (1980), the real price of public sector goods and services fell by an average of 12.5 per cent between 1961 and 1970, raising private sector profitability.

Innovation process in the ISI period

We now deal with the issue of what this setting meant for the process of innovation. Let us first stress that, overall, the array of policies coincided in stimulating investment. Public policy sheltered domestic industry from foreign competition, provided a stable macroeconomic environment, growing infrastructure and crucial inputs at low prices, and a tax system generous in its treatment to profits and supportive of their further reinvestment. In short, public policy created an environment extremely favourable to private investment. Investment did fluorish. For a long period, machinery and tools were imported at high rates, creating an important base for domestic industry.

In a different dimension, the overall macro framework was a suitable enviroment for the accumulation of competencies, a crucial ingredient in the process of innovation (Cimoli and Dosi, 1995). It is along these lines that government protection of new industries has been justified; that is, although a developing country may have a potential comparative advantage in manufacturing, its lack of experience does not allow it to compete with developed countries. It needs temporary protection against import competition: the so-called *infant industry argument*.

The idea that a domestic industry was being nurtured, that it was acquiring capabilities and improving its performance, stands well if judged by the evolution of productivity. As is shown in Chapter 4, during this period manufacturing showed reasonable increases in productivity. According to Samaniego (1984), productivity (measured by total factor productivity) increases ranked very well when compared to other countries. High productivity growth is also found by Blomstrom and Wolf (1989), although they study labour productivity, instead of total factor productivity. They focus on labour productivity gaps for the period 1965–84 between Mexican and US manufacturing, and find that these gaps decreased over the whole period, but the biggest catch-up took place during the second half of the 1960s, with a slowing thereafter.[1] Other studies (World Bank 1986, Hernández Laos and Velasco, 1990) obtain lower estimates of productivity growth and, as Ross (1993) points out, the most likely explanation for this difference – looking at the databases used – is that large and medium-sized firms had a better performance than small ones, and higher estimates are obtained when large firms are more represented.

We now examine more closely the role of some of the features of this policy framework. Consider first the government provision of basic infrastructure through public investment. Ramírez (1994) stresses that public investment in social and economic infrastructure greatly enhanced the productivity of private investment in Mexico. He tests for the Mexican case the hypothesis that public investment can foster – rather than crowd out – private investment. He warns that in its effort to eliminate wasteful use of resources, the Mexican public sector may err on the side of wasting the externalities associated with many public investments (this worry stems from the fact that public investment has declined continuously since the mid-1980s). He estimates a flexible accelerator investment model, adding variables which may be important for the Mexican economy, over the period 1950–90. One of his main results is that in his regressions to explain private investment, public investment does show a positive and significant coefficient. His estimates suggest that 'a ceteris paribus increase of 10 percent in public investment generates an increase in gross private capital formation of between 2–3 percent within one year' (pp. 12–13). In his 1989 cross-country study, Barro finds that one determinant of the investment–GDP ratio is the public investment–GDP ratio. He takes this ratio as a proxy for government infrastructure services, which affect private sector productivity. He obtains an estimated coefficient for the effect of public investment on total investment of 2.2 and writes that 'if taken literally, the coefficient of 2.2 in the regressions for i/y means that an extra unit of public investment induces about a one-for-one increase in private investment'. He then argues in favour of considering public capital, rather than public investment, as a measure of the flow of services provided by the government, and finds that the coefficient is still positive, although no longer significantly different from zero.

With regard to the promotion of imports of machinery and equipment, fiscal policy measures undoubtedly had a favourable impact on investment. Empirical support for this 'price effect' is provided by Ibarra (1995). Yet the other side of the coin was the poor development of the domestic capital good sector. A study by NAFINSA-ONUDI (1985) found that this sector was less developed in Mexico than in other Latin American and semi-industrialized countries. In Mexico, 90 per cent of machinery was imported, while the corresponding figures were 20 per cent in Brazil and 44 per cent in Korea. Moreover, these two countries were able to export capital goods: 27 and 20 per cent of domestic production, respectively. Another important, and sometimes overlooked, side-effect of the easiness of importing capital foreign goods was the hindering of the process of learning how to repair and improve the foreign technology embodied in these goods, an important ingredient in the construction of endogenous technological capabilities (Cimoli *et al.* 1998).

Summing up, during the 1960s government policies provided a protected environment from foreign competition and encouraged industrialization through the creation of basic economic infrastructure through public investment. At the same time, they permitted the imports of capital goods from abroad and discouraged – in relative terms – the production for foreign markets. This set of policies had mixed results on the process of acquiring domestic technological capabilities. On the one hand, an environment isolating domestic firms from foreign competition provided a well suited environment for learning complex manufacturing abilities and acquiring an industrial culture. The government role went well beyond that of setting these barriers, but also took the form of active participation in capital formation. On the other hand, this set of policies hindered the process of acquisition of learning capabilities by supporting domestic firms in the process of adaptation of imported technology (particularly, learning how to repair it and improve upon it). Finally, these policies also allowed firms to avoid searching to penetrate foreign markets. This too involves a process of learning and acquiring abilities which can help to improve the organizational design of firms and can generate spillovers into firms (Feder, 1988) with which they interact (for instance, suppliers). Moreover, by failing to establish a well defined temporal dimension for the duration of the protected environment, the overall protective policies removed the natural incentive to get ready to compete without help in the future.

Transition period and abandonment of the ISI pattern

The administration that took office in 1970 held the view that the government should take a more active role in the process of development. It began an era of attempts to modify the pattern of development that had guided Mexico's industrialization until then. Although the overall setting of protection continued, several efforts were made to eliminate some of its drawbacks. First, there was an attempt to remove the anti-export bias of previous years. In 1970 the Instituto Mexicano de Comercio Exterior (IMCE) was created, whose purpose was to help domestic firms to access international markets. In 1971 export subsidies called Certificados de Devolución de Impuestos (CEDIS) were introduced. Exporting firms were granted tariff rebates on imported inputs (a feature that is the essence of the *maquiladora* industry). In 1972 the Fondo de Equipamiento Industrial (FONEI) was created, with the aim of financing export-oriented activities. Finally, from 1977 to 1981 there was an attempt to rationalize protection and to deal with the origin of the anti-export bias: namely, the incentive to produce for a protected, easily accessible, less demanding domestic market. This rationalization took the form of replacing import licences with tariffs, as a first step to allowing foreign competition. Second, new sector-specific programmes were established. Prominent among them were the programmes for automobiles and for microcomputers. These programmes were different from the early fabrication programmes in that they granted import protection subject to the completion of requirements in both the domestic and foreign markets. Prices had to be within a certain range in the domestic market, and export targets had to be met on the external front. Third, the idea that the domestic capital goods industry was underdeveloped led to concrete policy measures. The subsidies to import foreign machinery, under Rule XIV of the tariff legislation, were removed and, instead, subsidies were established for the production of new capital goods. Moreover, the Certificados de Promoción Fiscal (CEPROFIS) gave fiscal incentives for the production and purchase of domestic capital goods.

These attempts to rationalize the pattern of development based on protectionism were largely offset by the government itself, by its management of macroeconomic policy. Starting in 1972, public expenditure began to grow, in accordance with the idea that the government should take a more active role in the development process. Since no reform of similar magnitude was undertaken to enhance public revenues, a public deficit followed, which was at the origin of the macroeconomic imbalances that would prove the difficulties of promoting expansive public policies to support domestic growth. It is important to note that international factors played an important role in this process, since without the abundance of financial resources for developing countries during the 1970s, the observed shifts in macroeconomic policy would not have been possible.

It is beyond the scope of this work to explain the reasons behind the abundance of financial resources for the developing countries in the 1970s, but a great part of the explanation lies in the increase in oil prices that generated huge surpluses in OPEC countries, which were transferred as petro-dollars to First World financial intermediaries that, in turn 'recycled' them to developing countries in the form of (mainly) loans. This abundance of financial resources generated both extremely low – even negative – real interest rates and the possibility of a large supply of credit. As is shown in Chapter 4, this translated into a very favourable environment for investment. Indeed, the contrast between the performance of investment in the 1970s and the 1980s is striking. In Mexico[2] investment averaged 23 per cent of GDP in the first decade and only 19.6 per cent in the second. The suspicion that international forces were at least partly responsible for this performance comes to mind as one examines other Latin American countries: in Argentina the corresponding figures were 21.7 and 16.1, in Brazil 24.5 and 17.9 and in Chile 17.9 and 16.3, respectively. For Latin America as a whole investment was 23 per cent of GDP during the 1970s and 17.3 per cent during the 1980s.

The evidence that the 1970s were very favourable to investment in developing countries – and the 1980s very unfavourable – goes beyond that provided by simple inspection of the above figures. Cohen (1993), in a cross-country study, finds that controlling for other relevant variables, investment in the developing countries was above average in the 1970s (by 2 percentage points) and below average (by 2 pertcentage points too) in the 1980s. Ramírez (1994) finds that, for Mexico, a 'dummy' variable associated with the oil boom of 1978–81 is significant, meaning that investment was higher during those years, even after controlling for the traditional variables used to explain its performance. During the 1970s, external factors favoured low interest rates and abundance of supply of funds, two crucial determinants of investment. The real interest rate is the traditional textbook variable affecting investment. Warman and Thirlwall (1994) find that for the Mexican economy the real interest rate negatively affect investment, with a statistically significant coefficient. Ibarra (1995) finds that a measure of the relative cost of capital services, which is constructed using the interest rate, the price index for capital formation, the producer price index and the corporate income tax rate, does have a negative sign (although it is not statistically significant). Several authors argue that the price of funds is not the only financial variable to be taken into account, but also the availability of funds. Ramírez (1994) argues that in Mexico this availability is in fact the real binding constraint when dealing with Mexican firms' financing. Warman and Thirlwall (1994) include the supply of credit besides the real interest rate as a financial explanatory variable of investment, to find that it is positive and statistically different from zero.

Thus, the abundance and low price of financial resources played a major role in the good performance of investment during the 1970s. It also played a role in allowing the government to make an important change in its macroeconomic policy, which we now examine. The Echeverría administration took office in 1970 and applied initially a very orthodox macroeconomic policy. To control deteriorating external accounts, contractionary fiscal and monetary policies were adopted. These policies produced a slowdown of GDP growth to 4.2 per cent, which was taken as additional evidence that a major shift in the overall policy was needed if the goals of the new shared development era were to be achieved.

In 1972 the Ministry of Finance attempted to reform the tax system so as to provide financing for an ambitious investment programme that would be a key component of a new mode of development, the so-called 'shared development' (Buffie, 1990). Although the tax reform attempt failed, public sector expenditure began to grow as if that reform had been a success. The fiscal deficit rose sharply as a consequence. Public sector expenditure grew from 22.3 per cent of GNP in 1970 to 32 per cent in 1976, while revenues increased only from 18.9 to 23.8 per cent during the same period. Thus, the fiscal deficit increased from 3.4 to 8.3 per cent of GNP during this period. In contrast with the stabilizing development, fiscal deficits were largely financed by borrowing from the central bank. The monetary base, which was growing by 19.3 per cent in 1971, grew by 33.8 per cent in 1975. Growth in public expenditure stimulated the economy. Real GDP growth accelerated from 4.2 per cent in 1971 to 8.4 per cent in both 1972 and 1973. Yet it soon produced signsof its fragility. Inflation accelerated as well. It jumped from around 5 per cent in 1971 and 1972 to 21.3 per cent in 1973 and 20.9 per cent in 1974. Coupled with a fixed exchange rate of 12.50 pesos to the dollar, this produced a rapidly overvaluing real exchange rate. This resulted in a deteriorating balance of payments. From 1971 to 1975, the current account deficit increased fourfold (from US $0.91 billion to $4.44 billion) and, interestingly enough, foreign indebtedness also quadrupled, from $6.6 billion at the end of 1970 to $27.9 billion by the end of 1976, with most of this debt being owed by the public sector. The private sector perception of this policy as unsustainable resulted in capital flight. When the central bank's reserves were being depleted, the government decided to devalue the peso by nearly 100 per cent, ending a long period of a fixed exchange rate, one of the cornerstones of the stabilizing development.

Soon after the October 1976 devaluation, an IMF stabilization programme was devised, to be implemented by the administration that took office in that year (the López-Portillo administration) during the following three years. It was a standard IMF-type programme, combining public sector austerity measures with trade liberalization. The public sector deficit should be reduced and the economy should be exposed to more foreign competition through a rationalization of the system of protection. During 1977, the stabilization programme was carried out as planned, and it yielded satisfactory results in terms of restoring macroeconomic balances. Yet a major factor appeared that changed the overall perspectives facing policy-makers. Mexico's oil reserves were discovered to be far greater than previously expected. Proven hydrocarbon reserves jumped from 6.4 billion barrels in 1975 to 16 billion by the end of 1977. The stabilization programme was abandoned in the first of its planned length of years.

In 1978, a new wave of public expenditure led growth began. Even though oil income grew in real terms by 30, 35.6 and 47.7 per cent in 1978, 1979 and 1980 respectively, the public deficit was not reduced. To the contrary, it even grew, from 6.7 per cent in 1977 and 1978, to around 7.5 per cent of GDP in 1979 and 1980. Public sector investment, which had declined by 6.7 per cent in 1977 in the context of the stabilization plan, grew by 31.6 per cent in 1978, 17.1 per cent in 1979, and 16.7 per cent in 1980. A massive inflow of foreign resources allowed this expansionary programme. An expansion of the monetary base, and growing inflation, followed. The inflation rate, which had been reduced to 17.5 per cent in 1978, increased to 18.2 per cent in 1979 and 26.3 per cent in 1980, producing a continuous appreciation of the peso. On the external sector, the expansionary policy translated into a growing current account deficit, which rose every year since 1977; from 2 per cent of GDP to 3.6 per cent in 1978, 3.6 per cent in 1979 and 5 per cent in 1980. This deficit was financed with public external debt, which grew from 36.4 per cent of GDP in 1978 to 41.2 per cent in 1979 and 49 per cent in 1980. But these increases would be dwarfed by what followed.

In 1981 the international oil market weakened. The restrictions that the government faced were now different. Yet it followed essentially the same macroeconomic policy. Public expenditure continued to grow in real terms. The peso was insufficiently adjusted. In an effort to curtail the current account deficit, import controls were accentuated. Yet this deficit reached a historical level of 6 per cent of GDP in 1981, having been 2 per cent in 1977, before the expansionary programme started. Private agents perceived that growing public and current account deficits were not consistent with a weakening oil market, and massive capital flight followed. Public external debt allowed lengthening of the overall macroeconomic policy course for some months. This debt, which amounted to $49 billion in 1980, grew from $74 billion in 1981 to $92 billion in 1982. Just as with the previous administration, during the last two years of the López Portillo administration a rapid growth in public foreign debt took place, which was largely used only to postpone an inevitable shift of policy. In the end, foreign banks were also convinced of the unsustainability of the policy course and the collapse followed.

We end this section by summarizing the impact of the changes that occurred during this period on the process of innovation. First, investment performance was on average very good – in part due to external factors. Second, public sector involvement increased in economic activities. In particular, more public attention and resources were devoted to education and technology-related activities than in earlier periods, enhancing the innovative capacity of domestic firms. Yet the fact that public investment increased in variability is important as well. Indeed, the 1976 failure of the shared development period was followed by a sharp reduction in public investment. The same would happen six years later. It is fairly clear that a steady level of public investment is far more useful than sharp increases followed abruptly by deep cuts.

The instability extended to other areas of public policy. Although trade protection remained high, it also became more volatile, strongly responding to trade balance behaviour. Thus import controls rose as the 1976 crisis approached, then were loosened in a liberalization attempt in 1979, then rose again until the proportion of imports subject to licensing reached 100 per cent in 1982. We claim that these shifts in trade policy do much harm to tasks that involve devoting resources to activities that render results in the long term, such as innovative activities. Of course, they closely mirrored the overall erratic behaviour of macroeconomic policy. Moreover, by showing the public that trade policy would adapt to balance of payment requirements, the government made it more difficult for future trade liberalization attempts to succeed, especially if surrounded – as was to be the case – by an adverse international environment and a huge external debt.

More generally, these two failed experiments adversely affected the incentives to innovate by beginning a series of recurrent crises. In both 1972–6 and 1978–82, the inflation rate accelerated, the real exchange rate appreciated and output grew rapidly, only to end up with a huge devaluation and a recession. These experiences encouraged entrepreneurs to take a short-term approach to business, to seek short-term profitability for fear of a drastic change of unknown nature in the longer term. This is very damaging to the support of technological capabilities, which take time to yield results.

New regulatory framework: deregulation and trade reform

The 1980s have been termed the 'lost decade' for Latin America. There is much truth in this assertion, as a look at almost any macroeconomic indicator would confirm. For instance, investment behaved very poorly, as already documented. Nutrition, health and other living standards indicators worsened dramatically. A crucial factor behind this behaviour was the burden of the inherited debt from the prosperous 1970s. Following the outburst of the international debt crisis and the ensuing poor performance of the debtor economies, several authors (e.g. Krugman, 1988; Sachs, 1988) draw attention to the fact that a high inherited debt could be damaging to investment. The magnitude of the distortions imposed by the debt burden even suggested the possibility that a partial debt forgiveness would be in the creditor's interest. Cohen (1993) estimates that the unanticipated and sudden transfer of resources from debtor countries to their creditors in the 1980s adversely affected investment behaviour. This shift in the service of the debt is significantly and negatively correlated with investment. He estimates a crowding-out coefficient of investment by debt service of 0.35 for the rescheduling countries. Similarly, Peraso (1992) finds that interest repayments on external debt in the mid-1980s did lower the ratio of investment to GDP.

Besides these inherited and external-led features, the 1980s were also a period of reform. A transition to a more limited role for the government and a wider role for the market was conducted. This new phase of the Mexican economy involved a process of privatization, deregulation, budget correction and trade liberalization.

Stabilization attempts, debt rescheduling and debt reduction

The years following 1982 were marked by the burden of the debt, distrust of government policies by the private sector and an adverse world economic environment. With respect to this last point, there was an extreme lack of funds from abroad: capital markets virtually disappeared for Mexico; there only remained 'concerted' lending, which essentially consisted in the rescheduled repayments. Various stabilization attempts failed in such difficult conditions.

Whereas in the period 1979–81[3] indebtedness was a tool in the hands of government to promote development, since 1982 foreign debt turned into burden for the economy. Instead of foreign debt being a complement to the country's own resources, the need appeared to seek resources to service it. Just as had happened six years earlier, towards the end of 1982 an IMF-sponsored programme was undertaken, under the name of Immediate Programme for Economic Reorganization (PIRE). This programme would allow Mexico to dispose of about $3.7 billion between 1983 and 1985, and had as its central features public deficit reduction and a real devaluation of the peso. As for the inherited debt, its first rescheduling took place in 1983. It consisted in postponing the repayment date of the principal. More specifically, the payment of $23.15 billion, due between August 1982 and December 1984, was rescheduled for eight years later. In addition, new loans were received to meet interest payments. Inflation did not behave as expected. Additionally, the government relaxed its fiscal policy. The ensuing unexpected behaviour of inflation on the real exchange rate, along with the loose fiscal policy, caused a balance of payment crisis in 1985 that forced the government to devalue the peso once more and to tighten its fiscal policy.

The 1985 Stabilization Programme required a second debt rescheduling, since the first one had reduced the repayments due between 1983 and 1985, but had set instead high repayments between 1986 and 1990. This second rescheduling made the profile of repayments flatter, reducing those between 1986 and 1990. The 1985 Stabilization Plan faced a huge fall in oil prices, from an average of $25.5 per barrel in 1985 to $12 in 1986. This fall was equivalent to 6.7 per cent of GDP, 48 per cent of export value and 26.2 per cent of public sector income. Due to the environment of a virtual non-existence of capital markets, the shock was absorbed by the country immediately in its entirety. In 1986 there was a drop of 3.6 per cent in GDP, which led the government to consider the possibility of declaring a unilateral moratorium on foreign debt. In a new process of renegotiation, in which the threat of a unilateral moratorium was credible, debt was rescheduled for the third time, and a reduction in the spread above LIBOR was achieved, as compared with the previous renegotiation. Nevertheless, this rescheduling was still guided by the premise that indebted countries would eventually repay all debt contracted before 1982, an idea that came under increasing criticism as, in Latin America as a whole, six years after the onset of the debt crisis, there were no signs of its end. Indeed, the persistence of the crisis was not exclusive to Mexico.[4]

In March 1989 US Treasury Secretary Nicholas J. Brady announced a new plan. This would shift the focus of the debt strategy, by abandoning the idea of looking for new concerted loans for eventual complete debt repayment, and seeking its reduction instead. In July 1989 an agreement in principle with Mexico was announced. As on other occasions, Mexico would be the first country in which the new strategy would be approved, and would serve as a benchmark for the treatment of other countries. This agreement shifted the focus of the international debt strategy, by abandoning the idea of looking for concerted loans for eventual complete debt repayment, and seeking instead its reduction.

The ensuing capital inflows and drops in domestic interest rates suggest that the agreement achieved a remarkable shift in expectations. This conjecture is confirmed more rigorously in econometric work by Claessens *et al.* (1993), who stress that the success of the agreement lay not so much in the reduction in the repayments scheduled, but in the reduction in the uncertainty of the possibility of meeting the required repayments. According to these authors, this uncertainty translated into uncertainty about the exchange rate, and thus produced a very high domestic interest rate.

Privatization and deregulation

During the period 1970–82 the number of government enterprises had grown enormously, from 391 in 1970, to more than 1,000 in 1982, reaching a peak with the nationalization of the banking system in 1982. The range of activities covered by these firms varied greatly, due to the diversity of reasons why they were created, ranging from the requirement for large initial investment – which made it very difficult for private investors to take advantage of profitable investment opportunities – to the government simply rescuing private firms to avoid the loss of jobs. During the administrations of Miguel de la Madrid and Carlos Salinas, the above process was reversed. In the former administration, the smaller enterprises were divested, and the government made clear its intentions of keeping control only of certain key enterprises, such as Pemex (oil), CFE (electricity), Ferronales (railways) and Conasupo (food distribution). The privatization process reached its peak during the first two years of the Salinas administration, with the sell-off of Telmex (telecommunications), Cananea (copper mining) and Aeronaves de México and Mexicana de Aviación (airlines). State-owned enterprises were reduced from over 1,000 in 1982 to 269 in 1991.

The opening of the economy in the second half of the 1980s created the possibility of greatly relaxing the previous regulatory framework.[5] According to policy-makers, during this period market forces were not capable of disciplining the behaviour of economic actors during the ISI era, for there was an environment in which few of these actors intervened in a small, closed economy, and thus there was no alternative to the government setting the rules that the market failed to establish. The opening of the economy created 'market' rules as an alternative to the previous regulatory framework. Deregulation affected vast areas of the economy. 'In three years, more than forty-five legal instruments (including laws and regulations) were changed', and price controls 'that had affected 198 generic products including 260,000 presentations' were eliminated (Fernández, 1995, pp. 314, 315).

We now discuss some activities in which deregulation has been remarkable. Road transport was one of the most emblematic areas. In Mexico, railways move only a fifth of the cargo that lorries move: road transport is the most important form of merchandise transport. Prior to 1988, regulation in the trucking industry established the requirement for a licence to operate, with incumbent firms heavily influencing the granting of these licences. Thus, regulation gave rise to important barriers to entry, and an oligopolistic structure emerged. This structure comprised two segments, one organized by routes for regular cargo and the other organized by products for specialized cargo on any route. As a result of these regulations, prior to 1988, it was very difficult to become a trucker. Moreover, restrictions on those allowed to transport cargo were also important. Among these, the distinction between regular and specialized cargo divided the market and limited competition. The existence of fixed routes impeded the necessary continuous reallocation of resources to deal with cargo imbalances among different routes, resulting in under-utilized capacity. The prohibition on private carriers transporting third parties' cargo, together with the fact that private firms 'usually have one-way transportation needs', also resulted in 'empty back haulages and under-utilised capacity' (Fernández, 1995 p. 317). In July 1989, a decree deregulated the trucking industry. Route restrictions were eliminated, and requirements for obtaining permits were reduced, clarified and decentralized. Restrictions on the type of load transported were removed (except for highly toxic and explosive products), and private carriers were allowed to transport other parties' cargo. The July 1989 deregulation was followed by a huge increase in supply, with the number of permits issued in the six months after deregulation representing a 21 per cent increase in the total formal trucking power, and by a sharp drop in prices, with the average effective tariff falling by 25 per cent. The transfer of resources from the trucking industry to the rest of the economy – as measured by the lower rates and increased supply – has been estimated at $1 billion a year.[6]

Other areas where deregulation is worth mentioning are petrochemicals, telecommunications, fishing and mining. The government changed the classification of petrochemicals, so that some of them were no longer considered as basic – and thus susceptible only to government production – but secondary. Many secondary areas were reclassified into lower categories. Overall, the reclassification implied freer action for private and foreign investment. In mining, the government introduced changes that increased the possibility of private exploitation of mineral areas. It also deregulated fishing, as it abolished previous licensing requirements for breeding and aquaculture, as well as marketing barriers, and relaxed restrictions on foreign investment, allowing a share of up to 49 per cent. With respect to telecommunications, we have mentioned that Telmex was privatized. Several other measures liberalizing authorization procedures for telecommunications equipment were also taken.

The effect of deregulation cannot be easily quantified. The most obvious effect is that it opened up new ways to do things; ways that were previously forbidden, or that were not developed for lack of pressure from competition. For instance, in package delivery completely new lines of services were established.[7] In the trucking industry, the fact that trucking services became more reliable and of higher quality had an impact on the possibilities for the rest of the economy. Higher reliability and quality led to new ways for companies to manage inventories. In extreme cases, previous unreliability had led companies to close whole production lines because inputs did not arrive on schedule. In these cases deregulation led to the establishment of new lines of production. Summing up, deregulation seems to have had a positive effect on the modernization of the service sector.

Trade reform

We now treat in detail the issue of trade reform. After a brief description of the government plans leading to trade liberalization, we deal with the issue of how it affected innovation, relying on investment and productivity.

In 1984, the Mexican economy entered a process of transformation into a more open one. This change took place amid conditions worthy of note. Indeed, the stabilization attempts that followed the 1982 crisis had not yet succeeded when trade liberalization began. In 1984 – between the 1982 and 1985 Stabilization Programmes – a plan to guide industry development and foreign trade, PRONAFICE (Programa Nacional de Fomento a la Industria y al Comercio Exterior), was issued. It was supposed to cover the 1984–8 period. The main idea of this plan was to combine export promotion with selective import substitution and gradually and selectively to rationalize protection. The trade liberalization envisaged in PRONAFICE began to materialize in December 1984 with the first liberalization measures, and in a July 1985 decree that liberalized 65 per cent of imports, while increasing tariffs to act as a counterbalance. In 1986 liberalization proceeded smoothly and Mexico entered the GATT. During this year, oil prices plummeted in what constituted the single most important external blow to the 1985 Stabilization Programme. The process of trade reform was not to escape the misfortunes of the stabilization attempts. Yet the result was neither the suspension nor the delay of the scheduled programme of liberalization, but its acceleration. In December 1987 PRONAFICE was effectively abandoned. As part of the first of a series of constantly renewed incomes policy stabilization agreements – the so-called PACTOS – trade liberalization was abruptly accelerated. In the PACTOS, trade liberalization was viewed as a major instrument in controlling inflation. Just as in the mid-1970s, trade policy was responding to macroeconomic problems. But this time it was not a current account deficit triggering protection. Instead, it was inflation leading to faster liberalization. At the same time, exchange rate management partially replaced the protection that tariff and permits were previously providing. Indeed, during 1986 and 1987 the peso was constantly depreciated, so that the protection domestic firms were losing from trade restrictions was compensated by an expensive dollar. From 1988 onwards this 'exchange rate protection' gradually deteriorated, and domestic firms began to feel the pressure of external competition.

Trade reform and investment

Although the major determinants of the poor performance of investment during the 1980s were not policy-driven, we nevertheless examine what role public policy may have played. The combination and timing of policies, together with the difficult conditions under which they were undertaken, did not provide economic actors with any reasonable certainty as to what to expect in the longer term. The public was left wondering what policy would ultimately prevail, and thus made decisions based on the very near future. Why was this so? First, it was the precedent of two deep crises in the 1970s, both preceded by promises of a new, sustainable mode of development. Moreover, previous experience suggested that, for a variety of reasons, the government could very easily shift the policy orientation. For example, the trade liberalization of the mid-1970s was abandoned as soon as the trade balance began to deteriorate. Second, the fact that the economy had to transfer resources abroad instead of receiving them – to service the huge external debt – in a very adverse international environment made the economy very fragile. Adverse circumstances could have led the government to shift policy, even though it did try to resist the temptation to do so. This is specially relevant for a trade liberalization policy. The public perceived that it could be reversed to manage a deteriorating external imbalance. Third, when plans were not matched by reality the lack of credibility continued to grow. Each failure of a stabilization plan reinforced this problem. Moreover, the sharp acceleration of liberalization in 1987 contradicted what the 1984 plan had established.

Many trade liberalization attempts in developing countries have been reversed. Not surprisingly, trade liberalization announcements are often received with scepticism. Trade liberalization that is believed to be only short-lived may have undesirable consequences. Calvo (1987) has stressed that it can trigger a glut of imports, particularly of durable goods, to take advantage of cheap foreign goods while they are available. Rodrik (1991) has emphasized that a reform that lacks credibility can deter investment, because potential investors will not want to commit resources to activities whose profitability might be only short-lived. Reallocation of resources may be delayed until it is known which policy will ultimately prevail. A trade liberalization programme may lack credibility for a variety of reasons. The public may perceive that the government will simply not find it in its interest later on to stick to a programme it has announced previously, especially if past experience suggests – as in the Mexican case – that the government sees no problem in changing plans. On the other hand, many circumstances, particularly a deteriorating external balance, may make it extremely difficult to avoid reimposing trade barriers. In the Mexican case, the enormous debt obligations, coupled with their permanent rescheduling and the adverse international environment, created much uncertainty about external balance behaviour. It is precisely factors provoking a deteriorating external balance that are the ones most often used to explain the reversal of a liberalization attempt. Thus, these factors are the natural candidates to measure the credibility of a trade liberalization programme.

Based on the above ideas, Ibarra (1995) obtains a measure of the credibility of survival of the Mexican trade liberalization, and then introduces this measure as one of the determinants of Mexican investment. Using data from 17 liberalization attempts in different countries, he finds that a deteriorating balance of payments, a falling real exchange rate and the use of expansionary fiscal and monetary policy all raise the probability of reversal. He then applies his estimates to gauge this probability for the Mexican case, to find that it reached high levels during different times in the period from 1985 to 1991. In particular, it reached a peak in 1986, the year oil prices plummeted, and it experienced an even steeper increase during 1988; that is, when the exchange rate stabilization plan began to work. Finally, he examines the effect of this lack of credibility – as measured by the variable just constructed – on investment, to find that it does have a statistically significant impact. He provides an estimate of the order of magnitude of this effect. The increase in the probability of policy reversal of the magnitude observed in 1988 may have caused a decline of about one-third in the rate of capital accumulation.

Trade reform and productivity

The trade reform that began in 1985 amounted to a complete overhaul of the Mexican economy. This had enormous effects on the way domestic firms behave; in particular, in the way they innovate. In this section we follow these changes by looking at the performance of productivity; in Chapter 4, productivity trends are analysed according to the differences of sectoral patterns and gaps with respect to the international frontier. Here, we rely on two different sets of studies. First, there are studies on the productivity of the Mexican manufacturing sector. These studies show good productivity behaviour after liberalization. We searched for the transmission channels that might be involved. Second, there are cross-country studies that look at the behaviour of productivity among countries with different degrees of openness to the international economy. Particularly relevant to these studies are the ideas that technological innovations spread beyond the country in which they are originated, and that the degree to which a country can benefit from foreign R&D depends on its degree of openness. Chapters 4 and 5 discuss more deeply the assessment of this spillover in the Mexican innovation system.

To address the first type of studies, we rely on work by Kessel and Samaniego (1995), Luna and Valdivieso (n.d.) and Tybout and Westbrook (1995), and on our own research. These studies differ in the databases they use, their level of disaggregation and the exact period they cover. Kessel and Samaniego (1994) use national accounts, and the nine divisions classification that these accounts provide. They use data from 1961 to 1989 and they focus on comparing the behaviour prior to 1985 to that following this year. Tybout and Westbrook (1995) use data from the Encuesta Industrial Anual, at the plant level, from 1984 to 1990. They classify plants in nineteen sectors. Luna and Valdivieso (n.d.) use this same database, but they emphasize the comparison between productivity growth in 1985–7 (the first stage of liberalization) and 1987–91 (when it was fully completed), and they use different levels of disaggregation, ranging from nine divisions to 126 classes. Our own work relies on data from national accounts, but we use a classification of 49 branches, and we also use data on capital assets from Banco de México. To measure the performance of productivity, Tybout and Westbrook (1995) estimate cost and production functions for the period 1984–90, and look for changes not only in productivity but also in average costs over this period. The other three studies focus on total factor productivity growth, which tries to capture the change in output not accounted for by changes in capital or labour inputs. They focus on the behaviour of productivity prior to trade reform as opposed to after the reform.

The evolution of productivity

Some studies find good productivity performance after liberalization. Kessel and Samaniego (1995), Luna and Valdivieso (n.d.), and Fernández (1998) find that productivity growth was higher after liberalization than before it. Tybout and Westbrook (1995) find that there was an important reduction in average costs (−6.84 per cent) and increase in productivity (11.17 per cent) in the period 1984–90. They do not compare these figures with any previous period because their focus is different: they are interested in decomposing this change into different sources. The changes in productivity growth after liberalization are important and statistically significant, according to the studies cited above. For instance, Kessel and Samaniego perform regression analysis to test whether the change in the rate of productivity growth was statistically significant. They run linear-piece regressions and find that the answer is positive. Their results for manufacturing as a whole show that the growth prior to liberalization was 1.1 per cent, which increased by 2.9 points after liberalization, to reach a growth rate of 4 per cent. This increase of 2.9 points in the rate of productivity growth is statistically significant. Thus, we can reject the hypothesis that productivity grew at the same rate after liberalization as prior to it.

Another important result is that, although when we consider manufacturing as a whole the rate of productivity growth did increase, there are important differences within the manufacturing sector. For instance, for the division of food, beverages and tobacco the corresponding regression shows no statistically significant increase in productivity growth. In contrast, in the division of basic metals, a situation of no growth changed into a rate of growth of 8 per cent, with the change being statistically significant. From inspection of the regressions of the different divisions, Kessel and Samaniego (1995) note the interesting fact that, after trade liberalization, productivity growth changed more in those industries in which it was having a bad performance, but it did not change much – or even showed no statistically significant change – in those industries in which it was already growing at high rates prior to liberalization.

Although the exact increases in productivity vary with the cut-off year and the databases used, the fact that productivity growth increased after liberalization is also obtained in the study by Luna and Valdivieso, as well as with the database we use. Moreover, the fact that there are important differences within manufacturing industry also remains true. In the study by Tybout and Westbrook (1995) no such increase in productivity growth is shown, because they do not perform this comparison, but they also find huge differences in the productivity and cost performance within the manufacturing sector. The natural next step, accepting that productivity did perform better after liberalization, is to find the channels through which liberalization could have affected productivity.

Channels of transmission

We do not have a complete explanation of the exact reasons that led to higher productivity growth, but we do have some relevant clues. Luna and Valdivieso (n.d.) point to the disappearance of inefficient firms, and the important role of small firms. With respect to the first point, they stress that 13 per cent of firms in their sample disappeared or merged in the period 1985–91. Moreover, this disappearance was greater for small firms than for big ones: the percentage of exits was four times higher for firms with fewer than 250 employees than for firms with more than this number. Besides disappearances being more acute for small firms, it is also true – and perhaps related – that changes in productivity growth are higher for small firms than for larger ones, as Luna and Valdivieso stress. Indeed, while annual productivity growth increased from −3.4 per cent in 1985–7 to 1.3 per cent in 1988–91 for firms with fewer than 50 employees, and from −2.2 to 1.3 per cent for firms with between 51 and 100 employees, it actually dropped from 2.8 to 1.1 per cent for firms with more than 500 employees. Thus, while the smallest firms (with fewer than 50 employees) increased their rate of productivity growth by more than 4 percentage points, the largest firms (with more than 500 employees) even suffered a reduction in their rate of productivity growth.

There are other potential suspects for increased productivity that we can discard, namely expenditure on technology, investment and scale economies. The first of these factors relates to firms purchasing technology to face the pressure of foreign competition. Yet there is abundant evidence that this was not the case. For instance, Luna and Valdivieso report that only 7.1 per cent of firms in their sample purchased technology in a systematic way. If disembodied technology did not play an important role in fostering productivity, what about modernization in the form of new equipment? The explanation cannot be as simple as a good investment performance, because it was in fact very poor during this period. Gross investment dropped by more than 11 per cent in 1986, and only recovered its 1985 level by 1990. Most surprisingly, scale economies were not important, either. It has often been argued that they play a major role in fostering productivity when economies are opened up, the idea being that by facing larger markets, manufacturing firms can take advantage of them, and reduce average costs. Yet Tybout and Westbrook (1995) analyse precisely this and conclude that scale economies played a minor role in the huge cost reductions experienced over the period 1984–90. They estimate that average cost reductions were of 6.84 per cent, of which only 0.79 per cent can be attributed to increased scale efficiency. Another 0.98 per cent is due to better allocation of production among the plants (share effect), and a big 5.07 per cent due to a 'residual' effect. This residual effect comprises all gains not attributable to scale or to reallocation. Thus, as these authors note, it is a 'catch-all' category, including improvements in organizational design and managerial effort, among many other potential sources of efficiency gains. Tybout and Westbrook (1995) perform a similar analysis for productivity, instead of cost performance. They find that productivity increased by 11.17 per cent for the overall manufacturing industry over the period 1984–90. This growth is decomposed to 0.55 per cent coming from the scale effect, 1.02 per cent from the share effect and 9.6 per cent from the residual effect. Thus, the scale effect remains quite small and the bulk of the improvement is left unexplained as a 'residual'.

Next, we examine the idea that the increased pressure from foreign competition forces firms to improve on such things as organizational procedures, layout design and managerial behaviour. Most of this view is supported by the case studies in Part 3. Here, the evidence is mixed. Tybout and Westbrook (1995) perform this kind of analysis. They pose the question of whether industries experiencing larger reductions in protection experienced better performance. Their answer is negative. They find no such association.[8] We also examine this point with our different data set. There are several measures of increased openness. One type of such measures are those under the control of the policy-maker, namely the proportion of imports subject to permits and the average tariff. We find, like Tybout and Westbrook, that there is no significant association between the amount of reduction in the average tariff and post-liberalization productivity growth. We also find that the growth of productivity after liberalization bears no relationship with the change in the coverage of import licences. In considering these results, however, we must stress that the effect of a system comprising instruments allowing for some discretionality is hard to determine; for instance, the sole existence of a permit does not allow us to know how much protection it really grants. Another set of measures of liberalization is given by the measures of nominal and effective protection, as defined by Ten Kate and De Mateo (1989). Both measures were heavily reduced with trade liberalization. Here we find more support for the hypothesis that letting foreign pressure in forces firms to behave more efficiently. We find that there is a statistically significant association between the reduction in nominal protection and subsequent productivity growth.[9] The branches with higher reductions in nominal protection tend to have higher increases in productivity afterwards. And an even stronger association is found between changes in effective protection and subsequent productivity growth.[10]

Another reason why a more open economy may produce faster productivity growth is because it can more easily appropriate technological advances from abroad. Consider an economy that raises its proportion of foreign trade. It raises both imports and exports as a proportion of GDP. The country will be capable, in particular, of raising its imports of capital goods, which carry with them technological advances from abroad, thus raising productivity as well.

The above argument is of great importance for the Mexican economy. In the years before liberalization, imports of intermediate and capital goods had been dropping. As can be seen by the evolution of trade figures, this tendency was reversed and huge increases in imports of intermediate and capital goods followed liberalization.[11] Imports of intermediate goods, which fell at an average annual rate of 4.1 per cent during 1981–5, grew on average by 16.2 per cent annually during 1986–90. Imports of capital goods showed an even more drastic growth: an annual fall of 12.3 per cent in the pre-reform period turned into a positive growth of 19.1 per cent for the post-liberalization period.

To test the hypothesis that imports of machinery and equipment embody improved technology that spurs productivity, we investigate whether a higher coefficient of imports of machinery is associated with higher productivity growth. The answer is positive: the branches with higher coefficients of imports tend to exhibit higher productivity growth, lending credence to the idea that capital goods from abroad are carriers of improved technologies.[12] A related, but more general, argument as to why increased openness fosters productivity is based on the idea that new goods are an important driving force for growth, as in endogenous growth models of creation of goods (Aghion and Howitt, 1989; Grossman and Helpman, 1989; Rivera-Bátiz and Romer, 1991). In these models, a wider variety of inputs allows the production of a higher output, and the creation of new inputs is the engine of growth. Openness is then important because a country with an open economy does not need to create new inputs itself. It can instead use those developed in the rest of the world. By specializing in the production of some inputs, while importing others, a country can benefit from the whole array of new products generated worldwide. But, on the other side, as is shown in the other chapters, openness can be a factor that inhibits local networking activities in the process of local diffusion of innovation. Similarly, if a sector of the economy both imports and exports goods, it can be indicative of some specialization. We found that a very crude measure of intra-industry trade was significantly associated with higher productivity growth. The further a branch is from being a single exporter or a single importer – but instead does both – the higher productivity growth it tends to exhibit.[13]

Cross-country studies

We now turn to evidence coming from cross-country data. Mexican studies may have difficulty in isolating the effects of trade reform because this reform took place amid many other policy shifts and external shocks. Cross-country studies provide an additional source of evidence on these effects, based on the experiences of a wide range of countries with different economic policies and different degrees of open-ness. We examine two sets of such studies. One of them, testing directly the relationship between trade and growth, is still open to debate. The other one, looking for spillovers of research and development from one country to others, has achieved neater results.

There is a wide literature on the empirical relationship between trade policies and long-run performance – either productivity or per capita income growth. Although most of these studies find a positive association between openness and performance, they have serious econometric and data problems, and the robustness of their results has been challenged since the frequently cited work of Levine and Renelt (1992). Three studies representative of the present state of this issue are Greenaway *et al.* (1988), Edwards (1997) and Harrison and Hanson (1999).

Edwards (1997) uses a data set for 93 countries over the decades 1960 to 1990 and finds that more open economies show faster total factor productivity growth. He proves nine different indexes of trade policy to confirm the robustness of his findings. His result holds for the different openness index he uses, and for different periods of the decades he analyses. Harrison and Hanson (1999), on the other hand, present evidence that cast doubts on the robustness of the link between more open trade policies and long-run growth, when a popular measure of openness is used. Green-away *et al.* (1988) concentrate on the link between trade liberalization and growth. They find that although liberalization does impact growth favourably, it does not do so in a straightforward way. Its effects are not instantaneous. Rather, they provide evidence of a 'J curve' effect. Taken together, the above studies suggest the need for further research to continue to clarify the empirical link.

Another related avenue of research is that on spillovers of research and develop-ment investment from one country to others. The importance of these spillovers is highlighted by the fact that 96 per cent of the world's research and development is performed in a handful of industrial countries (Coe *et al.* 1997). Thus, the ability to benefit from foreign research is crucial for a small developing country. International trade plays an important role in the spread of knowledge beyond national borders for two basic reasons. Foreign trade makes available products that embody foreign knowledge. But it also opens up channels of communication that enable the learning of new production methods, product designs and organizational set-ups, and to imitate and adjust foreign technology.[14] We now review findings from cross-country data supporting the idea that the ability to appropriate foreign R&D does depend in an important way on the degree of openness of a country.

Among the literature studying the extent to which the gains from R&D diffuse across countries, Keller (1997) studies R&D spillovers in a group of industrialized countries. After confirming that R&D does positively affect productivity, he goes on to study the extent of influence of foreign R&D on a country's domestic productivity in the same industry. He finds huge spillovers. R&D investment induces productivity gains in the same industry of another country almost equal (in the order of 50–95 per cent) to those induced at home. He also finds spillovers between different industries within one country, but they are smaller than those across borders. Thus, this study emphasizes the benefits from foreign research in the same industry over those from domestic research in other industries.

Helpman (1997) highlights the importance of international trade in across borders spillovers. He states that there is a close relationship between the gains a country can reap from R&D activities in other countries, and its openness to the international economy. Helpman claims that countries more exposed to the international economy gain more from foreign R&D activities. For a sample of 22 industrialized countries (21 OECD countries that do not include Mexico, plus Israel), Coe and Helpman (1995) also show that returns on R&D accrue not only to the performing countries, but also to their industrial country trade partners. Moreover, they show that foreign R&D has stronger effects on domestic productivity in more open economies. They find that for the smaller countries, foreign R&D is even more important than domestic R&D as a source of productivity growth.

In the study most relevant to our discussion, Coe *et al.* (1997) estimate the effect of R&D performed in the industrial countries on the productivity growth in developing countries. They provide quantitative estimates of this effect based on a sample of 77 developing countries which includes Mexico. They find that spillovers are stronger when countries are more open to international trade. More specifically, countries with higher imports of machinery and equipment – as a fraction of GDP – exhibit higher benefits from developed countries' R&D. In fact, in their preferred specification, foreign R&D affects developing country productivity only through its interaction with imports of machinery and equipment. Coe *et al.* find that a 1 per cent increase in the R&D capital stock in the industrial countries raises output in the developing countries by 0.06 per cent on average. But for the East Asian economies – which show a higher import share of machinery and equipment – the corresponding increase would be almost double, at 0.11 per cent. Thus a country with higher imports of machinery and equipment benefits more from an increase in foreign R&D, and a country with higher foreign R&D capital stock (one which trades more with industrial countries that invest heavily in R&D) gains more productivity from an increase in imports of machinery and equipment.

Conclusions

The ISI period revealed that some stylized facts can be drawn on the process of accumulation of technological capabilities. In Mexico as in other developing economies, innovation in the process of industrialization depends heavily on borrowing and adapting technologies from abroad. This acquisition of superior technologies prevailing in the developed world is closely related to the investment process, and, during the stabilizing development, all the micro and macro policies interacted to spur investment. Macroeconomic policies provided a stable, predictable economic environment that gave certainty as to the conditions under which investment projects would be carried out and firms would work. The role of government went well beyond that of providing a stable macro framework. This certainty was accompanied by a set of fiscal measures that further favoured the investment process, facilitating imports of machinery and equipment, and spurring reinvestment of profits. Firms were protected from foreign competition, which provided a suitable environment to learn how to operate the imported technologies, to acquire production skills associated with them and to engage in the problem-solving activities that allow incremental innovations to flourish as by-products of the production process itself ('learning by doing' and 'learning by using'). Yet the government failed to provide a well defined, credible schedule for the duration of the protected environment, thus removing the natural incentive to get ready to compete with foreign goods in the future.

These same drawbacks of the process began to generate growing problems, including external imbalances due to the lack of exporting capacity of domestic firms, and failed to improve the unequal income distribution. Partly as a response to these problems, there were attempts in the 1970s to shift the policy orientation. On the one hand, the government tried to moderate the excesses of protectionism. On the other hand, it decided to take a more active role in the development process to relieve social ills. To achieve this, it relied to a great extent on public expenditure. Yet this resulted in fiscal deficits that ultimately proved to be unsustainable, led to recurrent crises and rendered the efforts to moderate protectionism useless. In these crises the inflation rate accelerated, the real exchange rate appreciated and output grew rapidly only to end up in a huge devaluation and a recession. These experiences encouraged economic actors to take a short-term approach to business, to seek short-term profitability for fear of a drastic change of unknown nature in a longer horizon, and were very damaging to innovative activities, which take time to yield results. Moreover, these failed experiments left a huge external debt to be dealt with by future administrations, as well as a history of failed attempts to reduce protectionism, which would set a precedent and make more difficult the success of future attempts.

The 1980s were a 'lost decade' in terms of investment, growth and improvement of living standards. Yet they also established a transition to a new mode of development. This alternative pattern of development was characterized by healthy public finances, reduced external debt, limited public regulation and – perhaps most important for our analysis – a completely different orientation of Mexican industry. These new features of the Mexican economy involved a process of privatization, deregulation, budget correction and trade liberalization.

The new mode of development entails a new way to link the Mexican economy with the rest of the world, and it is too soon to establish definite conclusions, since innovation is a long-term phenomenon. Yet there are reasons to believe that openness should be beneficial to the innovative process. First, there is the evidence from comparative analysis of national innovation systems that one important condition for firms' effective innovative performance is their 'being exposed to strong competition and being forced to compete' (Nelson, 1993, p. 510). Second, a more open economy will entail in particular greater facility to import capital goods, which carry within them technology from abroad. Third, and closely related to the previous argument, new goods are often the form that technological advances take, as in endogenous growth models of creation of goods (Rivera-Bátiz and Romer, 1981; Aghion and Howitt, 1989; Grossman and Helpman, 1989), in which a wider variety of inputs allows the production of a higher output, and the creation of new inputs is the engine of growth. Openness is then important because a country with an open economy does not need to create new inputs itself. It can instead use those developed in the rest of the world. By specializing in the production of some inputs, while importing others, a country can benefit from the whole array of new products generated worldwide.

The previous arguments appear to have some support from both Mexican data and cross-country studies on across borders spillovers of R&D. However, anticipating some results from the chapters in Part 3, most of the spillovers remain within the successful exporter firms. Yet local linkages with other firms and institutions are highly eroded. In fact, as is stressed in Chapters 4 and 5, in the Mexican case the problem remains that other measures of firms' efforts to innovate – R&D expenditure, patents, etc. – and the capabilities to capture technological flows locally continue to show a poor performance, which seems to indicate that just taking advantage of the benefits of an open economy is not enough. Thus, other aspects of the creation of innovation process which are not analysed in the present section need to be addressed for a thorough explanation.

Notes

1. These authors also study the role of multinational corporations in the catching-up process. They find that: (a) multinational corporations exhibit higher productivity than local firms, but this gap is decreasing; (b) the rate of catch-up of local firms to the multinationals is positively related to the degree of foreign ownership in an industry; and (c) the rate of convergence of Mexican industries to their counterparts in the USA is also stronger in branches with higher presence of multinational corporations. They conclude that multinational corporations have helped to disseminate superior technology from abroad. However, Unger and Oloriz (Chapter 5) reach a different conclusion.
2. Data on investment performance in Latin American countries are taken from Ramírez (1994, Table II, p. 5).
3. Data in this section are taken from Lustig (1992) and Cline (1995).
4. Interest payments arrears in Latin America had been growing steadily, from $3.7 billion in 1986 to $8.6 billion in 1987 and $9 billion in 1989. Latin American economies showed no signs of recovering growth. It seemed ever more difficult, due to divergent bank interests, to mobilize 'concerted' lending. Debt prices in the secondary market had dropped between 30 and 40 cents per dollar. All these facts led to a shift in the international debt policy. With the ongoing strategy, it was perceived that the economies under the burden of the debt would not grow but their payments arrears would. In addition – and above all – there was the perception that private banks were reducing the exposure in indebted countries, to the detriment of the official creditors, the IMF and World Bank. This would eventually be translated into a state of debtor countries still trapped in the debt problem, with official creditors holding the debt instead of private banks. Official resources, after all, would have bailed out the banks without really solving the problem. The social uprising of February 1989 in Caracas, spurred by the austerity plan of the Carlos Andrés Pérez administration, reinforced the idea that a shift of strategy was necessary.
5. The data in this section are taken from Fernández (1995).
6. Another effect of deregulation was the increase in domestic production of lorries, which registered an impressive growth of 32.7 per cent in 1989.
7. The activity of custom brokers was also deregulated. In Mexico, the law establishes that customs transactions must be performed by custom brokers, a regulated profession. The process of entry into the profession kept the number of brokers low, and brokers' fees were set by law at a percentage of the value of merchandise. These fees acted, in effect, as an import–export tax. In 1989–90, brokers' activities were deregulated. The previous access scheme was modified and the official rate suppressed. In less than a year, the number of agents doubled, firms were allowed to name customs representatives and fees declined sharply. Also due to regulatory changes, private package delivery companies – almost non-existent prior to

deregulation – began to operate in Mexico. When the government stopped impeding the operation of these specialized companies, a new industry developed, with both Mexican and international companies, such as DHL and UPS. The effects on the rest of the economy are difficult to quantify, but one notorious effect is that firms no longer had to rely on their own private messengers, thus releasing resources for their own core competencies. Moreover, the appearance of these services opened the possibility of new innovative ways for many goods to be marketed.

8. In fact, they find evidence of a small association of unexpected sign between changes in openness and scale efficiency: increased openness slightly worsened this type of efficiency. This result stems from the fact that, according to these authors, in most industries the larger plants were already operating at their minimum efficient scale prior to trade liberalization.

9. More precisely, let TFPG be the total factor productivity growth from 1986 to 1991 as defined by Solow (1957) of the manufacturing branches (branches 11 to 49), and let CHPN be the corresponding changes in nominal protection during the period of trade liberalization (from the last quarter of 1984 to the last quarter of 1987) as obtained by Ten Kate and De Mateo (1989). A simple linear regression yields (heteroscedastic consistent errors in parentheses):

$$\text{TFPG} = 0.0399 - 0.0016 \text{ CHPN}$$
$$(0.114) \quad (0.0016)$$

where CHPN is significant at a 5 per cent level (p value $= 0.0230$). The data for output and labour come from national accounts, those for capital from the Encuesta de Acervos, Depreciación y Formación de Capital of Banco de México, and the two oil-related branches have been dropped because of problems in the measurement of their capital stocks.

10. Using the change in effective protection as an explanatory variable for post-liberalization productivity growth one obtains a p value of -0078 in a simple bivariate regression.

11. Imports of consumer goods increased by even more, but even after this growth, they accounted for only 11 per cent of total imports.

12. Let R5152 be the sum of the coefficients of imports from branches 51 and 52 (electrical and non-electrical machinery, respectively) according to the input-output tables for 1990. A simple bivariate regression yields (heteroscedastic-consistent errors in parentheses):

$$\text{TFPG} = 0.0523 + 0.8624 \text{ R5152}$$
$$(0.97) \quad (0.2676)$$

where the p value associated to R5152 is 0.0024.

13. Although more level of dissaggregation is called for to capture intra-industry trade, a preliminary simple measure (GL) defined as one minus the result of dividing the difference between exports and imports (in absolute value) over the sum of exports and imports (a measure that decreases as a branch gets closer to being either a pure exporter or a pure importer, in which case it takes on the value of zero) yields:

$$\text{TFPG} = 0.0720 + 0.0160 \log \text{GL}$$
$$(0.127) \quad (0.0064)$$

where number in parentheses are heteroscedastic-consistent errors, and a p value of 0.0154 is associated to log GL. A multiple regression including the three previous explanatory variables yields:

$$\text{TFPG} = 0.0547 - \underset{(0.0007)}{0.0015} \text{CHPN} + \underset{(0.3156)}{0.5135} \text{R5152} + \underset{(0.0082)}{0.0160} \log \text{GL}$$

the p values are 0.04 (for CHPN), 0.11 (for R5152) and 0.06 (for log GL).

14. Coe and Helpman (1995) cite numerous case studies supporting the fact that important learning channels do appear as a consequence of international trade.

CHAPTER FOUR

Production System and Technological Patterns

M. Capdevielle, J. M. Corona and C. Hernandez

Introduction

The Mexican industrialization process has followed two different paths. During the first path, between the 1940s and 1970s, industrialization was achieved through import substitution (ISI), and the Mexican economy registered an elevated growth rate. In particular, during the 1960s, Mexican manufacturing industry grew at an average of 8 per cent annually, combined with a high level of stability. The 1970s registered an average annual growth rate of 6.5 per cent, with oscillations. The 1982 economic crisis demonstrated that the import substitution growth model was exhausted, and the Mexican economy began a new path that was characterized by the search for macroeconomic stability, the opening of the economy to trade and government deregulation. With the new economic path, manufacturing activity has shown a lower average GDP growth rate during the past two decades (in the 1980s, Mexican manufacturing grew only 2.12 per cent, while this growth rate reached 4 per cent during the 1990s).

The low economic growth performance during a period of nearly two decades is a factor that could have radically influenced the pattern of acquisition for technological capabilities and the transformation of the production system.[1] Investment in new capital assets was reduced during the 1980s, thus affecting the possibility of introducing new technology incorporated in machinery and equipment. Despite the relative recovery of investment since 1988, this recovery has not been sufficient to reach historic levels or to compensate for the lag in investment produced by the crisis that began in the early 1980s. Furthermore, with a new international context of accelerated incorporation of new technologies and new paradigms, this macro situation has to be considered as a crucial factor in order to understand the Mexican production and innovation system.

In this chapter, we describe two aspects of the manufacturing production system: (a) its performance in terms of current production structure; and (b) the efforts addressed to upgrade its technological capabilities. This analysis is carried out using different indicators, and we will see how these indicators evolve.

The first section deals with the technological sector's main economic performance, as measured by indicators such as average labour productivity, total factor productivity, production composition, productivity gaps and – with respect to the international technological frontier – gaps in intra-industry productivity, patenting intensity, international competitiveness and specialization. In the second section, we discuss the main efforts aimed at the acquisition of innovative knowledge and the diffusion of this knowledge, taking into consideration an approximation for indicators on these efforts, such as the technology embodied in capital goods and machinery, relative salaries, R&D expenditure and knowledge flows across different sectors and firms.[2]

Production structure and performance are analysed according to different statistical classifications in order to identify each industrial group and technological sector. Technological change processes are different for the distinct industrial activities, in the ways in which technological gains are generated, disseminated and adapted, which permits a classification of the distinct industrial activities according to said characteristics. To the extent that some technological classification of sectors is need for an analysis of the whole industrial structure and its difference from other economies, we will use the Pavitt taxonomy as defined and presented in Chapters 1 and 2. As a matter of fact, this taxonomy was built considering the firms' and sectors' main sources and efforts that follow a strategy to improve their technological capabilities. Moreover, each of these technological sectors could be viewed as a meso-technological system with very specific ways of creating technology. At the present time, it is possible to identify unequivocally each meso-sectoral innovation system in terms of the following issues: to what extent the sector depends on the technology embodied in capital goods and equipment; how much the sector's competencies are related to the absorption of human capital that has a higher level of skills; whether or not the sector's competencies can be explained by the amount and the type of R&D expenditures; whether sectoral competencies are related to knowledge flows from other sectors and from firms within in the same sector; and if this capacity or lack thereof may be explained by addressing the issues mentioned above or if it in fact depends on other features which are more difficult to measure and which require specific case studies in order to understand them, e.g. organizational changes or tacit knowledge embodied in human resources (Dutrénit and Capdevielle, 1993; Capdevielle *et al.*, 1997). Part III, which is more directed towards the meso and sectoral systems, provides an in-depth description of the specificity of each sector and the type of firms that conform it.

The structure of the production system and its performance

Added value and industrial employment

Table 4.1 describes the manufacturing industry classified as per ISIC-Group Industries, STAN-OCDE codes, which correspond to the Mexican Industrial Classification census at the sub-sector level. Table 4.1 shows the distribution of added value for both Mexican and US industries during two different periods: 1970–4 and 1990–4. Sub-sector 38, metal products and machinery, has increased its share of added value within Mexican manufacturing industry; in fact, between 1990 and 1994 its added value share reached 26 per cent, increasing at a rate of 25 per cent since 1970–4. It should be noted, however, that this remarkable growth has been led by the higher growth rate for motor vehicles; other sectors, such as office and computing machinery and manufactured metal products, show a more modest increase in their participation. Some important change are also visible in sub-sector

Table 4.1 Added Value Shares in the Mexican and US Manufacturing Industries, 1970–1994

Sectors	Mexico		USA	
	1970–4	1990–4	1970–4	1990–4
38 Metal products and machinery	20.5	26.0	37.5	42.5
Fabricated metal products	3.7	4.1	6.6	6.8
Non-electrical machinery	2.8	2.4	6.8	9.3
Office and computing machinery	0.3	1.0	0.9	1.8
Electrical machinery	3.2	3.2	4.1	3.9
Radio, TV and communication equipment	3.1	2.5	2.2	6.7
Shipbuilding and repairing	0.1	0.0	0.9	0.5
Motor vehicles	6.3	11.0	7.2	4.6
Aircraft	0.0	0.2	4.6	4.2
Other transport equipment	0.5	0.8	0.3	0.1
Professional goods	0.4	0.8	4.0	4.7
31 Food, drink and tobacco	25.9	26.0	12.8	10.3
35 Chemicals	17.6	16.8	13.3	17.8
Chemical products	2.4	3.3	2.8	2.4
Industrial chemicals	5.4	5.6	3.9	5.3
Drugs and medicines	2.6	2.6	1.5	4.0
Petroleum refineries	4.7	2.4	2.7	2.0
Rubber and plastic products	2.5	3.0	2.4	4.1
32 Textiles, footwear and leather	15.2	8.9	5.7	5.2
36 Stone, clay and glass	5.6	7.6	3.1	2.3
34 Paper and printing	4.5	5.2	12.7	11.4
37 Metals	5.8	4.9	8.5	4.3
Iron and steel	4.6	3.4	6.0	2.7
Non-ferrous metals	1.2	1.5	2.5	1.6
33 Wood, cork and furniture	3.4	3.3	4.7	4.3
39 Other manufacturing	1.4	1.8	1.8	1.9

Source: The Structural Analysis Database, STAN/OCDE.

36, stone, clay and glass, in which the added value participation has increased from 5.6 to 7.6 per cent, from 1970–4 to the 1990–4 period. In contrast, the share in added value in sub-sector 31, food, drink and tobacco, has remained stable during both periods, while sub-sector 32, textiles, footwear and leather, has almost halved its share, from 15.2 to 8.9 per cent between 1970–4 and 1990–4.

If we compare the Mexican production system to that of the United States, the result is that the United States is even more concentrated in sub-sector 38, in which participation in added value amounts to approximately 42.5 per cent of total added value between 1990 and 1994. It must be stressed, however, that contrary to what is seen in the case of Mexico, the greatest proportion of this share is due to industries other than motor vehicles, such as non-electrical machinery, office and computing machinery, radio, television and other equipment. Under these circumstances, we can see that a different process of specialization takes place within sub-sector 38; in the United States, specialization is markedly directed at technologically complex products that often are linked with the electronic industry, whereas in Mexico this sub-sector is increasingly leaning towards production of automobiles and auto parts (the specificities of this sector in Mexico compared to other developed economies are analysed in detail in Chapter 15).

The fact that the share of total added value in the chemical sub-sector (35) is quite similar in both production systems could be misleading. The growth rate of added value participation is different: in the United States, participation increases from 13.3 to 17.8 per cent, while this share remains stable in Mexico. Furthermore, composition within the sector varies greatly between the two countries in terms of technological complexity: higher participation in drugs and medicines in the United States and less sophisticated chemical products in Mexico. More detailed analysis of the main specificities of the chemical and pharmaceutical sectors are developed in Chapters 11 and 12.

Sub-sectors 31, food, beverages and tobacco, and 32, textiles, footwear and leather, maintain a greater participation in Mexican manufacturing production than the equivalent in the United States. This shows a production structure in which the Mexican economy is more specialized in basic goods that represent a significant part of the domestic market consumption. Meanwhile, sub-sector 36, stone, clay and glass, has a higher share in Mexico than in the United States. The aforementioned sectors foods (31), textiles (32) and stone (36) are principally directed towards domestic demand, and the firms that predominate in these sectors are those that form part of the large national groups that developed during the import substitution period (Capdevielle *et al.*, 1997).

In terms of employment in the above-mentioned sub-sectors, a similar pattern seems to arise. In Mexico, employment is highly concentrated in the following sub-sectors, listed by degree of importance: 38, metal products and machinery, 32.5 per cent; 31, food, beverages and tobacco, 20.1 per cent; 32, textiles, 15 per cent; and 35, chemicals, 12 per cent. Sub-sector 38 is an activity that is labour-intensive in relation to the other Mexican manufacturing industries; in fact, participation in employment is greater than participation in added value. It is especially remarkable that the metal products and machinery sub-sector is more labour-intensive in Mexico than in the United States.[3]

Sectors and technological patterns

In terms of the technological classification of sectors proposed here (supplier-dominated sector (SD), scale intensive sector (SI), specialized suppliers (SS) and science-based sector (SB); see Chapters 1 and 2), it is worth mentioning that production of mature goods prevails in Mexico by an ample margin; the SD and SI sectors jointly contribute more than 85 per cent of total added value and employment (see Figure 4.1), whereas the participation of the SS and SB sectors is much lower. Particularly, employment in the SD sector accounts for an average of 55 per cent of total employment in the manufacturing industries; furthermore, in this sector, the personnel employed are principally workers who have a low level of skills (Sobarzo Fimbres, 1997).

The SS maintains a reduced importance in both indicators, after initial growth during the 1970s and a relative contraction during the 1980s. Meanwhile, the second group (SB) has constantly increased its contribution to added value, at a rate that is inferior to the rate in the United States, even though its participation in employment

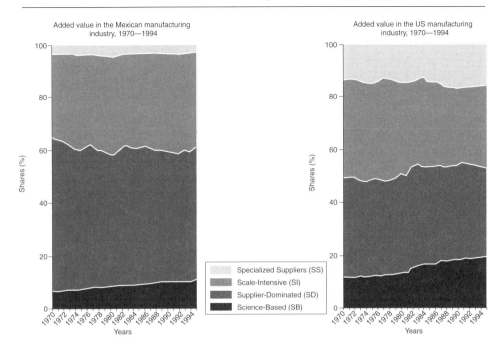

Figure 4.1 Distribution of Added Value in Terms of Technological Sectors for the Mexican and US Manufacturing Industries, 1970–1994.
Source: The Structural Analysis Database, STAN/OCDE, 1997.

is stable. In the United States, in contrast, both the SB and SS sectors registered permanent growth in their contribution to added value, although since the mid-1980s their participation in employment has decreased. This means that the most technologically advanced sectors in both countries have reduced the intensity of employment in relative terms. In brief, the picture that emerges in Mexico is one of a production system that is characterized by notable stability in its technological specialization, while there is a predominance of the more traditional sectors. In fact, when comparing added value and employment distribution, it should be noted that: (a) in general, and even in developed economies such as the United States, the SS and SB sectors' share of employment is consistently lower than that of the SD and SI sectors; (b) in Mexico, the share of these two sectors, SS and SB, is much smaller than their corresponding share in the United States; (c) in the United States, added value and employment in the SS and SB sectors has grown over the past few decades, while in Mexico the SS sector has decreased its participation and the SB sector has increased its participation; (d) the ratio of added value to employment in the SB and SS sub-sectors is much lower in Mexico than in the United States. This last point clearly indicates that in both sectors, SB and SS, production activities are labour-intensive.

Production structure and sectoral patterns: the main trends

The comparisons so far have attempted to highlight the main differences between manufacturing in the United States and Mexico, through sectoral technological patterns. In the United States, the importance of the SB and SS sectors has increased, and these sectors are largely focused towards producing knowledge-based goods, equipment and capital goods. In contrast, in Mexico the participation of all four technological sectors within the manufacturing industry has been remarkably stable. However, the participation of the SB and SS sectors within Mexico's industrial structure has barely grown from the small portion from which it started; furthermore, their share in added value and employment has not changed significantly. In general, it is possible to affirm that the structural change during the period under consideration was greater in the United States than in Mexico, while it must be taken into consideration that a less developed economy has greater potential for change.[4]

Nevertheless, in comparing the proportions of employment and added value among the different technological sectors, we must be aware that the internal composition of each sector also differs. In particular, in the SB and SS sectors, a great many of the technologically advanced products are produced and phases of production processes are carried out in the United States but not in Mexico. For instance, most computer manufacturing firms established in Mexico limit their activities mostly to assembly, while in the United States the computer manufacturing firms carry out more complex activities, such as R&D and industrial design. Not surprisingly, such a situation could lead to the generalized assumption that, overall, production lines in Mexico lack those key technological links in and of themselves. Furthermore, the technologically sophisticated activities in the majority of these production lines are currently being carried out abroad, and the domestic productive apparatus has little or no involvement. Therefore, this lack of integration in the chains of technology within domestic industry leads, in turn, to an alarming void of critical mass in terms of the institutions required to foster and support sophisticated technological activities.

The new Mexican industrialization path, in the context of the opening of the economy to increased competition, for some sectors has implied integration in production lines at an international level, in which Mexico has specialized in the links that have a low level of technological intensity. This situation is expressed in the breaking of domestic links, particularly for the production of goods with a high level of technology (SB) (De la Garza, 1994; Hernández Laos, 1998). The rupture of domestic links has diverse effects: on the one hand, it permits ties with foreign suppliers which have raw materials that offer advantages in terms of quality and price, which permits the introduction of improvements and indirect innovations through these inputs, and increases competitiveness. On the other hand, foreign competition replaces productive activities and organizations, some of which are not necessarily inefficient but must face unfavourable macroeconomic conditions (the high cost of money, insufficient infrastructure, negative external factors, etc.). Likewise, a sectoral specialization of this nature limits the effort, flow of knowledge and extraordinary profits that are associated with the more dynamic activities and those that represent greater technological opportunities.[5]

Finally, the analysis of the manufacturing industry pursued thus far, considering the distribution of added value and employment across sub-sectors according to the STAN classification, and the technological sectors established in Pavitt's taxonomy, reveals several significant specific facts concerning the Mexican production system.

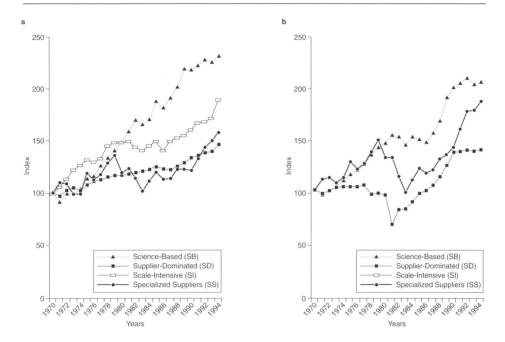

Figure 4.2 Average Labour Productivity (a) and Average Total Factor Productivity (b) for Each Technological Sector, 1970–1994.
Sources: Acervos de Capital, Banco de México and STAN/OCDE.

First, the manufacturing industry shows a notable rigidity in adapting to and incorporating the accelerated technological change in the world economy. Second, the pattern of productive specialization is, to a great extent, directed towards technologically mature products that have a lower level of income elasticity, a fact which is demonstrated by the high participation of the SD and SI sectors within Mexican manufacturing industry.

Average labour productivity and total factor productivity

As can be seen in Figure 4.2, average labour productivity in manufacturing industry has enjoyed continuous growth between 1970 and 1994. It is possible, however, to distinguish two distinct paths. From 1970 to the 1982 crisis, added value and employment grew at higher rates, although the former outperformed the latter. Then, after 1982, added value continued to grow, but at a lower rate, while employment remained rather stagnant. The technological sectors that registered the greatest increases in labour productivity were SB and SI. However, there is a difference between these two sectors. In the first, SB, the increase in productivity was based on an accelerated growth of added value, while in the second, SI, the productivity increase is explained by a marked reduction in employment.

Preliminary analysis of total factor productivity (TFP) has revealed gradual growth in the 1970s, principally due to progressive increases in net capital stocks and employment, similar to that of added value. At the beginning of the 1980s, there was a drop in the TFP, followed by stagnation of the same. From 1986 onwards, total factor productivity registered accelerated growth, as we have asserted in Chapter 3. It must be stressed, none the less, that this remarkable growth is due, first, to the slow growth in production and, second, to stagnant employment levels and a reduction in capital stocks. It is important to appreciate the cyclical character of the TFP, which was significantly reduced during the 1982–6 crisis and which has increased during the periods of higher rates of growth.

In the SB sector, the only sector in which both capital stock and employment have increased, the growth of TFP can be explained by the efficient utilization of labour and capital. For the remaining sectors, capital stocks decreased since 1982, while employment was stagnant in the SI and SD sectors, or contracted in the SS one. For the SI sector, the observed technological change appears to be associated with entrepreneurial activities, in particular with the changes in the firms' organizational strategy (quality circles, just in time, etc.) that allowed these firms to rationalize their labour force without a considerable capital investment. At the meso and micro levels this view is supported by the case studies in Part III of this book.

Based on the analysis above, it would appear that efficient utilization of capital and labour should be the principal force behind productivity growth. However, in the case of Mexico, after the 1982 crisis it was rather difficult to differentiate between the results of this optimization process and those generated by the combination of stagnant employment levels and a reduction in investment in capital goods. Thus, there is a sharp contrast to what has happened in the more industrialized countries, such as the United States, where growth of productivity in the manufacturing industries has occurred through significant increases in investment combined with diminishing employment.[6] Nevertheless, since the beginning of the 1990s, it would appear that this trend is beginning to be reversed; that part of Mexican industry which is focused towards export markets is increasingly investing in capital goods and is making a considerable effort to introduce technology through intermediate commodities, organizational changes and highly skilled human capital (see Chapters 5 and 10).

International gaps in productivity

Several important implications concerning the approach followed throughout this work appear to support an analysis of gaps in productivity as an approximation for the differences in technological capabilities. At any point in time, it is possible to draw two major conjectures, which can be tested: different countries might very well be unequivocally ranked according to the efficiency of their average production techniques, and, in the product space, of the (price-weighted) performance characteristics of said techniques and outputs, regardless of relative prices. Hence, broad differences also appear concerning the countries' capacity to develop new products, as well as different time lags in replicating these products, after they have been introduced in the world market. Indeed, the international distribution of innovative capabilities regarding new products is at least as uneven as that of production processes. For example, considering international patents as an approximation for innovativeness, the existing empirical evidence suggests that membership in the innovators' club has been restricted over the entire past century to all but a dozen developed countries. The only major new entry was Japan (Dosi *et al.*, 1990).

However, patents are only an approximation for innovation, and as such are not a good performance indicator for less developed economies, since the less developed economies usually favour other appropriation mechanisms, such as industrial secrecy or know-how (Pavitt, 1984).

Moreover, development and industrialization processes are strongly linked to the inter- and intranational diffusion of best practice techniques. In a related fashion, as we have already mentioned, at any point in time, there is likely to be only one 'best practice' technique for production and productivity levels which corresponds to the technological frontier. In the case of developing economies, the industrialization process is, thus, closely linked to borrowing, imitation and adaptation of established technologies from the more advanced economies. Such processes of adoption and adaptation of technologies are, in turn, influenced by each economy's specific capabilities.

The productivity ratio between Mexico and the United States can be viewed as an approximation for gaps in technological capability, considering this ratio as a way to approach the distance between production practices in Mexico and those at the international frontier. Comparative analysis of the changes in productivity in Mexico and the United States reveals an increase in the gap in productivity from 1970 to 1995, although this difference is not always linear. Even though this differential remains stable during the import substitution phase, it grows significantly during the 1980s (the period of the crisis) and then decreases as the economy is opened to increased foreign competition through trade reforms and institutional changes (new regulatory framework and NAFTA).

In terms of each of the technological sectors, the gap in productivity has decreased for the SD and SI sectors, whereas it has increased with regard to the SB sector. Because of the association between a technological sector and the nature of the innovativeness of the goods that each sector produces, particular attention should be devoted to the increasing gap in the SB sector and the diminishing gap in the SD sector. The differential in the SB sector may be explained by the notable growth in productivity that this sector enjoyed in the United States. By analysing the gaps with the international frontier, it readily can be seen that international diffusion of the more advanced technologies follows a slower pace than the rate at which the technological frontier expands. Obviously, this is particularly seen in the more innovative products. In contrast, in the more mature products in which production processes are easily replicated and adapted, the distance between Mexico and the technological frontier is much lower, as is seen in a narrower gap. Under these circumstances, there is expansion of the inequality in productivity in the most dynamic sectors, and this inequality is only reduced in the mature sectors beginning in 1986; this shows that the system was 'slow' to imitate and disseminate new technologies. Therefore, it is not possible to maintain that the new technologies offer 'windows of opportunity' (see Pérez, 1992) for Mexican manufacturing, although in isolated cases this could be true.[7]

Inter-industry gaps in productivity

Another mechanism to assess Mexican industry's technological performance is by measuring the gaps in productivity in firms belonging to the same sector, as well as by contrasting the average productivity of the four major players (establishments) in each sector with respect to the average labour productivity of the sector as a whole. Such an indicator could provide an idea concerning the distance between the 'sectoral frontier' and the rest of the firms and establishments in the sector. If this gap decreases, it could be safely assumed that the intra-industry diffusion of technology has increased (that is, the ratio between the average productivity of the sector and that of the four major firms has been reduced). Conversely, a wider gap would indicate that the four players, which established the 'sectoral frontier', were more successful in developing efficient production techniques and processes than the rest of the sector.

This indicator was developed by Casar *et al.* (1990), who demonstrated that during the 1970s, the intra-industrial dissemination of best practices was carried out most intensely, reducing gaps among firms. Conversely, since the 1980s, this indicator shows that the productivity gap has increased for all sectors, implying that the rate of diffusion for the best technological practices in the industry as a whole is slower than the leading firms' capacity to adopt said practices.[8] Paradoxically, and in contrast to what occurs at an international level, in which the gap expanded even in the sectors that are most technologically intensive (SS and SB), within Mexico this expansion corresponds to the mature sectors (SD, where the number of small firms has increased).[9]

Thus, from the analysis above, two facts can be readily observed: first, as emerged from the previous section for the period 1970 and 1995, the gap in technology with respect to the international frontier has increased throughout the manufacturing sector; second, the gap between the four major domestic players (establishments) in each technological sector and the rest of the firms within each one of these sectors has increased as well. This, in turn, enables the identification of two different velocities within the Mexican manufacturing industry: (a) that of a group of establishments with the most developed capabilities for catching up with the technological frontier; and (b) that of the remaining firms in manufacturing industry, in which the gaps with international and domestic best practices are increasing (Brown and Domínguez, 1999).

Propensity of Mexican manufacturing industry to patent

The patents granted in Mexico were almost entirely given to foreign firms (98 per cent). Some aspects related to the new trends in patenting activities should be stressed. First, some of the foreign firms that patent in Mexico do not have production activities within the country. Second, patenting activities are quite often related to business strategies for the purpose of preventing potential competitors from producing certain commodities or utilizing particular production processes. The ownership of a patent for a particular commodity or product enables firms to import the goods directly without getting involved in local production activities. The percentage of patents granted by sector[10] for the period from 1980 to 1996 is indicative of sectoral appropriateness criteria at an international level; therefore, it cannot provide a good indication of technological performance in Mexico, since it is not associated with endogenous sectoral innovation capacity. In other words, in

Mexico, patent activity is principally associated with MNEs' commercialization policy, which is aimed at preventing local production and imitation (a more detailed analysis is developed in the appendix to Chapter 7).

Patenting activities in domestic firms are almost nil, amounting to 2 per cent[11] of the total patents granted. Furthermore, this share is highly concentrated in the SI and SD sectors. It is interesting to note that the combination of the above-mentioned sectors forms a proportion of expenditure on R&D which is equivalent to participation in patenting. However, the SI sector does have a greater tendency to patent, and it is for this reason that, although it has a lower level of expenditure, it does patent more (Basberg, 1987).

The former (SI) accounts for up to 63 per cent of the patents granted to domestic firms; furthermore, this sector carries out 38.6 per cent of firms' total R&D expenditure. However, and rather paradoxically, these firms make the least relative effort as measured by R&D expenditure in terms of total sales. The latter (SD) has the largest absolute R&D expenditure (44 per cent) and represents 21 per cent of the patents granted. None the less, we must remember that R&D may be directed towards several goals, and the outcome of R&D is not always patentable. In addition, even when R&D activities translate into innovations which may be patentable, this does not necessarily happen, since patenting instead depends on the peculiarities of the sectors and agents involved. For instance, at the international level, the SD sector shows a low propensity to patent, which may be the reason for this sector's poor share in total patenting; in contrast, the SI sector, more often than not, encompasses large industrial groups and domestic firms that for their size, concentration, innovation capabilities and greater propensity to patent have a much higher level of patenting despite lower relative efforts in terms of R&D expenditures.

Another significant fact is that the subsidiaries of foreign firms have an extremely low participation in domestic patenting, which is entirely out of balance with their R&D expenditures. If it is true that their R&D expenditures, as a percentage of their total sales, is lower than that of domestic firms, their contribution to R&D expenditure in Mexico is more than one-third of the total. However, their domestic patenting level is irrelevant, even more so considering that most foreign firms in Mexico are concentrated in sectors with a high propensity to patent at an international level. Such a situation denotes a patenting strategy within the international corporation that centralizes these activities and does not patent through its local subsidiaries.

In summary, patenting activities of the firms located in Mexico, domestic as well as foreign, is very reduced. In addition, the patenting that the non-resident firms carry out does not necessarily have any relation to domestic productive activity, but corresponds to trade strategies that are interested only in domestic market sales. The reduced level of patenting in domestic firms, although it does correspond to domestic R&D expenditure, is quite distinct from the pattern that predominates at an international level. The fundamental difference lies in the low percentage of patents granted to the SB sector and the high participation of the SD sector. This situation can be only partly explained by the importance of Mexican manufacturing in both sectors. Basically, it expresses the low integration of production and specialization in the segments with a lower technological intensity, as well as a strategy followed by domestic agents. In the United States, the importance of patenting in the sectors based on science is much greater than their contribution to the national product, while in Mexico these two rates are similar.

International competitiveness and internationalization

Since the late 1980s, the Mexican economy has entered into a process of opening itself to world markets, which provides a new definition for the context within which firms operate, as described in Chapter 3. The Mexican economy has integrated its production system with the international production system, although it is worthwhile to stress that this integration has happened at varying speeds; as a result, some industries, such as automobiles and electronics, have come out on top. The increase in definitive manufactured exports and the volume of *maquiladora* industry trade have structurally transformed the sectoral composition of Mexico's foreign trade. The share of Mexican manufacturing exports in world trade has increased notably in the most internationally dynamic sectors, which have a higher degree of integration in world trade – mainly regarding the SB and SS sectors.

The specialization in Mexico prior to 1982 was predominantly based on a generalized inter-industry trade pattern (Casar *et al.*, 1990; Mattar and Schatan, 1993). For the most part, Mexican imports were capital goods and strategic inputs, while exports corresponded to the SI sector. The years 1986–96 were characterized by a change in the composition of international trade; thus, intra-industry trade acquired more relevance. By the 1993–6 period, intra-industry trade represented more than 70 per cent of the volume of trade (imports plus exports), which was mainly led by the SI sector (see Capdevielle *et al.*, 1997, 1999). This phenomenon occurred even without taking into consideration the *maquiladora* industry, which by nature requires intra-industrial trade.

The *maquiladora* export industry is the most dynamic activity in the Mexican economy. It has increased its participation in imports and exports constantly since 1980 (Table 4.2). In 1980, *maquiladoras* represented 14 per cent of Mexico's total exports, while this level increased to 43 per cent in 1998. During the same period, the volume of trade multiplied fifteen times and the magnitude of the positive trade balance increased seven times (to more than US$8 billion (current) in 1998, which represents approximately 6 per cent of total exports). The *maquiladora* industry's share of manufacturing exports is more intense in the sectors in which the innovative content should be higher. Exports from the *maquiladora* industry account for about 71 per cent of total manufacturing exports in SB, 67 per cent in SS, 55 per cent in SD and 18 per cent in SI. Mexican exports from the *maquiladora* industry, as well as those corresponding to intra-industry trade, are mainly targeted at the most dynamic markets in the United States. Meanwhile, Mexico's definitive exports – that is, exports that do not include temporary exports or *maquiladora* exports – are addressed to the less dynamic sectors in the US market.[12]

The existence of a phenomenon such as that of the *maquiladoras* poses a problem, in the present perspective, considering the effects of such a presence on the network with the local industry and institutions that support innovation. In particular, as far as the creation of backward linkages is concerned, Capdevielle *et al.* (1997) observes that there is a problem in the lack of local sourcing by the *maquiladoras*, which

Table 4.2 International Trade, 1980–1998

Year	Export				Import				Balance			
	Total	Maquila	Manufacturing	Non-manufacturing	Total	Maquila	Manufacturing	Non-manufacturing	Total	Maquila	Manufacturing	Non-manufacturing
1980	18,031	2,519	3,571	11,941	21,089	1,747	16,852	2,490	−3,058	772	−13,281	9,451
1981	21,802	2,998	3,834	14,969	25,428	2,085	20,620	2,723	−3,627	913	−16,786	12246
1982	21,306	2,503	2,999	15,804	15,065	1,748	12,019	1,298	6,240	755	−9,020	14,506
1983	22,889	3,211	4,805	14,873	10,450	2,490	6,278	1,682	12,439	721	−1,474	13,191
1984	25,113	4,232	6,028	14,853	13,735	3,235	8,660	1,840	11,378	997	−2,632	13,013
1985	23,114	4,400	5,553	13,162	15,860	3,305	10,869	1,685	7,255	1,095	−5,316	11,476
1986	17,986	4,657	6,524	6,805	13,845	3,589	9,241	1,015	4,141	1,068	−2,717	5,790
1987	22,969	5,913	8,677	8,379	15,655	4,583	9,865	1,208	7,313	1,330	−1,188	7,171
1988	24,934	8,242	9,966	6,725	22,813	6,343	14,720	1,750	2,120	1,899	−4,754	4,975
1989	27,264	9,557	10,148	7,559	26,951	7,231	17,699	2,021	314	2,326	−7,550	5,538
1990	30,565	10,415	11,157	8,992	31,227	7,749	21,414	2,064	−662	2,667	−10,257	6,928
1991	30,980	11,490	11,956	7,534	36,263	8,551	25,535	2,177	−5,283	2,940	−13,579	5,357
1992	32,813	13,268	12,422	7,123	44,130	9,900	31,466	2,765	−11,317	3,369	−19,045	4,358
1993	36,154	15,227	14,387	6,540	45,548	11,457	31,443	2,647	−9,394	3,770	−17,056	3,893
1994	42,195	18,206	17,192	6,797	54,991	14,184	37,397	3,410	−12,797	4,022	−20,205	3,387
1995	53,318	20,849	24,319	8,150	48,567	17,548	27,699	3,320	4,751	3,301	−3,379	4,830
1996	62,308	23,963	28,618	9,727	58,069	19,799	32,862	5,408	4,239	4,164	−4,244	4,319
1997	70,063	28,656	31,976	9,432	69,667	23,050	41,401	5,216	396	5,605	−9,425	4,216
1998	84,852	36,605	38,702	9,545	90,203	31,192	52,611	6,400	−5,351	5,413	−13,909	3,145

Non-manufacturing activities are agriculture, livestock, beekeeping, hunting and fishing, mining, products and nonspecific services.
Source: based on Economic Indicators, the nation's Central Bank, 1980–1998 (Banco de Mexico, Indicadores Económicos), 1980 Dollars.

means that the *maquiladoras* make very limited purchases of Mexican material and domestically produced knowledge inputs.

Sectoral technological patterns of efforts and competencies

Embodied technology

Considering Mexican manufacturing industry as a whole, the capital intensity index increased continuously from 1970 to 1981; during this period, the growth rate for capital stocks was greater than that for employment. During the 1980s, investment levels decreased drastically, translating into much lower levels of knowledge acquisition through the technology embodied in capital goods and equipment for all of Mexico's manufacturing sectors in general. In fact, from the 1982 crisis onward, a reduction in this index is visible, following the absolute reduction of capital stocks and stagnation of employment. In terms of sectoral technological patterns, it is possible to distinguish different behaviours for each of the sectors. During the import substitution period, all sectors gained in learning capabilities through the technology embodied in capital goods; from 1985 to 1993, capital intensity in the SD, SI and SS sectors diminished, while the SB sector followed an opposite trend. None the less, we should mention that SI is the sector with the highest capital intensity. Thus, by looking into capital intensity trends, some preliminary conclusions can be made. First, Mexican industry's investment in capital goods and equipment decreased sharply during the late 1980s and early 1990s. Second, the average age of capital goods and equipment is increasing, in comparison to previous historical phases.[13]

Relative wages

Relative average wages throughout the sectors can serve as an approximation for the differences in human capital incorporated in each sector, according to skills and competencies. Wage indexes in Mexico and the United States are compared; the almost opposing trends that these two countries follow are readily visible. Salaries in Mexico follow a more erratic behaviour for the whole period considered, together with a quite drastic decrease after the 1982 economic crisis (Sobarzo Fimbres, 1997). To the contrary, wages in the United States across all four technological sectors follow an upward trend, which seems to be stronger in the case of the SB sector.

The main reason for the gap in wages (hereby understood as the ratio of average industrial salaries in the United States and Mexico) is the cyclical changes in the Mexican economy. It is possible to identify three distinct cycles between 1970 and 1993: during most of the 1970s, this gap seemed to be narrowing; in the 1980s it became increasingly wider following the economy's structural adjustments; and it finally began to narrow again during the 1990s. If we analyse the relative sectoral wages trend (average sectoral wage compared to the average manufacturing wage) we can see that the lower relative wages are associated with the SD sector in both economies. However, we must stress that it is precisely this very same sector that accounts for the largest share of employment in Mexico, while it has a much lower share in the United States (about 55 and 38 per cent of total manufacturing employment, respectively).[14]

Sectoral expenditure on R&D

Tables 4.3 and 4.4 illustrate the fact that, in Mexico, firms' R&D expenditures as a percentage of total sales remain at a very low level, a fact that is further aggravated by the very limited dispersion of expenditures among the technological and productive sectors. SB and SS carry out the largest R&D effort. In terms of the firms that engage in R&D activities, it must be noted that these activities are, to a great extent, limited to the large domestic firms, although there is a small group of domestic small and medium-sized enterprises within the SB sector that do carry out some R&D. By comparing R&D expenditures in the United States and in Mexico, it is readily seen that in Mexico R&D averages a mere 0.58 per cent of total sales, as opposed to 3.12 per cent in the United States. Furthermore, R&D in Mexico varies between 0.35 per cent and 1.6 per cent of total sales, whereas it represents between 0.18 per cent and 20.19 per cent of total sales in the United States (see Table 4.3). When comparing sectors, Mexico, paradoxically, shows a higher effort as a percentage of total sales in sectors such as food, beverages and tobacco, textiles, footwear and leather, and metals, with respect to the same sectors in the United States, where, so far, the most significant efforts are mainly concentrated in sectors such as office machinery, computers, motor vehicles and electronic equipment.

As was briefly stated in the paragraph above, R&D in Mexico is rather homogeneously distributed among the different productive sectors, a fact which is in sharp contrast to what happens in the United States. In the traditional sectors, R&D in Mexico as a percentage of sales is usually higher than in the United States. However, in the technology-intensive sectors, R&D in Mexico is much less significant. This difference indicates a pattern of increasing international specialization in these industries, or even in certain segments of the production lines that are less technology-intensive. To illustrate this point, the case of the automobile sector should be considered. Although the Mexican automobile industry has shown an increasing dynamism and importance in terms of added value, employment and, particularly, exports, it must be stressed that the automotive R&D expenditures in Mexico are twelve times lower than their counterpart in the United States (see Table 4.3). Moreover, if firms' expenditures on technology transfer or acquisition of technology from external sources are analysed, we can see that this is, in general, vastly superior to R&D expenditures, in particular for the SS and SD sectors (ENESTYC, 1992, where technology transfer includes different sources, such as acquisition of equipment, patents, royalties).

When the structure of technological sectors between the United States and Mexico is compared in terms of added value and R&D expenditures (see Table 4.4), it should be noted that:

• industry in Mexico is more specialized in those sectors which, at the international level, have much lower levels of R&D expenditure;

Table 4.3 R&D Shares in Mexican and US Manufacturing Industries, 1989–1991

Manufacturing industry	USA	Mexico	Gaps
Food, drink and tobacco	0.31	0.69	45
Textiles, footwear and leather	0.19	0.48	40
Wood, cork and furniture	0.18	0.35	50
Paper and printing	0.36	0.42	86
Chemicals			
Industrial chemicals	2.97	0.6	495
Pharmaceuticals	11.85	0.99	1,194
Petroleum refining	1.57	0.73	214
Rubber and plastics products	1.05	0.68	154
Stone, clay and glass	0.91	0.84	109
Metals			
Ferrous metals	0.29	0.46	63
Non-ferrous metals	0.73	0.85	86
Metal products and machinery			
Fabricated metal products	0.59	0.27	217
Non-electrical machinery	1.65	0.86	192
Office machinery and computers	20.19	0.54	3,724
Electrical machinery	3.2	0.74	431
Electronic equipment and components	9.87	1.01	976
Motor vehicles	4.91	0.39	1,250
Other transport equipment	13.72	1.4	980
Instruments	5.9	1.6	369
Other manufacturing	1.36	0.63	217
Total manufacturing	3.12	0.58	543

Average values, expenditures on R&D as a percentage of companies' total sales.
Source: based on National Employment and Wage Survey (Encuesta Nacional de Empleo, Salarios, Tecnología y Capacitación en el Sector Manufacturero), INEGI-STPS, Mexico, 1992; Structural Analysis Database, STAN-OCDE.

- it could easily be supposed that production activities in Mexico do not require consistent R&D efforts, such as those carried out mostly in developed economies, since local production appears to be specialized in those links in the production line that require lower efforts in terms of R&D;
- the differences in those sectors in which the Mexican economy has shown increasing international specialization and intra-industry trade, as well as a higher presence of foreign firms, would imply that the MNEs and large domestic firms have established a specific strategic behaviour with regard to the geographical localization of production and technological (R&D) activities (see Chapter 5).

As an exercise, we hereby attempt to quantify the magnitude of the R&D efforts that Mexico would have to pursue in order to reach the international technological frontier. In this case, such a frontier is deemed to be the United States (see Table 4.4). Even though it is clear that the extent of the required efforts is indeed large, emphasis is placed on the efforts that Mexico would have to carry out to reach the same R&D expenditure levels as those in the United States. Thus, if Mexico did make the same effort while keeping the same sectoral composition of production, it

Table 4.4 Sectoral R&D Shares in Terms of Mexican and US Manufacturing GDP, 1989–1991

Technological sector	Added value Mexico (%)	Added value USA (%)	R&D Expenditures Mexico (%) (A)	R&D Expenditures USA (%) (B)	Gaps (A/B)(100)
Science-based (SB)	9.08	18.65	0.79	8.89	8.9
Supplier-dominated (SD)	49.49	36.66	0.58	0.56	103.6
Scale-intensive (SI)	37.69	29.97	0.50	2.55	19.6
Specialized suppliers (SS)	4.30	14.73	0.99	4.23	23.4
Total manufacturing	100.00	100.00	0.58	3.12	18.6

Source: Based on the Structural Analysis Database (STAN), the Analytical Business R&D Database (AMBERD) and National Employment and Wage Survey (Encuesta Nacional de Empleo, Salarios, Tecnología y Capacitación en el Sector Manufacturero), INEGI-STPS, ENESTYC, 1992.

would require an R&D expenditure of 2.21 per cent of total manufacturing sales, instead of its current level of 0.58 per cent. Although such a figure would represent an increase of 1.63 per cent in R&D as a share of total sales,[15] it would none the less imply a threefold increase in current R&D.

However, from examination of the most recent data on R&D (1994), a significant increase in the Mexican manufacturing industry's R&D expenditures is readily visible: from 0.58 per cent in 1991 to 0.96 per cent in 1994 (ENESTYC, 1995), which leads us to three considerations. First, R&D seems to be targeted at those activities related to the modernization of production processes and improving the organization of production (Cimoli *et al.*, 1998; Part III of this book). Second, this growing expenditure is highly concentrated in those sectors of the economy that export (that is, automobiles, glass, cement, office machinery and computers, electronic equipment, etc.). Third, the increasing R&D expenditure occurred over the period in which the Mexican economy reached its peak growth; as such, it would come as no surprise if, after December 1994, the *tequila crisis* disrupted these increasing efforts.

Knowledge flows: internal and external knowledge sources

In this section, the mechanisms through which firms develop their knowledge base, via their internal capabilities or their external linkages, are described. Particular attention is devoted to knowledge flows, which generally take into account the existing relationships between the productive entities – firms – and the knowledge producer, such as universities and institutions that support innovation. The analysis is based on the results of a survey carried out on a large number of manufacturing firms in different branches of industry.[16] The survey considered technological knowledge to be a key element in firms' innovation activities, in terms of both processes and products. Firms' technological knowledge was assessed, considering both internal and external sources of knowledge. Internal sources are related to personnel's skills, the R&D department, engineering for production process, etc.

External sources of knowledge refer to the interactions within which products, personnel and equipment are exchanged among other firms, and between firms and institutions (von Hippel, 1988; Lundvall, 1992).

In Mexico, the survey results show that domestic firms consider internal sources of knowledge as more important sources for their innovation activities than external ones. About 59 per cent of the firms qualified internal sources as very important, while only 32 per cent claimed that external sources were important. In the four technological sectors, the activities and skills of engineers and technicians and the experience of the labour force constitute the most relevant sources of knowledge. This is particularly true in the firms that form part of the scale-intensive and science-based sectors.

Analysis of external sources shows that other firms are the most important source of technological information and knowledge, especially in the specialized suppliers and supplier-dominated sectors. Government or university research centres are not a relevant source of information for Mexican firms; this fact is rather remarkable in the case of firms within the science-based sector, since this sector is strongly linked with these centres in the advanced economies. In Denmark, for instance, 29 per cent of firms claim that universities are an important source of technological knowledge, whereas this measure is only 7 per cent in Mexico. Hence, it could easily be claimed that Mexican firms are more inclined to innovate based on their internal techno-logical capabilities. The firms' linkages with other organizations and institutions in the innovation system are not significant; this is undoubtedly a weakness in the generation and diffusion of innovations throughout the system.

User–producer relationships in Mexican industry

A key element in firms' interactive learning processes is captured in the relationship between the producer and the user (Lundvall). Our analysis of the supplier–user relationship has revealed that the interaction between a firm and its suppliers and clients is characterized by a low intensity in which the exchange of information, experiences and technological knowledge is very scarce. This is certainly true if we analyse the relationship between a company and its clients, as well as its relationship with its suppliers.

An alternative approach for analysing technological knowledge flows is presented in the knowledge flows matrix (Table 4.5). This matrix, which has been built based on the information supplied by the survey, portrays the direction and intensity of knowledge flows between the different technological sectors. For example, we found two outstanding facts: (a) both qualitative and quantitative knowledge flows occur mostly among firms belonging to the same technological sector; (b) within the industrial system as a whole, the greatest number of flows take place between the scale-intensive and the supplier-dominated sectors.

Analysis of Table 4.5 yields the following results: 54 per cent of the suppliers in the science-based sector are firms located in the same sector; 23 per cent are in the scale-intensive sector, while only 3 per cent are in the supplier-dominated sector. The principle knowledge flows in the specialized suppliers sector are stable within the sector itself (42 per cent of its suppliers are from within the sector) and with the scale-intensive sector, which represents 36 per cent of its suppliers. The scale-

Table 4.5 Matrix of Knowledge Flows from User to Producer (Percentage Share of Supplier Firms for Technological Sector)

User	Supplier			
	Science-based	Specialized supplier	Scale-intensive	Supplier-dominated
Science-based	54.3	20.0	22.9	2.9
Specialized supplier	0	42.0	36.4	21.6
Scale-intensive	16.5	16.5	52.9	14.1
Supplier-dominated	2.6	27.6	53.9	15.8

Source: Survey on user–producer relationship in Mexico. Master of economy and technological change management, UAM-Xochimilco, 1998.

intensive sector and the supplier-dominated sector maintain strong ties with the scale-intensive sector.[17]

If the matrix is studied from the point of view of suppliers' nationality, we find a very relevant fact. It is clear that the firms in the specialized suppliers sector have established the majority of their technological links (54 per cent) with their foreign counterparts. Meanwhile, the bulk of their most important clients are in the supplier-dominated sector (52 per cent) and the scale-intensive sector (37 per cent). The SS sector fills an important role as a catalyst for technological learning within firms. In Mexico, however, owing to the limited size of the SS, such a role has been only partially fulfilled.[18]

Moreover, the technological information that the specialized suppliers sector generates does not remain in this sector; the technological knowledge passes directly to the same type of sector abroad, or it reaches these firms indirectly through their domestic subsidiaries. Thus, there is what we can call a 'drain of technological knowledge'. Due to the weakness of the specialized suppliers sector, its reduced size and the low level of complexity in the merchandise that it produces, technological knowledge does not accumulate in the firms located in Mexico; instead, it is drained off to a parent company that is located in one of the developed countries. This has become a vicious circle, which limits domestic capacity in the dissemination and generation of technological knowledge through the role that the specialized suppliers sector plays.

Conclusions

A first result regards a reconsideration of the theoretical basis that sustains recent policies. The acquisition of technological capabilities is not a 'linear and instantaneous' process. From this perspective, technological capability is a dynamic and heterogeneous phenomenon, which is built over time and through a complex learning and innovation process that is the result of a constant and efficient effort to generate knowledge. For example, the analysis of the composition of technological sectors and their evolution over time permits observation of a high level of stability in the technological specialization oriented towards traditional activities that are characterized by a mature technology. On the one side, this specialization of the

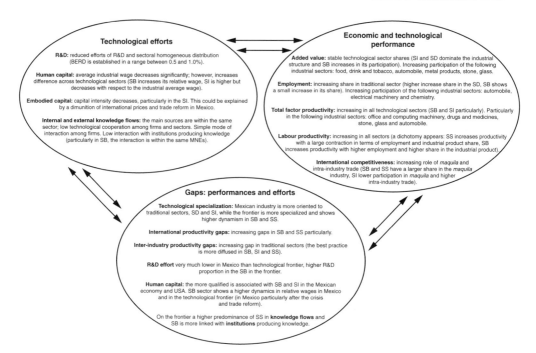

Figure 4.3 Description of the Production System: Technological Effort, Performance and Gaps.

production system limits its own technological opportunities. On the other, low technological opportunity is the main element that explains the reduced efforts and lower quasi-rents. Thus, a 'vicious circle' is established.

Figure 4.3 summarizes the most important technological features which describe Mexico's manufacturing production system, as well as the gaps with the international frontier, in terms of performance and efforts. The specificities of the Mexican manufacturing industry have established a pattern of linkages and opportunities which is, to a large extent, the engine behind other agents' performance within the innovation system, together with the main efforts of the production system itself. This is visible through a number of specific linkages and resources (with different intensities) that the manufacturing system demands from its institutional counterpart in terms of R&D efforts, human resources in science and technology, etc. It could thus be said that in Mexico nearly all technological efforts are targeted at a production system in which the specialization and composition is directed towards mature activities.[19]

With regard to sources of new technological knowledge, the vast majority of firms rely almost exclusively on their internal sources. In addition, most knowledge flows take place in the interior of each sector, while technological cooperation is generally low among the different firms and sectors. The interactions of firms with the institutions that produce knowledge is very poor, a fact which is most keenly felt in those firms belonging to the SB sector. In other words, it seems that the productive system demands a relatively low level of technological effort due to the type of sectoral specialization in which traditional activities with mature technology predominate. The tendencies in the recent changes in the composition of production and the new specialization in international trade have permitted the production of modern goods and a high dynamic in trade, but they are the result of productive processes that have low levels of integration, and they are found only in those segments that are intensive in the use of labour, combined with reduced technological requirements. This situation, to date, has not stimulated the development of productive capacity and technology.

Mexican manufacturing industry seems to be notably rigid in terms of permitting changes within its technological structure, when the specificity of the sectoral technological patterns is considered. This is particularly notable in the SB sector's slow relative growth rate and the SS sector's remarkable stability in terms of added value and employment. It can be said that the economy's specialization pattern leans towards the more mature technological products, as is readily verified by the high participation of the SD and SI sectors in Mexican manufacturing industry.

This specialization pattern has been established within a context in which both the international and the domestic inter-industry gaps in labour productivity have increased. In effect, as previously discussed, not only has the international gap increased for the whole manufacturing sector, but the domestic gap between the four major players (establishments) in each sector and the rest of the sector has also increased. It is thus possible to identify two distinct velocities within Mexican manufacturing industry. There is, within this industry, a reduced group of establishments with an increasing capacity to catch up to the technological frontier. In the remainder of manufacturing industry, the distance to both the international and the domestic best practice has increased significantly. The reason is that the increasing capacities of the firms in the first group have not been diffused to those in the second. It is precisely in such a situation that institutions could play a determinant role in anticipating and fomenting opportunities to enhance linkages and efforts throughout the production system. Despite the economic opening, the lack of domestic diffusion of the best productive practices and the inability to incorporate technological changes in products and processes impede domestic diffusion of the benefits of technical progress, and competitiveness is sustained on the basis of cheap and unskilled manual labour. Likewise, the reduced level of economic growth in general, and in the manufacturing industry in particular during the past two decades, is associated with a low level of investment; this limits the renovation of capital reserves and the technological innovation incorporated therein.

The results observed in the technological and sectoral composition of production, as well as the indicators of efforts and productive and technological performance, do not indicate a significant structural transformation. The Mexican economy has not shown sustained growth, nor has it recovered the levels achieved before the 1982 crisis. The industrial structure has not changed significantly, despite the extraordinary growth and structural change in international trade. Lastly, the effort and performance indicators offer rather unsatisfactory results, even when these are unequally distributed among individual economic agents. The specialization in foreign trade in the highly dynamic sectors does not show a corresponding significant change in the domestic productive structure.

The analysis of the efforts made and the results obtained in the development of technological capabilities in the Mexican manufacturing industry permits us to affirm that the new development model does not sustain the domestic generation of said capabilities. We must, however, consider that the available information, in general, only permits an evaluation of average values, within which some agents could have a quite distinct performance from the average, and it is possible that such agents could define the form of generating technological capabilities in the future. The time that has passed since the beginning of the adjustment process and the structural change is not brief, but it could still be insufficient to evaluate the phenomenon, which will only be clear in the long term. However, the tendencies are worrisome, given that it is clear that macroeconomic stability cannot be sustained in the long term, and the productive deficiencies and the expansion of the technological gap with the most developed economies are growing in a context of accelerated technological change.

Notes

1. During import substitution, Casar *et al.* (1990) concluded that technical progress is strongly associated with market dynamics. This affirmation can be verified in the total grouping of manufacturing, as well as in the performance differential between specific activities.
2. Other works that propose similar indicators for efforts and performances are Buesa and Molero (1992) and Unger (1985).
3. Likewise, these very same differences are readily noted when comparing them with the whole of the OECD area.
4. The structural change indicators elaborated on the basis of the data shown in Table 4.1 are 28 per cent greater for the United States.
5. There are two reasons for the changes in the Mexican technological sectors' market shares between 1970 and 1994. The first is of a cyclical nature, and captures the effects on the composition of these market shares that were caused by the repeated economic crises that the country has endured. To clarify this idea, it would seem that most of the goods that are associated with domestic demand and that are not readily tradable in international markets (SS and SD) are quite closely related to economic cycles. Thus, they decrease their market share during economic recessions, while, on the contrary, internationally tradable goods (SI) appear to increase their market share during the very same periods. A second explanation deals with the overall production trends in which the shares of SB and SI sectors have increased, offset by reductions in the SD and SS sectors. The growth of the SB and SI sectors' market shares is the logical outcome of an increasing demand for the goods associated with these sectors, as well as their growing share in world trade. The SS sector, in contrast, followed an inverse trend: during the last stage of the import substitution phase (1970–81), its share of production increased, only to be later reduced during the subsequent economic phases (e.g. stabilization and liberalization).
6. See The Structural Analysis Database, STAN-OCDE, 1996.
7. Likewise, we must consider that the relatively slow growth of the Mexican economy during the 1980s and 1990s can be considered as a factor that limits the incorporation of new technologies (see Casar, *et al.*, 1990; Dutrénit and Capdevielle, 1993; Unger, 1993, 1994).
8. Moreover, this intra-industry gap does not behave identically in all four sectors. It is, however, remarkable that the gap is not only wider but is also increasing at a higher rate in the least advanced sector in terms of technology, SD, while it increases at a lower rate in those sectors facing stiffer competition, SB and SS, regardless of the more accelerated rate of technology diffusion in these sectors. These findings could be related to the predominant

pattern of competitiveness that prevails in each one of the sectors; thus, SB, SI and SS, which compete in the international markets, are somehow more capable of adapting and diffusing technologies.

9. None the less, the existence of this productivity differential requires us to suppose that these firms must have other factors that make them competitive, such as lower wages, flexibility or specialization in niches of production for non-tradable goods.

10. We analysed the number of patents granted to the firms classified by sectors of technology, according to principal areas of production, whatever the nature and area of the patent. This classification identifies more than 50 per cent of the patents granted. Only the patents granted to firms were considered, not those granted to independent inventors or research institutions. The period analysed is 1980–96.

11. The total number of domestic patents is quite reduced, which is why the total value of the 1980–96 series was analysed.

12. Hernández Laos (1994a, b) argues that dynamic competitive advantages – such as technological change and economies to scale – statistically are not a significant source of the current competitiveness in Mexican industry. Mexican exports' competitiveness is fundamentally sustained by the devaluation of the exchange rate and the intensive use of cheap and low-skilled manual labour.

13. Nevertheless, we should remember that the prices of capital goods have been affected by trade reform, while Mexican firms' possibility of obtaining capital goods and equipment at lower prices was also reduced. (For example, during the same period, the price of capital goods in the United States decreased.)

14. Another interesting observation arises from the comparison of relative sectoral wages between the United States and Mexico. After the crisis at the beginning of the 1980s, relative sectoral wages appear to follow a similar trend in both economies. Thus, even if the gap in wages between the two countries is rather large in absolute terms, it is also true that the differences among sectors in the interior of both economies have followed remarkably similar trends since the early 1980s. For instance, relative wages for the SB sector caught up with the SI sector in Mexico during 1993; the same intersection in the United States' relative sectoral wages can be observed in 1985. Thus, Mexican industry seems to be beginning to discriminate between wages, in terms of sectoral technological specifications, as is done by its counterpart in the United States. None the less, the growing trend in wages in the SB and SS sectors is clearly more notable in the United States, where demand for human resources with higher skills and competency is increasing.

15. It is supposed throughout this exercise that there are no economies to scale in the development of R&D activities, which would make it even more difficult to reach a competitive level of expenditure, depending on the magnitude of said economies for the different sectors.

16. Survey on user–producer relationship in Mexico, Master of Economy and Technological Change Management, UAM-X, 1998.

17. Indeed, as we have said, it is these two sectors in which the flows of technological knowledge are concentrated. This is not surprising, since, as we have previously shown, these two sectors form the bulk of Mexican industry; they are the two oldest sectors, as well as the two that currently contribute the greatest share of employment, added value and technological effort.

18. The relative size of Mexican firms, in which there is a clear predominance of the Pequerías y medianas empresas (PYMEs) or small and medium enterprises (SMEs), places an even greater limitation on the flow of knowledge, given that a structure in which PYMEs predominate requires more intensive ties to be competitive and to develop productive and technological capacity, which permits the creation of 'goods to scale' that cannot be achieved by each individual productive organization. As existing studies show, in the French and Italian

industrial districts the small firms can be competitive only through very close productive and technological ties, which unite their technological and productive versatility by the scale acquired through the interaction of various small producers.

19. As we mentioned above, Mexico's R&D efforts are rather poor in comparison to those at the technological frontier. Under these circumstances, it is a paradox that the sectors that have a low effort in the development of technology consider internal sources as the most relevant for the development of their innovative capacity. This situation demonstrates their lack of ties with other agents and with the institutions in the national innovation system (research centres, universities, linkage centres, etc.). R&D efforts, which recently have registered growth, are highly concentrated in the export sectors (automobiles, glass, cement, office machinery and computers, electronic equipment, etc.).

CHAPTER FIVE

Globalization of Production and Technology

K. Unger and M. Oloriz

Introduction

Our analysis of Mexican globalization aims to illustrate the effect of globalization on the development of technological capabilities or competences. To this end we believe it important to distinguish between two types of firms: first, firms and industries dominated by foreign firms (FF, subsidiaries and joint ventures); second, firms and industries under the control of domestic firms (NF, including conglomerates and minority foreign participations). This distinction is applied to analyse production capacity and technological flows in recognition of the kind of interaction expected to occur within and between certain types of industries, and also between firms localized in Mexico and abroad.

We show that there is a different industrial specialization of FF and NF. Such a pattern of specialization is important, because it determines their respective contributions to the dynamism of the economy, namely to capital investment, the balance of trade, technology transfer, R&D practices and productivity gains. The combined effect of all these areas also illustrates the contribution of FF and NF respectively to the development of national technological capabilities or competences. Some more specific thinking about each type of firm and their anticipated effects may prove useful. We anticipate, and show, that foreign firms turn more to imports and less to domestic producers in areas where intermediate commodities are really relevant. Prominent examples can be obtained from case studies such as those elaborated in other chapters of this volume, including industries such as the automobile and autoparts industry, electronics, telecommunications equipment, electrical appliances, pharmaceuticals, fine chemicals and plastic products. National firms, on the other hand, tend to rely on the natural resource advantage of domestic materials content, for both exports and domestic sales, while relying extensively on the international market for standard technology in the form of technical assistance and new equipment and machinery. The technological maturity of remaining industries in the hands of large national firms may also be crucial in the sense that, for the most part, they are only concerned with incremental, minor process innovations, as a source of complementary competitive advantage. This is the case for national firms in typical mature industries like clothing and textiles, shoes, glass, cement, steel, beer, corn/wheat flours and other food products. Most of their technological efforts are guided towards saving energy and improving their use of raw materials.

The interactions defining this specific distinction between FF and NF evolve around key technologies, shared knowledge or skills, or producer–supplier relationships and, consequently, the patterns of knowledge flows can differ markedly. Foreign firms dominate the most modern high-tech type industrial sectors, while national firms control most of the more mature resource-based industrial sectors, as indicated in the examples listed in the previous paragraph. In this case, one can anticipate different channels for the acquisition of foreign technology at the different stages of operations of foreign and Mexican firms. One straight channel is the foreign firm as a channel for entry of new technology incorporated into new firms, new plants, new production processes, new equipment, new products and, consequently, new organizational changes. Another channel is the contribution of foreign firms to domestic technological activities (R&D, patenting and inventions, training activities, quality control). A third channel is the transfer of foreign technology, either intrafirm transfers for foreign firms or arm's length acquisitions from independent foreign technology suppliers. These channels, as much as their technological content, determine quite different contributions to the system of domestic capabilities. Below we extend other more specific evidence in these three respects.

A final analytical concern, though one very difficult in practice, is to capture the dynamics of the system. Both groups (foreign and national firms) will be considered in the modes of how these are nested in the technological sectors according to the Pavitt taxonomy. An exercise which attempts to answer some of the questions raised at the end of Chapter 2 is here extended. Production capacity and technological capabilities are analysed, considering the sectoral technological specificities, and in particular referring to the main linkages expected to develop across the sectors of Pavitt's taxonomy. Briefly, specialized suppliers produce product innovations and capital inputs for the other sectors, whereas through the production of components and advanced materials the science-based industries generate positive effects which propagate to the whole system. The scale-intensive and supplier-dominated sectors are the major users of equipment and advanced quality components of the other two, more innovation-intensive groups of industries. All the linkages between the four groups are fundamental to increased production capacity, in particular those which establish themselves between the most innovative and the traditional and natural resources-based sectors. The flows of interactions depicted in Figure 5.1 are at the heart of the national innovation system. Pavitt's sectoral classification is adjusted to Mexican industry to show if and how the production and technological flows between the domestic sectors are replaced by international linkages such as imports, subcontracting, intrafirm technology transfer and whole technology packages. In this context, we adopt Pavitt's taxonomy to analyse the technological 'localization' of foreign and domestic firms and their interplay with the Mexican industry, to suggest that the form in which globalization has proceeded resulted in more modest technological gains than anticipated. These issues are addressed through the use of several economic and technological indicators, listed in Table 5.1.

Table 5.1 Economic and Technological Indicators

FF and NF: international and domestic linkages
  GDP, exports, exports to GDP (Table 5.2)
  FF in GDP (Table 5.2)
  Exports and imports ratios (Table 5.3)

The importance of foreign firms and foreign investment
  FDI to total investment
  FDI in sectors
  FDI important projects and countries of origin

Foreign technological sources
  Technology expenditures: foreign and domestic suppliers
  R&D and technical collaboration with other enterprises

Fixed capital investment
  Fixed capital investment (Table 5.4)
  Capital intensity and productivity (Table 5.4)

R&D and technological transfer
  R&D ratios (Table 5.3)
  Technology transfer ratios (Table 5.3)
  Balance of payments by technological concepts

Technology embodied in equipment and intermediates
  Imports and imports to total supply (Table 5.2)
  Adoption of modern equipment
  Trade balance of high-tech products
  High-tech exports

FF and NF: their international and domestic linkages

Here we deal with the FF and NF in the recent context of development of the Mexican economy: the trade reform, deregulation and the transformation associated with the increasing openness and interactions with the rest of the world. Firms have generally changed their modes to interact with both the rest of the domestic economy and the world via different channels related to manufacturing activities. The evidence on the relative dynamism experienced by FF and NF could be summarized on the basis of production, trade and technology indicators as follows.

First, total manufactures GDP experienced high growth at more than 11 per cent between 1988 and 1993 at constant pesos, while FF increased their participation in manufactures output. The growth rates of FF's output averaged 12.2 per cent in the same period.[1] As a result, the participation of FF in Mexican industry reached 28.5 per cent in 1993 (Table 5.2).

Second, growth rates vary among sectors. The FF in science-based (growing at 23.5 per cent from a relatively small base at the origin) and supplier-dominated industries (growing at 15.3 per cent) grew at faster rates; FF in scale-intensive activities also grew successfully at more than 8 per cent a year. Important sectors in the dynamism of science-based industries are pharmaceuticals, fine chemicals, office and computing machinery (whose dynamism was mainly due to exports, especially

Table 5.2 Manufactures Output of Foreign Firms, Exports and Imports, 1988–1993

Technological sector	Manufactures GDP, 1993[a]	% FF in GDP in 1993	X/GDP 1993	Annual growth exports[b]	Annual growth imports[c]	M/(M + GDP) 1993
Science-based	14,829.8	64.2	0.56	170.0	72.6	0.37
Supplier-dominated	73,137.3	18.8	0.21	−1.0	63.0	0.23
Scale-intensive	76,157.8	30.1	0.21	27.7	58.2	0.24
Specialized suppliers	3,772.3	43.2	0.81	96.3	52.2	0.66
Total	167,897.3	28.5	0.26	24.9	60.7	0.27

[a] Millions of dollars; [b] exports growth 1990–3; [c] imports growth 1988–93.
Source: PETYC-CIDE Project data, based on SECOFI and INEGI.

of relevance in *maquiladora* exports of the computer industry) and electronic equipment for radio, TV and communications. Leading sectors in the growth of FF supplier-dominated industries are food, beverages, clothing, paper and electrical appliances. The most dynamic sectors in scale-intensive industries are plastic products, non-ferrous metals, home appliances and the auto industry. On a different path, the FF specialized suppliers, comprising producers of machinery and equipment of specific and common use, and precision equipment and instruments, experienced very moderate growth. Most of their production of machinery and equipment was reconvened to plants in the home country, which may now be the main suppliers of imported equipment, while retaining some basic assembly operations.

Third, excepting the supplier-dominated industries where FF are prominent in beverages, paper products and some food lines mostly oriented to local demand, the other three industry groups also experienced export growth at extremely high rates (Table 5.2). Export growth is higher in the same sectors where FF have a larger presence; that is the science-based, specialized suppliers and scale-intensive sectors (Table 5.2). The ratio of exports to output for the science-based and specialized suppliers sectors had climbed to 56 and 81 per cent respectively in 1993, though the production of both, and especially of specialized supplier goods, remained very limited.

Fourth, the FF that dominate the production of science-based and specialized supplier industries, and FF in some of the most important scale-intensive industries (like automotive, plastic products and housing appliances), achieve successful export performances but also reduce domestic content on a large scale. The net contribution to the balance of trade is much less than the export ratios indicate. These effects of foreign firms on the balance of trade deserve to be examined in more detail, as we do below, before turning to the important implications of increased imports for the innovation system.

Fifth the trend to increase imported raw materials and intermediates has become a general practice for both FF and NF in order to attain or improve international competitiveness: an increase of import ratios for all firms in the survey (ENESTYC, 1992) close to 4 percentage points from 1989 to 1991. None the less, FF have adopted much larger levels of imports content since they began. The difference in ratios of

Table 5.3 Imports, Exports, R&D and Technology Transfer According to Market Orientation, 1991

	Imports[a]		Exports[b]		%R&D[c]		%Technology transfer[c]	
	FF	*NF*	*FF*	*NF*	*FF*	*NF*	*FF*	*NF*
Total	49.5*	19.6	30.3*	7.1	0.57	0.68	2.83	3.28
Exporter	70.0	19.1	76.3	70.5	0.31	0.30	1.88	1.57
Non-exporter	43.1	19.6	9.4	3.9	0.69	0.73	3.26	3.51
Science-based	52.3	28.6	16.5	4.7	0.86	1.20	3.42	2.47
Exporter	87.5	51.8	82.6	78.1	0.36	1.30	2.12	4.58
Non-exporter	41.4	27.8	4.9	3.2	0.99	1.20	3.76	2.37
Supplier-dominated	41.8	20.4	10.4	5.6	0.66	0.60	3.27	3.41
Exporter	67.0	18.7	92.5	85.2	0.69	0.40	2.49	3.35
Non-exporter	41.3	20.3	3.8	2.8	0.64	0.60	3.31	3.51
Scale-intensive	51.6	17.1	41.2	10.0	0.41	0.70	2.20	3.09
Exporter	65.3	15.5	73.5	59.5	0.16	0.20	1.25	0.52
Non-exporter	47.7	17.1	16.6	5.7	0.63	0.80	3.11	3.59
Specialized suppliers	60.1	21.9	42.8	6.8	0.96	1.20	5.49	4.62
Exporter	80.0	20.5	92.1	79.0	1.39	2.80	9.73	10.74
Non-exporter	45.4	21.9	10.4	5.3	0.65	1.10	2.39	4.39

[a] Weighted average: raw materials to total inputs; [b] Weighted average: exports to total sales; [c] Weighted averages to firms incomes; * FF > NF accepted with 95% confidence.
Source: PETYC-CIDE Project data, based on ENESTYC 1992.

imported raw materials and intermediates for the FF and NF firms is indeed significant: 49.5 to 19.6 per cent (Table 5.3); thus clearly indicating the lesser degree of integration within the national economy of FF. When comparing exporters (those with over 50 per cent of sales through exports), the difference in import ratios is even more acute: 70 per cent for the FF and 19.1 per cent for the NF (see Table 5.3); though for non-exporters the import ratios are also substantially different, at 43.1 and 19.6 per cent respectively. In general, export and import ratios are significantly correlated but the coefficient is substantially larger for foreign firms.[2]

Sixth, the imports ratio is particularly high for FF in specialized suppliers (60.1 per cent) and science-based industries (52.3 per cent) (Table 5.3) but there are other sectors, and particularly the export-oriented FF within them, which seem also to be engaged in basic assembly operations. When comparing FF exporters with NF exporters within Pavitt's types of sectors, the percentage differences in import ratios are around 50 per cent, given that the NF are exporting on the basis of domestic resources; the difference also holds within the science-based sectors, even if NF in this group are more dependent on imports than other NF (Table 5.3). For most of the FF, imports of intermediates may be their main or only link with advanced technology from abroad. In fact, the imports ratio of FF exporters in the dozen leading sectors of FF are above 80 per cent (an exception is made of the auto industry exporters, at a non-trivial rate of 64.3 per cent). These sectors include most of those where FF are relevant:[3] automobile, electronic equipment, clothing, metal products, electrical appliances, plastic products, home appliances, transport equipment (excluding autos), office machinery, professional instruments and all lines of machinery and equipment. Such differences between FF and NF may have to do with the relative industrial specialization of each type of firm, but it is clear that national firms are producing closer to the logic of natural domestic advantages, whereas foreign firms belong to global strategies that at present are dictating lesser interactions with Mexican material suppliers.

Seventh, as might be expected, FF also privilege foreign sources of technology. The evidence from a survey conducted by CONACYT (1997b, pp.52–4) shows their large reliance on foreign technology acquisitions over national sources of technology.[4] The survey included a number of foreign and national firms, not a formally representative sample; but the results serve as an indication of technology transfer practices. In other sections below we analyse that survey in more detail.

The importance of foreign firms and foreign investments

As can easily be seen on the basis of the dynamics reviewed in the previous section, foreign firms and foreign direct investment (FDI) are very important to the Mexican industrial system. This section further examines their importance. We first focus on the recent evolution of foreign investment and then some implications about the role of foreign technology are advanced. In this latter respect, it may be right to accept the premise that the prospect of acquiring access to modern technology is perhaps the most important reason why countries try to attract foreign investment (Blomstrom, 1991, p. 93). Following Dunning (1981), the branches or subsidiaries of MNEs enjoy, among others, the advantage of access to many of the endowments of the parent company, including R&D and other cheaper inputs, at very low marginal cost (Chesnais, 1988, p. 500). At the end of the section we come back to some related concerns.

FDI is usually a total technology package that involves product and process technology from the parent office of MNEs, plus machinery, equipment and material supplies from compatible suppliers to the rest of the MNE (intrafirm imports), and in some cases R&D competences as well. This section explores how Mexican globalization is evolving through FDI. The analysis of foreign investment seems to indicate that the following trends have emerged.

First of all, the participation of foreign firms in Mexican industry is relatively large and increasing, totalling 28.5 per cent in 1993, as seen in Table 5.2. Their importance is most evident in the science-based industries (FF account for 64.2 per cent of output) and the specialized suppliers (43.2 per cent of output), but is also quite considerable in certain key scale-intensive industries, like automobiles and fine chemicals.

Most important has been the rise of investment in the stock market (*cartera*) in contrast to moderate increases in FDI. Foreign investment grew very significantly during the 1990s, from US$5.0 million in 1990 to $15.6 million in 1993. And though it collapsed during 1995, the ratio of foreign investment to GDP increased from less than 1 per cent during the early 1980s to around 4 per cent in the 1990s. The largest share of this increase is investment in the stock market, whereas FDI has also reported some good, even if more moderate, increases.

There is a heavy concentration of FDI in certain manufacturing sectors. Twenty out of 54 industries accumulate 86.1 per cent of total FF output and most important are the auto industry, chemicals and pharmaceuticals, and machinery/appliances, which account for more than half of the total. These sectors, however, are showing a declining importance *vis-à-vis* services activities (finance, trading, real estate). Most important for our concern with innovation is the declining importance of FDI in manufacturing. Since 1988, FDI in services has become more important than in manufactures, including new firms and the expansion of foreign corporations in banking and finance, retail and wholesale trading, hotel chains, commercial centres and other major real estate investments. The contribution of many of these activities to domestic competitiveness, notably organizational changes improving communications and financial services, can be important, though the overall impact on the innovation system of these activities may be less important than the impact of dynamic and innovating manufactures.

The same trend not in favour of manufactures was projected to remain at least until the year 2000. In the list of the few very large FDI projects for coming years seven modern manufacturing projects account for about 40 per cent of total investment (close to US$5,000 million), including two of the large soft drinks producers. However, the single most important projects do not belong to manufactures but to basic infrastructure contributing modestly to direct technological competences: basic petrochemicals (Nova in JV with Pemex for $2,000 million), shopping facilities (Reichmann: $1,100 million) and gas distribution (Trans Canada $1,000 million). The relatively important manufacturing projects are expansions in electronics (Philips and GE) and automobiles (Ford, VW and Nissan), though none of these accounts for more than $500 million.

More than half of total FDI is still of US origin, though the proportion in the stock of FDI declined from 69 per cent in 1980 to 61.2 per cent in 1995. The US FDI in manufactures also declined to 63.1 per cent of total US FDI in 1995, alongside the rise of US FDI in wholesale trade, finance and other industries. And within manufactures, there is also a change in the composition of US FDI in favour of the food and drinks industry (in general less inclined to export but more to import) and a substantial decrease in chemicals and transport equipment (undisputed leaders of the recent years' exports surge). This change in the composition of US FDI (and probably of other FDI, as suggested in the trend for total FDI) may explain larger increases in imports than in exports associated with FDI. Thus, the large foreign firms (as much as some very large national firms) within the manufacturing industry reduce the extent of industrial processing and increase imported content in order to improve their international competitiveness in domestic and foreign markets. Their specialization can take the form of product mandates or specific lines of business (as in the change to basic chemicals away from fine specialities), specializing in components (as in autoparts) or in labour-intensive assembly and integrated solutions to domestic customers (as with IBM and others in the electronics industry).

Reflecting on the implications of these trends for technological capabilities, we take the side of those that examine critically the assumption that FDI is one of the main and straight channels for acquiring technological competences, including ultimate access to higher levels of R&D capability. We are more in line with those arguing that the international allocation of R&D and, more broadly, the allocation of technological capabilities within MNEs is likely to remain centralized in parent firms, particularly in the aftermath of trade liberalization (Eaton *et al.*, 1994, p. 91).

According to this view, trade liberalization tends to favour more specialized production by the subsidiary for global markets and its R&D functions will diminish, while the MNEs internalize the research that is central to them. Thus, technological competence is likely to remain more concentrated than competence in production and assembly (Eaton *et al.*, 1994, pp. 94–6). However, we are also convinced that centralization depends on a variety of factors, including the NIS and the size and the technical characteristics of the home and host countries and of particular industries (Eaton *et al.*, 1994, p. 92), thus justifying a fuller exploration of the concrete operations of FDI and other sources of technological capabilities in Mexican industry.

Foreign technological sources

An important source of technology for Mexico is foreign. Estimates of the participation of local technology suppliers in a recent survey have shown that domestic technology operations (defined as the sum of both income and expenditures on technology sales or acquisitions to or from domestic sources) make up less than 7 per cent of total technology transactions, while foreign technology spending represented 98 per cent of total spending in the same firms surveyed. These results are highly associated to operations of subsidiaries of MNEs, including a few Mexican firms and their foreign affiliates (CONACYT, 1997b, p. 53). Foreign firms accounted for about 82 per cent of technology expenditures. Particularly, the importance of foreign technology for the innovation system of Mexican industry is still largely founded on the industrial base inherited from the import-substituting industrialization decades, which relied on imports of technology. For the most recent industrial phase related to trade reforms and deregulation, foreign technology and foreign investment were again expected to be the main industrial carriers. In this and later sections we estimate the recent contribution of foreign firms to R&D and technological flows with regard to different channels: the overall fixed capital investment, R&D efforts and collaborations, imports of intermediates and equipment, and technology transfers including foreign patents.

These may also relate to other more indirect (and difficult to measure) technical competences recently proposed in other OECD studies, such as knowledge flows in the form of collaborative industry activities and technology diffusion. Technical collaboration among enterprises as well as their more informal interactions have come up-front as one of the most important knowledge flows in OECD economies. R&D collaborations between firms are growing rapidly in some of those countries, but there is no evidence of this taking place in Mexico.

First of all, R&D spending is extremely low in Mexican firms at somewhere around 0.5 per cent of sales. Second, and more to our purpose here, estimates from data in the INEGI-CONACYT survey on R&D, conducted during 1997, show equally moderate efforts on R&D internally and externally to the firms: 0.25 and 0.22 per cent on sales during 1995 respectively. Third, FF and NF are very similar in their relative efforts: 0.45 and 0.47 per cent on sales respectively (proportions in the same range from an earlier survey are analysed below). However, the FF are much less inclined to spend on R&D externally to the firm in collaboration with local firms, local institutions or individuals (ratios of 0.36 and 0.09 per cent intra- and extra-respectively), while the still humble investment on R&D by NF is more balanced, at 0.22 and 0.25 per cent respectively.[5]

Other informal linkages and contacts may be important, including relationships among users and producers whereby knowledge and know-how are transferred, but their contribution to innovative capacity within Mexico is not evident either, even if most of these linkages within Mexican industry have not yet been definitely established. It may be that the existence of these linkages could be tested through cluster analysis and more firm surveys (OECD, 1997a, b).

Fixed capital investment

Among the main sources of technological competence are investment-related competences. These derive mainly from FDI and new and complementary investment by nationals, which usually translate to the incorporation of modern machinery, equipment and physical installations. Most of these may be imported capital goods and other imports of the latest vintages to allow local industry to improve their international competitiveness, and may usually accompany technology transfers and other capabilities. Furthermore, much new technology is embodied in the capital goods purchased, as OECD studies have begun to show (see Chapter 3). For all these reasons, investment in machinery and equipment is important and it is natural to expect that FF become an important source of these investment-related competences. However, the recent performance of Mexican FF is not encouraging.

In Table 5.4, we can observe that fixed capital investment in manufactures fell from 1988 to 1993, when translated into constant prices. The fall was particularly large for foreign firms, which reduced fixed capital by 24.0 per cent in the same period. This fall meant that FF reduced their share in total fixed capital from 28.9 to 24.0 per cent in 1993.[6] The reduction was most acute in scale-intensive industries (36 per cent) and specialized suppliers. The really important reduction in fixed investment took place in scale intensive industries, both FF and NF. Leading FF industries in this contraction are autos, steel and steel products, sound and TV components, non-ferrous metals, cement, tyres, glass containers and housing appliances. The NF scale-intensive contraction of investment is very high in public enterprises in refinery, basic petrochemicals, fertilizers, iron and steel products, and copper, and the beer industry, pastries and auto parts also reduce fixed investment.

Other industry groups also tend to reduce investment. The reduction of FF on specialized suppliers, for example, is compensated by some moderate expansion in local firms. This trend is led by metal parts and equipment for the supply of energy. A trend to the contrary is the important gains in fixed capital for both FF and NF in supplier-dominated industries such as soft drinks, certain lines of clothing, pasteboard, polyethylene products, tiles, metal wires and others of lesser importance. These traditional industries have been investing in fixed capital at the same pace as they expand employment; thus they seem more active in modernizing their production facilities than others. Foreign firms reduced fixed investment per employee significantly from 136.4 to 82.2 thousand pesos, closing the distance from national firms (75,100 pesos in 1993; Table 5.4). In fact, by 1993 NF tended to surpass the FF

Table 5.4 Investment, Capital Intensity and Labour Productivity in Foreign and National Firms, Proportional Variation, 1993–1998

Sectors	Fixed capital[a]		Capital intensity (K/L)[b]		Productivity (VA/L)[b]	
	1993	Proportional variation	1993	Proportional variation[c]	1993	Proportional variation[d]
Total	248.9	−0.08	76.7	−0.26	57.1	0.11
FF	59.8	−0.24	82.2	−0.40	77.9	0.07
Science-based	5.7	0.15	60.7	−0.13	114.4	0.28
Supplier-dominated	13.8	0.32	47.3	−0.03	60.9	0.31
Scale-intensive	37.9	−0.36	138.6	−0.46	92.2	−0.08
Specialized suppliers	2.4	−0.45	34.8	−0.48	43.1	−0.05
NF	189.2	−0.02	75.1	−0.20	51.1	0.13
Science-based	3.9	0.09	65.7	0.13	78.3	0.18
Supplier-dominated	82.6	0.33	44.4	0.01	34.9	0.14
Scale-intensive	96.4	−0.22	198.7	−0.23	113.1	0.28
Specialized suppliers	6.3	0.36	54.1	0.26	37.4	0.14

[a]Billions of pesos at constant 1993 prices; [b]thousands of pesos per worker; [c](variation) / (K/L 1988), [d](variation) / (VA/L 1988).
Source: PETYC, CIDE Project data, based on INEGI.

in capital intensity in most of Pavitt's groups (except the supplier-dominated). Let us examine the sectoral trends behind this result.

Closely similar to the trends on investment reviewed above, the group of FF in scale-intensive sectors led the reduction in capital intensity. Mostly as a result of significant increases in employment, the overall capital intensity of FF in scale-intensive industries decreased by 46 per cent. This result is the consequence of two predominant trends within the industries that make up this group: one trend is simultaneously reducing fixed investment and increasing labour employment, the other is reductions in employment in a lower proportion than falls in investment. Notable examples of the first kind are the automotive industry, radio and TV sets and components, housing appliances and plastic products. These industries account for 63.0 per cent of total scale-intensive exports, and might illustrate the kind of labour assembly practices of FF that also limit fixed investment to gain export competitiveness.

Examples of the other kind, where reductions in employment are proportionately lower than drastic falls in investment, are observed for FF in sectors mostly oriented to domestic markets, such as tyres, cement and iron and steel. Here FF rationalize in the use of both factors of production, probably correcting for previous excesses.

Within the FF, specialized suppliers also decreased capital intensity substantially by 48 per cent (Table 5.4), but their importance in total investment and employment is very moderate. But not only FF seek rationalizing measures. Most of the NF in scale-intensive sectors also tend to rationalize their production, while reducing substantially fixed investment. This trend shows in very substantial reductions in both investment and employment in the NF in steel, basic chemicals and petrochemicals, oil refinery and beverages. A few other sectors, like paper products, glass and cement, also rationalize in the use of labour (reduce employment) while undertaking some new investment. Yet another pair of sectors show significant increases of both new investment and labour: synthetic fibres and autoparts NF.

Thus, the modernization measures of FF and NF in scale-intensive sectors are varied, but the most important seem to involve preferential measures to increase assembly labour or to dispose of redundant labour while using more intensively installed capacity, at times with some investment in new machinery and equipment.

As a result, labour productivity shows significant improvements in general (Table 5.4), despite the negative trend of foreign scale-intensive and specialized suppliers, which by 1993 had moved their mix towards more labour-intensive assembly of lower productivity. The latter seems to predominate in export-oriented activities of FF, which also had reduced domestic integration in industries such as the automotive industry and plastic products (very important in scale-intensive exports), and most machinery, equipment and instruments.

R&D activities and technology transfer

According to ENESTYC (1992), only one-third of the firms invested in R&D during 1991.[7] The R&D ratios were also very low: 0.57 and 0.68 for foreign and national firms respectively (Table 5.3).[8] As expected, the ratios are larger for firms in the science-based and specialized suppliers industries, though the ratio does not exceed 1.0 per cent in any of the FF groups of industries. Perhaps more revealing are the lower R&D ratios of export-oriented FF in science-based and scale-intensive sectors. The basic labour assembly nature of these FF exports shows in their comparison to non-exporters in the same sectors: 0.36 per cent in exporters (mainly electronic equipment) against 0.99 per cent in non-exporters in science-based (pharmaceuticals and fine chemicals) and 0.16 per cent in exporters against 0.63 per cent in non-exporters of scale-intensive sectors (Table 5.3). These same FF had turned themselves even more into labour assembly by 1995, when their R&D ratios, according to other CONACYT (1997a, b) surveys, shrank to 0.25 per cent. The main industries in specific sectors are listed in the following paragraph.

The acquisition of technology from outside the firm, i.e. technology transfers involving licences, technical assistance, know-how and the like, also takes place in a limited range of firms, about one-half of the firms surveyed (ENESTYC 1992). On the whole, the other half is not involved in R&D or technology transfer (48 per cent of the firms). Spending on technology transfer follows very much the same pattern as R&D spending, although FF and NF specialized suppliers (and the more so those exporting capital goods and instruments) tend to spend more than the others: about 10 per cent on sales (Table 5.3). Again the most revealing data are the lower spending ratios of export-oriented FF in the assembly or basic processing of science-based industries (mostly electronic equipment), supplier-dominated (clothing, metal products and electrical appliances) and scale-intensive products (typically comprising firms in the auto industry, plastic products, home appliances and other transport equipment). Formal alliances of foreign firms with national firms have a declining trend after the FF found free trade and full ownership a better option to make business after 1986.[9] But the results advanced above with respect to the minor importance of technology operations taking place among Mexican industry and Mexican technology suppliers reveal poor development of local technical competences. Firms privilege foreign sources of technology, even if in this practice they deprive the Mexican innovation system of most of the externalities in learning and other benefits from conducting R&D and from interactions between local industries and producers of technology.

The evidence on R&D activities and technology transfer among FF and NF shows that local interactions of this kind are scarce and scattered. Most foreign firms conduct technology exchanges with other FF (including their own parent companies), but very few FF do have exchanges with domestic firms. The opposite occurs with national firms: they relate more frequently to other domestic firms, spending about three-quarters of their technology transfer with NF suppliers, and only the other quarter spent on foreign sources. However, there are still some good numbers of firms, about one-half of those surveyed, with no technology exchanges.

Other surveys on technology exchanges detail the above findings in four respects: (a) only some firms, not all of those prominent in their own industry, take part in technology transfer;[10] (b) most of the transfer involves foreign sources of technology; (c) the main technology contracted or acquired is patents, technical assistance and industrial property rights; and (d) the spending in general is relatively low but firms in science-based industries and the specialized suppliers spend a little more in external technology than others (CONACYT, 1997a, b). However, these findings need to be taken as preliminary trends only, since the survey was not based on formal sampling selection.

More generally, the results of R&D, patents and other contractual features summarized above indicate that local learning and the development of domestic capabilities do not occur automatically after the FF undertake control of an industry. Only one-third of the firms, at the most, are undertaking R&D in Mexico, as shown above. Those with technology transfer expenditures make up fewer than one-half, and those entirely passive (i.e. without R&D and technology transfer) make up about one-half of all firms. The ratios of R&D and technology spending do not indicate any significant contribution to domestic innovation capabilities, and this is even more pronounced in large FF, as shown in smaller weighted averages.

Foreign exchanges are far more important according to the deficits on the technological balance of payments of both types of firms for 1993: the foreign firms' deficit was US$11.3 million and the national firms' $2.5 million. Operations with domestic sources of technology accounted for surpluses of less than $0.2 and $0.6 million for each type of firm.

In relative terms to total sales, foreign firms in this limited sample generated a deficit two times larger. Major technology spending is related to foreign patents, foreign technical assistance and foreign industrial property rights. Technical assistance and property rights are also relatively important in operations with domestic sources, both in spending and as the technology concepts most frequently contracted. However, the very high average cost per foreign patent acquired surpasses by far the importance of the large number of technical assistance (TA) and property rights (PR) contracts. In relative terms (to sales) patents are also more important than other technology elements.[11]

Foreign firms in science-based industries spend more than others in absolute and relative terms. For them it is very important to spend on patents and technical assistance. At the other extreme, the FF and NF specialized suppliers have lower deficits on technology transfers because they are suppliers as well as acquirers of technology. However, these are a small number of firms anyway, most of them small in size. The slow recovery (or fatal absence) of these firms has important implications for the system's technical capabilities. These firms, which include capital goods and instrument producers, are themselves technology suppliers and should be seen as priority depositories of innovation capabilities.

To sum up, the pieces of evidence elaborated so far may be important for their implications for the national innovation system. One way to approach this is by reference to Figure 5.1, contrasting well integrated systems to the flows observed in the Mexican NIS. The limited role of specialized suppliers and science-based industries in the Mexican context has now been clearly established on the basis of the evidence reviewed before, which highlighted the following points.

The FF specialized suppliers moved production to plants in their home countries, while retaining here some basic assembly operations. These firms reduced considerably their fixed investment in Mexico. These and the foreign scale-intensive industries moved their mix towards more labour-intensive assembly of lower productivity.

The science-based groups, both FF and NF in electronics and chemi-pharmaceuticals, had some expansion in new fixed investment, but their use of labour expanded more than proportionately as they also became more labour-intensive assemblers for the international markets.

The FF in science-based, specialized supplier and scale-intensive industries achieve successful export performances but also reduce domestic content on a large scale. The imports ratio is particularly high for FF in specialized suppliers and science-based industries but there are other export-oriented FF sectors also engaged in basic assembly operations. Thus, the modernization measures are preferentially to increase assembly labour while using more intensively installed capacity, at times (in science-based firms) with some new investment.

In close correspondence, R&D and technology acquisitions remain very modest. The R&D ratios are very low everywhere, including for firms on the science-based and specialized suppliers industries, and the more so in the export-oriented FF in science-based and scale intensive sectors. Technology transfer follows the same pattern as R&D spending. Again most revealing are the lower spending ratios of export-oriented FF in the assembly of science-based products and some supplier-dominated and scale-intensive products. Other more domestic oriented FF and NF specialized suppliers show lower deficits on technology transfers due to their own capabilities, given that they are suppliers as well as acquirers of technology, but these are a small number of firms in any event.

This summary about the results on producing, trade, R&D, patents and other contractual features suggests that local learning and the development of domestic capabilities do not necessarily follow under the FF leadership of industry. Most of the estimates indicate a rather limited contribution of these firms to domestic innovation capabilities, and this is probably more pronounced in the operations of large FF. Other firms and industries, including some specialized suppliers anchored to a few of the domestic competitive industrial clusters, should be considered for the development of deeper and more integrated innovation capabilities.

Technology embodied in equipment and intermediates

The source of foreign technology, imports of capital goods and parts, components and intermediates, is also very important in a country lacking its own complementary or competitive firms in these import-dependent areas of industry. For instance, and in accordance with the importance of domestic networking emphasized throughout this chapter, imports substitute for many important technological products; that is, imports are a very large proportion of total supply in the foreign-dominated industries of specialized suppliers (66.0 per cent) and science-based (37.0 per cent) sectors (Table 5.2). However, these industries, and in particular the capital goods producers, are at present widely recognized as important competencies to modern national systems. The challenge remains to argue for the local development of a certain level of technological competences in the capital goods industry as a crucial element for the long-term development of a number of key industrial clusters. The challenge involves developing the evidence on the importance of technological competences in production as much as in the use of capital goods, without raising the fear of a return to protection policies.

For one argument, it is clear that capital goods producers are an essential component of the user–producer link widely endorsed in the OECD studies of innovation over the past decade. Their importance needs to be brought into the recent picture of industrial specialization taking place under the guidance of trade liberalization in Mexico.

The most obvious concern in relation to the evidence presented above may be that the dynamics of export-oriented activities, in both FF and NF, will be very detached from domestic integration with capital goods producers, leading to an incomplete industrial specialization without evolving into more integrated innovative clusters. On the contrary, the evidence developed in this chapter indicates that both capital goods and sophisticated high value added intermediates remain mostly as imports from the leading industrialized countries. FF export-oriented sectors are even more detached from domestic sources. Let us now examine in more detail the issue of benefits derived from the dissemination of imported capital goods.

There is ample evidence on the importance of technology embodied in capital goods in a number of OECD firm surveys focusing on the dissemination of information technology, including computers, communications equipment, numerically controlled machine tools and other modern hi-tech technologies. For Mexico, the ENESTYC surveys produced evidence on the adoption of modern equipment, but our analysis indicates that the introduction of modern machinery and equipment (mostly confined to centres of numerically controlled manufacture) has not occurred on a large scale; only one-sixth of firms did it over the three years covered by the surveys, and the importance of this equipment on value terms is merely 5 per cent of the total value of machinery and equipment in 1989. These trends are in line with the modest performance of recent investment evidenced in both Chapter 3 and our account of fixed capital investment above. The introduction of equipment, on the other hand, has had mixed results: the only significant effect occurred in NF exporters who experienced an increase in export ratios (3.6 per cent on average), but they also raised their imports content in similar proportions. As for FF exporters and non-exporters in general (though acknowledging some few exceptions), their modernization drive has not justified or required new equipment, but merely a more productive rationalization of their labour-based activities.

The analysis of wider technological diffusion effects of changes embodied in equipment and machinery is usually limited, since the statistics do not reveal the source of equipment or technology, limiting their usefulness in tracking technology flows among actors within the NIS (OECD, 1997a, b). In the Mexican case, however, we can expect a very high proportion of imported sources of this kind of modern equipment, at least as much as with most other capital goods scarcely produced in the country. In other words, the specialized suppliers of particular importance for the integration of the innovation system and crucial in the networking are for the most part absent in Mexico. Thus, not only may we be constraining the access to much of the new technology embodied in the capital goods, but also the easiness of importing capital goods is hindering the process of learning how to repair and improve the foreign technology embodied in these goods, as stressed in Chapter 3.

One kind of complementary information on the sources of technology is obtained by analysing trade flows of hi-tech goods, which include many sectors of capital goods (in the specialized suppliers and science-based industries) and other hi-tech intermediates. Mexico's performance on high-tech trade departs from Pavitt's sectors but needs the complement of trade orientation of industrial operations. The trade balance on high-tech goods runs generally in deficit (excepting years like 1995 when imports were severely constrained), but recent deficits are highly ameliorated by trade surpluses in science-based goods and the contraction in imports of capital goods and other specialized supplier goods. The influence of electronic exports is clear in this result, with exports from the *maquiladora* industry and exports related to temporary imports compensating for other imports.[12] *Maquiladora* exports and temporary exports are different in kind from high-tech exports of higher integration to domestic inputs. For the latter, the results are different: imported high-tech goods and intermediates for domestic use (definitive imports) are four to ten times larger than corresponding Mexican exports. The performance described above indicates the shallow assembly nature (high import dependency) of most Mexican exports of high-tech goods, since most of these are *maquila* and temporary exports of science-based and specialized suppliers' industrial goods of very high import content. These are led by foreign firms in some modern industries, but we have to be cautious in equating their performance to a Mexican capacity to compete in high-tech activities.

Conclusions: a sectoral cluster analysis of global and localized technological flows

As a first step, and prior to examining and designing the main channels and flows characterizing the Mexican economy, attempts were made to substantiate the following general points: (a) FF are the most dynamic agents in the response to the international competitive pressures of the past decade; (b) the FF and NF larger exporters activating different channels to incorporate foreign technology remain an important source of technology and production inputs; (c) FF and the larger NF rely extensively on foreign sources of advanced technology, though in doing this they are spreading the globalized effects of the more competitive parts of the Mexican innovation system; (d) the assembly of exports and import commodities flows dominate and explain the main pattern of technological flows and sectoral linkages with the domestic economy.

Instead, liberalizing technology transfer in the 1990s was assumed to bring a gradual but generalized increase in technological capabilities, which could eventually lead to R&D and other local innovation efforts and competencies. Our evidence indicates poor results, suggesting that industrial adjustment has occurred preferentially through process innovation, such as the improvement of production organization, skills improvement and adaptation of machinery and equipment – not the renewal of fixed capital – for FF and NF obtaining better competitiveness performances. A more detailed analysis of the modes that take place in the Mexican firms and sectors is presented in Part 3 (Chapters 10–16).

Moreover, the main changes could be observed in how sectors and types of firms (considering FF and NF) are interlinked with the foreign production networks and technological sources. Particularly, the pattern related to R&D efforts and other modes of transferring technology has been dominated by the greater integration of imported inputs in most competitive sectors. Their direct contribution to R&D and technology transfer is not substantial. The evidence on R&D activities and technical collaboration (technology transfers) shows that efforts and local interactions of this kind are scarce and scattered. The transfer (importation) of foreign technology involves many steps. The processes of technology acquisition, adaptation, starting up and learning on the job need to be analysed by separating the role of different actors of the NIS into such phases. In practice, the extent of packaging into these phases is very significant. Local learning may be closely linked to unpackaging, doing, using, copying, repairing, and so on. The most ideally extended diffusion process of technology (the 'distribution power' of the system, as it came to be named recently) involves many firms, institutions and individuals accumulating capabilities within the national system while they participate in these operations as suppliers, competitors, users, advisors, etc. Access to much of the new technology embodied in imported capital goods precludes their production domestically, and the easiness of importing capital goods is hindering the process of learning how to repair and improve the foreign technology embodied in these goods.

We have also shown that the industrial specialization of FF and NF defines two relatively independent clusters of weak domestic integration to the most technologically dynamic science-based industries and specialized suppliers. The pattern of how the Mexican industry has been globalized could be viewed by following the incomplete web of domestic interactions between competencies and technological flows across the four types of sectors: science-based, specialized suppliers, scale-intensive and natural resource/traditional supplier dominated sectors. For the most part, the supply of goods of the two earlier sectors are imports; and exports of these and scale-intensive goods include large proportions of *maquiladora* type of exports.

The interaction of the four types of sectors in Mexico is highly oriented to external linkages with the world globalized economy (see Figure 5.1). A sectoral cluster pattern of FF dominated by production flows in terms of imports (intermediate and capital goods) and exports (assembly components and goods, and some commodities) has clearly emerged, whereas technological flows are highly integrated with the world economy in terms of imported equipment and intermediates. The cluster pattern of NF is mostly specialized in resource-based traditional goods and scale-intensive commodities, and thus more integrated to domestic intermediates, but also highly integrated to global sources of technology in the form of imported capital goods and foreign technology transfers.

Figure 5.1 is useful because it summarizes schematically the most important results of this chapter as regards the composition of Mexican industry and the flows of goods and technology within the Mexican NIS. There are four major results. First, industry is heavily concentrated in the traditional industries of both the supplier-dominated and scale-intensive groups of sectors. By contrast, science-based and specialized suppliers account for a very small fraction of manufactures GDP: 8.8 and 2.2 per cent respectively (compare with percentages above 15 per cent for each group in the USA in Chapter 4). Second, the uneven participation of FF with much larger weight in the smaller sectors of science-based and specialized suppliers, relatively high participation in some scale industries like automotives and chemicals, and a much lower importance of FF in the traditional industries. Third, the dynamics of inter-industry flows is simply not working to improve R&D efforts and linkages with the institutional framework for two main reasons: *maquiladora* operations dominate the production of science-based components, thus allowing for very limited links and flows to other domestic suppliers of intermediates; the imports of equipment to be used all through the industrial system substitute for the learning capability that could accrue to domestic specialized suppliers of equipment in a well integrated NIS. Fourth, it follows naturally that technology is not a major concern for FF or for NF in most industries. Technology from the MNE is available to the FF in Mexico and most of the NF in traditional industry can import it. The economic incentives to develop their own capability through R&D and more intensive technology transfers do not seem to be there.

The analysis of recent Mexican industrial restructuring has shown that a new specialization pattern has emerged with particular roles for FF and NF separately. Mexican industry develops in a highly unbalanced industrial structure specialized in a few sectors, where NF dominate most of the traditional and resource-based mature industries (mostly in the supplier-dominated and scale-intensive sectors like food and beverages, steel, glass, minerals, cement and basic petrochemicals), complemented with a few sectoral and production chains of FF where economic activities are coordinated and integrated by large MNEs across the geographic boards with highly integrated linkages in production and innovation processes (think of the automobile industry), and *maquiladora* type linkages which are highly integrated to intrafirm imports rather than to domestic production capacities (as in the modern science-based sectors of computers and telecommunications led by foreign firms). None the less, all types of firms are integrated with countries that lead in international trade and technological innovations, becoming dependent on imports of technology, as well as on imports of the most technologically dynamic products and intermediates. As is also stressed in Part III, the net effect of all this is some improvement in most aspects related to productivity and organizational

FLOWS IN A DOMESTIC INTEGRATED NIS

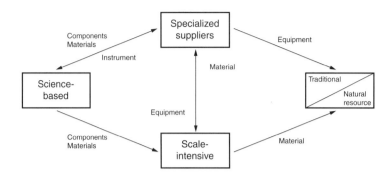

FLOWS IN A GLOBALIZED SYSTEM

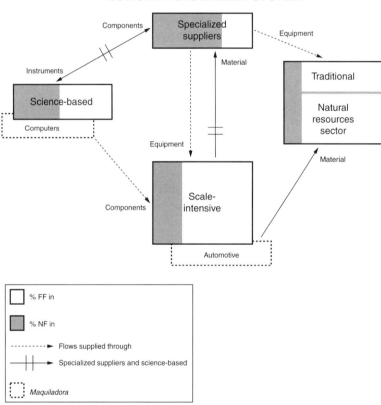

Figure 5.1 Globalization of the Mexican NIS, Technological Flows and Sectors.
Source: adapted from Guerrieri (1993).

changes, though the dynamics of the industrial and technological systems linked to FF and NF are not contributing to the development of national technological capabilities in terms of local efforts and linkages with local firms and institutions.

Notes

1. If growth is estimated in dollars converting pesos into the exchange rate of each year, the rates are much more moderate at 3.2 per cent a year for total GDP and 3.8 per cent a year for FF's output.

2. The correlation coefficient for export and import ratios of FF is 0.67, significant at the 95 per cent interval.

3. The equivalent import ratios of NF exporters in similar sectors as much as in other sectors are much lower, around the 20 per cent level.

4. On a macro scale, the coverage ratio of Mexico's foreign technological balance of payments in comparison to other OECD countries is one of the lowest ratios, around 20 per cent, i.e. expenditures on royalties are five times larger than incomes (CONACYT, 1997b, p. 161).

5. There are also some important sectoral differences within FF and NF but they may be mainly related to the sampling composition of the survey, which inhibits us from pushing into the details. There is more on this in the R&D section, comparing exporters and non-exporters.

6. Take into account their participation in output at 28.5 per cent in 1993 (Table 5.2).

7. Data from a sample of 5,071 firms.

8. The R&D ratios are substantially lower for the firms successful in exports (0.31 and 0.30 respectively). Similar results apply for the half of firms that take part in technology transfer: the ratio for foreign and national firms oriented to exports are half the ratios of the domestic market-oriented firms. Thus, export performance is not supported by technology efforts, which in the event seem mostly relevant to compete domestically.

9. The scope for more privatizations has also been reduced considerably.

10. The survey aimed to include a large number of firms, but not a formally representative sample. First, merely 24.2 per cent of 2,400 firms originally sampled declared technology transfer payments, but fewer than one-half of them (43 per cent) provided the requested information. In the final count, only 155 questionnaries proved useful for our estimates.

11. The importance of patents in technology transfer may be taken cautiously because it depends on a few very large firms transferring a limited number of costly patents, most of the them as intrafirm transactions.

12. More than 90 per cent of these exports are telecommunications equipment and components.

PART II

Institutional Infrastructure and Networks

Institutions and the National Innovation System: an Introduction

M. Cimoli

The concept of institutions and their role in the NIS

Among different proposals, our focus is mostly based on the intellectual debate around the evolutionary approach. It is particularly within this context that our analysis is developed along the lines of certain fairly stylized points, without loss of generality, such as: (a) the fact that firms are nested in larger systems that include institutions, organizations and networks; (b) the role of institutions in terms of their capacity either to retard or to support innovation, and (c) the role of co-evolutionary processes as a source of changes in the production system and institutions.

Firms and networks

Extensive research has pointed out the linkages between technology and institutions. By explicitly referring to this perspective, one observes that the concepts such as paradigms and trajectories, which stem from the specific and cumulative nature of technology, have been related to the consequences derived from the existence of localized technical change. A general property, by now widely acknowledged in innovation literature, is that learning is local and cumulative. Local means that the exploration and development of new techniques is likely to occur in the neighbourhood of the techniques already in use and within a specific institutional framework. Cumulative means that current technological development often builds upon past experiences in production and innovation, and it proceeds via sequences of specific problem-solving junctures.

At the micro level, technologies are to a fair extent incorporated in particular institutions: the firms, whose characteristics, decision rules, capabilities and behaviours are fundamental in shaping the rates and directions of technological advance.[1] First, firms are embedded in rich networks of relationships with each other and with other institutional actors – ranging from government agencies to universities, etc. Second, a major element mentioned earlier linking microeconomic learning with national patterns of development is founded on the thread of incentives, constraints and forms of corporate organization in the broader institutional framework of the political economy of each country. Third, for our purposes, let us just mention that the micro- and mesoeconomic theoretical building blocks outlined above and drawn from an evolutionary perspective are in principle consistent with broader institutional analysis of national systems of production, innovation and governance of socio-economic linkages.

Institutions and opportunities

Regarding the above view, as suggested by Nelson (1996):

> while, at early stages of our intellectual development, we tended to stress the 'firms' as the locus of competences, in the sense of command over routines, I think we now have a much more eclectic and fluid set of notions about that, recognizing that some competences reside in particular individuals, some in particular organizations, some in networks, and some in broader structures. This latter set of notions has drawn us into analysis of entities like 'national innovation systems'. It is particularly here that we find the concept of 'institutions' attractive. We find it convenient, and natural, to characterize the development of, for example, the corporate research and development laboratory as an institutional innovation. Similarly, the development of the research universities, or the intellectual property rights system, or the pattern of relationships between employers and workers, we are inclined to talk of as institutional change. Here, we are a very long distance from our original notions about 'routines' and 'competences'.

According to the previous paragraph and pushing our interpretation further, the role of institutions within a NIS could be viewed as 'the magnet poles' – negative/positive – where institutions act as either a snare or a springboard, hindering or supporting the innovation process via incentives. Thus, on the one hand, institutions can be considered as a set of constraints on individual actions; on the other, individuals can use institutions as a springboard where the environmental novelty can be managed and new opportunities introduced. It is at this point possible to make a fundamental conceptual distinction between institution and organization (Edquist, 1997): the canonical definition of institution is associated to common habits, routines, established practices, rules or laws that regulate the relationships between individuals and groups at the macro, meso and micro levels. Organizations are formal and informal structures – private or public – aimed at reaching specific objectives which may be explicitly declared or not. Organizations (economic, social and political) are seen as the engine of institutional change through their demand for investment in knowledge, the interactions set by them between economic activity, scientific knowledge, and institutional structure, and, finally, through the gradual changes on informal rules which occur in the course of their activities. Under this approach, the above contradictory view is solved, considering that institutions define the set of opportunities of a society and the potentiality to manage environmental novelty, whereas organizations exist in order to exploit such opportunities and novelties. In doing so, however, they develop and gradually alter institutions, so that the characteristics of institutional change are depicted as intrinsically evolutionary.

Institutions and co-evolution

In this view, it is straightforward to acknowledge a bidirectional relationship between the technological patterns developed by the production system – as proxied by measures of the distribution of different characteristics such as sectoral specialization, R&D efforts of firms, innovative competencies, ownership and persistent behavioural traits – and the institutional functions such as providing incentives for modernization and innovation activities, producing human capital and knowledge resources. This constitutes the core of the co-evolutionary outlook as emphasized by Nelson (1994). A description of the co-evolutionary path between production system and institutions is built up in this book: see, for example, Figures 7.1 and 10.1.

A central fact that should be borne in mind for understanding the role played by the Mexican institutions within the innovation system is that over the past forty years the development pattern of the country has undergone profound modifications. The economic context from the 1970s to the early 1980s has changed deeply, from an import substitution model to a more open economy. In addition to this, the 1980s also witnessed the introduction of a brand new regulatory framework characterized by major trade reforms, privatizations and the NAFTA agreement. The discussions in Chapters 7, 8 and 9 set forth a description of the way in which different institutions have acted as engines of changes in Mexico, defining their functional specificities and inter-linkages with the production system. Emphasis is placed on the identification of competencies and functional role within the institutional scene; at the first level of the analysis a distinction is made among institutions dedicated to support innovation (Chapter 7 and the appendix note on intellectual property rights), to train human resources (Chapter 8) and to produce and transfer knowledge (Chapter 9). In this context, it should be understood as a fact that organizational learning can follow a multiplicity of evolutionary paths. However, it is fundamental to recognize that the rates and directions of learning are not at all independent from the ways that the structure of organizations emerge, change, develop particular problem-solving capabilities, diversify, etc. The formal and informal structures of organizations are examined in Chapter 7.

Institutions in the Mexican innovation system

Institutions supporting innovations

Casalet, in Chapter 7, deals with the Mexican institutional matrix, identifying its competencies and functions. Within the different functional roles of institutions, different types of specific and concrete organizations are distinguished and analysed: (a) organizations whose competencies are devoted to providing incentives for innovation, by means of fostering modernization in firms' through credits, promoting exports of non-oil products, assisting in the development of production chains with SMEs, providing assistance on intellectual property rights issues, etc.; (b) highly specialized R&D centres aimed at supporting innovation in specific sectors and firms, of which some play a strategic role within the Mexican economy – energy, oil, water, electricity, etc. – because of the relatively large amount of public funding they provide and their subsequent role in the distribution of power within the system; (c) organizations dedicated mainly to human resource development (postgraduate training or other), technological services and R&D projects, to which more regional and specific competencies are associated, partially due to specific governmental efforts towards decentralization and establishment of regional productive networks; (d) organizations devoted to providing information and reducing uncertainty across firms and other institutions as regards market standards like certification, quality and training. These institutional frameworks are of recent creation, funded by both the public and private sectors, and are identified throughout this work with those specific and concrete organizations that link the different actors of the system creating network, working as a bridge for knowledge and information.

Moreover, without attempting to propose a general taxonomy of institutions, it is of great importance to distinguish between the main established categories, formal and informal, private and public organizations, specifically dedicated to support innovation (technological and services centres, universities, etc.). Emphasis is placed on understanding and mapping the Mexican institutional matrix according to the geographical localization and competencies of each organization within the innovation system, where the term competencies means, in a very rough sense, the different activities carried out by specific organizations aimed at fostering innovation. To a certain extent it could be said that this is an attempt at coming up with the institutional design of the country, where each organization is mapped among a network composed by firms and other organizations.

Institutions supporting human resources

Valenti, Varela and Castillo, in Chapter 8, describe the educational system, considering its capacity in terms of the human resources produced by it together with its linkages – or lack thereof – with the production system. The main objective of any education system is to produce sufficient high quality human resources which can then be absorbed by the production system in order to increase its innovative efforts by means of complex skills, conscious efforts and competencies. Nowadays there is plenty of empirical evidence clearly showing that technological upgrading requires investment in human resources, while maintaining high quality, advanced curricula throughout different technical subjects. Moreover, it is also recognized that competencies in education – that is, an educational organization capable of producing human resources with formal qualifications – cannot be directly transformed to those in human resources with regard to production and innovation. The competencies incorporated within the educational system cover only partially the requirements for creating skills; on-the-job training and learning are also important. However, high educational competencies are a necessary condition for skills, technical experience and innovative efforts within industrial activities; as such, the interaction between the educational and production system is the main issue explored throughout this section.

Institutions supporting knowledge production

Casas, de Gortari and Luna, in Chapter 9, deal with the portion of the institutional system that specializes in producing knowledge and its linkages with the production system. However, the interplay between basic research and economic performance is a complex phenomenon and most of its benefits cannot be quantified due to the infinity of channels through which spillovers are realized: new instruments, skills developed by people participating in basic research, individual mobility, access to national and international networks etc.

Knowledge production has traditionally been located in universities, which are increasingly assuming a predominant role in its distribution and in establishing linkages with industrial activities. In Mexico, as in many other countries, most of the applied and basic research is centred on the universities, mainly funded from public resources. It is within this context that interplay between basic research and economic performance becomes attractive in the midst of the numerous possible relationships within an innovation system; in this sense, several of the main findings of recent studies on related issues should be kept in mind (SPRU, 1996). This report found that 'the overall conclusion emerging from the survey and case studies are that: (i) the economic benefit from basic research are both real and substantial; (ii) they come in a variety of forms; and (iii) the key issue is not so much whether the benefits are there but how best to organize the national research system to make effective use of them'.[2]

In this context, possible changes in the linkages between universities and the production system are discussed in the light of society's expectations and increasing budget constraints, which have the joint effect of favouring research that pursues more immediate and direct benefits. Also in this chapter, a great deal of attention is placed on the linkages and networks between universities and production systems. A taxonomy is proposed, considering the following quantitative and qualitative indicators: (a) types of science-based institutions of higher education that collaborate with industry; (b) the origin of these collaboration initiatives; (c) determinant factors for collaboration; (d) objectives of collaborative relationships; (e) types of knowledge flows; (f) types of relationships between the collaborating entities; (g) funding; (h) factors hindering university–industry collaboration.

Notes

1. According to the interpretation which is being presented, the existence of heterogeneity will manifest itself not only at the level of technical efficiency, but also at that of profitability, as different rates of learning influence the firms' ability to survive and expand, and thus affect industrial structures. Firms are crucial (although not exclusive) repositories of knowledge, embodied, to a large extent, in their operational routines, and modified over time by the higher level rules of behaviours and strategies (such as their search behaviours and the decisions concerning vertical integration and horizontal diversification). This idea is central in the characterization of companies' technological capabilities proposed in Nelson and Winter (1982) and Nelson (1993), as well as in the idea of competence proposed by Dosi *et al.* (1992), whereby 'a firm's competence is a set of differentiated technological skills, complementary assets, organisational routines and capacities that provide the basis for a firm's competitive capacities in a particular business' and 'in essence, competence is a measure of a firm's ability to solve both technical and organisational problems'.

2. Particularly, the main findings are: (a) from the numerous attempts to estimate the interplay between research and productivity, it has been found that a positive and significant rate of return associated with the impact of research on productivity is obtained; (b) basic research is, first and foremost, a source of useful information to be drawn upon in the development of new technologies, products and process; (c) basic research may be especially good at developing the ability to solve complex problems, which often proves of great benefit in firms and other organizations confronted with complex technological problems; (d) participation in basic research is essential to obtain access to national and international networks of experts and information; (e) the tacit knowledge and skills generated by basic research are specially

important in newly emerging and fast moving areas of science and technology; (f) personal links and mobility are vital in integrating basic research with technological development (particularly, in terms of linking basic research to postgraduate training); (g) new instrumentation and methodologies are important, both within science and as a form of output or economic benefit from basic research.

CHAPTER SEVEN

The Institutional Matrix and Its Main Functional Activities Supporting Innovation

M. Casalet

Introduction

During import substitution, the institutional structure was attributed to support for the industrialization process, production needs and investment for the development of large projects. In the 1970s, once the industrialization phase had been consolidated, highly specialized sectoral institutions prevailed, providing solutions to new management requirements for scientific personnel and supporting critical industrial sectors – electric and nuclear energy, oil and water – at the same time driving the scientific and technological activities schedule within national institutions. Government policies were important in order to carry out specific projects, considering both the operational and financial aspects. Liberalization policies, privatization of public enterprises and public subsidy to support demand for technological services have modified the modes of linkages and interaction between production system and institutions. During the 1980s and 1990s new institutions appeared and the older ones changed their activities and organizational configuration. Given this, particular attention is dedicated in the present chapter to the bridging institutions. These institutions are dedicated to support services for firms and other institutions (such as standardization, quality and certification, particularly to SMEs) and the reinforcement of inter-management activities. Bridging institutions have several origins, and financing can be public, private or mixed. The analysis is also devoted to the role played by the SEP-CONACYT Centres, a research system formed by different specialized institutions and decentralized in different regions of the country. Its regional distribution and linkages with a high heterogeneity of firms contribute to shape a specific intermediate structure supporting the innovation process. Within this institutional framework, our principal interest is the nature of networks that have been created and the features of the linkages generated by institutions and firms.

This chapter analyses the main features of the evolutionary process that link the production system and the institutional framework dedicated to supporting innovative activities. The first section contains an analysis of the historical evolution of the institutions from the import substitution period to the recent scenario characterized by a highly liberalized and globalized economy. In the second section, a distinction

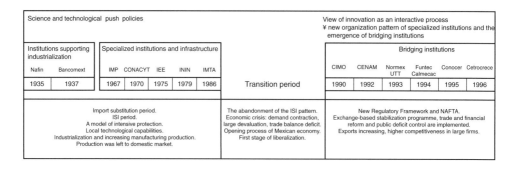

Figure 7.1 Evolutionary Path of the Mexican Institutions Supporting Innovation.

between different institutions is made on the bases of main functions performed in the Mexican system. These functions are derived from the role played in the creation of different competences in firms (providing incentives for modernization, supporting information exchanges, uncertainty reduction and specialized research and development activities). A deeper analysis of the functional activities and actual configuration of bridging institutions is developed in the third section. The regional setup of SEP-CONACYT Centres is then analysed. The last section is dedicated to the conclusions, and an appendix considers intellectual property rights.

Historical path of the Mexican institutions

In order to understand the historical evolution of Mexican institutions' supporting innovation, it is fundamental to bear in mind that Mexico's development path has undergone profound modifications over the past forty years. The economic framework that was in place from the 1970s to the early 1980s changed from an import-substitution model to a more open economy, further altered during the 1980s by the introduction of a new regulatory framework characterized by major trade reforms, privatization and the North American Free Trade Agreement (NAFTA). Figure 7.1 shows the different historical economic settings and the evolution of the institutional framework.

During the 1970s and early 1980s scientific and technological policy in Mexico aimed at creating institutions that supported innovation. Specialized institutions such as IMP (Mexican Institute for Petroleum), IIE (Electrical Research Institute) and later ININ (National Institute for Nuclear Research) and IMTA (Mexican Institute on Water Technology) came into existence during this period, with the main purpose of addressing quite specific technological and sectoral issues. The expansion of the public sector, together with protected private industrial activity, strengthened this inward orientation of institutions and industrial sector. These were almost exclusively orientated towards the highly protected internal market whose regulatory framework aimed at fostering domestic industry. During this period, the industrial sector pursued economies of scale, production capacity and better organization of production process. However, on the other hand, the quality of products and the requested standardization norms were hardly ever attained (Katz, 1984, 1995; Cimoli, 1988).

During the import-substitution phase the creation of institutions, along with their financing and orientation, fell directly into the government's sphere of activity. Throughout this phase policies were aimed at consolidating the specialized infrastructure of the country, together with the prompt installation of institutions that foster the productive sector, which would correspond to the industrialization demands of the country and diverse sectoral problems: such as IMP, IIE, CONACYT, ININ, IMTA (Marquez, 1982; CONACYT, 1996a). It should be noted that the institutions that emerged during this period lacked institutional and inter-sectoral articulation. They were, in fact, a response to the initiative of either researchers or government functionaries in the context of the implementation of broader state policies that required a specialized infrastructure to face the process of industrialization and the needs of domestic firms. These institutions have played a substantial role in the adaptation and development of local technology for large public firms and new regenerating researcher groups in science and knowledge production. After two decades, it follows that this specialized infrastructure was developed through excessively bureaucratic self-contained organizations, which had little concern for the actual outcomes of these initiatives and, furthermore, lacked any control over the institutions' achievements. Organizations had little concern for achieving any particular objectives since funding was secured *ex ante* and it was not necessary to carry out evaluations to monitor fund allocation. In addition to this, it was difficult to conduct coordinated activities of inter-institutional exchange as each institution operated independently and was not actively encouraged to work with the productive system.

The 1980s brought a rupture in the import substitution path. Over subsequent periods, the opening of the economy fostered a part of the productive sector, within the new modernization process, to adopt new technologies and introduce organizational changes. New forms of cooperation among firms (mainly SMEs) and regions were envisaged in order to address this demand. Bridging institutions are a response to this new era of the institutional creation of a market of services for firms, particularly SMEs, as well as to the new role of the private sector in providing incentives and funds for this institutional scheme (David, 1994; Casalet, 1995; Katz, 1997a, 1997b). As already mentioned, during the 1980s new policies were set in place, aimed at opening the domestic market and reducing state control on production and prices, which further changed the pattern of development into one aimed at gaining participation in the international market.

Institutions and modernization: a new interactive pattern

More specifically, from 1985 onwards, protectionism was reduced in conjunction with declining import tariffs, directed towards increasing exports and private investment instead of public spending. At the same time, modification of the national regulatory framework began with changes to the Law of Foreign Investments in 1989, tailoring it to the new international scenarios. It was within this context that in 1991 the Mexican Investment Council was created in a joint effort by the private and public sectors. Within the existing financial institutions, both Nacional Financiera (NAFIN), the national development bank, and the Banco de Comercio Exterior

(Bancomext, literally the Bank of Foreign Trade), which had been created at a much earlier period, redefined their scope. In the case of the former, since 1988 its orientation was chiefly directed towards providing credit support for SMEs. As for Bancomext, it was expected to have an active role in promoting non-oil exports. It was thus foreseen that both institutions would support production activities and competitiveness, promoting linkages between SMEs and creating new forms of business cooperation: inter-firm collaboration, programmes for developing domestic suppliers and so on (NAFIN, 1998a; Bancomext, 1997a, 1997b).

More recently, in the 1990–4 National Plan for Modernization and Foreign Trade, yet another new strategy emerged through the redefinition of the role of the state. This entailed a contribution in the creation of an economic setting that would lead to efficient participation in the international competitive markets and stimulate private investment and employment. The plan aims at a new institutional framework that supports relationships between firms, users and suppliers, immersed in more regional settings. From this new 'plan', the creation of technological capabilities should no longer be considered an isolated activity, occurring in specialized laboratories or inside large firms; innovation should involve the combination of incremental developments and improvements, as well as activities designed to improve quality. However, the central idea of this 'plan' remains that the incentives for an upgrade of technological capabilities are obtained exclusively from the growing integration in the international market and the foreign investment captured by the Mexican economy.

Particularly, within this framework organizations are supposed to adopt more flexible organizational schemes with less pyramidal decision-making processes, in addition to, through budget constraints, no longer enjoying unlimited subsidies. The latter is also evident in the financial strategy, as organizations' survival depends increasingly on their ability to develop self-funding schemes, through more transparency in their operations and offering high quality services. The cases of several large institutions, such as IMP, ININ, IMTA and IIE, can provide an illustration of the argument above. Institutional change means both the emergence of new institutions and the decline and disappearance of old ones. How many resources are put to use on a day-to-day basis on innovation activities in small firms, in networking between firms and in training and education in connection with the diffusion of innovation, is anyone's guess. The allocation of resources to innovation activities is not clear; in some cases, it is the result of deliberate managerial decisions within a firm, or of politicians via governmental support for specific technology development programmes. Finally, some resources are allocated by institutions (private or public associations), or the allocation of these resources is influenced by them. Thus it is difficult to give a general pattern of the allocation of resources for innovation. Resources may also be allocated haphazardly; for example, as a result of the lack of information, managerial control and power distribution across the political coalitions. For example, one can think of the political cycles, built upon the 'sexenios' (six-year presidential term transition) and the absence of an evaluation process of institutions and their objectives. In fact, this process of institutional reform is not linear. While institutions are trying to come up with a more rational organizational reform which would permit a more efficient utilization of their resources and technological sources for production activity, there exist, at the same time, within these institutions, power groups and coalitions built across the government which hinder the implementation of these changes since, more often than not, these groups follow their own agendas. In these circumstances, evidence is emerging that a 'distribution of power' based on politics (and group coalitions nested in the overall institutional system) produces adverse mechanisms that condition the objectives of each organization.

During these years, the process of institutional restructuring continued under rapid changes in the economic context at the national and international levels. The appearance of new institutions, referred to here as 'bridging institutions', should be perceived as an attempt to address the requirements posed by the globalization process, market liberalization and structural reforms. The term bridging institutions comprises different types of institutions which none the less share the common feature of playing a central role in the establishment and strengthening of exchange relationships among firms, as well as between them and other private and public organizations. Although these institutions are not R&D centres in the traditional sense of the term, they carry out a significant function in the improvement of the firms' problem-solving activities in production, marketing, information, quality standardization, exports, etc.

Bridging institutions are the new institutions that address the changes in the relationship of firms with the demands of the market. The new dimensions of competitiveness have forced firms and the country to invest increasingly in intangibles: technology, skills, organization, information testing and quality control. Nevertheless, the sole creation of this new support infrastructure, at both the national and regional levels, does not suffice to ensure a network that links with the production system. In fact, the activity of such a network depends on the relationship among the different types of competencies offered by these institutions, together with the learning processes developed by them, a more flexible relationship-based organizational culture and their relationships with their users (Richardson, 1972; Planque, 1990; Teece and Bennet, 1997).

Policies oriented to modernization and the new demands arising from particular firms and from industry as a whole push organizations to adopt more efficient and flexible structures. These policies suppose that firms are demanding quality control, normalization, verification of processes and technological modernization. A great deal of this demand is focused on information services in the context of the new information technology (Internet, computer-based information networks, etc.). In addition to this, coming from firms' demands there seems to emerge specific pressure towards supporting innovative processes where interaction plays a central role, as it does in the articulation of SMEs with large firms, and in connecting those instances offering technology (bridging institutions, centres for technological development, consultancies, etc.) with users (Bianchi, 1997; Dini and Katz, 1997).

The future development of bridging institutions is still rather uncertain. The vast majority of them do not have enough elements for assessing their own performance and evaluating their human resource training programmes, either internal or resulting from their work with firms. Nevertheless, these institutions may be considered as the germ of a new organizational culture based on training oriented towards new exigencies of competitiveness inside firms, and towards improving their competitive position in the market place (Kluth and Andersen, 1995).

Functional matrix of Mexican institutions

In this section, a distinction of different institutions is made on the basis of main functions performed in the Mexican system. From the rationale of the previous section, in constructing an institutional taxonomy for the Mexican case, the historical path of the country and its effects on the creation and development of technological capabilities have to be considered in conjunction with theoretical methodological contributions developed in several case studies. Table 7.1 groups the basic activities aimed at the creation of technology carried out by public institutions, as well as intermediate organizations directed at consolidating a service market in the country. Table 7.1 thus constitutes the basis for the articulation of activities and institutions whose specific competencies and results are further disagregated in Tables 7.2, 7.3, 7.4 and 7.5.

Table 7.1 depicts an institutional functional matrix where institutions are taxonomized according to the main modes and activities to support innovation. Four types of functional activities are identified. The first type of institutions thus identified, as seen in the first row, covers a rather comprehensive set of tasks: to provide incentives to support modernization through various financial schemes; to support firms producing non-oil commodities in an attempt to diversify the production of the Mexican industrial structure; to develop production and technological chains or linkages; and those devoted to issues regarding intellectual property rights, invention and innovation through patents (Aboites and Soria, 1997). The second group of institutions is dedicated to providing information and reducing uncertainty, in particular activities to enhance product and process quality, certification and standardization and training labour force. Institutions in the third group are concerned with achieving rather specialized innovations within specific production sectors, such as oil, nuclear energy and water. The fourth group of institutions is formed by those that carry out basic research oriented to fundamental science and technological development across regions of Mexico. A more detailed characterization of each group follows; further details for each group can be found in Tables 7.2–7.5.

Institutions devoted to providing incentives

This group is chiefly composed of NAFIN and Bancomext, institutions that provide financial incentives to foster the development of SMEs, whose main responsibilities are to provide financial credit and support, assistance for modernization efforts, and technical assistance. Table 7.2 shows the historical path of these two important institutions in Mexico, including their evolution, objectives and how these have changed over the years, their place in the macroeconomic setting and their programmes, results and coverage. Some of the most outstanding of these features are outlined in the following paragraphs.

With regard to NAFIN, a significant period starts in 1989 when the institution leaves its role as a banking institution for state-owned companies and focuses on SMEs. As a development bank, NAFIN channels up to 98 per cent of its funds to foster productivity, quality and competitiveness in these firms. This transformation coincides with the reassessment of SMEs as credit subjects and the redirection of funds to increase their productivity and job creation. Towards the end of 1994 the institution was again reorganized in the light of Mexico's economic and financial

Table 7.1 Functional Matrix of Mexican Institutions Supporting Innovation

Function	Subset	Organizations
To provide incentives	To support company innovation and modernization with credits	CONACYT (programmes: Fidetec y Forccytec) NAFIN
	To encourage non-oil exports Development of productive chains for SMSF Intellectual property rights to knowledge and ideas	Bancomext Bancomext, NAFIN, SECOFI, CONACYT IMPI
To provide information and reduce uncertainty	Standardization Certification Quality Training	IMNC Normex Calmecac Cenam IMPI Fundameca Infotec Centro-Crece ADIAT
Highly specialized research and development	Energy sector institutions, creators of technical support for the country, and of highly specialized knowledge	IMP IIE ININ IMTA
Research and development in the basic sciences, and regional technological development	Training at postgraduate level Consultancy services Research	SEP-CONACYT Centres

ADIAT (Mexican Managing Directors Association of Applied Research and Technology Development), Bancomext (Foreing Trade Bank), Calmecac (Mexican Certified Quality, Civil Association), Cenam (National Centre of Metrology), CCTC (Centre for Total Quality and Competitiveness), CETINDUSTRIA (Technological Centre of Information and Industrial Linkage), CIMO (Programme for Integral Quality and Modernization), C.P. DISEÑO (Promoting Centre of Design), Crece (Centre for Business Competitiveness Development), CONACYT (National Council of Science and Technology), CONOCER (Council for Standardization and Certification of Labour Skills), IIE (Electrical Research Institute), IMP (Mexican Petroleum Institute), Infotec (Fund of Information and Documentation for Industry), ININ (National Institute of Nuclear Research), IMPI (Mexican Institute for Intellectual Property, IMTA (Mexican Institute of Standardization and Certification), FIDETEC (Fund for R&D and Technological Modernization), Forccytec (Fund for the Strengthening of Scientific and Technological Capabilities), FUNDEC (Mexican Foundation for the Innovation and Technology Transference in small and middling Enterprises), Fundameca (Mexican Foundation for Total Quality), NAFIN (National Development Bank), NORMEX (Mexican Society for Standardization and Certification), PRAEM (University-Enterprise Linkage Programme), PIEMBT (Incubator programme for Technology-based Enterprises), UTT (Technological Tranference Unit).

collapse, and its consequences of economic and political uncertainty. Both NAFIN and Bancomext responded to the crises with emergency schemes, restructuring credits and streaming the network of non-banking financial intermediaries to face growing insolvency of their clients, principally that of credit unions and other fostering entities which were the financial intermediaries most hurt by the 1995 crisis. New programmes and activities were pursued, in an attempt to address some of the most pressing concerns, such as enhancing production chains (via programmes targeted at suppliers), training entrepreneurs, assisting firms to achieve higher quality standards (Entrepreneurial Development Programme) and enlarging the financial guarantees programme for SMEs (NAFIN, 1995, 1997, 1998a, 1998b; Casalet, 1995).

Bancomext (see Table 7.2) aims at promoting non-oil exports and foreign investment. It should be mentioned that there is no other institution of its kind in Latin America and even less so with such a comprehensive view as that of Bancomext (Bancomext, 1997a, 1997b). This comprehensive vision is directed at identifying the needs and opportunities in foreign trade; hence the variety of promotional and information products and services offered by its 37 branches located throughout the country. Bancomext is constantly on the lookout for those sectors with the greatest potential for international trade and those where Mexico has competitive advantages, carrying out periodical studies on industrial growth indicators and international trade of foreign and domestic competitors. Finally, it also tries to identify, assess and diffuse new business opportunities arising in international markets, with 29 commercial offices and seven modules located in those markets that offer the greatest potential opportunities for business.

Like NAFIN, Bancomext is currently redefining its mission with the view of increasing the national content of exports, and fostering the modernization of subcontracting activities which should provide a firm ground for new modes of interaction among firms based on quality control, normativity and high quality outcomes, in addition to opening up new export markets and consolidating existing ones. Last but not least, work is also carried out towards incorporating SMEs in export activity.

It is clear that the route for both institutions towards achieving their new objectives is to promote suppliers' programmes and the integration of SMEs into productive chains, with a renewed interest in innovation networks that could play a key role in the process of openness through firm reorganization aimed at redefining specialization within a fruitful cooperation context. Production should be fostered in correlation with those public institutions whose programmes contribute to technological modernization via the improvement of learning abilities in SMEs through inter-firm cooperation (SECOFI, Ministry of Trade and Industrial Promotion), information networks and linkages with research centres (SECOFI, CONACYT; see Table 7.2) (SECOFI, 1997a, c, d).

Specialized institutions

Highly specialized research institutions address the needs of sectoral growth in the country and aim at strengthening the technological competencies of several fundamental sectors. Such institutions are going through a reorganization phase as well, with the purpose of reorienting their policies to deal with increasing pressure to attain higher efficiency and search environmentally friendly technologies (IMP, INTA, ININ, IIE) and more efficient utilization of resources. It is worthwhile to note that the most acute deficiencies of their trajectories are owing to the poor insertion in stable technological cooperation networks, domestic or international. The severe discontinuities present in the institutional trajectories of these specialized institutions, which are often associated with political power centres (a political elite that, despite all, have been determinant in ensuring their existence as a means of providing the interchange networks and funding for projects (see Table 7.3)).

Basic research institutions and their regional activities

These institutions make up the SEP-CONACYT system. This system is composed of applied and basic research centres, technological development, services and high level training centres. Their regional insertion represents an attempt at decentralizing scientific and technological activity, along with a means for the construction of regional networks of firms, local government and other research and technical training institutions. SEP-CONACYT Centres cover a broad variety of subjects in research and graduate training – of which some, such as the PhD programme in astrophysics, are unique in the country – at both national and regional levels in an effort to enhance the competitiveness of regions and sectors. In addition to the above, SEP-CONACYT Centres also encourage the creation of technology-based firms and provide technical consultancy services to the private and public sectors. Some of these centres function as sectoral technological centres, providing information services, databanks and specialized seminars, while others work as specialized consultancy firms in engineering, administration and information, often assuming mediation roles, and carrying out activities related to normalization and quality control (Table 7.4).

Institutions devoted to provide information and reduce uncertainty

The institutions most often associated with the generation of an ambiance of confidence and certitude, namely 'bridging institutions', were a result of the 1992 Federal Law of Metrology and Normalization. The priority for these institutions is to offer complementary institutional development of a market of services targeted at the conformation of technological competencies of firms, especially SMEs. Such institutions arise as a real option for firms to gain familiarity with the application of international norms and standards in production, strengthen new inter-firm cooperation mechanisms between SMEs and larger firms, and generate networks of exchange of technology, information and technical assistance – electronically or via personnel – between research centres and firms. Bridging institutions should complement and broaden the support granted by the institutions described in the above sections, with additional training programmes for entrepreneurs and, more importantly, through their ability to articulate and mediate in the formation of efficient systems and waive mistrust between actors (Hilebrand *et al.*, 1994) (see Table 7.5).

Bridging institutions: their specificities and organizations

In the 1990s, as stated before, a new process of interaction has taken place in which firms and institutions have been forced to pool their efforts in the creation of new competencies to face the present demands with regard to quality, production, design, organization and so on, on top of working towards the creation of new social and cultural scenarios where 'interaction' becomes the most important mode of creating and transferring knowledge (Granovetter, 1985; Lee, 1997; Maklund, 1997). In Mexico, bridging institutions are currently concerned chiefly with building incipient models of technological knowledge flows and offering technological services, such as funding for technological innovation projects and advice on intellectual property rights.

The identification of the population of bridging institutions within the Mexican NIS proved to be extremely complex for a variety of reasons. The main reason is that bridging institutions carry out their intermediation role throughout an extremely wide range of activities. They operate under different legal regimes. Most of these institutions date from the beginning of the 1990s, which in turn implies that they are currently in a stage of gestation and consolidation on the services market, along with the fact that their services are still largely unknown, and, to a certain extent, characterized by spontaneity, further increasing this sector's heterogeneity. Evaluating the performance of bridging institutions is difficult, partly because of problems inherent in the role of intermediation performed by this type of institutions. It is hard to assess the performance of this mediation role by means of traditional indicators, such as patents, publications, personnel or budget. As pointed out by Hertog *et al.* (1995) in their study of the Dutch innovation system, 'data on these institutional and policy oriented factors are mainly qualitative and descriptive in nature. The performance of a diffusion infrastructure, where networking and linkages for mutual learning are essential features, cannot be grasped by quantitative data.'

It should be stressed that the elements that determine institutional competencies cannot be evaluated by what emerges from the external regulatory framework, or by considering only quantitative indices. Institutions are characterized by distinct histories, modes of responding to the macro setting, routines and scopes. Hence 'competencies' should be considered together with the specificities of each institution and its specific modes of interacting in an overall context. The main functions of these bridging institutions can be classified into four categories: technological modernization (technological support, technological information services); training; services of standardization and certification; and promotion of a culture of quality.

With regard to the legal regimes under which bridging institutions are ascribed, the distribution is as follows: 41 per cent of the institutions studied were civil associations; 41 per cent of these are autonomous, while the remaining 59 per cent maintain some type of integration with other organizations. It is worth mentioning that the presence of federal organizations among the institutions analysed is due to the provision and administration of special services that fall into the governmental sphere. In many cases, these federal organizations carry out functions that can be associated with those developed by bridging institutions, as exemplified by IMPI (the Mexican Institute of Intellectual Property Rights); CENAM (the National Centre of Metrology); and CONOCER (the Council for Standardization and Certification of Labour Skills).

A significant number of these institutions have achieved financial autonomy; in effect, 38 per cent of them are economically independent from external financial sources, mainly through the sales of their services, which is important, since the vast majority of these institutions, upon foundation, depended on external funding – either federal or from the private sector. However, a significant number of these institutions still depend on public or private sector resources for their survival, despite the revenues generated by the sale of their services. With regard to users of their services, it is interesting to note that a great majority of their clients are predominantly small and medium-sized firms, with a scant presence of micro firms, despite the fact that they are (allegedly) a top priority for practically all bridging institutions.

Bridging institutions are seldom directed towards one industrial sector in particular; in fact, 63 per cent indicated that their clients belong to 'manufacturing industry' and were not able to provide any further detail. Representatives of these institutions claim that this lack of specialization is precisely their marketing strategy in the light of the still scarce demand for their services from the production system. This claim, along with the fact that these institutions are relatively young, could support the allegation that bridging institutions are in fact trying to maximize their potential client base. Yet, the trend observed in a few of these institutions is towards finding a particular niche in the market, and hence towards specialization.

Concerning the personnel employed by bridging institutions, two interesting facts are readily visible. First is the predominance of small institutions: 69 per cent have fewer than 15 people in their permanent staff. Second, in 72 per cent of the institutions few of the personnel have graduate degrees or some other type of specialization. One final observation that may help a better understanding and interpretation of the data presented so far refers to the age of these institutions, that is, 94 per cent of the institutions studied are less than ten years old.

Private consultants as bridging institutions

Following the OECD's definition of 'Bridging institutions', which is the same one utilized throughout this chapter, privately owned consultancy firms do not qualify as bridging institutions. However, these firms carry out a number of activities through which they fulfil functions identified as inherent to bridging institutions. For this reason, a brief assessment of private consultancy firms within the Mexican NIS is prepared, where these firms are included and considered as bridging institutions as well. In numerous national experiences, private consultancy firms play an important role in the generation of a new organizational culture, as well as in bringing basic knowledge and new technologies to potential (local) users. In the study of the Dutch NIS by Hertog *et al.* (1995), it was shown that private consultancy firms play a leading role as agents through which technological knowledge is diffused. Their presence in the development and expansion of industrial districts in the Third Italy has been equally important. In the latter case, these firms acted as driving forces behind the development of new technologies and forms of productive organization, while at the same time they also had an active role in the fields of marketing and design, thereby opening up new opportunities in international markets for the firms within these Italian districts (Brusco, 1982; Baudry, 1995; Bellardi, 1989).

According to the data, the priority areas of specialization continue to be 'organizational activities' and 'project planning and design'. However, it must be noted that 10 per cent of the consultancy firms studied claimed that they specialized in 'technical support'. A more detailed analysis shows that 2.3 per cent of consultants offer services of 'certification of processes and products', 7 per cent offer 'technological development services' and 9.2 per cent offer services of 'production advice'.

The sector of consultancy firms in Mexico is as yet unstable and heterogeneous. Presently, these firms are also enduring a process of change in the light of the new economic scene. At their earlier stage Mexican consultancy firms catered chiefly to government, working on nationwide infrastructure projects mainly through engineering projects. During the 1980s, as was the case with many other institutions, private consultants changed their activities, in an effort to meet the new services demanded by other private firms (Casalet, 1995). These new activities represent an attempt to address the need to create a service market aimed at entrepreneurial development, complementing the present deficiencies in the brisk advent of this market. In fact, a sizeable portion of this market is currently held by foreign consultancy firms, particularly from the USA, relying on their easy access, prestige and international experience, and challenging the quality of the services offered by their domestic counterparts.

Among their services private consultancy firms are beginning to include, albeit slowly, activities related to assistance and technology transfer, and the development of a new production culture, and are more concerned with bringing quality services to the client, design, quality control and providing export opportunities. According to the directors of the National Chamber of Consultancy Firms, one of the issues facing this sector lies precisely in the vagueness and flexibility of the very concept of consultant. Over the past few years, Chamber representatives have pointed out that, 'in recent years, there has been an enormous increase in mobility, due to the entry of many people who are trying their luck in the consultancy market. The problem is that the very notion of consultant is extremely vague, thus enabling anyone to believe that he/she is qualified to be a consultant. This in turn has led to a high rotation rate in the sector; in other words, that firms come and go, because they do not manage to survive.' Certification of consultants is hence one of the central problems regarding the confidence levels in this market: currently, the Council for Standardization and Certification of Labour Skills (CONOCER) is working on setting up a Standardization Committee for the consultancy sector, which would constitute the first step in setting up norms to be used when assessing a person's competence to be a consultant. However, a number of difficulties need to be overcome before this committee becomes fully operational. This is not a simple process, as accurately pointed out by some Chamber representatives, and it would seem that the market is by far the best selection mechanism despite the fact that the whole sector may very well pay a high price over the next few years.

The SEP-CONACYT system centres

The SEP-CONACYT system deals with a diversity of themes in basic and applied research, human resource training, and technological development. However, the origin, profile and evolution of each of the centres differ greatly. This makes the system a loose collection of centres, some operating since 1941 (COLMEX, Colegio de México, and INAOE, Instituto Nacional de Astrofísica, Optica y Electrónica). Since their transfer under CONACYT's administrative control did not follow a specific organizational normativity, the system transformed into a complex bureaucratic net. The 1995–2000 Programme of Science and Technology states that 'the SEP-CONACYT system is an effective instrument in the decentralization of scientific and technological activity, as well as an efficacious means of linking scientific research to the technological and social needs of the country'.

The system presently comprises 28 research institutions that can be regrouped by their objectives and specialities into the following sub-systems: exact and natural sciences (nine centres); social sciences and humanities (nine centres); technological development (seven centres) and an additional two centres, devoted to providing information services (INFOTEC, Fondo de Información y Documentación para la Industria), and to financing grants for higher education (FIDERH, Fondo para el Desarrollo de Recursos Humanos). The centres' organizational modes are civil associations (non-profit making organizations), decentralized public organizations, public trusts and decentralized organizations (which are profit-making).

Technological activities of the centres

The SEP-CONACYT system can be viewed as an attempt to decentralize scientific and technological activities and, as such, it is spread throughout the country. This enables the various centres to learn about the specific problems of the regions within which each centre is located, and to implement research and training strategies designed to meet the region's concrete requirements. Technological development is important within the activities of the various centres. Almost half the centres (45 per cent) studied here are involved in technical development, while fewer than 20 per cent carry out basic research. Applied research is carried out at 40 per cent of the centres. It should be noted that the three activities that received the highest frequency among the centres studied can be considered as related to technological development: 92 per cent of the centres carry out design and manufacture of processes and products; 77 per cent are involved in consultancy and technological assistance; and 69 per cent work on the evaluation of production and products. These activities indicate that technological capabilities are based on incremental innovations and not on innovations that imply drastic transformations in processes and products. Also noteworthy is the relatively high importance assigned to the organization of seminar, forums and lectures, which is one way in which the centres can generate linkages not only with the productive sector but also with other academic institutions. Fewer than half of the centres sold the results from their applied research. Projects are negotiated on a one-to-one basis with a single firm, leaving open the possibility of time management conflicts between industry and centres, through more direct communication between the patterns involved.

A key aspect of the SEP-CONACYT system refers not to its insertion at the regional level, but to its ability to establish technological cooperation networks, both inside and outside the system, with other higher education institutions, firms and public organizations for training human resources and the development of projects in the productive sector. The multidisciplinary and multiregional nature of the system opens up opportunities for complementarity and specialization. The system itself might be considered as a network, albeit loosely integrated and not self-sufficient, inasmuch as it relies on external agents for developing some of its projects.

The relationships within both of the subsystems, of basic sciences and of technological development, are not frequent. This is also manifested by the degree of utilization of the technical infrastructure of the centres, in particular in those activities related to certification, since the centres have been selected by SECOFI to carry out such a function at the regional level.

The centres in the scientific subsystem do not pool efforts with other centres for offering services, or certifications, congresses or lectures. The linkages of these with other centres or institutions are directed chiefly towards research and training, while technological centres have created more linkages covering technological issues. The services most frequently offered by technological centres to firms are consulting services, technical assistance, organization of technological training seminars and forums and, to a lesser extent, project assessment, design and manufacture of products and processes and definition of norms and procedures.

As to the impact of these services in the performance of firms, it seems that, from the results of firms surveyed, the aforementioned services have been helpful in reducing production costs, opening up new areas for innovation and reaching new export markets, as well as consolidating their position in the domestic market. It is readily visible that their impact is still limited, presumably because of the low demand from firms, despite the importance of innovation activities in the current competitive context, although demand has steadily increased during the past few years, probably due to the magnitude of the economic crisis and the ensuing need for firms to look for new market niches; in 1998 most of the technological centres' service capacity had increased.

Most of the firms benefiting from the centres' services are domestic medium-sized ones, probably because these are the ones that, on the one hand, have accumulated a certain knowledge of their markets and, on the other cannot afford to set up their own development facilities. It should be noted, however, that this interactive process between firms' demand and centres' supply is changing and evolving on a daily basis. Firms are increasingly aware of the benefits of utilizing technological support services, in particular to establish a new quality culture increasing their linkages with the outside world. The centres themselves are leaning towards a new definition of technology, better linked with the institutional – organizational dimension, which would imply new managerial and organizational skills.

Conclusions

A description of the institutional matrix within the Mexican innovation system has been attempted, considering the main transformation it has endured over time, along with its actual configuration in terms of the specific and concrete competencies of organizations and entities that support innovation activities. It has been possible to distinguish four functional activities within the institutional matrix: first, organizations devoted to providing incentives for modernization and innovation activities (CONACYT-Fidetec, NAFIN; Forcytec, where some of them are specific programmes to support industries and innovation), as well as organizations and banks aimed at supporting both non-oil exports and firms' networks for SMEs (Bancomext, NAFIN, SECOFI, CONACYT); second, 'bridging institutions', organizations dedicated to providing information and reducing uncertainty by standardization, certification, quality and training (IMMC, Normex, Calmecac, Cenam, IMPI, Fundameca, CIMO, Infotec, Centros-Crece); third, highly specialized research and development organizations offering support for specific knowledge areas (IMP, IIE, ININ, IMTA); fourth, organizations devoted to research and development in the basic sciences, regional technological development and training at the postgraduate level (SEP-CONACYT Centres).

The evolution of the institutional matrix thus constructed has also been presented throughout the different development phases of the Mexican economy, alongside the changes in the institutional dimension regarding both the relationships among the macro, meso and micro levels and the competencies of each organization supporting innovation. It must be noted that this whole process is believed to result from the co-evolutionary interaction between the institutional matrix and the productive structure. The new demands arising from firms and industries are actually pushing organizations to adopt more efficient and flexible structures, which can be seen in the cases of several large organizations, such as IMP, ININ, IMTA and IIE. However, the path towards institutional reform is not at all linear; as a matter of fact, while entities are working towards building a rational organizational task which would allow for more efficient utilization of their resources and technological sources in production activities, there are still strong power groups and coalitions nested at the interior of these same organizations, built across the government, whose existence poses serious risks on the successful implementation of these changes. The process along which the Mexican institutional matrix has evolved shows that 'coordination' and 'networking' activities between specific organizations are very rare. Within each type of functional activity – providing incentive, reducing uncertainty, specialized and research activities – and between them substantial coordination and dialogue between organizations are very scarce activities (Figure 7.2).

Policies oriented to supporting modernization and small and medium firms are crucial in the explanation of the institutional path. In fact, along these lines, the portion of the production system most exposed to international competition has increased its demands on services dealing with quality control, normalization and verification of processes and of technological modernization. It should be mentioned that a significant share of this demand is focused on information services, within the context of the new information technology (Internet, electronic information networks, etc.). In this circumstance, bridging institutions have an incipient role of nesting firms in networks where these are linked with other firms and institutions. However, as it is stressed in Part III, most of the successful exporting firms develop their linkages with firms and institutions localized in advanced economies.

Organizations such as NAFIN played a key role in the construction of the industrialization process of the country, providing financial resources for the public sector and generating an important support infrastructure for public firms during the import-substitution phase. Later, emphasis was placed on the development of SMEs through credit and technology. Nowadays, the role of NAFIN as development bank has changed, diminishing its importance in favour of organizations such as Bancomext, whose activities are closely linked with the opening up of the economy and the globalization of the markets. With regard to the specialized institutions that played a central role in the creation of technological competencies during the industrialization of the country (IMP, IIE, ININ, IMTA), what is presently relevant is the sale of

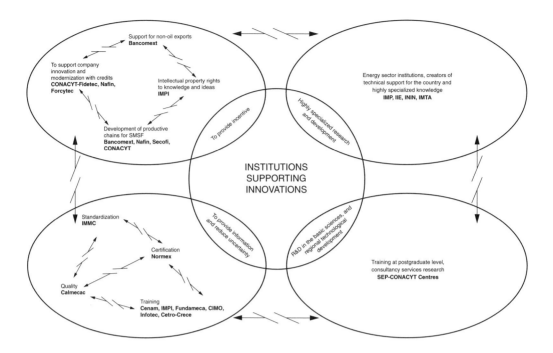

Figure 7.2 Mexican Institutions: a Non-articulated Network.

services and the loss of interest in research. Such organizations are suffering the effects of privatization: the diminution of budgetary resources. They are increasingly concerned with the needs of the domestic and international markets, having to meet higher quality and better competitiveness criteria, favouring these activities over research. This situation is bound to be also present within the SEP-CONACYT Centres, particularly in the technological development subsystem, whose activity could be reduced to a simple function of technical consultancy if it is not complemented by support for research inside the centres, in connection with the centres in the exact and natural sciences. In general, on the one side, the new process, within which most of the organizations dedicated to applied and basic research have reduced their efforts in these activities, can be seen as a necessary transformation to survive in a new constrained world; on the other side, if most organizations assume this pattern, a negative impact on the pre-competitive research system as a whole might follow. Finally, it can be readily seen that direct support targeted at the consolidation of public and private institutions aimed at technology is still very incipient and atomized. If such a situation were to prevail in the future, given the generalized perception of organizations and policy-makers of the difficulty of creating an articulated system, the consequences would most probably be dire for innovative activity. Furthermore, organizations and policy-makers more often than not have only a partial conception of what technology is, reducing it to 'technical information' and assigning little value to organizational aspects that are of particular importance in the institutional dimension and that suppose a lengthy process of learning.

Table 7.2 Programmes Oriented to Supporting Industrialization and Technology

Institutions	Evolution and objectives	Specific programmes
SECOFI	1993 To foster inter-firm cooperation and the creation of associations for acquiring equipment, and technological inputs and assets.	Firm integration. Weak achievements, lack of continuity. In 1997 there were 226 integrator firms with 7,036 associates, mainly from agribusiness and fisheries.
SECOFI Fideicomisos Privados	1996 To provide entrepreneurial assessment services. To link firms with institutional funding sources. To provide information services. To link firms with public and private institutions and organizations.	Support CRECE centres, regional centres for entrepreneurial competitiveness. Creation of a network of consultants. 26 centres in several states.
CONACYT	1991 Programme to foster technological modernization. Fund for Research and Development for Technological Modernisation (FIDETEC) Programme for developing technological and scientific capabilities (FORCYTEC) Programme for academy – firm linkages (PREAEM) Incubators for technology-based firms (PIEBT)	Fund for Research and Development for Technological Modernization (FIDETEC) Programme for developing technological and scientific capabilities (FORCYTEC) Programme for academy – firm linkages (PREAEM) Incubators for firms with technology-based firms PIEB
CONACYT (FORCCYTEC)	1991 Financial risk instrument that supports applied research and development of pre-competitive and mature technologies. Improvement of manufacturing competencies. 1996 Changes in the fund's rules	1994 Lack of significant results Support to the furniture research and development centre (Guadalajara) Plastics (Guadalajara) Centre for entrepreneurial competitiveness (Saltillo) Mexican institution for metrology and normalization (D.F.) Centre for food processing innovation 1995 Severe problems – Modification of operational rules
CONACYT FIDETEC	1991 Creation of the Fund for Research and Development for Technological Modernization (FIDETEC), with the objective of fostering pre-competitive R&D, including adaptation, transference, technological improvements of products and processes.	Reduced impact. SMEs are the most benefited from this fund. In 1997 it transforms itself to reduce paperwork, direct credit is granted. Guarantee and shared risk programmes.
PIEBT	1996 Promote the development of technology-based firms with the support of regional governments, commercial banks, firms and academic institutions.	Scarce results. In 1995, only 5 of 11 projects were granted funding. In 1996 this number was reduced to 3.

Table 7.2 *continued*

Institutions	Evolution and objectives	Specific programmes
PREAEM Participation of SECOFI, Conacyt and Infotec. Technological Services Information System (SISTEC)	Created in 1990, promotes the association and cooperation between firms and academy. 1997 Provides information on the capacity of existing technological services by means of a database on the services offered by applied research and technological development centres, and specialized consultancy firms.	During the period 1991–3 70 projects were approved, but only 7 in 1995 and 5 in 1996. Provides information on the capacity of existing technological services by means of a database on the services offered by applied research and technological development centres, and specialized consultancy firms. Still under implementation.

Institutions providing financial incentives

NAFIN	1934 Creation with the purpose of allocating resources to develop the country's infrastructure, through credits, promotion and support to SMES. 1940 Promotional bank: promotes large federal government projects and public firms. 1953 Financial activity aimed at industry and infrastructure. Capitalization and creation of instruments directed at fostering domestic savings. 1960 Creation of trust funds.	Direct promotion of firms defined as of strategic importance, such as Fábrica de Papel Atenquique SA, Altos Hornos de Mexico SA, Celanese Mexicana SA, Viscosa Mexicana, Sosa Texcoco SA, among others. FOGAIN was created in order to support to SMEs and FOMIN. Creation of the National Borderline Programme, of the National Productivity Centre, of Plan Lerma (1964), of the Trust for Pre-investment studies, of FOMIN (industrial support fund) in 1972, Fonacot, FONATUR, FONEP (1967), among others.
	1970 Financial restructuring of strategic sectors: iron and steel, hydrocarbons, electrical energy, railways, mining, telephones. 1980–8 Decentralization of economic activities, regional promotion and support for SMEs. 1988–94 Second level bank, emphasis on SMEs. Preference given to manufacturing industry. Support for large companies that favour productive linkages. Favouring an entrepreneurial culture by training. Emphasis placed on increasing productivity and modernization.	State funds to promote micro-industry started with funds from SINCAS. Financing for long-term and/or riskier projects. Single programme to finance modernization (Promin): • guarantees programme; • first level credit options; • programme of risk capital; • support programme for member companies; • training services and technical assistance; • trusts, valuation and diagnostic services; • investment bank; • strategic alliances.

1994-5	Promotion of policies and actions to promote the competitiveness of SMEs. Creation of the National Council for SMEs. Support for the financial system, education, health and nutrition. Support for the UD, manufacturing industry, production of food, drinks and garments.	Recovery programme for outstanding debt. Not possible to restructure debt through non-banking financial intermediaries.
1996	Restructuring of financial inter-production. Promotion of productive activity. Alliance for agrarian industries, investment in infrastructure, financing and training. Alliance for growth (ACE).	Single programme for financing modernization. Risk capital programme of direct share contribution. Purge of the network IFNB Stock Exchange, subcontracting of the Securities Exchange in Queretaro. Strategic alliances.
1997	New orientation for NAFIN.	Restructuring of PRODEM Development of programmes for suppliers, and sectoral programmes. Creation of agencies.
Bancomext		
1937	To increase exports.	
1950	To encourage exportation of Mexican goods.	Participates in the organization of foreign trade. IMPEXMAL. COMPROMEX. National Centre of Foreign Trade Information (IMCE).
1981	Multiple bank. International competitiveness of Mexican companies and promotion of non-oil exports.	Creation of organizations orientated towards foreign trade
1993	Integral support for SMEs.	FINAPE (agrarian and fisheries) FOPYME (for SMEs with debts up to 6 million pesos) Promotion System for Exportable Supply by Subcontracting of Processes (SPS)
1995	Mexico Exports: a regional approach. Investment bank with participation in development projects for exports and the attraction of domestic investors. Development Programme for Suppliers.	
1998	Support for SMEs exports. Programmes for suppliers intensified. Integral services offered to entrepreneurs.	ADE/restructuring in UDIS. Telemarketing. Directory of exporters.

Table 7.3 Specialized Research Institutions

Institution	Date of creation and legal regime	Objectives and programmes	Results to date
IIE	1975	Fulfil the demand for electrical energy, operate complex electrical systems, research on electrical systems.	40 patents on joint projects with industry. Most significant innovations: analysis on Mexican fuel oil, planning and design of simulators and development of polymeric concrete.
	Funded by the Federal Commission of Electrical Energy (CFE).		Gasification of fossil fuels for generating electricity.
		Programmes:	Agreements with UNAM's Instituto de Ingeniería and firms to manufacture hydraulic turbo-machinery.
	Decentralized public organism, with legal personality. Own financial resources.	● Modernization of information and telecommunication networks.	Agreement with the ININ on oceanographic studies in the Gulf of Mexico.
		● Communication networks, research on optic fibres.	Programme SIDETT, developed jointly with CFE (integrated system for computerized design of transmission towers).
		● Artificial intelligence.	
		● Geothermal energy, effects on the environment.	
IMTA	1986	Develop the technology and human resources necessary to ensure proper handling of water, on both the short and long run.	1992 applied for patent for the following technological developments:
	created as a decentralised organism of the SARH		● Removal of iron and manganese in water.
	1994		● WC water deposit without ironwork.
	Due to re-structuring of the field, it now reports to the Environment Ministry.	Programmes:	● Control valve for hot water.
		● Creation of new areas, hydraulic laboratories, water quality, isotopic hydrology, treatment of residual water and hydrogeochemistry.	● Universal bank for domestic appliances.
	1993		● Appliance for rehabilitating lakes utilizing air.
	Diversifies its income by providing services to different clients; works for PEMEX, water operators, consumer associations, etc.	● Centre for Water Research (CENCA) agile detection of cholera in water.	● 34 computer programmes registered in SEP.
		● Technology for estimating salinity in agricultural soil through satellite. Rehabilitation of saline soil by draining.	● Rehabilitation of lakes and lagoons over the Lerma–Chapala waterway.
			● Inventory of industrial water discharges.

			Programmes	
ININ	1979	The government operated this entity coordinated by the Energy Ministry. Funded by federal resources, moreover it sells services to firms and other institutions.	Contribute as national laboratory to the research and development of nuclear sciences and their applications. Carries on research and provides quality services. Programmes: • Scientific development; new materials. • Environment protection. • S&T transference, research and applications on radiation, research and services in Laguna Verde, services for firms. • Specialized Centres.	Competes with firms in the private sector on sterilizing and rehabilitation of products and raw materials. Metrology centre of ionic radiation (single of its type in the country), handling, storage and treatment of radioactive waste. Between 94 and 97, successful conclusion of 64 network projects, 25 with OIEA's support and a further 17 with CONACYT's. 1,405 technical papers published. 450 projects presented in scientific symposiums. Organization of graduate programmes jointly with UAEM and UAH. 474 papers in specialized books and journals. Active cooperation networks with: UNAM, INP, UAM, UAEM. Central de Laguna Verde, CFE, Comisión Nacional de Seguridad Nuclear, CONACYT, Japan Atomic Energy Research Institute, Los Alamos National Laboratory (USA), PEMEX.
IMP	1965	Decentralized public organism, with legal personality. Own financial resources.	It provides PEMEX technological support for developing the supply of hydrocarbons and their derivatives. Programmes: • Exploration, geological, geophysical and seismic activity studies. • Underground storage. • Development of equipment for refineries and petrochemicals. • Research on catalysts. • Basic engineering. • Human resource training.	Almost half of the 454 patents granted on catalysts. Development of 30 NOMs for analysing the quality of raw materials and additives utilized in drilling. More than 50 technologies for processing and generating design tools. Process simulator (SIMPROC). Projects: Catalysts FIES/FIDEPEMEX. Technological R&D. FIDEPEMEX and IFS (high education institutions). Graduate programmes.

For key, see Table 7.1

Table 7.4 General Information on the SEP-CONACYT System Centres

Subsystems	Centres	Geographic localization	Activities
Natural and basic sciences	CIAD	Sonora	Carry out basic and applied research in the following areas: biotechnology, enviroment, earth and sea sciences, electronics and telecommunications, information technology, basic sciences, materials, among others. Moreover, take part in the development of human resources through participation in graduate programmes.
	CIBNOR	Baja California Sur	
	CICESE	Baja California	
	CICY	Yucatan	
	CIMAT	Guanajuato	
	CIMAV	Chihuahua	
	CIO	Guanajuato	
	I. DE E.	Veracruz	
	INAOE	Puebla	
Social sciences and humanities	CIDE	Mexico City	Carry out studies on economics, public administration, public politics, sociology, public health, history, Anthropology, among others. Furthermore, take part in the development of human resources through their participation in graduate programmes (except TAMAYO).
	CIESAS	Mexico City	
	COLEF	Baja California	
	COLMEX	Mexico City	
	COLMICH	Michoacan	
	ECOSUR	Chiapas	
	FLACSO	Mexico City	
	MORA	Mexico City	
	TAMAYO	Mexico City	
Technological development	CIATEC	Guanajuato	Development of specific research for industrial sector. Consultancy services. Human resources training. Information services. Moreover, take part in the development of human resources through their participation in graduate programmes (except COMIMSA).
	CIATEJ	Jalisco	
	CIATEQ	Queretaro	
	CIDESI	Queretaro	
	CIDETEQ	Queretaro	
	CIQA	Coahuila	
	COMIMSA	Coahuila	
Services	FIDERH	Mexico City	Information services. Human resources training.
	INFOTEC	Mexico City	

For key, see Table 7.1

Table 7.5 Institutions Providing Information and Reducing Uncertainty

Industrial policy	Institution	Start and depends	Objectives and/or programmes	Results
To stimulate the diffusion, use and transfer of technology within the national productive apparatus (mainly in the sector of MSMSF).	UTT	1993 Autonomous (began in the form of a private sector trust fund, with support initially from CONACYT. Canacintra and IBM Mexico).	Consultancy and technological assistance. Commercial missions. Legal Aid nationwide (42 per cent of services given outside the Metropolitan area).	Approximately 3,000 clients attended; financial autarchy.
	Cetindustria	1994 CONCAMIN, CONACYT (through FORCYTEC) and FUNTEC.	Industrial network (development of computer skills). Attention to users (first level consultancy). Industrial technological linking (link-up). Administration of the TIPS programme, in the Federal District and Metropolitan area.	Too few users to meet expectations (problems with entry and diffusion within the market).
	FUNDEC	1994 CONCAMIN and SECOFI (its capital is made up of a trust fund comprising the resources obtained from the sale of LANFI shares).	Support programme for industrial groups. Development of technological culture. Funds for pollution prevention projects nationwide (especially Guanajuato, the Federal District, Monterrey, Yucatan, Mexico State and Veracruz).	Funding for industrial associations, leather, textiles, garments. Pollution prevention programmes. Human resource training.
	Promotional Centre for Design	1994 Private sector Trust Fund; comprising resources from BANCOMEXT, NAFIN, SECOFI, IMPI, CONACYT, IBM Mexico, Mexinox and Quorum A.C.	Evaluation of designs and corporate image. Formulation of design projects. Business diagnosis (technology of products, systems and manufacturing processes, etc.) the Federal District and Metropolitan area.	Attention to SMEs. 546 firms serviced in 1996; 686 in 1997. Most were small firms and with projects outside the Federal District. Main assisted sectors: food and beverages, agribusiness.
	ADIAT AC	1989 Civil association (non-profit making) made up of different Institutions and Companies (both public and private), from the productive and academic sectors, committed to Research and Technological Development.	Annual symposium. Prize for technological innovation. Technological circles. Computer network. National cover.	Programmes with affiliated institutes. Research on stimuli for firms. Awareness, of the legislative power, of the R&D problems.
	CDIDT	n/d Canacintra.	Diffusion of technology in the Federal District and Metropolitan Area.	Very few users.

Table 7.5 *continued*

Industrial policy	Institution	Start and depends	Objectives and/or programmes	Results
To raise levels of labour training and competitiveness of MSMSF.	CIMO	1988 The Ministry of Labour and Social Services (funds from the World Bank).	Integrated Training Service for MSMSF. National cover.	More than 125,000 companies attended.
To establish a national system of standardization and certification of labour skills.	CONOCER	1995 The Ministry of Labour and Social Services, and the Ministry of Public Education (through the Project of Modernization of Technical Education and Training, which is receiving World Bank support).	Coordination and promotion of the national system of standardization and certification of labour skills. National cover.	Fostered the creation of 13 standardization committees, and in the next year the expectation is to create 13 more.
Business training.	IMDT	1988 Institute of the National Chamber of Consultancy Firms.	Training for technical and professional personnel in consultancy firms. Promotion of the knowledge and use of technological development among consultancy firms. National cover.	No data available.
	CCTC	1991 Decentralized organization of CONCAMIN.	Business Training Programmes in the Federal District and Metropolitan Area.	No data obtained.
To stimulate and strengthen the system of standardization and certification of quality (1992 Federal Law on Metrology and Standardization).	IMNC	1993 Autonomous; sponsored by CONCAMIN, CONCANACO-SERVITUR, CNA and UNAM (when it began, it had a Trust Fund provided by CONACYT, through FORCYTEC).	Standardization, certification and verification of standards (NOM and NMX). Training in standards and quality. National cover.	57 leader companies were certified; training services to 1,500 people during 1996; financial autarchy
	NORMEX	1993 Autonomous; sponsored by Canacintra and the University of the Valley of Mexico (initially supported by the National Polytechnic Institute).	Standardization, certification and verification of standards (NOM and NMX). Training in standards and quality. Laboratory tests for environmental protection, chemical analysis, food and packaging. National cover.	More than 300 clients attended; financial autarchy (with certain difficulties during 1996).

	Objective	Year / Status	Functions	Results
Calmecac		1994 Autonomous (when it began, it had a Trust Fund provided by CONACYT.	Standardization, certification and verification of standards (NOM and NMX). Training in standards and quality. National cover.	Database of 3,000 clients (including rendered consultations and services)
CENAM	To modernize the national system of metrology (1992 Federal Law on Metrology and Standardization).	1992	Primary laboratory in metrology. Research, advice and training in metrology. National cover.	In 1995, 1,200 calibration services were carried out, approx. 1,800 in 1996, and 2,000 in 1997; sale of services has covered 18 per cent of the Centre's maintenance costs
IMPI	To modernize and strengthen the national system of intellectual property rights (1991 Law on Promotion and Protection of Intellectual Property Rights).	1993 Autonomous Federal Institution.	Administration of the national system of the rights to intellectual property rights. Training and services of information on rights to intellectual property (patents and trademarks). National cover.	In 1997, 4,612 patents were granted. Between 1980 and 1998, a total of 52,281 patents were granted. No sectoral data are available.
FUNDAMECA	To stimulate a culture of quality in the national productive apparatus.	1987 Autonomous.	To stimulate a culture of quality. National prize for quality. National cover.	More than 750 companies have participated in the national prize for quality

Appendix: a note on intellectual property rights

J. Aboites and M. Soria

This note is based on a broader study on the changes that have occurred in Mexican intellectual property right laws (Aboites and Soria, 1997). During the second half of the 1980s, important changes took place in the regulatory framework for intellectual property rights (IPRs) in the industrialized and less developed countries. The reasons behind these changes were, on the one hand, governments' and firms' growing acceptance of the importance of knowledge assets in international trade; and, on the other, the US government's pressure during the GATT negotiations – the Uruguay Round – to harmonize institutional norms regarding intellectual property rights. Underlying this proposal, most developed economies support the idea that the heterogeneity of IPRs in GATT member countries produces serious distortions in world trade, and particularly discourages foreign direct investment (GATT, 1994). The debate has concluded with an international proposal that was called *Trade Related Aspects of Intellectual Property Rights* (TRIPS). This initiative was passed in 1993, when GATT/WTO member countries approved TRIPS during the Marrakech Conference.

Mexico has accepted this norm and introduced changes in the domestic law that regulates IPRs. A new norm has been introduced, together with the consolidation of the trade reform which began during the second half of the 1980s, and which concluded with the signing of NAFTA and Mexico's membership in the OECD.[1] The IPRs that correspond to the previous industrial property law (1976) have changed radically. The new law incorporated most of the reforms carried out between 1987 and 1997 in such important issues as: (a) a breeder's rights; (b) an integrated circuit's layout design; (c) industrial secrecy; (d) computer programs; and (e) industrial designs.[2] Under these circumstances and considering the characterization of the core patent cycle as *granting, protection* and *use* (ONU, 1990; Doer, 1999), we can briefly describe the main structural changes. The changes in the *granting of patents* (1991) included new areas of patenting (pharmaceuticals, biotechnological and chemical products), as well as the acceptance of the novelty test from the Patent Cooperation Treaty (PCT) member countries (1987). The changes in *protection* were based on the duration of the period of patent protection: this period was ten years in 1976, and it was extended to twenty years in 1991. As for *use*, the importing of a patented product was again incorporated in 1991. This right to exploit patents was the centre of a controversy during the 1970s, given that it would permit transnational companies to import patented products without having to produce them locally.[3] Thus, transnational companies used patents to block competition and to protect their markets. Some studies have shown that this use of patents has inhibited the development of domestic productive and technological capability, since it does not favour the diffusion of technology.[4]

The changes in the IPR's regulatory framework, the liberalization process and the structural reforms, like the privatization, have impacted on the patenting activity pattern. Comparing the evolution of patenting activities in two periods, before trade liberalization (1978–86) and during the process itself (1987–96), we can state that: (a) before trade liberalization, patent applications by residents and non-residents decreased; (b) during the process itself, non-resident applications grew considerably, while resident patenting continued its tendency to decrease.[5] As a result, there was strong growth of patenting by non-residents, compared to total patenting.[6]

In this context, two important trends can be observed: (a) the flow of total and non-resident patent applications is closely linked to domestic and foreign direct investment during the 1978–96 period; and (b) there is no significant relation between resident patenting activities and the evolution of total private sector investment. Thus, the evolution of non-resident patenting has met NAFTA's expectations in the sense that direct foreign investment increases the flows of patented technology. The United States is the country that has increased its participation the most (60 per cent), despite a decrease during the 1995 crisis. Europe and Japan follow.

The evolution of patent applications by type of patent-holders (firms, research institutes, universities or individuals) shows two tendencies. During the 1991–4 period, there was growth of applications by all patent-holders, whereas in the 1994–6 period there was a substantial decrease in three types of patent-holders. Between 1991 and 1994, the most important growth in patent applications was from firms, universities and research institutes. Individual persons had the lowest growth. Between 1994 and 1996, there was an overall decrease, universities and research institutes being the most affected. It is important to point out that firms are the main patent-holders, since eight out of ten patents belong to firms, specifically multi-national corporations.

Chemicals, metal products, machinery and equipment are the sectors in which 88 per cent of patent applications are concentrated. They are also the most active sectors in the number of patent applications during the 1991–4 period. In the chemical sector, the growth of patent applications is linked to PEMEX, the government-owned petroleum monopoly, as well as to the important petrochemical industry that has developed around this state-run company. The rest of the manufacturing sectors, specifically the traditional ones (food and beverages, textile, leather, etc.), have less relative importance and less activity in patent applications. During the 1995 economic crisis, all manufacturing sectors *registered* reductions, except for electronic technologies; R&D intensive manufactures from multinational firms (pharmaceuticals, biotechnology and others) were noteworthy because of their dynamism in patent applications.

This leads us to suppose that there are two factors that block the diffusion of technology that is codified in patents, so that it does not reach the domestic productive system: (a) the majority of the transnational companies patenting is for commercialization (by importing patented products or to block competition); and (b) the transnational companies support their R&D effort at home and, preferably, develop network with institutions and high technology firms in developed economies. An important conclusion that is derived from the previous statement is that NAFTA met expectations of increasing foreign direct investment, but the same is not true for the local diffusion of technology flows. In other words, the transnational companies mostly patent to commercialize, thus favouring the creation of networks abroad.

Thus, new technologies are being patented in the Mexican patenting system. None the less, this non-resident patenting in pharmaceuticals and others does not show a spillover that has influenced domestic innovative activity. This fact appears to show that growth of non-resident patenting does not generate endeavours in local innovative activity or in the creation of networks that contribute to the strengthening of the nation's technological capability. In other words, the strong growth of non-resident patents serves more to block the development of dometic industry's technological capability. This is particularly true for the pharmaceutical industry; for example, there is no incentive for R&D, or for linkages between universities and domestic companies related to the generation of new molecules that are national discoveries (Chapter 12).

Despite this fact, there has been a reduction in domestic patenting. Thus, despite the increase in non-resident patents, there is not an adequate diffusion of the technological knowledge that arrives in Mexico from abroad. This suggests that the existing networks are not stimulated for the diffusion of this type of technological information towards the national agents, which is a distinguishing characteristic of the Mexican innovation system. This is the case in the domestic pharmaceutical industry. Another characteristic that distinguishes the system of patents registered is that applications for patents in electronic technology are relatively low. In effect, despite the boom in electronic exports, there has not been a significant increase in patenting activity. This is another facet in the lack of integration in the Mexican national innovation system.

In general, we can affirm that the changes in intellectual property rights in Mexico have strengthened the transnational companies' strategies by permitting the diffusion of their innovations through trade, instead of through the creation of local innovation and technological networks.

Notes

1. In the principal agreements that Mexico has accepted from 1976 to 1997, the following must be emphasized: *Chapter xvii on intellectual property, NAFTA (1994); TRIPS-OMC (1994); Patent Cooperation Treaty, OMPI (1995).*

2. The most outstanding were the following: (a) an increase in the duration of the patent; (b) the elimination of barriers in patenting (pharmaceuticals, biotechnology, etc.) and in the importing of products; and (c) an increase in the types of intellectual property rights (integrated circuits, biotechnology, etc.). In addition, this implied a harmonization of Mexico's intellectual property rights with those of the industrialized countries.

3. This form of using patents was considered in the 1942 Industrial Property Law and was repealed by the 1976 Inventions and Trademark Law. According to GATT (1994), prohibiting the import of a patented product is a practice that distorts international trade and, thus, is an obstacle to free trade.

4. Among recent studies, see Raghavan (1990).

5. In 1986, slightly fewer than 1,000 patents were granted, while in 1993 more than 6,000 were granted.

6. In 1982, 92 per cent of patents were granted to non-residents; in 1996, non-resident patents represented 96 per cent of total patents. Since almost 93 per cent of the patents registered between 1987 and 1996 were non-resident patents, total patenting grew during these years.

CHAPTER EIGHT

Human Resources and Competencies

G. Valenti, G. Varela and G. del Castillo

Introduction

This chapter is based on some stylized facts that are recognized as the basis for the good performance of a national innovation system (NIS) (Nelson, 1993; Cimoli and Dosi, 1995; Kim, 1997a; Lall, 1997), namely: (a) the competencies in terms of knowledge, skills and abilities that the human resources in science and technology (HRST) acquire and develop over time; (b) the existence of efficient interactive networks between the main actors in the system; and (c) the linkages with networks at an international level. Particularly, this chapter is focused on the HRST's recent evolution and their relationship with the other parts of the Mexican innovation system.

Most studies on innovation systems recognize that the competencies incorporated in HRST must be viewed as pre-competitive sources that determine the set of abilities and experiences that enable firms to purchase, utilize, adapt, improve and create technology efficiently at a micro level. Moreover, experts have recognized that a nation's HRST is the result of processes that are determined and addressed by different institutions and policies. There are three main actors in the process that develops HRST competencies: governmental agencies, higher education institutions (HEIs) and production system (firms and sectors). Governments establish norms, make decisions and carry out actions that have a significant impact on how HEIs and firms operate. They establish the rules of the game and develop the incentives within which the other two actors carry out their activities. HEIs provide education and research and development (R&D) services within such frameworks. It is important to stress that the upper secondary and tertiary level institutions are, in fact, the main sources for the HRST. Finally, the firms that employ personnel in production and R&D activities acquire and address the specific requirements for production activities: the competencies that are originated in the educational system.

The first section of this chapter describes the analytical approach through which the importance of the HRST is explained as a determinant for the performance and the linkages of the actors that participate in the NIS. The second analyses government's policy on higher education and science and technology activities. This text makes a comparative analysis of the Mexican government's participation in higher education (HE) and in science and technology (S&T), through the amount of funds that authorities spend on education and S&T. We then present a brief description and analysis of: (a) the flows of enrolments and outflows in the Mexican education system by levels of education, fields of knowledge and type of HEIs; (b) the HRST stock; and (c) a brief profile of the quality of education programmes in engineering and basic sciences. The following text concentrates on the interplay between HIEs and the productive system and on the analysis of the employment conditions for engineers and basic scientists. The final section presents conclusions.

HRST and their linkages with the NIS

International experience proves that for the NIS's effort, competences and perform-ance, a satisfactory interplay between the government, HEIs and firms depends on the quantity and quality of human resources that HEIs produce, as well as firms' adequate absorption of HEIs. Moreover, it is possible to claim that there is a positive correlation between the amount of HRST (together with the quality of training on a core set of basic knowledge and orientation towards the productive sector) and the NIS's performance.[1]

Furthermore, the risk of obtaining a low NIS performance is greatly reduced if there is a sufficient supply of highly skilled HRST (Chi-Ming and San, 1993; Kim, 1993, 1997a; Walker, 1993; Scott, 1995). In fact, upon observing those cases in which the NIS shows a poor performance, it can be readily seen that more often than not such a result is associated with policy failures, in the sense that policies favouring quantitative over qualitative increases in education were pursued. One of the most illustrative examples of such a failure is the Korean case (Kim, 1993, 1997a, 1997b). A second indication of a weak NIS is when the supply of highly skilled HR is not efficiently absorbed by the productive system. The most acute symptom of this is the so-called 'brain drain phenomenon', whose negative effects on NIS performance have been studied in Taiwan (Chi-Ming and San, 1993).

Policy failures are not limited to economies with a low per capita GDP. Several studies show that education policies in the UK, during the 1960s and 1970s, failed to provide proper incentives to include courses with a high technological content at the secondary education level, and there was also a lack of linkages with the productive sector. This policy resulted in poor training in technical-instrumental capacity and inferior problem-solving abilities in the engineering and basic sciences programmes (Walker, 1993; Scott, 1995). The importance that the absorption of HRST in the productive sector has on the NIS should come as no surprise (Vithlani, 1996; Hayward, 1997). Firms' strategies and decision-making processes ultimately depend on their management and labour force's professional profile; those firms in which engineers and scientists account for a relatively high share of the labour force are more apt to develop technological and organizational changes and to improve their performance, while their goals are clearly oriented towards growth.

On the basis of these premises, we develop the rest of this chapter considering the interaction of government policies related to HEIs, HRST competencies and link-ages with the production system. Three hypotheses support this analysis: (a) the first is that HRST competencies are, at least partially, a function of government and HEIs policies (e.g. expenditure on education and R&D); (b) the second argues that firms' technological capabilities are associated with HRST competencies and the firms' abilities to adapt and use these competencies at the production and manage-rial levels; (c) the last argues that another important element that configures the NIS is the interaction between competencies relative to HEIs and the abilities (skills, knowledge, etc.) required by a production system.

Throughout this text, the competencies related to HEIs (HRST stock and flows[2]) are measured through a variety of indicators, in order to identify changes in the composition, behaviour and distribution of enrolment in secondary and tertiary education levels (e.g. undergraduate and graduate levels). For graduate levels, the analysis is carried out according to several parameters, including field of knowledge (natural and exact sciences and engineering and technology[3]) and type of HEI (public and private, universities and technological institutions). Average growth rates are also computed for the period between 1985 and 1995, with special emphasis on the fields of knowledge particularly relevant to the NIS: basic sciences, engineering and technology.[4]

The interplay between competencies in the HEI and the production system is assessed using the following variables: employment by types of professional training; firms' personnel educational profiles; and firms' technical and innovative performance in relation to their educational profiles.[5]

Governmental policies

During the past 30 years, higher education and science and technology policies, in terms of the formation of human resources, have been characterized by three fundamental stages.

First, during the 1970s, the Mexican government paid special attention to higher education. The focus was on quantitative rather than qualitative results. Consequently, the higher education system grew in terms of the absolute number of enrolments,[6] as well as in the number of institutions and programmes.[7] To add to this effort, the National Council for Science and Technology (CONACYT) was created.

Second, during the 1980s, the expansion phase was affected by the severe economic crisis which began in 1982 and which caused significant reductions in the funding assigned to higher education (see Chapters 2 and 3 of this book). This especially affected public HEIs (specifically the universities, where 90 per cent of their income was derived from government subsidies). Financial restrictions also had a direct impact on university professors' salaries and on R&D and research equipment expenditures, such as for laboratories and workshops. At the end of this decade, most of the studies and evaluation agree that: (a) the graduate programmes had insufficient human resources and some had poorly qualified human resources for teaching, an inadequate stock of material and equipment for the research activities; (b) the content of such programmes was often poorly connected with long-term research and lacked relevant information on the labour market's requirements (CONACYT, 1987/8); (c) the weak relationship between secondary and tertiary (e.g. higher education) levels and the HEI's poor linkages (particularly public HEIs) with the production sector.

Third, at the beginning of the 1990s, policies were primarily oriented towards quality, the introduction of quality assessment and the creation of government funds for financing HEIs.[8] The aforementioned directions were supported by four mechanisms: (a) the National Research System, which seeks to be registry of researchers in

Mexico; (b) the Excellent Graduate Programmes Register, which classifies those academic programmes that due to their quality deserve special financial support from the government;[9] (c) the creation of a new type of HEI, the technological university,[10] which is based on close relationships with local industry in different parts of the nation (e.g. *Universidad Tecnológica de Aguascalientes, Universidad Tecnológica de Tula-Tepeji, Universidad Tecnológica de Netzahualcóyotl*); and (d) the creation of the Higher Education Modernization Fund (*Fondo para la Modernización de la Educación Superior*, FOMES), which grants additional support to the HEIs on the basis of specific projects directed towards the improvement of institutions.[11]

In summary, we can say that fundamental characteristics displayed by the higher education system throughout the past thirty years are: (a) weak linkages between different levels and institutions within the education system (Schmelkes, 1996); (b) low participation of private funds in the financial sources of universities; (c) failures in the implementation of evaluation policies; (d) resistance to evaluation by some HEIs and academics (Valenti and Varela, 1997) and the predominance of quantitative instead of qualitative evaluation; and (f) weak linkages between the higher education system and the productive sector (SEP, 1989; Muñoz Izquierdo, 1990, 1996; Bazúa and Valenti, 1991; Casas and Matilde, 1997b). Advances have also been made during the past ten years. Specifically, the general evaluation policy has produced a better information on the actual system in terms of how the HEIs function, and it has modified the decision-making processes at an institutional as well as at an individual level; it has notably stimulated professors' interest in graduate level studies, and has achieved an improvement in the wages paid to professors.

Government expenditure on education

Through different indicators, this section describes and compares government expenditures devoted to HE. The pattern of government expenditure on education was rather haphazard during the past twenty years, as a result of the financial crisis. During 1980–2, expenditure increased significantly compared to what was spent throughout the 1970s. Between 1983 and 1988, mainly due to the 1982 financial crisis, this amount decreased abruptly. However, from 1989 onwards, the government made a new and sustained effort to reach pre-crisis expenditure levels (Ornelas, 1995).Turning to total government expenditure on higher education as a percentage of the GDP, in 1992, Mexico displayed one of the lowest rates of higher education expenditure as a share of the GDP: 0.5 per cent, as against 1.2 per cent in the United States and 2.1 per cent in Canada (see Table 8.1). The third indicator refers to government expenditure on higher education as a percentage of total government expenditure: in 1995, direct government subsidy to higher education was 18 per cent of the total expenditure for the three principal education levels (other countries assigned a greater percentage: United States, 23%; Canada, 26%; Turkey, 35.6%). The fourth indicator considers higher education expenditure by source funds as a percentage of GDP: Mexico budgets a similar percentage of expenditure on HE as the other OECD countries. The difference compared to some of the more advanced OECD countries is that the share of direct government subsidies is greater in Mexico (77%) than the OECD mean (54%) (compare United States, 47%; Canada, 61%;

Table 8.1 Major Expenditure Indicators on Education and R&D

	Mexico	USA	Canada	Spain	UK	Turkey	OECD average
Public expenditure on HE (% GDP), 1992[f]	0.5	1.2	2.1	0.7	1.0	0.5[a]	n.ap.
HE expenditure by source of funds (% GDP), 1995[g]							
Direct public subsidies	0.8	1.1	1.5	0.8	0.7	0.8	0.9
Public subsidies to households	n.a.	0.02[b]	0.51	n.a.	0.19	0.05[b]	0.11
Private funds	0.24	1.24[b]	0.45	0.25	0.11	0.08[b]	0.67
Annual expenditure per student (US$ = PPP), 1995[g]							
Primary level	1,015	5,371	n.a.	2,628	3,328	710[b]	3,595
Secondary level	1,798	6,812	n.a.	3,455	4,246	510[b]	4,971
Tertiary level	5,071	16,262	11,471	4,944	7,225	3,460[b]	10,444
Expenditure on R&D (% GDP), 1998[h]	0.36[c]	2.8	1.6	0.9	1.9[d]	0.5[c]	2.2[d]
R&D expenditure by source of funds, 1997[h,i]							
Government	66.2[c]	31.9	32.3	43.6	30.8	56.6	31.4
Private	17.6[c]	64.3	48.9	44.7	49.5	36.8	62.3
Other funds	16.2[c]	3.8	18.7	11.6	19.8	6.6	3.8

[a]1980 data; [b]1994 data; [c]1995 data; [d]1997 data; [e]1996 data; n.a., not available; n.ap., not appropriate.
Sources: [f]World Bank, *World Development Indicators*, 1997; [g]OECD, *Education at a Glance, Indicators*, 1998; [h]OECD, *Science, Technology and Industry Scoreboard 1999: Benchmarking Knowledge-based Economies*, 1999; [i]CONACYT, *Indicadores de Actividades Científicas y Tecnológicas*, Mexico, 1996.

UK, 70%; Spain, 76%; Turkey, 86%). The fifth indicator refers to government expenditure per student and by education level. In 1995, Mexico registered one of the lowest levels of expenditures on education in each of the education levels (primary, secondary and tertiary) compared to the OECD mean (see Table 8.1). During 1995, Mexico (and Turkey) reported an average expenditure that was also lower than the OECD average; Mexico also registered more significant differences in expenditures at the different education levels, in particular between basic and higher education. During that same year, expenditure on higher education by students in Mexico was nearly six times greater than that for basic education, while this ratio was only slightly greater than 3:1 for the other OECD countries. In other words, Mexico not only spent less per student, but this expenditure was also highly unbalanced in terms of the educational level.

From the above trends, we can conclude, comparatively with other developed economies, that fewer resources are addressed to HE by Mexico. Moreover, financial resources are allocated according to cyclical economic crisis. Finally, private funding of education is scarce.[12] Diverse diagnoses have shown that policies and resources are oriented to support quantity achievement, with little regulation concerning quality (e.g. the stimulation of competitiveness among the HEIs for funding based on quality and results and a low presence of logic in accountability within the HES: Bazúa, 1997; Valenti and del Castillo, 1997; Kent, 1998).

Human resources in science and technology

Government participation in S&T also has a central role in terms of the competencies. This participation is shown by the following indicators. The first refers to expenditure on S&T as a percentage of GDP. Mexico lags notably in comparison to other OECD countries. Mexico's R&D expenditure amounts to 0.36 per cent of GDP, much lower than the OECD average and much lower than the expenditure levels of the leading countries (OECD average, United States) or even those of Canada and Spain (see Table 1). The second indicator corresponds to R&D expenditure by source funds. In Mexico, the majority of the funds assigned to R&D activities come from the government, while in the United States and Canada the majority of the financial resources for R&D come from private funds (see Table 8.1). The third corresponds to the number of scientists, engineers and technicians involved in R&D. In countries with more dynamic economies and a higher R&D expenditure, personnel devoted to these activities are counted in thousands per million of population, while in Mexico there are only 213 scientists and engineers and 73 technicians (per million of population) engaged in these activities (see Table 8.2). Within the OECD, Mexico and Turkey have the lowest absolute number of R&D personnel. The fourth indicator refers to the number of people devoted to R&D in the productive sector. In 1995, Mexico had only 4,466 people devoted to R&D working in the productive sector, while the UK had 146,000 (Table 8.2). Even more revealing than the sheer number of people is the fact that only 12 per cent of the total personnel engaged in R&D are within the productive sector in Mexico, whereas this sector accounts for up to 50 per cent of such personnel in other countries. This shortage of R&D personnel is more clearly visible in the results from the 1996 national survey on organizational and technological change, in which only a few of the firms surveyed claimed to hire personnel with graduate degrees. Furthermore, even in those cases, highly qualified personnel accounted for a remarkably low share of the total number of employees, whereas the firms with rates that were slightly higher were those with a large proportion of foreign capital.

A comparative analysis of the four indicators in their totality shows that Mexico budgets less financial resource for R&D, and there is a shortage of private funding sources, the same as in higher education. Human resources are even more scarce; but the rate of growth of human resources is very significant.[13] Another element in the case of Mexico is that the human capital dedicated to S&T is mainly employed by the public sector (universities and research centres); this shows, as we demonstrate below, that there is a lack of coordination between the private productive sector and the public education system.

Primary, lower secondary level and enrolment in HEIs

The features that characterize the basic education level (primary and lower secondary) and enrolment in HEIs are as follows. At the basic education level, important advances have been observed in the rate of school attendance by age group, in that it is quite similar to the level in the advanced countries, particularly at the primary level and to a lesser degree at the lower secondary level, with some lags above all in rural zones. However, there are problems in the quality of the teaching–learning process and in the type of competencies that, in terms of knowledge, the students

Table 8.2 Indicators of Human Resources

	Mexico	USA	Canada	Spain	UK	Turkey	OECD average
Educational enrolment (% of age group), 1996[f]							
Secondary level	61	97	105	122	133	56	n.ap.
Tertiary level	15[a]	81	90	51	50	18	n.ap.
Scientists and engineers on R&D per million persons, 1985–95[f]							
Scientists and engineers	213	3,732	2,656	1,210	2,417	261	n.ap.
Technicians	73	n.ap.	1,073	342	1,019	26	n.ap.
Scientists and engineers (% labour force aged 25–34), 1994[g]	434	887.1	698.4	658.8	1,186.8	440.7	744.8
% population aged 25–64 completed tertiary level, 1996[h]	3.7[b]	26	17	13	13	6	13[c]
Total R&D personnel, 1995[i]	33,297	n.a.	129,359[d]	79,988	270,000[d]	18,498	n.a.
Personnel devoted to R&D in universities and firms, 1995[j]							
Universities	19,433	962,700[d]	76,554[d]	47,857[e]	146,000[e]	15,854	n.a.
Firms	4,466	n.a.	65,225[e]	27,321[e]	148,000	3,634	n.a.

[a]1997 data; [b]1995 data; [c]OECD total data; [d]1993 data; [e]1994 data; n.a., not available; n.ap., not appropriate.
Sources: [f]World Bank, *World Development Indicators*, 1999; [g]OECD, *Education at a Glance, Indicators*, 1996; [h]OECD, *Science, Technology and Industry Scoreboard 1999: Benchmarking Knowledge-based Economies*, 1999; [i]OECD, *Basic Science and Technology Statistics*, 1997; [j]OECD, *Main Science and Technology Statistics*, 1997.

acquire at this education level, as shown by Guevara Niebla (1992), Schmelkes (1996) and Santos (1999) which point out that a significant part of the student population at this level shows at least three learning problems: (a) low levels of performance in general knowledge; (b) low levels of ability in terms of the development of capacity and logical structure as the basis for future acquisition of scientific and technical knowledge and abilities (specifically in terms of knowledge in maths and natural sciences); and (c) a weak orientation towards a technological culture, particularly at the lower secondary level. These deficiencies, which are formed at the basic level, affect the academic development of many students as they continue through the upper secondary and tertiary education levels.

The upper secondary education level shows one of the lowest rates (61%) of enrolment by typical age group (Table 8.2). In addition, the number of students enrolled in secondary education as a percentage of total population aged 5–29 is only 4 per cent, while the OECD average is well above 10 per cent. Statistical evidence has shown that young people in Mexico have less inclination to engage in technological training in upper secondary education than in the more advanced economies. In 1992, the percentage of young people engaged in these types of programmes was 42 per cent in Mexico; the proportion in countries such as France, Italy and Germany was greater than 50 per cent.[14] It should be mentioned that the least attractive option seems to be professional technical education (in 1994 it represented only 18.1 per cent of total enrolment at the upper secondary level in Mexico). Although the programmes offered in professional technological education are purportedly designed to meet the productive sector's needs, little of the basic theoretical and instrumental training that is essential in forming a good technician is provided.[15]

The weak ties between the production system and the education system have to do with *failures* at the upper secondary level and the low technological opportunities of the productive sector. At the upper secondary level, the programmes of study with a technological orientation are rigid in more than one sense. First, it may be impossible to continue studies (in that they are terminal degree programmes); second, it has not been possible to coordinate quality models to transmit scientific-technological knowledge (Bracho, 1990); third, the exchange with the productive sector in most cases is limited to social service and professional scholarly internships. In terms of the productive sector, the problems are of a distinct nature: first, employees do not believe that technical education degrees are desirable (Villa Lever, 1996); second, the great majority of the companies, particularly the micro and small companies, do not have the capacity to modernize, which means that they have a very scant demand for technically specialized human resources.

At the tertiary level (undergraduate and graduate or postgraduate studies) the following tendencies were observed: in 1997, at the international level Mexico show the lowest rates of enrolment by typical age group (15 per cent) with respect to other countries, such as the United States, the UK, Spain and other Latin America countries (Table 8.2).[16] From the mid–1980s to the mid–1990s, in Mexico the annual growth rate for enrolment in engineering was one of the largest, similar to that of countries with developed and dynamic economies, with the exception of the United States.[17] Between 1985 and 1995, significant growth was observed for the first time enrolment rate for private HEIs,[18] compared to public HEIs, at both education levels. At the undergraduate level, the annual growth rate for public HEIs was much less (1.1 per cent) than for private HEIs (7.8 per cent). At the graduate level, the annual growth rate for private institutions was nearly double (12 per cent) that of the public institutions (6.3 per cent). This change in trends may be explained by two causes: (a) the degree of saturation of public universities' enrolments; (b) students' recent preference for a particular type of private HEI, in which programmes are more closely linked with the production system and firms via the HEIs' network of relations and the institutions' accrued prestige.

Flows in the HEIs by field of knowledge

The analysis of HEI flows is made on the basis of two key indicators: first-time enrolment rate (inflows) and completion rate (outflows) from the higher education system according to levels, undergraduate and graduate (postgraduate) from 1985 to 1995. Both indicators are analysed according to type of HEI (public and private, universities and technological institutions) and by fields of knowledge.

At the undergraduate and graduate levels, first-time enrolment according to type of HEI and by field of knowledge shows the following tendencies for the 1985–95 period. Growth of the annual first time enrolment rate at a graduate level (7.4 per cent[19]) is greater than that at the undergraduate level (2.2 per cent). In Mexico, there is also higher enrolment in the area of engineering and technology than in basic sciences, at both undergraduate and graduate levels. In 1995, first-time enrolment in undergraduate education showed a notable concentration in engineering and tech-nology, representing up to 32 per cent of total first-time enrolment. Conversely, first-time enrolment in natural and exact sciences was just 2 per cent. At the graduate level, the figures show that the area of engineering and technology concentrates 16.03 per cent of the total first time enrolment students at a national level, while natural and exact sciences accounts for 5.69 per cent.

For the same period at the graduate level, the highest annual growth rate was for engineering (10.2 per cent) and natural and exact sciences (9.9 per cent). At the undergraduate level, from 1985 to 1995, first-time enrolment in engineering and technology showed greater growth in public technological institutes. Enrolment in universities and private technological institutes remained predominantly within the administrative and social sciences. Despite the fact that enrolment in public universities is more diverse, it is in these institutions that the majority of basic scientists are trained, while private universities have practically no students in these fields. Enrolment in natural and exact sciences in public or private technological institutes is also low. At the graduate level, the greatest increase in enrolment in graduate courses in engineering and technology was in private technological institutions. Enrolment in natural and exact sciences increased more in public and private universities. Such dynamics in private HEIs can be partially explained by the low number of students that had been attending these institutions in 1985.

Although the absolute number of highly skilled human resources has increased, firms have not fully felt the direct impact on their innovative performance. The majority of these resources remain within the academic sector[20] because firms have a low demand for highly skilled personnel, and because of the weakness of the linkages between HEIs and industry, particularly in terms of R&D activities (Casas and Luna, 1997b). We can also see that public and private universities have a distinct integration model with the productive sector. Based on some studies of graduates (ITESM, 1993; Valenti *et al.*, 1997) and on interviews with experts, it is possible to infer that there are two different models for the way in which graduates form part of the labour market, depending on whether they have studied in public or private institutions. The graduates from public HEIs tend to occupy intermediate and high level positions in activities directly linked to the firms' productive processes. The graduates from private HEIs (e.g. *Instituto Tecnológico y Estudios Superiores de Monterrey*) work in management areas that are more linked to management activities.

Completion rates

The Mexican education system is characterized by low efficiency in its completion rate. According to SEP data, in 1994 the national average of titled graduate students, six years after enrolment, was under 30 per cent (Reséndiz Núñez, 1998). If the rate of non-graduate students is considered, completion efficiency for 1995 increases to 70 per cent, in terms of students enrolled five years earlier. This last figure marks an increase in the rate of completion efficiency from the 1985–90 period, which was close to 50 per cent. Between 1984 and 1994, the total outflows annual growth rate more than doubled for those registered in first-time enrolments (4.8 and 2.3 per cent, respectively); the greatest share of these corresponds to business and social sciences and engineering. Conversely, the natural and exact sciences' outflows growth rate was notably small and even negative in some instances.[21] Public technological institutes contributed more engineering and technology graduates, whereas at the postgraduate level the natural and exact sciences were runners up in HRST output for the period, particularly from public universities.

Graduate levels reveal the dynamics of postgraduate studies: between 1984 and 1994, the annual growth rate for completion was 10.5 per cent, while at the undergraduate level the value was 4.8 per cent. However, the baseline for these increases is quite small in absolute numbers.

Analysis of the first-time enrolment rate and completion rate at the tertiary level helps us to infer that, at least in the short term, the technological capacity with regard to human resources is mostly characterized by professionals in the area of engineering and technology, compared to a very small share of professionals in the natural and exact sciences. In the medium and long term, the tendency improves at a postgraduate level.

From the perspective of developing a NIS, there are two worrying trends that should be addressed: on the one hand, the HEIs generate insufficient technological competencies, since fewer and fewer people are trained in basic and exact sciences; and, on the other, the productive sector has a poor absorption rate for basic and exact scientists, since the stock of scientists is employed mostly in the education sector. In addition, the academic formation that engineers receive is more diversified, since it combines knowledge and application, while the education that the basic scientists receive is more one-dimensional. The formation that the engineers receive allows them to insert themselves in different areas and moments in the productive processes, which does not happen with the scientists whose professional formation leaves them with less ability to do this. In this way, the labour market favours engineers more than scientists (Bosworth, 1981; Valenti *et al.*, 1997).

HRST stock between 1985 and 1995

Given that the HEIs are the source of HRST stock, it was considered appropriate to review these institutions' output rate, as well as other types of indictors that show the low availability of HRST in Mexico, from different points of view. These indicators are as follows.

In Mexico, there is a low rate of enrolment (3.7 per cent) at the tertiary education level for the 25–64 age group. Other OECD countries register much greater rates, such as the United States (26 per cent) and Canada (17 per cent) (Table 8.2).

During 1985–95, of the total number of professionals that graduated at a national level (1,424,014), nearly 30 per cent were in the areas of engineering and technology and the natural and exact sciences. This output flow represents approximately 129,500 graduates per year, of which 36,754 pertain to our fields of interest.[22] According to data from the 1990 Census, of all the professionals that graduated from the two areas of interest for this chapter, human resources in science and technology accounted for 21.9 per cent of total employed professionals.[23] Of this percentage, 16.3 per cent were engineers and technologists and 5.6 per cent were natural and basic science professionals. Of all the graduates employed in activities directly related to productivity, engineers and technical personnel represent 19.4 per cent of this human resource, whereas natural and basic science professionals account for 2.6 per cent. Total output from engineering and from the natural and exact sciences in 1992 represented 8.2 per cent of the economically active population within the 25–34 age range. In contrast, in the United States, Canada and Spain, availability of tertiary level human resources in the two areas is at least 16 per cent of this age group for the economically active population.

About quality in curricula

The behaviour of the first-time enrolment rate and the completion rate at the tertiary level have been accompanied by a government policy that introduced several evaluation mechanisms aimed at identifying quality setbacks in higher education. Among these mechanisms two dealt directly with quality in higher education: the Registry of Excellent Graduate Programmes (*Padrón de Excelencia de Posgrados*) maintained by CONACYT, and the Interinstitutional Committees for Evaluating Higher Education (*Comités Interinstitucionales para la Evaluación de la Educación Superior*) or CIEES, which forms part of the National Commission for Higher Education (*Comisión Nacional para la Educación Superior*) or CONPES.

These committees have had to deal with a lack of objective and reliable information regarding the professional careers of graduates, together with the assessment of employers and of graduates themselves, concerning the suitability of graduate training in meeting the private sector's present and future needs. In addition, these committees face the absence of a methodology to carry out such evaluations in terms of quality and pertinence parameters. Recently, efforts were made to overcome these deficiencies, mainly by the CIEES, CONACYT and CENEVAL.[24]

Despite these challenges, throughout the past four years the CIEES for engineering and basic sciences have been designing their own reference frameworks and methodologies. They have made substantial advances in the assessment of the quality and relevance of the professional training that public HEIs (universities and technological institutes) offer in their respective fields. The problems that have been detected can be classified into four areas: (a) a lack of highly skilled academic personnel who keep up to date in their field of study; (b) the use of obsolete teaching methods that fail to utilize recent technological advances in the teaching–learning process and poor development of problem-solving skills, fundamentally those in basic sciences; (c) poorly equipped and often archaic workshops and laboratories, which are inadequate for training in experimentation and application models, and a lack of textbooks that combine theory and concepts with instrumental training; and (d) misconceptions regarding the current formation, specifically between scientific formation and the formation of scientists.

Interplay with the production system

In Mexico, the principal characteristics of employment conditions and salaries, according to areas of study, are as follows:

1. There is a marked difference in the job opportunities available for engineers and basic scientists. In Mexico, engineers are employed in both the secondary and tertiary sectors of the economy, while job opportunities for basic scientists lie predominantly within the education sector.
2. Although the patterns of absorption of engineers into the labour market in Mexico are similar to those observed in other countries, this is not necessarily

the case for scientists. In other countries, scientists are employed in industry, government and professional services.

3.   The labour market induces particular dynamics in the flows of human resources, and two facts are clearly discernible: (a) engineers usually enjoy better positions and salaries than those offered to basic scientists (this is particularly true in the case of young professionals); (b) job opportunities for engineers are much more diversified among the different economic sectors (INEGI, 1993; Valenti *et al.*, 1997).[25] It should be noted that this trend is also present in other countries.

To sum up, this employment pattern provides a warning sign of the extremely rigid conditions that prevail, not only in the supply of education services in the natural and exact sciences, but also in the absorption of these resources by the productive sector. These findings should serve as a guide for the HEIs in terms of the ties that they should seek with the workplace. Because professionals in industry and services are facing increasing demands on their performance, the degree of adjustment in training programmes, with the workplace's demands in mind, is a key element in any NIS performance. Indeed, professionals are dealing with more intense pressures to achieve higher levels of knowledge, intellectual skills, attitude, aptitude, leadership and teamwork (Valenti *et al.*, 1997). These results coincide with the observations concerning the assessment of the quality and relevance of professional training that the CIEES carried out for engineering and basic sciences, as was discussed in the previous section.

Firms' training profile

Some insight on what happens at the micro (firm) level comes from the analysis of two national surveys: the Technological and Organizational Change Survey (ENACTO), and the Survey on Employment, Salaries, Technologies and Training in the Manufacturing Sector (ENESTYC).

The results obtained from the ENACTO survey show that there is a significant relationship between the human resources' education level and the firm's techno-logical profile: the higher the proportion of skilled employees, the greater the firm's propensity to incorporate modern technology. This is also relevant to the firm's innovative performance. It is important to remember that the firm's innovative capacity is assessed by the new products, processes or services it introduces and by its R&D efforts. Despite the poor absorption rates for professionals, only a low proportion of firms hire personnel with no instruction at all. In summary, two facts are worth noting: (a) few firms hire personnel with graduate studies and in those that do they are a very small proportion of the total; and (b) the hiring of trained personnel is more numerous in firms with a high share of foreign capital.

Similar findings were extracted from ENESTYC. What makes this analysis important is that the technological sector[27] is the principal determining variable, given that there are significant variations in the education profiles of employees within the different technological sectors. The following tendencies can be seen through the indicators:

1.   Productivity *indexes*[28] by sector. The scale-intensive sector has the highest productivity, with science-based industries coming in second. Productivity

indexes are lower for the remaining two sectors, supplier-dominated and specialized suppliers.

2.   The firm's innovative profile (as measured by product and process innovation). Of all the firms that innovate, the greatest proportion of innovative firms incorporate a higher number of personnel who have completed tertiary education.[29] The relationship between the firms' education profiles and their propensity to innovate was particularly noticeable in the science-based sector.

3.   Type of machinery and equipment. The survey discovered that computerized equipment is mainly introduced in the sectors with a more highly skilled labour force, while manual machinery and equipment is more prevalent in firms belonging to those technological sectors that have lower training profiles.

4.   The opening of Mexico's economy to increased foreign trade had a positive impact on productivity in the companies that possess the human competencies to increase productivity.

In summary, in Mexico, as well as in other countries, human capital is a determining variable in innovation processes. In particular, human capital has played a significant role in the companies that have modernized during the economic opening. However, personnel with a high level of preparation still have a low participation in the productive sector, given that the majority of the productive system is formed by micro and small companies that have not entered the technological modernization.

Conclusions

Some of the most important efforts and competencies in an innovation system are those incorporated in the HRST, which can be viewed as a pre-competitive source that determines the set of abilities and experiences which enable firms to purchase, utilize, adapt, improve and create technology efficiently on a micro level.

There are three main actors in the process of the development of HRST competencies: government or governmental agencies, HEIs and production system (firms and sectors). Governments set norms, make decisions and carry out actions that have a significant impact on the operation of HEIs and firms, formulating the rules of the game and the incentives within which the other two actors carry out their activities. The HEIs provide education and R&D services within such a framework. Finally, firms hire their personnel, who are products of the education services, for their own development as well as the development of their R&D services, in this way defining their productive performance. Several issues and results are relevant here.

Throughout this chapter, we have identified the following tendencies: (a) insufficient amount of HRST; (b) the recent introduction of quality assessment and accountability of government funds destined for the HEIs; (c) a low participation of private funds in the public HEIs and in R&D activities; (d) a growing importance of private HEIs compared to public HEIs; (e) weak linkages between the upper secondary and tertiary education levels; (f) insufficient education quality in the distinct education levels (from the primary levels); (g) limited ties between the education system and the productive system (with distinct linkage models for the public and private universities). Some of them need further explanation.

Over the past thirty years, government and educational organizations devoted special attention to the development of their secondary and tertiary education levels. During the 1970s and part of the 1980s, this led to policies in which implementation was mainly oriented to fostering enrolment at these levels, although there was little concern about quality or results.

Since 1985 there has been significant growth in enrolment in engineering programmes, and there has also been an increase in the importance of public technological institutes. Basic and exact sciences, on the other hand, have shown signs of stagnation, in particular at the undergraduate level, in which public universities have catered for the greatest portion of students in these fields. Although efforts have been made, Mexico's supply of technicians, engineers and scientists is still insufficient, as are its enrolments at the secondary and tertiary levels. This is particularly true when compared to the enrolment rates for the typical age groups at each level in other OECD countries. Another important issue is the low number of personnel employed in R&D activities, and the fact that R&D is oriented towards government research centres and universities.

Enrolment rates at the graduate level are low, since the vast majority of students select business and social sciences. The growing trend in enrolment, specifically in social and administrative sciences and engineering and technology, could indicate that the increasing preferences for certain programmes, in particular over the past ten years, has been greatly influenced by the job opportunities available in the labour market. In addition, it is also a symptom of the problems that the public HEIs have in resolving their operational problems, particularly in the area of teaching. The growth rates for enrolment in tertiary level institutions was greater in the private than in the public HEIs.

The quality standards and curricular flexibility throughout the HEI's programmes have not been encouraged with the same effort as enrolment. An important implication of this issue can be seen in the prevalence of obsolete programmes which do not address the problems associated with the acquisition of the problem-solving skills that professionals demand. These programmes do not encourage research activities at the graduate level, and they fail to provide important linkages with the productive system. Some reasons can be identified: (a) an inconsistent history of expenditure on education and R&D; (b) the low participation of private funds in HE and R&D; and (c) a lack of emphasis on the outcome and impact of the training that HEIs offer, a trend that began to reverse itself during the 1990s.

Since Mexican firms show low R&D intensities and hire few professional employees, and even fewer highly trained human resources (e.g. PhDs), there is a poor absorption rate for HRST within firms. This low human resource profile has greatly hindered proper linkages with the production system within the Mexican NIS at a time when firms' performance often depends on the cognitive and technological competencies of their human resources. Empirical evidence has shown that the firms that hire larger proportions of engineers and professionals show a greater propensity to introduce modern technology and innovate. The opposite is also true: the firms that have fewer professionals within their labour force seem to have rather stagnant innovation and technological profiles.

A still unresolved challenge is to consolidate a technological education subsystem that would be responsible for training technicians, engineers and scientists. It has not been possible to make scientific and technological studies attractive from the lower secondary to the tertiary education level. There are two principal factors that contribute to this situation: first, there is a lack of linkages between academic programmes at the different education levels; and, second, science graduates receive lower salaries than other types of professionals (for example, engineers). The chances of science graduates finding better jobs are also fewer than for engineers, because the productive sector does not always have the conditions to absorb these graduates, since they carry out scant R&D activities and they innovate very little (see Parts 1 and 3 of this book).

Notes

1. In countries such as the UK, Korea and Taiwan, the building and/or rebuilding of HRST competencies was possible, to a great extent, because of the central role education played in the process of linkages with the production system (Kim, 1993, 1997a, 1997b; Walker, 1993; Scott, 1995). Similarly, the reforms introduced in higher education systems during the 1980s in countries such as the UK, Germany, the Netherlands, Spain and Sweden were centred on fostering and perfecting linkages with the production system. Special emphasis was placed on ensuring the quality of the teaching–learning processes and better developing the programmes and formation profiles, keeping in mind the productive sector's needs in different technological specializations (Hunter, 1981; Brennan *et al.*, 1996).

2. Stock should be understood as the data concerning the availability of the amount of HRST, in a particular geographical unit and at a certain moment (OECD, 1997a). Flows should be understood as the movement or behaviour of HRST over a period of time, usually a calendar year.

3. In this document, basic sciences includes natural and exact sciences, and engineering and technology includes all engineering careers, architecture and industrial and graphic design.

4. We accomplish this by using international indicators compiled and published by organizations such as the OECD, UNESCO and the World Bank. For Mexico, the data used in the analysis are mainly extracted from official information sources, including ANUIES (National Association of Universities and Institutes for Higher Education), CONACYT (National Council for Science and Technology) and INEGI (National Institute for Statistics, Geography and Systems), as well as from the results of several national surveys regarding employment, technological change and R&D in firms and institutions. In addition, this comparative analysis is based on the mean value of selected indicators for the OECD region versus their values for the Mexican case. Some data are also contrasted with the UK, a country with a heavily industrialized economy, and with two other nations with intermediate development that have a greater similarity to Mexico, namely Spain and Turkey. Mexico's two major trading partners are also reviewed (e.g. the United States and Canada), and finally data from other Latin American countries are utilized whenever possible.

5. The data utilized in this part of the study rely heavily on different surveys together with two longitudinal studies on the graduates from two large universities, one public and the other private: *Encuesta Nacional sobre Cambio Tecnológico y Organizacional* (National Survey on Technologial and Organizational Change,ENACTO); *Encuesta Nacional de Empleo, Salarios, Tecnología y Capacitación en el Sector Manufacturero (National Survey on Employment, Wages, Technology and Training in the Manufacturing Sector,* ENESTYC*); Encuesta sobre Investigación y Desarrollo Experimental* (Survey on Experimental Research and Development, IDE-1993).

6. Between 1970 and 1984 enrolment in graduate studies increased by 550 per cent and in undergraduate studies by 389 per cent.

7. Special attention was also devoted to two other issues: (a) enrolments and programmes at the graduate level; (b) the creation of a binary higher education system, which was designed to incorporate both universities and technological institutions.

8. The new mechanism that the government favoured was the allocation of additional special funding, guided by the results of an evaluation procedure. These changes fundamentally were: (a) incremental funding for HEIs with ties to projects designed to improve institutions; (b) incremental funding for graduate studies scholarships for Mexican students in Mexico or abroad; (c) incremental funding for domestic research; (d) special funding programmes designed to link HEIs and industry; and (e) incremental incomes for research based on academic productivity.

9. This growing interest resulted in a comprehensive reassessment of national graduate programmes, which CONACYT organized in 1985. Nowdays, CONACYT manages 80 per cent of the government funds destined to grant scholarships to postgraduates students, in national postgraduate programmes and programmes abroad.

10. In 1991, from the perspective of the formation of human resources, one of the responses to the opening of the Mexican economy to increased trade was the creation of a system of technological universities, inspired on the French model, the *Instituts Universitaire de Technologie*. The purpose is to form mid-level technicians (ISCED 5) using a pedagogical model that incorporates ties with the productive sector (Villa Lever, 1996). Mexico now has 36 technological universities, which are distributed throughout 19 states.

11. The FOMES is oriented towards the following aspects: (a) developing the human factor; (b) modernizing administration; (c) influencing the transformation of the structures that organize the teaching–learning process; (d) expanding coverage of demand for educational services; (e) intra- and inter-institutional linkages of actions in the HES; (f) linkages among education levels; (g) promoting the development of areas of excellence that strengthen the national identity; and (h) strengthening university linkages.

12. Other studies show that education requires constant and balanced spending to succeed; this spending must be targeted at securing a predetermined quality level. Thus, it is necessary to develop an appropriate combination of expenditure policies and to design and implement mechanisms that guarantee that institutions have adequate performance, placing special emphasis on academic programmes. The more developed countries, in which a NIS is consolidated, are characterized by having consistently maintained a substantial expenditure on education over a number of decades, as well as by their efficiency in allocating this expenditure (Germany, Japan).

13. Today, Mexico and Turkey show the highest annual growth rates for R&D expenditures; in general, these types of rates are associated with countries that show lesser economic development within the OECD area, probably reflecting the greater effort that these nations make to improve their capacities. In addition, the number of people engaged in R&D activities within Mexico's productive sector grew considerably in 1994, presumably due to the new S&T policies adopted since 1990.

14. OECD data, various issues from 1996 to 1997.

15. For example, the CONALEP *(Colegio Nacional de Educación Profesional Técnica)* (1994) study shows that the majority of its graduates are employed in the service sector, particularly in computer departments, trade and administrative areas, while a lesser share is employed by industry. In general, technical secondary education has not been successful in enabling graduates to apply efficiently their acquired knowledge in the workplace; the result has been an extremely low supply of qualified technicians.

16. Furthermore, fewer than 10 per cent of enrolments at the tertiary level are for post-graduate studies.

17. For more information, consult the NSF's Science and Engineering Indicators (1998, Chapter 2).

18. For the specific case of Latin America, Vessuri (1993) explains that it can be observed, as of late, that public HEIs have lost importance in the formation of human resources compared to private HEIs, especially in terms of tertiary education (post-secondary) and higher education. He argues that this shift in enrolment trends is the outcome, among other things, of the relative ease with which private HEIs can address particular demands, as well as the high academic quality of their staff and lecturers.

19. It is important to consider this figure cautiously, given that the absolute numbers from which it is formed are very small.

20. Even though there is no generalized empirical evidence on this issue, these authors claim that such is the case, supported by the notably low R&D activity level that Mexican firms report (OECD, 1996a, 1997b, e) and by the results of the study on graduate students upon completion of their studies at *UAM-Iztapalapa* (Valenti *et al.*, 1993).

21. The decreasing interest in basic sciences in Mexico can be considered to mean that the supply of scientists has been greatly reduced. In addition to their already reduced share in the total number of employed professionals according to the 1990 National Population Census, enrolments and outflows from 1985 to 1995 followed a decreasing trend. Even though the general overview of human resources in engineering is somewhat more positive, it can be considered as a cause for concern.

22. Despite the low availability of HRST during 1985–95, the specific weight of engineering and technology and the natural and exact science areas in the total graduate register grew from 25 per cent in 1985 to 30 per cent in 1995. Engineering and technology grew even more markedly. At the postgraduate level, 17.5 per cent of the 120,699 students that completed their postgraduate studies relate directly to the two areas of study. Again, at the masters and specialization levels, engineering and technology prevailed over the natural and exact sciences. However, in doctorate studies the latter surpassed the former. The average yearly output at the postgraduate level was 10,969 graduates.

23. Data were calculated using the 1990 *Censo de los Profesionistas en México* (The Mexican Professionals Census), Mexico, INEGI, 1993.

24. The National Evaluation Centre for Higher Education (*Centro Nacional de Evaluación para la Educación Superior*) or CENEVAL has participated in several of these evaluation processes, albeit at the individual level through the application of knowledge tests.

25. According to the study on UAM graduates, there are four elements that tend to have a greater incidence on the probability of obtaining high remuneration in professional performance: the field of study; a high academic performance during studies; a successful insertion in the labour market after completing studies; and a job in the private productive sector.

26. An empirical study carried out in the UK (Bosworth, 1981) found that the patterns of insertion in the labour market are quite different for engineers and scientists; the kind of training that each one receives is an important determinant in this difference.

27. The technological sectors considered herein are those defined by Pavitt, namely: science-based, specialized suppliers, scale-intensive and supplier-dominated.

28. Productivity is calculated as follows: added value/total employees (Casar *et al.*, 1990).

29. Firms were classified by their labour force's education profile, according to the following criteria. Firms with low-skilled labour force are firms where at least 50 per cent of the labour force has completed primary education. Firms with high-skilled labour force are those where at least 25 per cent of the labour force has completed tertiary education.

CHAPTER NINE

University, Knowledge Production and Collaborative Patterns with Industry

R. Casas, R. de Gortari and M. Luna

Introduction

This chapter analyses the general characteristics of the scientific base accumulated in institutions of higher education (HEIs) and the way in which research activities developed by these institutions[1] relate to the innovation activities within firms. The aim of the chapter is to identify the forms by which knowledge flows between the two sectors.

There are three arguments which support this chapter: the first relates to the non-linear model of innovation, which is conceived as an interwoven process, possible by virtue of complex interactions between firms and other sectors, such as educational institutions and government agencies (Nelson and Rosenberg, 1993; Gibbons *et al.*, 1994; Etzkowitz and Leydesdorff, 1997; Cimoli and della Giusta, 2000). The second argument relies on the importance of the university scientific base in the innovation process; those institutions, considered to be repositories of basic research, are proving to play a relevant role in that process. However, their participation does not seem to be direct, but adopts an indirect path, making the non-linear model of innovation more plausible.[2] The role of universities in countries such as Mexico is particularly important as in universities are concentrated the greater part of scientific competencies for knowledge production. The third argument refers to two differentiated orientations of university–industry collaboration: one is related to collaborations based on human resource training, mainly professionals, and the other focuses on collaborative activities based on scientific research, in which researchers, professors and postgraduates involved in HEI research activities participate together in attending to specific demands from industries. This chapter focuses on the second orientation.

The study of the relationship between HEI scientific competencies and the manner in which networks of links are set up with firms is carried out on two levels of analysis that are related to the general methodology for the study of the Mexican innovation system:

1. On a macro level of analysis, an assessment is made of the scientific competencies which universities possess as compared to those generated in government institutions and in industry. By the use of different indicators, their

historic development and specific characteristics are identified and compared against international indicators. From this, HEI general scientific and technological capacities can be inferred.

2. On a meso level of analysis, the links between the university scientific base and industry are identified. The aim is to discuss, on the one hand, the magnitude of this phenomenon and, on the other, the dynamics of those interactions. The magnitude is assessed by means of quantitative indicators previously obtained from surveys applied to both HEIs and firms. The dynamics of relationships are analysed by means of qualitative indicators elaborated from different sources. A taxonomy is built on both types of indicators. This chapter highlights the regional outlook and identifies those fields of research in which collaborations are more dynamic, with an attempt to determine whether this aspect relates to the various types of HEIs, their research competencies and the economic characteristics of the regions.

Evolution and current trends of science competencies[3]

In universities in Mexico as well as in other developing countries are concentrated the country's greatest efforts in science, which has for the most part been supported by government budgets. This fact contrasts with the very low participation of industry in research and development (R&D) activities and its financing.

Historically and in very broad terms with regard to the evolution of science and technology (S&T) policies, specific players and institutions have held the role in the promotion of this kind of activity, of which different stages can be identified: (a) in the first stage, the academic elite was the main participant, promoting support for S&T activities during the 1970s, this being continued by the government in the early 1980s; (b) industry and the market emerged as the main players in S&T policies by the end of the 1980s; (c) an interactive, or networking model for policy-making, involving the joint participation of all three sectors, appears to be the feature of the 1990s (Casas and Luna, 1997b). It is worth mentioning that the last type of arrangement is very closely related to a non-linear conception of innovation and, therefore, to a relative increase in collaborations between universities and industry.

During the 1970s, research capacities were concentrated to a large extent in Mexico City (which contributed 75 per cent of the human resources devoted to R&D) and particularly in the National Autonomous University of Mexico (UNAM). At that time, as occurred in other Latin American countries, the role of science and technology was reassessed by government. From 1971 to 1981, the federal expenditure on S&T[4] tripled as a percentage of the gross domestic product (GDP), increasing from 0.15 to 0.46 per cent (Lustig, 1989). Consequently, universities experienced unprecedented growth in enrolment and a significant increase in research capacities due to the allocation of resources to improve infrastructure and the creation of new institutions.[5] On the other hand, the early 1980s were characterized by the dominant authority of the government in an extensive planning project and in the definition of S&T development priorities. During the middle half of this decade, also characterized by a severe economic crisis, GDP fell by 26 per cent and federal expenditure experienced a negative growth (Lustig *et al.*, 1989, p. 19). Research salaries also experienced a considerable drop. Within this context, the National System of Researchers (SNI)[6] was founded in 1984 to reverse the negative trends and the depression of research activities. This stage was characterized by an institutional approach to S&T development, very similar to a linear model of innovation, having as its main goal an increase in the S&T supply. This view was complementary to that of the private sector: within the framework of a closed economy and protectionist policies relative to industry, this sector showed very little interest in the development of scientific activities or in the use of the knowledge produced by universities.

By the end of the 1980s, together with the opening up of the national economy, a market integration model of S&T development emerged as dominant. According to this new economic approach, the production of knowledge should be driven by the demands of industry. Planning was replaced by assessment and particular attention was paid to the quality and pertinence of the production of knowledge. In addition, the intervention of industry in the financing and operation of educational and technological systems was encouraged. Despite the importance of market criteria in the design of policies, the government continued to play a central, albeit different, role in R&D activities. The main purpose of government policies would be to create conditions for the better performance of Mexican industry in a new economic context.

A new stage based on an interactive model oriented towards a trilateral relation-ship among government, academia and industry is the feature of the 1990s. In theory, this approach would imply an equilibrium between the industrial and institutional parties in the building of networks and partnerships.[7] We document the character-istics of this stage in the following sections.

Stylized facts in scientific capacities in Mexico

When we analyse the distribution of expenditures and personnel devoted to R&D, the distribution of research by fields, the general trends in scientific production, and the distribution of projects by research type, some stylized facts in science capacity can be drawn:

- Whereas government is decreasing its participation in R&D expenditures (from 50 per cent in 1993 to 33 per cent in 1995) and government research institutions are decreasing the concentration of R&D personnel, industry and higher educa-tion institutions are increasing theirs. Furthermore, the increase in R&D expenditure of the private sector only occurred between 1993 and 1995 (8 to 21 per cent) (CONACYT, 1996b, 1997c).
- As far as S&T competencies in the 1990s are concerned, it is noticeable that between 1990 and 1996, after ten years of negative growth, there was some recovery in the federal expenditure on S&T, with a growth rate of 6.4 per cent (CONACYT, 1997c).
- When taking into account the distribution of the percentage of expenditures in R&D activities within the HEIs, it is worth pointing out that public HEI still contribute the major proportion, even when private HEIs increased their expend-

iture slightly in these activities in 1995.[8] In private universities, R&D activities are financed by non-governmental resources, and come mainly from donations from the administrative boards and from research contracts with industry and other sources (OECD, 1994).

- With regard to personnel devoted to R&D activities, although separate information is not available for public and private HEIs, it is important to note the total number of SNI members for each of those types of HEIs between 1994 and 1996. From data obtained for 1996 (CONACYT, 1997c), public HEIs concentrate 66 per cent of SNI members, while private universities have 2 per cent. Among public universities, UNAM has 34 per cent of SNI members, public state universities, 16 per cent; the National Polytechnic Institute (IPN), including the Centre for Research and Advanced Studies (CINVESTAV), reached 9 per cent, and the Autonomous Metropolitan University (UAM) 6 per cent. This distribution reflects the fact that resources of excellence in S&T still show a trend towards concentration in few institutions, mainly located in the centre of the country (56 per cent).

- In terms of areas of research, personnel of excellence devoted to R&D activities are mainly found within the biological, biomedical and chemical sciences, and then in physics and mathematics. Personnel in the engineering and technology area, which observed important increases during the period of 1987–91, shows from 1992 a trend to decrease, currently representing 21 per cent of the total members of this system (CONACYT, 1997c).[9]

- Scientific production is difficult to assess adequately, given the severe limitations of information available in the country.[10] The best approach for evaluating scientific production should take into consideration the quantity, quality and relevance of scientific production, by means of a combination of national and world indicators (PETAL, 1990, p. 466). Some quantitative indicators of scientific production with a national approach are already available. The total rate of increase in papers published from 1980 to 1995 has been 97 per cent. It is worth mentioning that significant increases in this rate were observed from 1987 to 1988, (16 per cent) and from 1988 to 1993 (19 per cent) (CONACYT, 1997c).

- In using other complementary sources of information, it is observed that scientific production by fields of research, in the case of UNAM, is concentrated[11] in the biological and health sciences, which report the major amount of publications, a trend that corresponds to the concentration of personnel. Similar trends were obtained from an analysis of publications by SNI researchers in 1991. The greatest productivity was for medicine, biology, physics and chemistry, while lower productivity was observed for certain fields of engineering. This pattern of production by fields of research implicitly refers to both basic and applied sciences, it being difficult to evaluate which predominates.

- The only data available for making international comparisons are those of the Institute for Scientific Information (ISI). According to this source, Mexican scientific production is below the average of the industrialized nations, and also of countries in the Latin American region such as Brazil. The entire body of scientists in Mexico produced in 1995 an average of 2,258 publications, while in industrialized countries the average ranged between 54,536 (Japan) and 257,414 (USA). The disciplines with the greatest number of scientific publications between 1981 and 1996 were clinical medicine (18 per cent of the total publications), physics (17 per cent) and plant and animal sciences (11 per cent) (CONACYT, 1997d). The greatest Mexican participation in world scientific production is for astrophysics, agriculture and plant and animal sciences (CONACYT, 1997c).

- From citation analysis (CONACYT, 1997d), the major impact factor was for the fields of immunology, molecular biology and neurosciences. Clinical medicine, which stands first in production, occupies the eighth place in impact. This is an example of how citation analysis based on international sources could reflect diverging impacts for fields of national and local interest. Clinical medicine is a field oriented to research on illnesses affecting the Mexican population, and is very probably of low interest for world science.

- Regarding journal impact, the *Revista Mexicana de Astronomía y Astrofísica* and *Salud Mental*[12] have achieved, between 1990 and 1992, an important impact factor when compared internationally (CONACYT, 1997d). Other journals, such as *Revista Archivos de Investigación Médica* and *Revista Mexicana de Física*, are increasing their impact in recent years.

- With citation impact analysis, journal impact analysis and the average of participation of Mexican science in world production (CONACYT, 1997d), it can be argued that Mexican science is important in different fields. The main competencies are found in astrophysics, clinical medicine, molecular biology, neurosciences, agricultural sciences and geosciences. However, it appears to be weak in engineering sciences. The quantitative indicators already available, most limited to ISI coverage, must be complemented with an assessment of the quality and relevance of research activities, with both a national and international perspective.

- With regard to the location of research, a process of institutional and geographic decentralization has been noted. UNAM, in particular, is contributing to a decentralized research policy and reducing its participation in R&D activities, in favour of public state universities, the SEP-CONACYT Centres system[13] and, to a lesser degree, in favour of private universities and public technological institutes. However, scientific competencies are still concentrated in public institutions; thus, between 1991 and 1996 they received 96 per cent of the projects financed by CONACYT and 97 per cent of the funds allocated through research promotion programmes.[14]

- Historically, research has been oriented towards applied and experimental rather than basic science. Currently, however, the distribution of expenditures among these three types of research is very similar (CONACYT, 1997d). With respect to research fields, it can be observed that PACIME[15] has favoured basic sciences over applied sciences (which include biology and engineering) and other sciences related to the social concerns of the country, such as health and natural resources. Even if the data are weak for defining the specialization patterns in science by fields of knowledge, it is useful to argue that Mexican research seems to be stronger in biomedical (including biotechnology), clinical medicine, physics and earth sciences, with both a basic and applied approach, than engineering and technology.

The magnitude of university–industry collaboration: some indicators

Historically university–industry relationships have been weak in Mexico. However, beginning in the 1990s, there has been more interest from HEIs in increasing their collaboration with industry. Various factors have contributed to the growth in relationships between university and industry, at both national and international levels,[16] the most important being the North American Free Trade Agreement (NAFTA), the guiding principle behind the educational modernization programme in the late 1980s and the intervention of the private sector in the financing and functioning of the educational and technological systems.

Such factors have led to the introduction, from the late 1980s, of different policies and mechanisms by government, firms and HEIs in order to promote more frequent collaborations (Casas and Luna, 1997a and b). On behalf of government, mechanisms to increase private sector participation in education and professional training directed to the needs of Mexican society were applied. In terms of HEIs, mechanisms such as professional practices, school–industry programmes, external advisory councils with the participation of the private sector, alumni associations and centres for technological administration are some of the outstanding measures introduced. And finally, as to firms, some large enterprises have signed formal contracts with HEIs, and some important entrepreneurial associations have explicitly expressed their desire to cooperate with the government and the educational sector for the definition of industrial and technological policies.

Two different orientations should be distinguished when referring to university–industry relationships (Casas and Luna, 1997a and b).[17] The first involves collaborations based on the training of professionals and business advisors oriented towards satisfying the organizational and technical demands of industry. This orientation has been adopted mainly by private universities, which were created to address the demands of industry. In view of the new economic model currently applied in Mexico, this trend has been intensified by most public higher education institutions, which are introducing mechanisms and programmes to make human resource training adequate for the demands of industry.

The second orientation refers to collaborations that are established on the basis of research competencies and are conducted for the development of products and processes, their improvement or specialized technological services addressing the interests of industries. This is a new trend that can be found in the larger public institutions of higher education, which concentrate research and personnel resources in S&T and are at present developing mechanisms to established formal agreements, mainly with large firms. Some private universities that during the past decade have built capacities in research activities are also involved in developing research projects of interest for industry.

One of the main differences with regard to this second trend is the role played by public and private universities. Public universities develop research oriented towards basic science and this is supported mainly by their own university budget. Private universities are oriented mainly towards diagnosis and consultancy activities utilizing resources from industry and governmental programmes and to a lesser degree by their own budget.

In order to have a rough idea of the magnitude of university–industry relations, we utilize here quantitative indicators from several surveys applied to both HEIs[18] and industries.[19] It should be clarified that these surveys deal with both orientations of collaboration referred to previously. These surveys are relevant to document the following: the organizational structures, the financial resources, the quantity of projects, and the intensity of the use of the university knowledge base.

Organizational structures

One indicator of the recent changes regarding relationships with industry is that more than half of the institutions surveyed have introduced organizational struc-tures to administrate and promote those interactions. They respond to different approaches to collaboration. In large universities, mainly public such as UNAM, IPN and the University of Guadalajara, specific centres exist for link-up activities; in other institutions, such as technological institutes, specific departments are in charge of linkage and technological administration. Private universities have also created specific units to integrate their activities with industry, an example being the structure of the Monterrey Technological Institute (ITESM-Monterrey Campus), where each department develops its own strategy.

In some cases, these activities are integrated into extension departments; in others, they are part of the offices for academic exchange or are incorporated into postgraduate departments. The majority of link-up activities based on research are coordinated directly by faculties or by postgraduate and research divisions, although they exist as specific link-up units within the institution. The existence of these types of units does not involve, in the majority of cases, a centralization or concentration of decisions for collaboration. Rather, in some cases, linkage units operate on a decentralized model in which each research centre seeks better mechanisms for interrelating with industry, depending on its fields of research, and on its technical and experience capabilities. It would seem, according to Gould (1997), that a mixture of centralized and decentralized structures offers the most advantages.

Financial resources

With regard to financial resources in public as well as in private HEIs, the greatest support for collaboration comes from their own budgets, while companies provide a very reduced amount of funding. Despite the existence of government programmes for link-up activities, these support the HEIs in a very limited manner.[20] The resources obtained from the collaboration with industry, although they continue to be very low in comparison to the HEIs' total budget, have increased over the past few years.[21] In addition to the financing obtained from industry, HEIs also sought out other external financial sources to support their research activities. All these sources have allowed some HEIs to increase their research competencies by means of laboratories and equipment and to be in a better position to attend to demands from the industrial sector.

Quantity of projects

Scarce information has been gathered in Mexico, similar to other OECD countries, that could be useful to evaluate the quantity of university–industry projects. A broad assessment of the quantity of these relationships is that during the past decade joint projects have been scarce and university–industry collaborations were weak. However, according to the ANUIES Survey (1997), between 1994 and 1996 HEIs increased their collaboration projects, oriented to both human resource training and research activities, on an average of 89 per cent. The highest rates were for private universities (238 per cent), followed by public technological institutes (93 per cent), while public universities increased projects by 41 per cent. This information reveals that during the period of 1994–6, HEIs have intensified their relationships with industry, very probably as an effect of policies and mechanisms already introduced.

However, if we consider the number of projects supported on research activities separately, the trend is quite different. From a survey applied in 1997 to 1,322 firms in the manufacturing sector (CONACYT, 1997a), 63 per cent were developing innovative activities. The results reported that only 4 per cent of these firms had established collaborative agreements with universities for the improvement of products and processes; most were Mexican firms. Of those enterprises, 42 per cent reported that agreements with universities were significant, while for 35 per cent, the relationships were moderately significant and, for the rest, were of minor importance.

Data obtained from the two previously mentioned surveys indicate two important points: first, the relative weight that each of the actors gives to collaborative activities, and the fact that innovative firms do not seem to be interested in knowledge produced in HEIs; second, HEIs establish relations with a wider spectrum of industries and not specifically with those characterized as innovative ones. This trend is also explained by the broad group of objectives of collaborations, among which services stand out.

From the previous discussion it seems that HEI had little participation in the development or improvement of technological process and products by industries. In fact, some recent studies (Casas and Luna, 1997a and b) have documented that many projects are based on informal interactions, and are established with small and medium firms, which are not characterized by innovative activities but by the assistance of the HEIs to solve specific organizational or technical problems. Other studies carried out within the framework of the OECD (Laursen and Lindgaard, 1996; Vithlani, 1996) in Europe and the USA have also shown that collaborations between these two sectors have limited direct impact on the innovative performance of firms and result in few exploitable product or process developments (OECD, 1996a, p. 3). We can highlight here that the indirect impact of universities in the innovation process is a feature of both developed and developing countries.

Intensity of the use of university knowledge by firms

Collaborative projects generally involve a variety of activities, among which research and technological development are at a medium level of intensity. As far as research is concerned, there is a variety of linkage activities, such as basic research, joint research, technological development, technology transfer, technology licensing and technical assistance. However, most of the activities in this category are related to technical assistance, engineering and information services, these demands from industry being conditioned by the existence in HEIs of facilities, including laboratories and equipment.

The existence of infrastructure (laboratories and equipment) is a precondition for HEIs to be able to respond to industry demands (ANUIES, 1997). But the accumulation of knowledge at the academic level, expressed in tacit knowledge embodied in the scientific personnel, is also a precondition for collaboration, as other studies have documented (OECD, 1996a; Vithlani, 1996). Some private institutions have made great efforts to contract PhD academics and to obtain sophisticated equipment in order to interact with industry through specialized services, such as in the case of ITESM.[22] On the other hand, public institutions such as UNAM and IPN satisfy the need for specific technical services to industry, given the infrastructure capabilities they have accumulated.[23]

In view of the characteristics of the accumulation of research in HEIs, these constitute a source of information for industry and an opportunity to observe the progress being made in certain technological fields. In some specific cases (ANUIES, 1996; CONACYT, 1997; Casas and Luna, 1997a and b), it has been shown that there is a demand for tacit knowledge on the part of firms, through the mobility of personnel and the use of publications and patents produced by the universities, which represent codified knowledge.

However, the degree of intensity in the utilization of this knowledge continues to be low for specific industrial sectors. In the case of the automotive industry (see Chapter 15), only 2 per cent of firms hire R&D services from public universities and 0.7 per cent hire from public and private technology centres. As for the pharmaceutical industry, links with universities and public research organizations are short term, specific and informal, and are generally reserved for such activities as clinical tests but not for basic research (see Chapter 12). Regarding the chemical industry (see Chapter 11), it has been argued that 'very few chemical companies have approached universities or research centres for technological developments', but Arvanitis and Villvicencio additionally argue that the weakness of the relationships with universities is a wider problem in dealing with the difficulty that companies have in establishing linkages with any type of suppliers or technical associates.

Despite the low intensity of the use of university knowledge by firms in quantitative terms, some important foreign firms established in Mexico, such as Procter & Gamble, Ciba-Geigy AG, AT&T Corp., Hoechst AKT, Bayer AKT, the BASF Group, Rhom and Haas Company, and Motorola, Inc, have developed formal collaboration agreements with certain large universities (UNAM, UAM and, to a lesser degree, the Autonomous University of Nuevo León and, among the private universities, the ITESM and the Universidad de la Laguna) (IIS-UNAM, 1985). These agreements, of very different natures and with a variety of objectives, have lasted for several years and have been very useful as a knowledge flow mechanism, facilitating personnel mobility and the transmission of tacit knowledge. This fact proves to be important as such firms, included among the main ones taking out patents in this country (CONACYT, 1997a, 1997b), are recognizing the importance of those HEIs that concentrate research capacities in Mexico.

The dynamics of university–industry collaboration

The study of the dynamics of collaboration between universities and industry enables us to appreciate that such relationships are possible through complex interactions that may be considered inherent to the interactive or non-linear model of scientific-technical knowledge production.

From data obtained from several programmes that have supported collaboration in various different regional environments[24] and the use of other sources of information,[25] it was possible to gather a group of qualitative indicators of the current dynamics of collaborations based on research activities.[26]

The regional dimension

University–industry collaborations in Mexico are taking place on a regional basis, given the geographic proximity between research institutions and specific problems related to local natural resources and industrial activities. Some regions stand out (the Centre, the Northeast, the West and the Bajío region) for their greater dynamism regarding linkage; other regions may be considered as intermediate (the North-Central states of the country), whereas some others are characterized by their lower level of linkage (mainly the states in the South and Gulf regions and the Northwest).

Although it is possible to identify a certain profile or regional specialization from the frequency of the links made between specific areas of knowledge and economic sectors, undoubted are the great diversity that exists regarding the type of academic institutions involved, the type of fields of knowledge, the profile of demand or type of firm, the objectives of the collaboration and its geographic scale, and the technological sectors involved.

The complementary nature of formal and informal relations

With regard to the type of relationships which are established, although formal relationships have acquired importance during the past few years, informal inter-actions continue to carry considerable weight. The majority of the sources consulted report only the collaborations already established on a written agreement or contract. However, informal relationships carry a significant weight in the process culminating in the setting up of a formal agreement; they are also relevant in the links between academic institutions and innovative firms that have developed new products and processes.[27] Other studies have documented that 'the effects of networking and gate-keeping, via informal contacts, can be substantial' (OECD, 1996a).

The diversity of initiatives

Relationships between academy and industry based on research activities do not appear to follow a pattern regarding the origin of the initiative, which may come from different actors. Among the most common, the following initiative origins were identified: (a) large national or foreign companies; (b) business associations or local agricultural organizations, particularly where small and medium-sized firms use traditional technologies; (c) micro and small innovative firms; and (d) researchers or groups of researchers in universities and from academic institutions in general.

Links are generally of a spontaneous nature, stemming from bonds of trust and personal relationships. However, the consolidation of collaborative relationships frequently depends on the support provided by governmental programmes and on the facilities offered by the academic institutions in terms of economic, institutional and legal resources. In the process of setting up collaborative bonds there is, consequently, a dynamic relationship between supply and demand.

In the case of UNAM, we found examples which document both directions of the initiative. In considering the data from 1995 and 1996 jointly, the distribution of initiatives for linkage registered the following behaviour: in 1995, of 80 agreements for collaboration handled by the Centre for Technological Innovation (CIT), of the aforementioned university, 23 per cent responded to the demand from industry, while in 1996, of the 87 agreements, 43 per cent came from the firm's initiative (CIT-UNAM, 1997).

The variety of objectives

With regard to relationships based on research, the objectives are diverse. In the most dynamic regions, collaborations concerned with the development or improvement of products and processes are predominant (32 per cent), followed by scientific and/or technological research (24 per cent), administrative diagnoses on production (19 per cent), and optimization of production (12 per cent). However, the objectives of collaboration are usually multiple and occur simultaneously or successively. They include the training of firm personnel by the universities or of students at firms, human resource formation at the undergraduate and postgraduate levels, and technological services that could be routine or could require highly specialized knowledge.

An example is the Instituto Tecnológico de Celaya, which bases a large portion of its relationships with regional firms on interactions generated through the formation of human resources at both the undergraduate and postgraduate levels. However, these relationships have generated new objectives, such as specialized services, consultancy, the improvement of technology and some research projects for firms.

The interdisciplinarity of knowledge flows

The attempts to generate links with industry produce various types of transfer of knowledge. These range from the traditional knowledge inherent to a particular discipline to that produced in an interdisciplinary mode. In the current globalization environment, this implies cross-border knowledge, more characteristic of the new technologies. On reviewing the agreements set up through the CIT-UNAM, we note that these have involved both relationships in traditional scientific fields (mechanical engineering and chemistry, agronomy, veterinary) and participation in fields characterized by new technologies (biotechnology and material sciences).

The complexity of regional configurations

While analysing the characteristics of collaborations in various regions of the country, it was possible to discover that their construction is extremely complex. Although geographic proximity plays an important role, we frequently find links which go beyond, crossing state, regional and national boundaries to encompass economic sectors. This is the case for the mining sector cluster in the Northwest of the country which, although its original nucleus is at the State University of San Luis Potosí and the mining industry in that state, it is expanding towards other states in the region that have mineral resources. It involves other mining companies and HEIs, such as the Instituto Tecnológico de Saltillo and CINVESTAV, both located in Coahuila. This cluster crosses Mexican borders, establishing collaborations between Mexican institutions doing research in mining with institutions in Canada.

The building of networks between various participants

If the academic institutions are taken as a unit, collaboration with other entities carrying out national and international research is extremely frequent. But even if the firm is taken as a unit, one sees that collaboration based on research sometimes involves links that combine relationships, among which the following stand out: (a) firms that establish relationships with different types of public academic institutions; (b) firms that collaborate with public and private universities (particularly at the state level); (c) firms that interrelate with various kinds of institutions, such as public and private universities, Mexican or foreign academic institutions or research centres.

An example of the first type of collaboration is the scientific exchange network in agriculture in the Bajío region. It allows the flow of knowledge on agricultural problems between different types of institutions that carry out research in this field[28] and maintain a close interaction with different associations of local agricultural associations and cattle farmers in the region. Furthermore, with the initiative of the CINVESTAV-Irapuato, and given the demand for research on the part of producers, a postgraduate programme was created aimed at strengthening the research into food and biotechnology within the region (Paredes López *et al.*, 1996).

With regard to the second and third types, relevant exchanges are observed in the Northeast region between the ITESM, Monterrey Campus and the Universidad Autónoma de Nuevo León. The latter also interacts with a group of large national and foreign companies established in the state of Nuevo León.

It is worth mentioning that despite the significant weight of individual firms, the participation of business associations and local producer associations stands out in fostering collaborative activities with universities.

The diversity of sectors

There is no pattern at the national level regarding the collaboration of universities and industry by type of firm, differentiated by size or by the sector to which they belong. The relationships between fields of knowledge and industrial branches are extremely irregular, particularly where areas of knowledge are connected to high technology fields. Additionally, there is no correlation between industrial sectors of high technology and innovation, because the development of products and processes is found in both traditional and novel technology sectors.

To illustrate the dynamic described above, the case of the University of Guadalajara, is noteworthy; its Department of Wood, Cellulose and Paper has formalized research projects with firms belonging to different industrial sectors. In this way, it simultaneously collaborates with paper-producing firms, with associations of furniture manufacturers and with associations of tequila producers.

Problems for knowledge flow

The main problems for the flow of knowledge range from the lack of an innovative culture on behalf of firms,[29] to the incipient institutional strategies for linkage activities in HEIs, to the inadequately defined technological and industrial policies of the government. In general, obstacles for university–industry relations are part of a broad complex of factors inherent to universities, industries and government.

Among the most important are the following: (a) a lack of coordination among the three participants; (b) limited financial resources and capital to sustain technological collaboration; (c) the dilemma between economic competitiveness criteria and adequate evaluation of scientific and technological activities; (d) the weakness of appropriate mechanisms for the flow of knowledge, particularly expressed in intermediate or interface structures; (e) the lack of definition of a legal framework to sustain collaboration; (f) the inherent conflict between public and private knowledge, and the consequent dilemma for academia between the unrestricted freedom of research and the secrecy demanded from industry; (g) the inadequate and almost non-existent policies and incentives for collaborative arrangements for innovation; and (h) the low value of scientific knowledge as conceived by entrepreneurs.

One problem that deserves attention is the legal framework. Definitions such as the pertinence or non-pertinence for patenting in HEIs and the way in which firms need to protect their innovations (patents or industrial secrets) affect knowledge networks. Secrecy is a problem for both universities and industries, for the former because they have to protect their research developments, and for the latter because the definition of demands or the flow of personnel affects the confidentiality of industrial technological strategies, an issue which limits collaboration with universities.

Taxonomy of university–industry collaboration

From previous quantitative and qualitative indicators, specific trends have been identified, from which we have built a taxonomy (see Table 9.1). The main characteristics that reflect the current status of university and industry collaborations are the following.

1. Science-based university industry collaborations are found mainly in those public national universities which concentrate major efforts in research, even when the quantity of relationships is still limited.

2. The existence of scientific competencies, in terms of both personnel and infrastructure in HEIs, provides a type of comparative advantage to universities with a science base. However, these capacities *per se* are not the only factor needed to establish collaborative activities. Governmental programmes and a culture of innovation in firms are necessary to complement that condition.

3. The initiative to establish collaborations comes principally from HEIs, i.e. from the supply side. Some institutions have created mechanisms and programmes to orient their research activities towards industry, while others do not have institutional support and rely on the negotiation of contracts with industry on the researchers themselves.

4. The objectives of collaboration are multiple and are scarcely oriented to innovation or technological development. Despite the existence of the two orientations of collaboration between university and industry, the empirical evidence reflects their interrelation; in other words, human resource training and other collaborative objectives based on research are frequently interwoven.

5. Knowledge mainly flows through mobility of graduate students and researchers. This is a pattern followed by both private and public universities. In fact, graduate student mobility is at present the most efficient way to begin to build knowledge networks to respond to the demands of the productive sectors. In view of this, the dominant trend of knowledge flow between universities and industries in Mexico is accomplished through tacit forms.

6. Collaborative activities between universities and firms are based on formal, spontaneous and sporadic relationships, and even if the ingredient of informal relationships remains strong and contributes to the consolidation of collaboration, the dominant trend is to formalize them through agreements and contracts for specific purposes. However, these relationships tend to be spontaneous and do not constitute a part of institutional policies induced by HEI policies, or by industrial or government strategies.

7. Funding for linkage activities derives mainly from university budgets. The level of funding from industry is particularly low for public HEIs. This is a problem that deserves attention, as some universities assume expenses that correspond to firms. Public HEIs have not yet developed an entrepreneurial culture and do not have a clear definition regarding the cost of knowledge. This is the case for public technological institutes and other public universities that devote part of their postgraduate teaching efforts or the use of the infrastructure and research time to respond to the demands, which only contribute a low percentage of the real cost of collaboration.

8. From previous observations, it is worth highlighting that the dominant problem regarding university–industry collaboration is the lack of coordination among the participants. However, the lack of a governmental technology and an innovation policy also prevents a major impact of university–industry collaborations that could favour and support regional development. This would allow the establishment of networks among research institutions, a recombination of science competencies and improved collaboration with industry and other economic sectors.

Table 9.1 Taxonomy of Science-based University–Industry Collaborations

Main characteristics	Current forms	Dominant trends
Types of HEIs, with a science base, collaborating with industry	• Public national universities • State public universities • Private universities • Technological institutes	• Public national universities
Origin of the initiative of collaboration	• Higher education institutions • Industry • Government	• Higher education institutions
Determinant factors for collaborations	• Scientific competencies in HEIs • Infrastructure in HEIs • Industrial capabilities • Government policies	• Scientific competencies and infrastructure in HEIs
Objectives of collaborations	• Innovation • Technology development • Product, process or production improvement • Specialized technical services • Routine services • Research activities • Graduate students for industry • Technical personnel training	• Technical personnel training • Product, process and production improvement • Routine services • Specialized technical services • Graduate students for industry • Research activities
Types of knowledge flows	• Codified (publications and patents) • Tacit (personnel mobility)	• Tacit knowledge (graduate student mobility)
Kind of relationships	• Informal/formal • Spontaneous/induced[a] • Sporadic/lasting	• Formal, spontaneous and sporadic
Main funding sources	• Government • Industry • HEIs	• HEIs
Obstacles	• Lack of coordination • Lack of financial resources • Market criteria v. collaboration • Public v. privatization of knowledge • Administrative slowness • Lack of policies and incentives • Under-valorization of scientific knowledge • Lack of interfaces and legal framework • Secrecy v. research freedom	• Lack of coordination • Lack of policies and incentives • Conflicts between public and private knowledge • Tensions between research freedom and secrecy

This taxonomy is based on the systematization of the main characteristics found in the analysis of the magnitude and the dynamics of collaborations.

[a] This characteristic refers to the existence or non-existence of institutional policies for linking activities.

Conclusions

In general terms, it can be stated that Mexico is considerably behind with regard to the production of knowledge on a global scale. When compared to other countries, such as the USA, Japan and the UK, Mexico shows a pattern of generation of knowledge in which government encouragement is weak,[30] there is no determined support from the business sector and the HEIs participate in R&D activities with the largest share.

Despite these general trends, over the past three decades the country has increased its incorporation into the world of science, developing its competencies largely in the HEI sector. The emphasis on basic and applied science has led some HEIs and knowledge sectors – biotechnology, astronomy, biomedicine, among others – to the forefront of knowledge. However, engineering and technology, even if they are being importantly developed in HEIs, are less supported by financing governmental programmes and by current evaluation criteria.

This chapter has demonstrated that science-based university–industry collaborations are still very weak. Despite this, information gathered by this study shows an emergent increasing trend towards collaboration and a rich horizon of possibilities for interactions between university and industry. The analysis has led us to recognize that these interactions are oriented to a variety of purposes and are not centred on the development of technology. Among different purposes stand out relationships oriented to the training of human resources, and collaborative activities based on scientific research, which take place simultaneously or consequently. This suggests that Mexican universities could be playing an indirect role in the innovation process, given that the transfer of tacit knowledge is currently the main means for collaborations.

The study of the dynamics between university and industry made it possible to appreciate that relationships are based on very complex interactions, which are providing a learning process and multiple forms of networking among the actors. This feature permits us to argue that an interactive non-linear model is beginning to be applied for the development of knowledge.

The decentralization process of research activities is creating the conditions for networking at the regional level. In fact, this study documented that important collaborations take place on a regional basis, given the geographic proximity between research organizations and the consideration of specific problems related to local natural resources and industrial activities. However, these efforts should be strengthened by regional policies to impact regional social and economic development.

From the above discussion, we can argue that university–industry collaborations constitute an innovative factor for firms, as much as their relationships with suppliers, customers or their own R&D capabilities. However, given that in Mexico research competencies are largely to be found in the HEIs, this factor should be of greater importance for firms. From the analysis carried out to this point, it is clear that the transfer of knowledge from academy to industry, to a greater extent, occurs spontaneously, and that increasing and consolidating that collaboration requires programmes and incentives from both universities and firms to foster it.

Quantitative and qualitative indicators were useful to build a taxonomy that identified the dominant trends in the collaboration between university and industry based on research activities. This taxonomy highlighted, among other elements, the leading role of universities in knowledge networking and the conflicts of interest derived from the privatization of public knowledge and the tension between research freedom and oriented research. These issues deserve serious consideration by university, government and industrial spheres.

In general, the most pressing concern regarding university–industry collaboration is the dispersion of efforts, the lack of equilibrium between the supply and demand of knowledge and the lack of the use of knowledge generated in HEIs by the production system. As was stressed in Part 1, the Mexican production system has developed an industrial structure characterized by low technological opportunities, low demand of knowledge produced locally and high interaction with firms and institutions localized abroad. This set of paths indicates a critical coordination problem that undoubtedly affects the configuration of the national innovation system.

Notes

1. In Mexico HEIs are a heterogeneous group of institutions with very different objectives and functions. Within this structure different sub-systems are distinguished: public universities (autonomous, national or state and technological) that mainly receive financial support from federal and state governments to pursue both teaching and research activities, and technological institutes, widespread throughout the country, with postgraduate programmes and research activities, that are supported by the Ministry of Public Education; and private universities that channel their own budgets for postgraduate programmes and research activities.

2. Different papers have documented the importance of knowledge produced in universities and the developing role these institutions are playing as R&D providers for the innovative process. Among others, the following are worth mentioning: Rosenberg and Nelson (1994), OECD (1996a, 1997b, d), Mansfield (1991), Etzkowitz and Leydesdorff (1997), Nelson (1993), Edquist and Lundvall (1993) and Johnson and Lundvall (1994).

3. The analysis in this section is supported mainly by three data sources: CONACYT (1976), various issues published in 1997 and Lustig *et al.* (1989). It is worth mentioning that Mexico does not have historically accurate series on the evolution of R&D activities from the 1970s to the 1990s. This is mainly due to the diverse definitions and the different components used to characterize S&T and R&D activities in different periods. For this reason, data only indicate general trends. During the 1970s, statistics referring to R&D included basic research, research oriented to sectors of application and research oriented to general knowledge of national reality (CONACYT, 1976), while during the 1990s, R&D includes basic, applied and experimental development, and is one of the components of S&T activities that integrate, in addition to R&D, scientific and technical education and scientific and technological services (CONACYT, 1997c, and other issues).

4. It is worth noting that S&T expenditure includes scientific and technical education and services (CONACYT, 1997c).

5. Among these were the Autonomous Metropolitan University (UAM) and the Centre for Advanced Research and Studies (CINVESTAV), an excellence centre that is part of the National Polytechnic Institute (IPN), which in the future would play a relevant role in the development of S&T in Mexico.

6. The National System of Researchers is a programme of incentives geared to recognize the work of the most productive and qualified researchers, by means of peer evaluation, resulting

in the assignment of a scholarship, for three-year periods, to compensate for the low salaries in universities.

7. Although this model has not been established, in the 1990s several trends were slightly but significantly reversed with regard to the amount and location of R&D activities in comparison to the trends observed during the 1970s.

8. Data for public and private HEIs in 1995 were elaborated by the authors from information included in CONACYT (1997d).

9. This was owing mainly to inadequate recognition of technological and engineering activities within the criteria of evaluation applied by SNI, which tended to favour scientific criteria rather than to include an adequate evaluation of activities developed by engineers whose products do not correspond to scientific activities.

10. The only sources available are the number of papers published in journals included in the *Science Citation Index* of the Institute for Scientific Information and other analyses of a bibliometric nature developed from that source, which in general present strong limitations for countries such as Mexico. Critical analysis of the use of these sources can be consulted in Velho (1985).

11. This level of aggregation of scientific areas offered by CONACYT has not succeeded in elaborating a comprehensive classification of scientific fields, and within the different programmes, leans towards science and technology, in which various classifications are used. This is a problem that should be addressed by policy-makers in order to achieve a more accurate information base on science and technology competencies that would support rational policies.

12. This journal from 1992 has the name of *Archives of Medical Research* and from January 1999 is edited in Mexico but published by Elsevier, New York. Its impact factor has raised from 0.392 in 1997 to 0.632 in 1998.

13. See Chapter 7 of this book, where these centres are analysed.

14. Through these programmes, CONACYT channels funds additional to those from research institutions. Their operation involves researchers competing to obtain funding and assessment of their proposals in terms of quality and the academic progress of the researchers involved.

15. The only available source for analysing research fields is the Program to Support Science (PACIME), operated by CONACYT from 1991/1996. This weakness has already been highlighted by OECD (1994), when analysing the distribution of funding by area of research.

16. A detailed analysis of these factors may be consulted in Casas and Luna (1997). In particular, the general introduction to the book and Chapters 3, 4 and 5 should be consulted.

17. It is very difficult to separate purely the linkage activities related to human resource training from those related to research activities, because they are often pursued simultaneously. Given this fact, reference is made in this section to collaborative activities based on research which frequently implies human resource training at postgraduate levels.

18. Information from the following surveys is used: *Encuesta sobre Vinculación Academia-Empresa*, CONACYT and ANUIES, 1996; *Oferta Institucional de Servicios Externos y Desarrollos Tecnológicos*, IPN, April 1996, and *Oferta de Servicios Tecnológicos de las IES y Centros de Investigación Tecnologica del país*, IPN, November 1996.

19. Information from the following surveys is used: ENESTYC, *Encuesta Nacional de Empleo, Salarios*, INEGI, 1995; *Encuesta Nacional de Innovación*, CONACYT, 1997, and *Encuesta sobre la problemática de la empresa mexicana ante el reto de la modernización*, *FASE II*, July 1994, Nacional Financiera, Mexico.

20. An example is the CONACYT Academy–Industry Linkage, which allocates resources for collaboration projects between HEI and industry. This programme supported, between 1992

and 1995, 95 projects, with an investment of 21,911,735 Mexican pesos, while from 1995 to 1997 it supported only seven projects with an investment of 1,310,733 Mexican pesos.

21. A recent survey (IPN, 1996a, 1996b) found that 44 per cent of the institutions surveyed obtain approximately 10 per cent of their overall budget from collaborative activities, and only 25 per cent of the institutions reported obtaining 50 per cent of their budget from those activities.

22. This is the case of the Instituto Tecnológico de Monterrey (Campus Monterrey), which has created the Centre for Environmental Quality, and established an infrastructure to offer analytical services to industry in the fields of air and water quality, dangerous waste products and sewage.

23. A very important case is the Faculty of Chemistry at UNAM, which develops specialized analyses for the pharmaceutical and food as well as to other branches of industry (Casas and De Gortari, 1997, p. 191).

24. Among others the Academy–Industry Link Programme and Regional Research Systems, are both operated by CONACYT. The aim of the former, begun in 1992, has been partially to support research projects for which there is private sector support. In general, projects are proposed by HEIs, which interest a potential user. The second most recently created programme operates on the basis of priority areas identified by forums where representatives of academy, industry and state governments participate and where relevant themes are defined for different regions of the country. After identification of the relevant areas, an invitation is issued for the submission of research projects, which must have the guarantee and financing of a potential user.

25. For this purpose, the information used was gathered for the study 'Successful Cases of Innovative Companies', Deputy Director of Scientific and Technological Policy, CONACYT and information presented in the study of Corona (1997). Also used was information collected for the ANUIES/ALO study, *Catálogo de Casos. Vinculación entre los Sectores Académico y Productivo en México y EU*, Mexico, 1996.

26. Very little information was found with regard to the dynamics of knowledge flows (mobility of personnel, co-publications, co-patenting, etc.). A study should be requisitioned for that purpose, which exceeds the remit of this chapter.

27. From a study of these (Corona, 1997) and considering exclusively the firms linked with the HEIs, it is seen that of a total 74 firms, 35.1 per cent, have informal relations with the HEIs and that a majority are lasting relationships, which represent 28.2 per cent.

28. As is the case with the Autonomous University of Querétaro (UAQ), the Autonomous University of Aguascalientes (UAGS), the University of Guanajuato (UGTO) and the Centre for Research and Advanced Studies in Irapuato (CINVESTAV).

29. Other chapters included in this volume document this situation.

30. Mexico currently dedicates 0.33 per cent of the GDP to expenditure to R&D, while other countries of average development, such as Spain, dedicate 0.80 per cent and industrialized countries, between 1.61 and 3 per cent (OECD 1997e).

PART III

Sectoral and Regional Innovation Systems

CHAPTER TEN

Co-evolution and Innovation Systems

M. Cimoli

Introduction

This chapter is concerned with the modes and patterns that describe the interaction between the production system and institutions, as well as the configuration of different cases related to the sectoral and regional systems of innovation. Particularly, in this chapter, the aim is to analyse how the technological pattern of production system and institutions have changed over time. These changes cannot be understood if we do not consider the evolution of the macroeconomic setting in Mexico during the past few years, as well as the principal changes introduced by the trade reforms and other specific policies that are more closely related to science and technology. This understanding will, in turn, enable us to explore innovation systems at the more meso and micro levels, where this definition will be related to the principal parameters that define the innovation process.

This chapter introduces the notions of innovation systems and clusters at a meso level utilized through the case studies in the following chapters. Chapters 11, 12, 13, 14 and 15 are devoted to specific case studies, namely the chemical, pharmaceutical, biotechnology, glass container and automobile industries. The rationale behind the choice of these specific sectors of the Mexican economy was not only their importance in the nation's total economic activities, but also principally because they illustrate four important issues within Mexican industry: (a) the historical evolution and importance (chemical industry); (b) the institutional changes that favoured or did not favour the development of science-based sectors in Mexico (pharmaceutics and biotechnology); (c) the importance of strategies and technological capabilities in a large domestic firm (glass container); and (d) the increasing international competitiveness (automobile). Chapter 16 is dedicated to a regional case study on the state of Aguascalientes, which has been able to upgrade its technological capabilities. Our analysis is based on the interplay between informal and formal knowledge flows, the sectoral pattern of technological capabilities and the role of institutions in increasing the context of globalization as the main element in providing an explanation for this upgrade in the region's capability.[1]

Production system and institutions: a co-evolutionary path

The content of this section is primarily based on the studies carried out in Parts 1 and 2 of this text and other works published recently.[2] Particularly, on the basis of analysis of the macroeconomic setting, the description of Mexico's production manufacturing system, the institutional Mexican matrix and the results of several of the surveys named above, we can see a pattern of how the production system and the institutions have co-evolved through the three different historical phases described in Parts I and II; that is, import substitution, transition and new regulatory periods.

In Figure 10.1, we have sketched a pattern based on the specific facts that explain the co-evolution process between the production system and the institutional framework. In this figure, it is straightforward to acknowledge a bidirectional relationship between industrial structure (using measures of the distribution of different characteristics as an approximation, such as firm sizes, innovative competence, ownership, persistent behavioural traits) and patterns of technological capabilities. Different rates of learning influence the ability of firms to survive and expand, thus affecting industrial structures. Conversely, any particular institution or organization – with its associated distribution of corporate features – influences and constrains what and how fast firms are able and willing to learn.[3] There is an impressive list of specific patterns of linkages and reciprocal influences that could, of course, be very lengthy. The fundamental point here is that the type of reciprocal influence which takes place in the Mexican case is not at all independent from the ways: (a) development policies evolve; (b) industrial structures emerge, change, develop capabilities, diversify, etc.; and (c) political design of institutional infrastructure. This is the core co-evolutionary view emphasized in Part II of this book.

Industrialization and technological capabilities

The analysis derived from the evaluation of the different historical phases of the county's development (from import substitution to the new regulatory framework) has revealed that a process of modernization of the production system related, particularly, to exporting firms has indeed taken place.

During the import substitution period, the sources of the industrialization process were established and a process of upgrading in technological capability began through the adaptation of plants and blueprints, as well as efforts to improve the organization of production. More specifically, let us briefly introduce the main results that have emerged from analysis of the capability to accumulate technology during the ISI period. Katz (1984 and 1987) and Cimoli (1988) suggest that: (i) a significant amount of technological learning and incremental innovation does occur; (ii) there is no inevitability in the learning-by-doing process, which on the contrary requires adequate organization, both within each firm and each environment; (iii) the degrees and direction of the accumulation of technology vary according to the nature of the firms, e.g. whether they are family, large domestic and multinational; (iv) the sources of the industrialization process were established and a process of upgrading technological capability began through the following: the adaptation of plants and blueprints, efforts to improve the organization of production, increasing capacity to obtain full production, long-term R&D-oriented activities and the imitation of products; (v) products have been characterized by low-quality standard (producer-user in terms of quantity and prices only).

In family firms, the technological upgrade during the initial phase is associated with the technical ability of the entrepreneur, who has transferred the technological

ISI period	Transition period	New Regulatory Framework and NAFTA.
A model of intensive protection. Local technologicical capabilities. Industrialization and increasing manufacturing production. Production addressed to domestic market.	The abondonment of the ISI pattern. Economic crisis: demand contraction, large devaluation, trade balance deficit. Opening process of Mexican economy. First stage of liberalization.	Exchange-based stabilization programme: trade and financial reform and public deficit control are implemented. Export increasing, higher competitiveness in large firms.

INDUSTRIALIZATION OF PRODUCTION SYSTEM	PRODUCTION SYSTEM	MODERNIZATION OF PRODUCTION SYSTEM
¥ Adaptation of plants and blueprints. ¥ Efforts to improve organization of production. ¥ Increasing capacity to obtain full production. ¥ Low quality standard (producer–user in terms of quantity and prices only). ¥ R&D long-term oriented activities and imitation products.	¥ Increasing role of large domestic firms and MNEs (increasing concentration). ¥ Higher participation in the international market (increasing intra-sectoral trade). ¥ More international integration (decrease in the linkages with local firms). ¥ Decrease in the number of domestic producers of intermediates and equipment. ¥ Competitive advantage based on static resource endowments (low labour cost).	¥ Increasing production capacity and improving organizational efficiency process innovation product quality. ¥ Increasing R&D oriented to production efficiency for export-oriented firms (quality, cost reduction, utilization of acquired machinery and equipment, personal training). ¥ Increasing international inter-firm linkages. ¥ Reduction of local linkages between firms.
PUSH AND SPECIFIC INSTITUTIONAL SUPPORT	INSTITUTIONS	INTERMEDIATION AND SERVICE INSTITUTIONAL SUPPORT
¥ Several public institutions contribute to the formulation of S&T policies: Ministry of Finance, Ministry of Industry, Ministry of Education, National Council for Science and Technology (CONACYT) and other decentralized institutions. ¥ Specific and sectoral institutions, science-based and strategic institutions are created.	¥ Lack of coordination between instruments, agents and services for technological development. ¥ Part of S&T policies falls under the supervision of CONACYT. ¥ Emergence of decentralized agents providing linkages across the existing actors.	¥ An institutional non-coordinated system appears, characterized by the dispersion of S&T policies. ¥ The emergence of bridging public and private institutions oriented to certification, quality standards and personnel training.

Figure 10.1 Co-evolution of Production System and Institutions.

knowledge, to build the equipment for production activity and the reproduction of the manufactured products. During this phase, effort is concentrated on product design activities; the quality of the product is improved, and attention is paid to product differentiation strategies. Conversely, the MNE's subsidiaries, in which production is mainly concentrated on standardized products, particularly autos, other durable consumer goods and traditional manufactures, have adopted the technologies developed by the parent companies in the industrialized countries. In the MNE's local subsidiaries, the technological flow between the subsidiaries and the parent firm influences the evolution of technological trajectories. In the initial phases, the effort is to adapt the blueprints and the equipment to the local environment through industrial engineering activities. In large domestic firms, the evolution of the technological trajectory is similar to that of the local subsidiaries of MNEs.

During the transition period, we can see that a large number of firms in different sectors have disappeared. In this context, it is important to remember that during the financial crisis the companies had significant problems in obtaining financing, particularly the SMEs. More recently, this analysis of Mexico's production system confirms that the nation captured a dynamic comparative advantage, but only in efforts related to modernization in the most successful export firms: subsidiaries of MNEs and large domestic firms. There was an increase in learning capacity, in terms of improving organizational efficiency, skills and production organization. This process can clearly be explained by the requirements necessary to compete in international markets, specifically related to quality and standard certification (for example, sectors such as automobiles, electronics and glass containers).

Modernization process and technological capabilities

Mexico's macro and trade policies have had a great deal of influence over the technological paths of its production system; another important factor is the new regulatory framework introduced by NAFTA. Promoters of liberalization and deregulation argue that a stable and open economic environment encourages insertion in the international arena, thus contributing to an increase in overall competitiveness (see Aspe, 1993). From this point of view, horizontal industrial policies should provide a more appropriate framework in order to upgrade techno-logical capabilities and efforts. In other words, policy-makers assumed that no measure other than letting the market operate through adequate price signals should be taken in order to grant the optimal allocation of resources and technological upgrading.

In general, the picture that emerges is one of a country that has faced a radical 'selection shock'. In this section, we discuss and review the pattern that emerges at the sectoral and firm levels. Improvement in technological capabilities has occurred mostly within large exporter firms; there has been little communication with institu-tions, and the response has been minimal in terms of the prevalent S&T policies. In other words, the learning and innovation process in Mexico has responded primarily to price and market signals, and not to the tailor-made S&T policies – which were, of course, designed to have an impact on this process, but were not properly articulated and lacked clear incentives, which were frequently addressed badly. These observa-tions are supported by one important fact: firms throughout the various sectors have heightened efforts to increase productivity and quality.

On the basis of the sectoral analysis and from the results of several surveys a picture of the historical path of each sector can be drawn (Corona, 1998; Lara and Corona, 1998; Lara, 1998; Vera-Cruz, A., 1998; Dutrénit, 1998; Arvanitis, 1998). Examples include the chemistry, brewery and glass containers sectors, in which R&D activities have been predominantly reoriented towards quality, cost reduction, standardization requirements and utilization of imported machinery and equipment. In the case of the pharmaceutical industry, the trend seems to show a significant influence from the new institutional framework; for example, the new intellectual property regulations. For example, firms mainly devoted to improving production processes have paid only scant attention to developing new active principles (sub-stances).

The automobile industry developed during the import substitution era, under the leadership of transnational companies, and during the most recent period it con-tinued its privileged position as an industrial policy objective (e.g. a highly protected sector). During import substitution, it maintained a very capital-intensive dynamic, combined with high relative wages, even though production technology was not competitive at an international level. At the present time, in the context of a restructuring of production at an international level, the Mexican automobile industry has demonstrated export capacity while reducing the gap in productivity compared to the United States. Likewise, the composition of domestic production has been specialized in the most labour-intensive segments and importing inputs that require a greater technological intensity. During the import substitution process, the technological capabilities that Mexico acquired were associated with adapting equipment and blueprints, as well as adapting design and products for the local market. Currently, firms are modernizing productive processes, increasing the degree of specialization and the dimension of scale to achieve international standards. Firms are developing local research capacity applied to production and improvement in organizational efficiency (see Chapter 15).

The chemical industry had support in the form of specific protection designed to stimulate the development of national companies, thus limiting the participation of transnational firms during the import substitution period. Based on Mexico's natural resources, production diversified, with active government participation in development and direct production. During this period, an institutional system developed to support such activity, creating specialized institutions and the development of specialized human capital. This sector makes an intensive use of capital and pays the highest wages of all Mexican manufacturing. None the less, despite institutional efforts, this industry's expenditures on R&D are relatively low compared to international parameters (see Chapter 11).

Under the leadership of domestic companies, the brewing industry is characterized by having made significant efforts in terms of the technology incorporated in capital goods and human capital. This industry presents significant economies of scale that were developed for the domestic market. Due to the characteristics of a homogeneous and tradable product it could relatively quickly and easily be reoriented towards the international market, particularly during the 1982–8 crisis years. This industry's R&D expenditure is double that of the United States. R&D is oriented towards production efficiency, improvements in quality, training of employed personnel and the merger of companies as mechanisms for learning at the international level, thus reducing costs and carrying out 'external benchmarking'.

The electronic industry is suffering due to a process that involves a significant transformation in the composition of production, and its *maquiladora* production predominates in this sector, and even production destined for the domestic market showed a significant reduction in the level of integration of domestically made electronics. Prices dropped significantly in relative terms, decreasing the importance of added value in manufacturing. This sector is led by transnational companies, and its efforts are oriented towards quality improvement, costs reduction, changes in the organization of production and in training of the plant's personnel.

In general, the evolution of industry seems to indicate a lack of effort in the creation of networks between firms – within a sector or between sectors – and the institutions. This situation is related to the type of specialization that has been followed, based on traditional natural resources, the use of less qualified labour and the increased dependence on imported capital goods. This has been accompanied by the disappearance of the following sectors: capital equipment and, generally, specialized suppliers. In addition, these firms have also experienced a diversification process and an international integration, which reduced the contribution of domestic subcontractors in important scale-intensive activities. This modernization process, however, has occurred mostly within the firms. Think of the case of chemicals, brewing and glass containers sectors in which R&D activities have been mainly reoriented to quality, cost reduction, standardization requirements and utilization of imported machinery and equipment (Cimoli, Cingano and della Giusta, 1998; Ortiz, 1994 and 1998).

Other technological patterns can be identified in the textile and footwear sectors, for example. In textiles, joint ventures and *maquiladora* firms are increasingly gaining importance and competing in the international arena. Here, the learning process is primarily characterized by efforts in training, just-in-time production and better commercialization. Family-run businesses – a large part of the textile sector – are characterized by inefficient organization and administration. Their main efforts are concentrated on increasing economies to scale and organizational efficiency as suppliers in the domestic market. In contrast, the footwear sector is one of the examples in which regional technology policies and institutions have supported the learning process undertaken by firms. Thus, these companies have increased their capacity to obtain better quality, as well as greater integration among the firms within the sector, accomplished by establishing an industrial district (for example, Nuevo Leon).

This upgrade in technological capabilities – achieved by some Mexican firms – has been associated and defined as a *modernization process*. In order to proceed to a more detailed description of the industrial restructuring process, Arteaga and Micheli (1997) have compiled a simple index that makes it possible to identify precisely the industrial activities with the highest concentration of companies involved in modernization processes. In this empirical exercise, modernization is principally associated with the acquisition of new capital goods and a new organizational pattern in production activities. Five indicators are used for computing the Index of Modernization Efforts: (a) introduction of automated machinery and equipment; (b) R&D efforts; (c) type of maintenance (corrective/preventive); (d) an automatic quality control process in place; (e) a quality control process by operation in place. Establishments fulfilling all five criteria can be considered companies in which the modernization process has been seriously pursued (high modernization efforts). The researchers then proceeded to determine the distribution of such establishments throughout the 52 manufacturing branches or industrial activities. Such identification can provide the basis for observing – according to a different classification – efforts in Mexico to address the modernization of the manufacturing industry.

This, in turn, permitted the researchers to assign a level for each of the industrial activities, according to the proportion of establishments pursuing high modernization efforts. The basic configuration revealed by the index is indicated in the following figures: industrial activities characterized by high efforts account for only 4.4 per cent of the total manufacturing establishments, but they generate 36.2 per cent of the total production value. Specifically, the activities with high modernization efforts are preserved foods, edible oils and fat, the sugar industry, tobacco, basic

Table 10.1 The Main Characteristics of Modernization Processes in Mexico, 1989–1991

Modernization effort	Number of establishments	Production value	Employment	Establishments involved in	
				Machinery modernization	Organizational changes
High	4.4	36.2	27.9	59.3	25.0
Medium	9.4	32.0	22.9	44.7	22.2
Low	42.3	23.5	30.4	26.1	18.2
Very low	43.9	8.3	18.8	28.6	12.7
Total	100	100	100	30.4*	13.9*

* Shares of the total establishments involved in machinery modernization and organizational changes respectively.
Source: Arteaga and Micheli (1997), data taken from *Encuesta Nacional de Empleo, Salarios, Tecnología y Capacitación.*

chemicals, artificial fibres, pharmaceuticals, plastic products, the basic iron and steel industry, metal furniture, the automobile industry and electronics. Industrial activities with lower efforts account for 43.9 per cent of the total establishments, but generate only 8.3 per cent of production value.

In the group of establishments pursuing high modernizing efforts, almost 60 per cent brought in machinery or equipment during the period analysed, while 25 per cent made changes in their labour organization (see Table 10.1). In the latter case, the most frequent modification was an increase in workers' technical knowledge (61.5 per cent of the establishments), followed by an increase in the degree of workers' autonomy or responsibility (53.4 per cent). Conversely, the least frequent change was in the number of assignments per worker (24.5 per cent).

Type of firms and their historical paths

The process described above appears to be dominated by two types of firms: subsidiaries of MNEs and large domestic firms. Both types show a higher capacity to compete in the international market; however, their historical technological patterns are different. MNEs have benefited from large incentives to set up production facilities within Mexico, due to the trade policy and, more recently, to NAFTA, in particular for firms from outside the North American region (Japan, Europe, etc.). The MNEs maintain strong links with their parent companies with regard to technological flows; their learning path is mainly by adapting capital goods equipment, increasing production capacity and improving process innovation and quality standards. Moreover, an effort to increase inter-firm linkages (producer/user) and personnel training is present. In this context, we distinguish between the MNEs, in which production involves locally available inputs other than the labour force, and the *maquiladora* industry. For example, one crucial difference between the two is the absorption of local inputs in some sectors such as the automobile industry; in contrast, in the *maquiladora* industry, reliance on local specialized inputs is much weaker. On the other hand, the pattern of large domestic firms cannot be understood without considering two main historical facts: their learning efforts during the import substitution phase; and their efforts to gain higher productivity and quality through their modernization processes in the 1990s (Capdevielle, Cimoli and Dutrénit, 1997; Cimoli, Cingano and della Giusta, 1998; Garrido, 1995, 1998a and b; Garrido and Péres, 1998).

During the import substitution process, these large local firms developed economies of scale that enabled them to compete in the international market, once they faced an open economy. This implied adapting plans, blueprints and designs in the domestic market, as well as an effort to improve organization and increase production capacity. However, some of these firms also developed R&D activities in order to generate their own knowledge base. Probably, the most remarkable experience during the 1970s was that of the steel producer Hylsa, a subsidiary of Grupo Alfa. This firm developed a production method, named Hyl, that resulted in a significant reduction in costs. This method began to be used by steel producers in other countries, and it became an international industry standard. Hylsa is not an isolated case. Other interesting examples include Visa-Femsa, the Modelo Brewery and Vitro, which produces glass containers. These firms developed their own R&D departments, which helped to reduce costs, and they successfully used imported machinery, as well as other innovations, to reduce costs (Dutrénit in Chapter 14).

During import substitution, these large firms specialized in the processing of raw materials for the production of commodities directed to the local market – particularly, food, tobacco, beer and soft drinks – or intermediate commodities, such as cement, glass, steel, chemicals and petrochemicals. A protected market and local demand allowed the development of both economies of scale and intrasectoral vertical integration, which comprehended the whole production process from the extraction of raw materials to the distribution of final commodities throughout the entire country. This process also implied that these firms adapted plans, blueprints and designs in the domestic market, based on technological alliances with the MNE as well as an effort to improve organization and increase production capacity. However, some of these firms also developed R&D activities in order to generate their own knowledge base. Moreover, as a result of the learning process that occurred during import substitution, the large domestic industrial firms created specific assets, accumulated managerial skills and developed specific organizational structures.

In the chemicals sector, Cydsa, Resistol (member of Grupo Desc) and Alpek (member of Grupo Alfa) made technological alliances with MNEs such as Dupont or Cabot Corporation. In the autoparts sector, firms like Nemak from Grupo Alfa or Tremec and Spicer from Grupo Desc also formed technological alliances with firms such as Ford, General Motors and Nissan, and consequently they became important producers for the significant automobile firms. Finally, in the food industry, the bakery company Bimbo was able to adapt and develop new technological sets for production, and Grupo Maseca created a new technology that changed the 'tortilla' industry (as a result, tortillas became an industrial product.)

In the 1990s, under the new regulatory framework, these large local firms were forced to restructure and reorganize their activities to be able to compete in a global context. In other words, they improved their productive competitiveness and strengthened their positions in the local markets. They benefited from the new technological inflow incorporated in capital goods, equipment and intermediate commodities, provided by the new open economy framework. Some traditional firms, like Hylsa, developed long-term investment programmes (in the case of Hylsa, the programme spanned the period 1990–7) that permitted them to reach the industry's international competitive standards. These firms also renewed their technology; at the present time, there are more than forty steel producers in twenty countries using the Hylsa method. Other firms, such as Cementos Mexicanos (CEMEX), developed new technological and managerial skills; CEMEX became the third largest cement producer in the world. In a different experience, DINA, an old state-owned truck manufacturer that is now under new private owners, used its technical-historical evolution to become a North American class producer which includes MCI in the United States.

During the 1990s, under the new regulatory framework, these large local firms were able to modernize their production process and organizations. That is, they improved their international competitiveness and production capacity, and they strengthened their position in the local and foreign markets. Since the mid-1970s, CEMEX had started to export to the southern United States, the Caribbean region and Central America. At the same time, it continued to increase its presence in the domestic market, through the acquisition of smaller firms, the construction of new production plants and the renewal of already existing plants. The company has also diversified its activity, by opening commercial firms in countries where its products are sold and by producing paper bags and concrete (Garrido, 1995, 1998a; Garrido and Péres, 1998).

During the same period, CEMEX also made important investments to purchase cement plants abroad, as well as to renew and open new plants within Mexico, such as the Tepeaca plant in the State of Puebla, which is of considerable size and has leading technology at world level that permits it to operate on a multiple plant system and to develop vertical integration at a multinational level. From the point of view of organizational structure, CEMEX has integrated its regional or country activities as a global structure organized in three important divisions. These divisions are highly articulated and centralized through a sophisticated – via satellite – computerized communication network. With this infrastructure, the executives of different subsidiaries all over the world keep in touch continuously through video conferences. This expansion of computer science within CEMEX has led the enterprise to create Cemtec, a new subsidiary whose mission is to qualify high ranking executives in this field: both from CEMEX plants and from other companies within the region, at international levels.

Visa-Femsa exported its brews to the United States, thus becoming a strong competitor with the big American and German brewers. Grupo Bimbo and Grupo Maseca have also successfully exported their plants and technologies to the United States, as well as Latin American countries. Finally, the newcomers on the horizon of large local firms discovered new roles for R&D and technological skills in the arena of global competition. This is the case of Empresas La Moderna, a member of Grupo Pulsar, formerly the biggest tobacco and cigar producer in the country, which has recently switched to agriculture based on biotechnology. La Moderna bought several international firms with strong skills in biotechnology R&D, and the company has made a strategic alliance with Monsanto to divide and share vegetable and legume markets in Europe and America. The main purpose of this change in activity is to specialize in horticultural and forest production and in the biotechnology frontier field. The latter was promoted by the merger with the Agrícola Batiz enterprise, the major Mexican producer and exporter of vegetables and legumes to the United States. Furthermore, Seminis, a seeds and grains firm, was created as part of the Agricultural Biotechnology Division of Empresas La Moderna. The initiative to form Seminis was a consequence of the positive results obtained with the biotechnological improvements that Empresa La Moderna made through its Bionova enterprise in tobacco production, basic input for Cigarrrera La Moderna. Furthermore, this was a product of the decision to restructure the Pulsar group investments, in order to achieve positions in a global industry, such as biotechnology. From this perspective, the group bought several international firms that produce seeds, such as Asgrow Seed, Petoseed and DNA Plant Technology Co. (DNAP). Specifically, with the purchase of DNAP, Grupo Pulsar acquired the most technologically advanced enterprise in the field of control and manipulation of genes to inoculate them in seeds, thus achieving a notable technological advantage. The company also acquired laboratories all over the world, with more than 500 researchers in the biotechnology field. Presently, the firm budgets 14 per cent of its invoicing in seeds and vegetables for R&D, and it plans to increase this figure to 18 per cent.

With the Seeds Division for vegetables and legumes of Asgrow Seed, La Moderna controls 22 per cent of the world market for this kind of seed, 39 per cent of the North American market and 24 per cent of the European market. In addition, La Moderna and Monsanto reached a cooperation agreement by which the latter would be the strategic provider of Seminis biotechnology, for the improvement of agricultural species by producing the next generation of seed. Furthermore, DNAP would work with Monsanto in the development and application of new technologies for improved fruits and vegetables. The agreement with Monsanto put Empresas La Moderna in a position to combine its germplasm bank, its R&D capabilities and its distribution network with frontier leading technologies. Likewise, Seminis and Monsanto recently agreed on a strategic alliance with Mandel-Bio, which gives La Moderna exclusive access to Mandel-Bio's genetic and genomic work and developments. Consequently, with regard to integration, Empresas La Moderna Seminis's international production, as well as its strategic development, is closely associated with Monsanto's international structure. In March 1999, Pulsar restructured the conglomerate, transforming Empresas La Moderna into Savia, which joins all the agrobusiness activities, including R&D.

In general, those big local enterprises operating in mature industries confront great dilemmas in terms of their future development. On the one hand, they can continue on the already walked path, broadening and stabilizing the product's life cycle by increasing economies of scale, efficiency and product differentiation; at the same time, they would decrease costs and increase added value, in order to keep their international position. On the other hand, the firm could opt to move its investments to new industries based on the development of knowledge through R&D, as well as innovative activities, which are fundamental for long-term growth, competitiveness and profitability. However, this option is problematic for most enterprises, because it requires important amounts of investment, as well as considerable technological, organizational and managerial capabilities.

Institutions that support technological capabilities

S&T policies and institutions have also changed throughout the different phases of development (Part II in this book: Casalet on the institutional matrix; Valenti, Varela and Castillo on human resources and universities; Casas, de Gortari and Luna on knowledge production and universities linkages). From import substitution to the most recent period, the improvement in human resources has not only been maintained but also grown continuously, based on a variety of instruments: scholarships, public financing, etc. An improvement in research centres and universities, in terms of personnel and publication quality, can also be observed.

Moreover, different types of institutions have been created. The emphasis during the first period was on specialized and public sector institutions, in which an institutional-push model prevailed. After the transition phase, and in the new regulatory framework, new institutions have appeared which are determined mainly by a new scenario in which firms are required to satisfy norms concerning the quality, standardization and certification of products and processes. In this context, bridge institutions that act as intermediaries aspire to and, increasingly, assume the linkages between the firms' demands and public knowledge, which satisfies the above requirements.

However, this phenomenon has appeared only recently and very few institutions are, in fact, assuming this role; moreover, it would appear that the response from institutions is mainly supported by public policies and the production system's needs. This co-evolution process, as in other countries, is not linear and coordination is not optimally determined. In particular, our analysis conveys the idea that these two systems – institutions and the production system (firms and sectors) – do really interact according to different sets of incentives. The picture thus emerging is a dichotomy, in which large and successful firms push their learning efforts in small linkages with local institutions and respond weakly to the pre-competitive incentives created, inasmuch as their efforts concentrate on responding to the incentives promoted by the nation's macro and trade policies. On the other side, institutions have difficulty in promoting linkages with an industry characterized by reduced technological opportunities (particularly for the firms that do not export).

The sectoral system of innovation: a clustering approach

In the technical literature, there are a variety of definitions for the term cluster. In the present work, however, and notwithstanding the NIS concept (or any other innovation systems at the meso and micro levels), this term is developed considering that a central and crucial aspect is the fact that innovation and innovative processes remain the main aspects to be explained.

A variety of concepts have recently been brought forward in order to define the nature of innovative activities: technological regimes, paradigms, trajectories, salience, guide posts, dominant designs, etc. There is a great amount of overlapping material in these concepts, since what they attempt to grasp is, basically, the main common features in sources, patterns and directions of technical change. In other words, these concepts are commonly associated with the advancement of innovation, as measured by changes in the fundamental techno-economic characteristics of artefacts and production processes (for a discussion and references, see Chapter 1). A comprehensive explanation of the above-mentioned concepts is not the purpose of the following discussion. The common ground relating these topics is that each particular body of knowledge shapes and constrains the rates and direction of innovation, regardless of market inducement. This does not imply that price signals are unimportant; instead, the firm's innovative activities are bounded by the available knowledge along either a narrow road or a modem highway, which none the less sets a definite path, no matter how broad this path might be.

It follows that it should be possible to observe regularities and invariances in innovation patterns that could display significant shifts when radical changes in the knowledge base appear. Consider, for example, the subsequent modifications in innovation patterns among the different firms and sectors as technology changed from transistors to integrated circuits, where the combination of laser and mechanical technologies appears. Changes in paradigms induce new narrow roads within modern highways, along which firms find new innovation patterns. To date, for an established paradigm and trajectory, it is widely acknowledged in the literature on innovation that learning processes are local and cumulative, and are, furthermore, incorporating and determining firms' technological competencies. By local we mean the efforts and technology competencies that principally surround the set of techniques that firms use. By cumulative we mean the significance of past production and innovation experiences as a key background to gain competencies for specific problem-solving activities and to absorb knowledge from the environment.

These general ideas can be applied at the sectoral level regarding, more specifically, concepts such as opportunity and appropriability conditions, cumulativeness of technological knowledge and the nature of the knowledge base. This could clearly be considered as a basis for understanding the reasons behind the existence of differentiated sectors. Sectors are different not only because they produce different goods (consider, for instance, automobiles and cakes, different products intended for different purposes) but also because they have different patterns associated with the opportunities presented by changes in their knowledge base, their capacity to capture such opportunities and the cumulative experience and historical path that underlie their current status. We should nevertheless add that the above statement does not mean that products have nothing to do with the ways they are produced; instead, this text emphasizes how technological patterns are developed (Dosi *et al.*, 1988; Winter, 1984; Dosi and Nelson, 1993; Carlsson and Stankiewicz, 1995; Malerba and Orsenigo, 1996; Breschi and Malerba, 1997).

It follows immediately from the previous discussion and Chapter 1 that when we are defining a sectoral system of innovation, the elements that we mentioned above need to be taken into consideration. It is in this sense that, within the framework of the Mexican innovation system, attention should be devoted first to the particular dynamics in the industrial sector that were developed under continuous pressure from both the macroeconomic setting and trade policy (Cimoli, 2000; Katz, 2000). Moreover, the institutional framework and geographical distribution that surround the sector are identified with a meso level that is combined with the sector's technological pattern. On the other hand, since the sectors are ultimately formed by firms, the technological patterns and dynamics of the critical set of firms within a sector determine the whole sector's innovation pattern.

It is only now that we may proceed to define a sectoral innovation cluster, in which coherence with the main approaches underlining the theory of innovation systems will be preserved. A sectoral innovation cluster can be defined as a group of firms that share a common way of making and developing artefacts that are determined by specific conditions of opportunity, appropriability, cumulativeness and knowledge base, which in turn are, in and of themselves, embedded in a framework of particular competitive relationships and institutional linkages. Moreover, the characterization of each sectoral cluster within the innovation system, according to the conditions mentioned above, allows us to provide a qualitative evaluation of the gaps between Mexico and other industrialized economies.

The conditions in which opportunities can be differentiated across sectors and reflect the likelihood for innovation in any given effort are associated with different sources. In some sectors, these conditions are related to scientific linkage with universities and other research institutions; for others, the main sources are internal technological efforts, based on R&D and the acquisition of equipment. Yet opportunities in other sectors are mainly generated through user–producer relationships. Appropriability conditions relate to the capability to apprehend the benefits of innovation. Some sectors could be characterized by high appropriability conditions, in which firms could successfully protect their innovations from imitation. In other sectors, knowledge is easily diffused and appropriated by a large spectrum of firms. Cumulativeness is linked to past experiences and the ability to develop new technologies. Cumulative conditions, however, are not easily applied to the concept of sectors, since they are endogenously determined within the firms. None the less, the dynamics that the sector follows, to a certain extent, are the dynamics of a critical set of firms and the competitive relationships among these companies. Knowledge base refers to the differences in the sector's scientific foundation and how this affects innovative activities. The knowledge base underlying a sector can be of a generic or specific nature; it can be achieved with varying degrees of complexity, with differences in integration in terms of scientific disciplines and competencies to acquire this knowledge.

We must point out that although the present approach appears to follow a technological-push model, we also have clearly acknowledged that such an approach needs to be combined with other crucial elements, such as the competitive relationships among the firms and the network of agents which interact with these firms, within a specific institutional and regulatory framework. To clarify the concept we mentioned in the previous paragraph, when speaking about competitive relationships, firms behave differently depending on whether they compete in local or global markets. It is possible to differentiate within sectors and industries on the basis of their competitive boundaries, from the more local to the national and up to the international competition arenas. Not only are competitive relationships in terms of products relevant; the modalities in which firms compete regarding the acquisition of equipments, intermediate commodities, etc. from local or foreign suppliers are significant as well. Moreover, the institutional and organizational frameworks within which firms (in some sectors) are nested are also important in determining and understanding the technological patterns present in a company's competitive profile.

It is clear that the two concepts introduced in the paragraphs above (the first referring to the technological base of the firm and the second related to competitive relationships) are interdependent in the co-evolutionary sense. In other words, it is not only opportunity, appropriability, cumulativeness and the knowledge base that determine competitive relationships, it is also the relationship between the set of these four aspects and the competitive relationships that determine one another.

In the following chapters, sectoral clusters are built up on the basis of the main features and specificities observed in the firms in each sector. The identification of the four conditions is the final step in a descriptive analysis of the main characteristics prevailing in the chosen sectors. In this context, innovative activities can be distributed across different regions or highly concentrated within some regions. As was noted in Chapter 1, innovation proceeds through the interaction of many different institutions within the system, involving some sort of informal and formal knowledge linkages.

In Chapter 16, we analyse how geographical specificity – in terms of local technological capability – can explain the transmission and communication of knowledge. Chapters 15 and 16 provide the example of a case of sectoral and regional convergence of technological capabilities in terms of the role played by the automobile industry in the state of Aguascalientes.

Notes

1. We should mention that the data for this study are based on several industrial surveys, which support our analysis at the micro level. Special surveys were carried out for each of the sectors, covering a large number of firms; several of the ENESTYC surveys for different years were used. Other surveys used were: the survey applied in the DGXII project on Science and Technology Policies in Mexico, the OSTROM and UAM surveys on the chemical sector, CONACYT's 1997 National Innovation Survey and CONACYT's 1995 and 1997 National R&D Surveys.

2. See Cimoli *et al.* (1998), Corona (1998), Lara and Corona (1998), Lara (1998), Vera-Cruz (1998), Dutrénit (1998), Arvanitis (1998), Arteaga and Micheli (1997), Ortiz (1998, 1994), Garrido, (1995, 1998a, b) and Garrido and Péres (1998).

3. Formal applications of this general idea are found in Nelson and Winter (1982), Winter (1984) and Dosi *et al.* (1993).

CHAPTER ELEVEN

Learning and Innovation in the Chemical Industry

R. Arvanitis and D. Villavicencio

Introduction

Technological and organizational learning in firms has received a great deal of attention in the innovation literature. Today, next to the analysis of the economic impact of innovations, and the strong efforts made to create models of the growth patterns by including technological change, the processes by which firms build their learning capabilities are an issue in themselves. Technological performance and innovation are largely the result of these processes. But at the same time, a debate has been opened about the origins and importance of the internal learning capabilities of firms and the influence of external factor, such as the macroeconomic conditions, the level of development of material infrastructure, the educational levels of the population and the institutional framework. All these have been wrongly opposed to the internal learning of a specific company. Indeed, the whole issue of the national system of innovation can be seen as an interrogation about the relations between these internal capabilities and the environment of the firms. Our study tackles the issue by looking at the specific case of the chemical industry.

After a brief overview of the trends in the chemical sector worldwide and a presentation of the general characteristics of this industry in Mexico, we focus our analysis on the technological behaviour of firms. Based on the research we carried out on several chemical firms in Mexico, we can conclude that the industry has shown undeniable learning capabilities, accumulated mainly in the past thirty years. Our approach stresses the fact that the answers given by firms have not been uniform. The learning experiences should ideally be seen as unique to a particular firm: all firms differ in their technological behaviour and consequently in their performances. The important fact here is that even when belonging to the same industrial sector, sharing the same market and institutional environment, firms can behave differently. What, then, makes such a strong difference? All sorts of answers can be given depending on the resources that one sees as more important, which shrinks down to looking at how these resources are channelled to the productive units as well as how the companies view their environment, their limits and advantages. The way companies diffuse knowledge among departments and organizational divisions, the way this knowledge is managed, the way 'knowledge channels' such as suppliers' or clients' needs are managed, contribute to the particular behaviour of a firm. The whole universe of chemical companies is examined in terms of technological regime differences where three large clusters are defined. As is noted in Chapter 10, each cluster can be characterized by its differences in terms of opportunity, appropriability, cumulativity, knowledge base composition and the technological linkages that firms establish.

Overview of the chemical innovation system worldwide

The chemical market is a very large one, representing one trillion US dollars in 1990, 1991, p. 104), dominated by very large companies. The largest one, Höescht, announced sales of 36,408 million dollars. European companies, which are the more important ones, tend to be multiproduct firms, including a pharmaceutical division, whereas American companies tend to be more specialized. By and large, the typical expansion policies until the early 1980s were based upon vertical integration. Nowadays, a turn has been made and most of the expansion strategies focus on specific markets through mergers and buying smaller specialized companies.

In the 1980s and until 1995, the world market prices for commodities fell regularly. After these sharp decreases in prices, the industry has been obliged to go through a thorough restructuring process that ended in more efficient plants, with firms looking at focusing on their 'core competencies' instead of diversifying their production. The sector has also been marked by numerous alliances and cooperative agreements on both commercial and technological grounds. The restructuring of the chemical industry world wide has been particularly important for the large European companies, such as Höescht, Bayer, Akzo and ICI.

The role of national state policies has been crucial in this period. In all industrialized countries, the state has been active in implementing all sorts of instruments, including subsidies and direct intervention (OECD, 1992a). But in most cases, the policies have been implemented through indirect action: strengthening public research and technologies programmes, procurement programmes, policies for human capital formation and mediation in salary negotiations with trade unions and active interventions in financial and fiscal matters (OECD, 1992b). Probably a quite efficient means of action, although difficult to measure, has been that of concertation, networking and the gathering of distinct actors from a variety of different social and economic contexts. The existence of cooperative and technological alliances has fostered a more rapid communication between the public and the private sectors in Europe, the USA and Japan. But some evidence indicates this to be true even in large developing countries. These types of cooperative technological agreements, joint ventures and similar technological alliances are particularly active in new technological markets such as combined polymers, new materials and biotechnological developments applied to chemical processing.

Companies, and not only state policies, have been protagonists of these networking efforts. Although it is known that large companies in the chemical sector have historically been active promoters of technological development in cooperation with university research centres, they now assist in the expansion of cooperative technological agreements (Hounshell and Smith, 1988). These take many forms and may combine distinct types of competencies and up to a certain point are learning experiences (Bruno, 1995). It is also important to remember that the chemical sector has been historically largely based upon a great ability to promote large investments, reduce costs by scale economies and distribute products on large global markets. After the profound restructuring of the 1980s, the sector has been more geared to innovation of processes rather than products, designing more flexible and efficient productive schemes (Arvanitis and Mercado, 1996).

Technology in the chemical sector is complex and cannot be reduced to a unique and simplistic view. One way to differentiate within the industry is to distinguish a more traditional industrial sector, linking basic chemical 'commodities' to products directly dependent upon them, and a second sector that relies upon the finer products with high value added and satisfies a demand for differentiated products. Recently some authors have introduced the notion of 'performance products' which can be both pseudo-commodities (high production of low cost products for specific uses) and specialities. The sector is a science-based sector according to Pavitt (1984), owing to the central role played by R&D and academic science. A more in-depth view of the sector would create a more complex image, with the coexistence of at least three divisions: traditional scale-intensive industries (mainly commodities and pseudo-commodities); firms which act as specialized suppliers tailoring products with traditional technological content to the needs of their clients; and science-based firms in advanced technological areas and markets. Most large firms typically belong to all three of them.

The chemical industry seems to be moving along the following lines worldwide: (a) increased market globalization; (b) a growing importance of 'clean' products or environmentally friendly products and processes; (c) products – and thus production – seem to meet clients' expectations more closely. These general lines imply a strong pressure towards efficient quality programmes, efficient production and 'just-in-time' or similar no-stock schemes, as competitive advantages. Thus knowledge on production processing is essential, as well as R&D product knowledge. Conversely, a large portion of production depends on low prices of inputs, which in petroleum producing countries such as Mexico is a competitive advantage. Traditionally, science and technology have been closely linked to the chemical sector; chemical engineering is one of the outcomes of this close link. Nowadays, the chemical sciences and engineering are undergoing large changes in order to address future challenges: (a) new synthesis techniques for combining molecules; (b) new catalysers and reactive systems that allow for shorter life-cycle products, more efficient and environmentally friendly processes; (c) alternative uses of traditional raw materials; (d) new materials with better performances and shorter production routes, or routes that allow new combinations of materials in the process; (e) the introduction of bioprocesses in traditional chemical industries (ACS, 1996; Arvanitis and Mercado 1996).

These trends are not uniformly applied to all companies and all industrial plants. However, they reveal the importance of functions inside firms that become vital: the ability to have a prospective view of the market and devise new strategies and the growing role of R&D and engineering clearly indicate these new trends. Problem-solving activities are to become increasingly complex, thus demanding a closer articulation of these productive functions, different knowledge and different types of actors. Innovation seems to be the product of an articulate network of institutions more than the sole product of the internal R&D effort of a firm. Table 11.1

Table 11.1 Comparison of General Characteristics of the Chemical Industry in Industrialized Countries and Mexico

	Industrialized countries	Mexico
Firms' characteristics	Large firms dominate the market; great number of small and medium-sized companies specialized in specific products in high-tech 'niche' markets. Firms growth mainly by mergers.	Large firms are medium-sized by international standards; few high-tech small companies. Firms growth by exports and to limited extent by mergers.
Production characteristics	High scale of production. High diversification of products. Multiproduct companies. High costs of inputs, mainly petrochemicals. Vertical integration from basic petrochemicals to final finished consumer market and semi-finished products (industrial markets).	Small scale of production. Limited diversification. Low product scope. Low cost of petrochemicals. Limited vertical integration due to the state monopoly on basic petrochemicals.
Strategies	Continuous introduction of innovative products. Numerous technological alliances between firms (large and small). Concentration to 'core activities'. More efficient production. Flexible schemes of production. Environmentally oriented strategies are dominating the R&D and innovation process; strong incentive for pollution prevention rather than 'end-of-pipe' pollution abatement.	Improvement of the quality of products, few innovative products. Very few technological alliances. More efficient production. 'End-of-pipe' pollution abatement, environmental behaviour responds to 'command-and-control' governmental strategies. Feeble voluntary environmental strategies.
R&D	High basic research intensity in firms, strong links with academic science and numerous independent R&D consultant firms.	Low R&D oriented towards basic processes and components in firms, few links with academia, no independent R&D.
Innovation	Highly intensive innovation process, in both products and processes.	Low innovation, mainly oriented towards adaptation of products to local markets and efficient production processes.
Markets	Large commodities markets, strong competition in 'global' markets. Very diversified markets for a large variety of specific types of products, with high value-added ('pseudo-commodities', 'performance' products and specialities).	Small commodities domestic markets; need to export in order to sustain large-scale production costs. Extremely small and rare markets for specialities, performance products and pseudo-commodities. Niche markets for products tailored to the needs of clients.

summarizes the main characteristics of the chemical industry in industrialized countries and compares them to those of the Mexican industry.

Some general characteristics of the chemical industry[1]

The coverage of what is broadly identified as the chemical industry varies according to the different products and subsectors considered. For the purposes of this section, by chemical industry we mean basic petrochemicals (other than the most basic products controlled by Petróleos Mexicanos, PEMEX), intermediate chemical products (including agrochemicals) and final products excepting pharmaceuticals. Rubber and plastic products are also excluded.[2] The share of the chemical industry thus defined in total manufacturing GDP averaged 8 per cent in the period 1970–93, increasing slightly over the last few years; for instance, for 1993 its share was 10 per cent (see Table 11.1). The evolution of the GDP illustrates the fact that the chemical industry on the whole has had a rather smooth and rapid growth since 1970. Petrochemical goods are growing more slowly and even experience a decrease after 1993. Specialities, which are included in the 'other chemical products' category, and are more oriented towards the national market, experience more heavily the depression of the national market that is generated by devaluations. Major multi-national companies have also increased significantly their capacities in Mexico, which explains the rapid growth of sectors such as detergents and cosmetics and the large 'other chemical products' category.

The chemical sector includes industries that are essentially capital-intensive. But there is also a large population of medium and small companies that are labour-intensive. Overall, the industry is a low employer: it represents only 4.5 per cent of the workforce (as compared to 5.7 per cent of the US industry), and as ANIQ's Anuarios Estadísticos shows, the employment level decreased in 1995 with respect to 1994.[3] However, the sector's productivity has risen notably, up to three times the average labour productivity of the manufacturing industry in 1993. According to the industrial census, in 1993 there were 2,269 industrial chemical plants with an average of 81 employees per plant. Such an average might be misleading because of the great differences in industry's structure: large firms with more than 250 employees, while making up only 7 per cent of the total number of firms, account for 53 per cent of the labour force, whereas medium-sized firms represent 32 per cent of the labour force.

The chemical industry in Mexico has been concentrating production in larger firms, and shows a clear focus, both in these large firms and in successful SMEs, on exports as domestic demand diminishes. It thus profits from the industry's comparative advantages, mainly cheap inputs from the petrochemical sector and labour, advantages which apply for petrochemical basic products, pseudo-commodities and some special markets. Investment increased considerably around the early 1970s and at the beginning of the 1990s. Foreign direct investment from large foreign firms, and joint ventures between these and domestic firms, have also been significant. It should be noted none the less that the majority of investments are concentrated in large groups of firms. The industry's GDP is distributed in the following way: final products, 46 per cent (soaps, detergents, cosmetics, lubricants, paints, varnishes and so on); intermediate goods, 20 per cent (polymers and fibres); basic chemical products, 15.4 per cent, basic petrochemicals, 15.5 per cent.

Intra-industrial trade grew from 24 per cent in 1980 to 57 per cent in 1990, with more chemical firms catering for firms within the same industry. Finally, it must be recorded that the chemical industry is highly concentrated. The degree of concentration in each branch does not seem to depend upon the type of products, scale of production, orientation of sales or other productive characteristics; thus the degree of concentration is most certainly the product of the firms' strategies.

With the North American Free Trade Agreement (NAFTA) a new framework seemed to be put in place, although the opening of the sector to international trade took place even earlier, between 1985 and 1987.[4] Since the NAFTA opened the US market to Canadian and Mexican products, up to 92 per cent of Mexican chemical exports consist of products with no tariff barriers in the USA.

Both exports and imports have increased at a remarkably high rate since 1987, growing at an average rate of 15 per cent from 1993 to 1996. Mexico is strongly specialized in inorganic chemical products (e.g. petroleum derivatives) although it is a petroleum producing country. Exports have focused on dynamic international markets, though even with large shares Mexican exports grow at a lower rate than world commerce. The degree of specialization is rather low, and is mostly concentrated in markets which are relatively small, as measured by their 'sectoral contribution' (the share of a market in OECD imports). Thus, on the whole, export behaviour seems satisfactory but fragile. Nevertheless, this overall pattern hides the fact that exports are very concentrated in a few companies and that the absolute figures for exports are quite low. Moreover, the trade deficit is a structural problem throughout Mexican manufacturing industry whose explanation is beyond the scope of this chapter. It should be noted, however, that in general, large exporters are also large importers; this is also the case in this industry.[5]

While larger companies tend to export, they are generally more exposed to competition and also more keen on attending to efficiency and productivity on a more permanent basis, rather than supplying a market at whatever cost. Thus changes in the economic environment that resulted from the NAFTA have translated into changing strategies of large firms (Unger, 1994). SMEs, on the other hand, are faced with harsher financial shortcomings and principally serve domestic markets that are rather small and less competitive by nature, since their behaviour is more tightly linked to clients and they have greater dependence on external technologies. SMEs also have a more cautious attitude towards growth and external sources of growth (Villavicencio *et al.*, 1995; CEPAL, 1996).

Employment in the chemical industry has a large share of skilled workers, technicians and engineers, who have traditionally been developed within the firms themselves. In addition to this, the growth of graduates in chemical engineering and similar careers has been quite regular over the years. Thus the industry, and also the state and academic institutions, could rely on a regular flow of high level human resources.

As far as research in chemistry is concerned, it is interesting to note that chemical disciplines account for 8.9 per cent of all scientific publications in Mexico. However, the dominant areas of research – synthesis of natural products, analytical chemistry – are not oriented towards applied science. This clearly indicates how far the

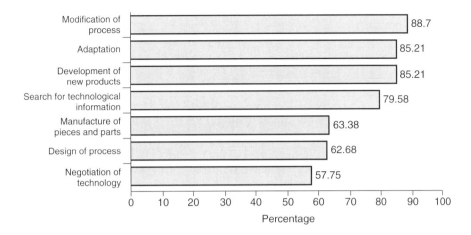

Figure 11.1 Internal Technological Learning Activities.
Source: ORSTOM-UAMX, Survey of the chemical sector, 1995.

Mexican research system is from the productive world, since even research on catalysis, a field with internationally recognized researchers, important publications and evident strategic interest for a petroleum-producing country, is mainly basic research (Arvanitis *et al.*, 1995, 1996). Recent efforts to link the academic world with the productive sector are few and very restricted.

Regarding patenting activities, the chemical field is the single most important field in Mexico: core chemical fields (organic and inorganic chemistry, agricultural chemistry, processes and petrochemicals) represented 23.6 per cent of the granted patents between 1980 and 1992, and 13,994 patents in the core chemical fields between 1980 and 1996, 15.21 per cent of the total registered patents.[6] The domestic firms' utilization of the patent system and industrial property is extremely poor, none the less. They applied for only 5 per cent of the total number of patent applications in Mexico, averaging between 400 and 600 patents per year since 1994, the year in which the new law of industrial property came into effect, which has mainly benefited foreign firms.

The learning capabilities in chemical firms

In Mexico, firms in the chemical industry have two important technological competencies. First, they are capable of modifying or improving production processes, adapting machinery and equipment according to their needs, by means of empirical activities based on the production and engineering personnel, activities that are often referred to when speaking of 'learning by doing'. Relatively few companies have experience in the design of new processes, which is a more complex activity indicative of a real design capacity. Second, they have capacities for developing new products, which constitutes the main orientation of innovative efforts. These new products may be the modification of chemical formulations, the copy of products or formulations and original formulations and products (see Figure 11.1).

It is difficult to assess the degree of novelty of new products. In most cases, novelty refers to the fact that the company introduces some product which is new to the Mexican market but usually exists in foreign markets. It appears that, although companies in the chemical sector have developed an important human resource base and effective technological capacities, they seem not to proceed to a more innovative behaviour. More than half the companies registered fewer than ten innovations in five years in products and processes. Only 12 per cent of surveyed companies introduced some new product not existing elsewhere. Thus the vast majority of chemical companies are moderate innovators looking mainly at copies or adaptations of already known products.

Most of the innovative firms developed their own R&D and engineering activities, and only few firms maintain cooperation agreements with external agents and institutions. In general, the main reasons for innovating are related to satisfying client's needs, increasing the quality of products, productivity and exports, in that order. The R&D activities of the firms are more important than is usually assumed from the official figures on R&D expenditure by the productive sector. We polled 87 companies out of the 1994 sample for whom we had verified data on R&D and sales. These 87 companies allotted a total of 176.7 million new pesos in 1994 for R&D activities. That represents an average of 2.76 million new pesos by company and 4.17 per cent of sales. If we include companies with no R&D expenses, the average R&D expenses amounts to an average of 2.24 per cent of sales. Furthermore, we have observed that almost a quarter of the companies do not have any serious R&D capacity. Effective R&D represents 45 per cent of our sample. The number of R&D personnel for the sample of 87 companies is 447, which represents 2.7 per cent of the total personnel in the sample.

Finally, if we observe the proportion of R&D expenses on sales, 18 per cent of the companies do not spend anything, 39 per cent spend less than 2 per cent of their sales and more than 40 per cent of the companies spend more than 2 per cent of their sales on R&D. Given the quite low innovative activities that we have mentioned above, it seems that R&D figures are quite high. In fact, a thorough examination of the content of R&D activities in most companies indicates that research organized by projects with medium-term objectives is very rare. Most R&D is dedicated to complementary activities: intensive search for information on technologies; service to production and marketing functions of the company, including the definition of client 'needs'. Additionally, and more importantly, compared to an homologous company of an industrialized country, the typical Mexican company will devote larger resources to developing its own research, information and training programme, all things that are rather difficult to find 'out there' in the vicinity of the company. Thus, the content of R&D activities is probably different in Mexican chemical companies than in, say, a German or a US company. What is different is the proportion of research 'projects' in Mexican companies. Probably, information search, technical support to production and marketing and other peripheral technical labours to the productive processes tend to be the bulk of the work in a typical R&D unit in Mexico. Furthermore, since most Mexican companies are buyers of foreign technology, the installation processes might be longer than in a country native to the technology. Distance, language, cultural differences and references all need to be digested by the local firm. This installation process might be a lot more important, and the R&D personnel will be typically engaged in this assimilation process.

The chemical companies usually adopt an 'autarchic' behaviour. Links with other institutions, public services, universities, research centres and so on are very weak. Links are strong with clients and foreign technology suppliers. They are moderate with universities as far as highly skilled engineers are concerned. The vast majority of companies never rely on outside sources of information when adopting strategic decisions. Our data show that companies have used their own developments for the productive technology improvements, as their own R&D capacities are the principal source of improvements in products and processes. Only half of the companies have narrow links with national companies for product and process developments and even fewer engage in links with universities and research centres.

Companies feel that when they wish to engage in an active development policy, even at a rather moderate level by adapting equipment or processes, or by engaging in minor innovations on products, there is nothing outside the company that might serve its information and knowledge purposes. Companies have to generate their own information and their own knowledge, and thus have shown to a large extent experience in searching for technological alternatives but a low negotiation capacity for foreign technologies (see Figure 11.1). Moreover, even for financial support public institutions are very little used by companies. So larger companies have more facility to grow because of larger in-house financial resources than SMEs.

Based on the above-mentioned survey, we can illustrate the external technological linkages of the firms (see Figure 11.2). The chemical industry prefers foreign suppliers of technology independently of size, origin of capital or market. Very few companies have approached universities or research centres for technological developments. The weakness of the relationships with universities is not related to the nature of the linkages with universities but to the difficulty companies have in establishing linkages with any type of suppliers or technical associates.

Foreign producers of equipment are largely preferred to local producers or commercial suppliers: 23 per cent of the surveyed companies had an exclusive contract with a foreign producer of equipment and 22 per cent had exclusive contacts with a commercial company that usually represented a foreign supplier. Only 9 per cent of the companies relied exclusively on a local equipment producer. The local supplier is usually a combined supplier with some foreign equipment producer. These figures illustrate both a preference of companies for foreign suppliers and a 'missing link' in industrial development. There are practically no reliable local producers of large equipment for industry. The capital goods industry is lagging behind in Mexico and the figures for preferences of suppliers translate this missing type of industry.

Links with clients are also very strong: 56 per cent of the companies sell more than 40 per cent of their production to their three more important clients. This proportion goes up to 30 per cent for those selling more than 60 per cent of their product to their principal clients. In the majority of cases the relations are on a long-term basis. The intensity of these links has to do with their markets: links are more intense with industrial clients.

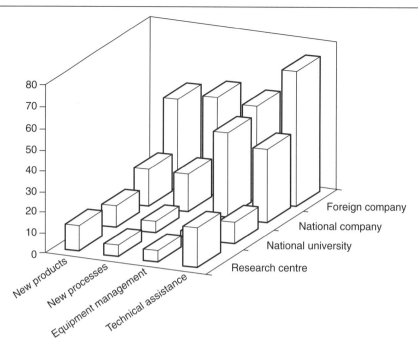

Figure 11.2 External Technological Linkages of Companies.
Source: ORSTOM-UAMX, Survey of the chemical sector, 1995.

Clusters of companies in the chemical industry

With regard to the chemical sector, it is easily seen that large firms within this industry, often backed up by foreign capital or large financial corporations, have kept up with the pace of international competition. They became more efficient, producing better quality products, reducing production costs and raising productivity, implementing lay-off schemes and investing in modernization. SMEs have endured a great deal more economic pressure and consequently are more reluctant to implement programmes requiring significant investments. Massive lay-offs as well as the closure of many SMEs were the trademark of the 1980s and 1990s; thus their figures for productivity and production should be carefully considered.

From the above discussion, it seems that firms with active development strategies favour an 'outward' pattern of behaviour, whereas smaller firms or less technologically active firms adhere to more traditional markets with a more 'inward' pattern. The first type of firms favours joint ventures and alliances and will, obviously, include subsidiaries of multinational firms. The second type is more idiosyncratic and favours local adaptation of technologies and in-house development.

There seems to be a second divide, probably more interesting to policy-makers, which might indicate some route for novel technological development policies, and which accompanies this first large cleavage. There seems to be some opposition in behaviour between companies that deal principally and quasi-exclusively with their foreign technical partners and those that have a preference for local developments.

This cleavage really covers a different priority as far as efficient process development is viewed, as opposed to new product development. One can thus identify a type of company that attends clearly to process development as an obligatory search for efficiency: 'be good or be dead' is their motto and to some extent they dominate the discourse on industrial development. Quality is the buzzword here. These companies look mainly at foreign technical partners and have exports in mind.

The other type includes companies also definitely interested in this expansion through exports, but with a more intense search for product development, adaptation and copy. These companies have a real internal R&D and engineering capacity, but are not only interested in processes. They favour product development mainly because of their types of markets. A typical case might be a company that produces intermediate polymers; that is, performance products. If the company wants to keep its market, the necessity is to find novel materials and new uses for their products. They need to do that based on both a grounded technological design capacity and a good prospective capacity. In a very unstable economic situation, like the one depicted in the preceding section, one dares to enter these activities only because there is the absolute certainty of not being challenged seriously by competition. This is also the great difference with similar companies in the other more industrialized countries of the OECD, which will deal more permanently with competitive uncertainty as well as the inherent uncertainty of technological development. But the comparison with European or US companies is of little help because of huge differences in the size of companies and markets.

In fact, the whole of this industry acts mostly as a market-based cluster, where firms rely heavily on themselves, often guided by the needs of their clients and an idiosyncratic development strategy which to a certain extent has kept firms isolated. It should be borne in mind, however, that the process of opening up the economy might alter the pattern described so far since it has modified the population – size and distribution – of chemical firms. Such a process will undoubtedly accentuate the differences between 'inward' based – promoting mainly internal technological learning – and 'outward' based strategies – relying principally on foreign technical sources of development – as well. It is expected that markets will play a key role together with those macroeconomic policies affecting them in the future development of the chemical sector. Moreover, in taking into account differences among types of firms we obtain three clusters that show similar characteristics (see Table 11.2) and belong to the same brand of 'technological regimes'.

Cluster I contains large corporations usually backed up by a financial consortium. These are usually leaders in their branch, and are mainly oriented towards export competition. They fear no competition and adopt international standards. The subsidiaries of multinationals usually belong to this type. But one also finds many nationally owned large companies, which usually belong to a large financial or industrial corporation.

One such case is CelQuim, a very large and old Mexican company, founded as the by-product of the vertical integration effort of a large industrial group in the north of the country. CelQuim is a complex industrial group producing polymeric material for the textile industry as well as for other industries. It was certified to ISO 9000 shortly after the norm was issued. It is a very dynamic producing group and has been driven by a tendency towards industrial excellence. The managers are among the

Table 11.2 Firms, Markets and Technological Regimes of the Clusters in the Chemical Industry

	Cluster I	Cluster II	Cluster III
Characteristics of firms	Large corporations, backed up by financial consortia including banks.	Large corporations, backed up by financial consortia including banks.	SMEs with little financial support.
Type of products	Commodities and specialities, mainly for industrial clients.	Commodities and specialities, mainly for industrial clients.	Common consumer products.
Markets	Export leaders. High competition.	Market leaders (domestic or foreign). Low competition and monopolistic positions.	Domestic markets (niche markets).
Sources of technology	Higher education (engineering). Alliances with foreign firms. Importance of clients and suppliers, especially PEMEX.	Higher education (engineering). Equipment suppliers. Input suppliers (PEMEX).	Higher education (engineering). Equipment suppliers. Clients.
Opportunity conditions	Low level of innovative activities, but strong learning patterns. Technology flows mainly through foreign partners and technology suppliers. Limited vertical integration R&D limited to production support.	Technology mainly based on internal R&D, product and process design. Limited vertical integration.	Dependence on suppliers of technology, mainly foreign. No integration.
Appropriability conditions	Complex technologies. Protection mainly through secrecy for national firms, and patenting for foreign subsidiaries.	Complex productive technologies. Difficult to imitate products. Low patenting; secrecy.	Easy to copy products (being themselves many times copied), simple processes. Secrecy; little incentive for protection of innovation.
Cumulativeness of technological knowledge	Assimilation of technologies through strong engineering. Efficient in seeking patterns of production. Strong quality programmes.	Development of new products and more efficient processes through R&D and engineering. Permanent R&D and development seeking. Strong internal learning.	Low development capacity. Adaptation and copying of products. Internal learning-by-doing based on use of technology. Old equipment and high gap with competitors.
Nature of the knowledge base	Complex, similar to foreign companies, without R&D capabilities but interaction of engineering and quality programmes.	Complex, science-based and linked to strong design and R&D capabilities	Simple, mainly based on strengthening productive capabilities.
Nature of linkages	Economic and information back-up by financial consortia. Few contacts with universities.	Economic and information back-up by financial consortia. Strong links to university research through R&D departments. Government support.	No contacts with universities. No government support.

best in the country, proud of the level, which they like to compare to similar North American companies. Technology is one of its basic assets and has been largely acquired or modernized through joint ventures with foreign companies. The associations with the foreign technology provider are an exchange on the basis of 'my market–your technology'. The company has given serious thought to opening a corporate R&D laboratory and has even hired a person who would fit the profile of an R&D manager. But after some exchange, the idea of setting up the laboratory was abandoned. The interesting fact about the company is that it maintains very thorough and strong links with universities in the country. It has been the driving force of a biotechnology project which now may be seen as one of the most accomplished technological developments in environmental technology. But excepting this very particular case, the group has been reticent on the idea of developing its own technology. So cluster I would include this type of company, where high quality production, high degrees of competitiveness and efficient management do not necessarily lead to more internal technology development, by choice or strategy.

Cluster II also gathers large companies, but of the more inward pattern type. They also are leaders but usually fight to keep exclusive markets and monopolistic positions. A good case is Pegado, a company that, although it now belongs to a large financial holding group, has been one of the most famous Mexican chemical companies. While its older business unit, the one that is oriented towards consumer products (mainly glue) is a brand known by all Mexicans, it is more the newer business units – the polymer and the intermediates producing units – that are dynamic and highly efficient companies. A common feature has been, historically, the need felt by the company to develop its own technologies. This has been accentuated by the fact that its principal foreign technology provider has broken its link to Pegado. Thus the company which had already created a corporate R&D unit increased its research activities, initially in an effort to provide support to the productive units. In fact, the R&D unit was quite strong and has been an active research unit even at academic levels, employing doctoral candidates and PhDs. Interestingly enough, its highly innovative activities are not the direct product of visible projects; they are the product of intense relations with producing units in some very select areas. In many cases, chief executive officers of the group have been threatening to close the corporate R&D unit if benefits are not directly linked to its status. It can also be said that the fruitful development of R&D – that is, R&D producing value for the company – has been possible only in these business units with a quasi-monopoly of the market. For the discussion here, we should mention that Pegado has not always been in a good financial situation and that it has suffered a lot from the restructuring of the chemical sector.

Many such companies can be found in Mexico. But the majority have probably not been as effective in overcoming the difficulties that are posed by the process of opening the economy to foreign competitors. Apart form the monopoly ingredient and the commitment to R&D, these companies share a strategic point of view of the chemical sector: they choose to enter markets where technologies are complex, needs are more niche-like and markets are less oriented towards commodities and more towards specialities; that is, high priced products.[7]

Cluster III gathers all SMEs that mainly ship in domestic markets. One good example is PETROPROD. It is a medium-sized company that specializes in intermediate petrochemical products. It has chosen to enter this market because 'raw petrochemicals', as they call it, is not paying sufficiently. It has a large array of R&D activities and its R&D department employs five persons on a regular basis, of which two are highly specialized engineers. The head of the company, the son of its founder, is also a chemical engineer and has always been interested in the technical part of his business, although he no longer directly intervenes in the productive operation of the company. The knowledge developed in the R&D unit has been so good that it developed a continuous-line process instead of its batch process. But it installed the process in a Korean chemical company in Korea rather than in its own production plants, because the size of its market would not permit it to absorb the production of a continuous line. Most companies that belong to Cluster III are usually interested in developing very strong links with their clients, up to a point where in some cases they depend too much on them. This is a way of avoiding large market changes. It should also be mentioned that most companies in this cluster are positioned in consumer products rather than intermediate chemical products.

Of course, this heuristic clustering of the chemical industry does not account for companies that are too small or too inefficient in their use of technology (but see Arvanitis and Villavicencio, 1998, for an effort to create a more comprehensive taxonomy). In fact, we can say that clusters of companies show differences in the technological regimes in terms of opportunity, appropriability, cumulativity and knowledge base and the linkages they have (see Table 11.2).

Opportunity conditions can be differentiated across sectors and reflect the likelihood of innovating for any given effort associated with different sources. The first type of firms (cluster I), exporters and quality oriented, are not as interested in innovation. They do have R&D and engineering, and could develop these capacities even more. But the R&D effort is mainly oriented towards production support and peripheral activities, as we have already pointed out. Technology flows mainly from their foreign partners, with whom they have strong links either through alliances (the foreign partner offers the technology and the Mexican counterpart offers the market) or because they act as subsidiaries of a foreign company. The second type is much more based on its own R&D effort. Usually these companies prefer not to deal with a foreign partner. Historically they have developed a strong R&D and engineering base. These appear to be more innovative companies and produce rather complex technological products. They use their internal capacities more fully than firms from cluster I. This is totally different from most SMEs belonging to cluster III, which depend on their technology supplier. Most companies in cluster III have to keep their production capacity alive and occupy their engineering personnel to strengthen their technology base. The very rare cases of innovative SMEs share common characteristics with the larger firms from cluster II: they have some R&D oriented towards innovative projects; they also try to avoid foreign sources of technology. But since these SMEs have little financial support, most projects are doomed or limited in scale.

Appropriability conditions are also very different in the three clusters. Cluster I firms use patents when foreign capital is in. Nationally owned firms are less oriented towards patents because they have little to patent. This is not the case for cluster II companies, which should be the natural clients of the patenting system. For reasons that are still not known, they avoid the use of patents and prefer secrecy or rely on the fact that most national competitors are unable to follow them. Cluster III companies are themselves strong copiers and low innovators and thus do not seek patenting. Even the more innovative SMEs avoid patenting, mainly for reasons of the high costs of this practice.

Cumulativeness is linked to past experiences and abilities to develop new technologies. Cumulative conditions, however, are not easily applied to the concept of sectors, as they are endogenously determined within the firms. Most of the elements in this category result from the above analysis of the learning pattern in each group of firms. The pattern for each category is defined as follows: cluster I, assimilation of technologies through strong engineering, efficient seeking patterns of production, strong quality programmes; cluster II, development of new products and more efficient processes through R&D and engineering, permanent R&D and development seeking, strong internal learning; cluster III, low development capacity, adaptation and copy of products, internal learning by doing based on use of technology, old equipment and a high gap with competitors.

Of course the net result of these differing patterns is a different knowledge base which also cumulates differently. Cluster I companies are producing good quality products that can be exported through efficient internal learning procedures based on foreign technological bases. Cluster II will be rather producers of novel products and will compete mainly because of a strong engineering and R&D capacity. The low technological development effort of cluster III companies restricts their production to adaptations of simple products using an empirical knowledge base.

For many firms, accessing scientific and technological information, competitor's achievements, and economic data, entails costs they are not always able to afford. Many of them get the information they need by creating and enhancing *external linkages* with other economic organizations and institutions like technology suppliers, universities and research centres, as well as promotional and financial development public agencies. In the chemical industry, technology support and equipment maintenance linkages are very strong, generally with foreign suppliers (see Figure 11.2). However, the linkage pattern is different in each of our three clusters.

In cluster I, firms usually have no difficulty in getting the necessary technical and scientific information. They do this through the channels that are instituted when setting up their alliances or technological linkages with an external – usually foreign – provider. Since firms belonging to this cluster usually do not run their own R&D centre, they have to rely heavily on the R&D facilities of a 'mother' company (this will be the case for a subsidiary) or of the foreign partner (usually the case for the Mexican owned companies). Linkages for the development of new products or adaptation of processes will rarely be with universities or public national research and technical centres.

Firms in cluster II rely heavily on their own R&D facilities. They will try to develop their own research links with external R&D centres and universities. They will get involved in government-supported innovation programmes that will provide them with financial support, human resources training or long-term joint ventures with public research centres.

Finally, cluster III firms will rely or not on external linkages with universities or research centres based mainly on very short-term benefits. But mostly these companies will tend to have as few external linkages as possible, except with their basic equipment provider. Most of these companies, being SMEs with strong financial limitations, will tend to avoid any involvement in cooperation they tend to consider as costly. These 'autarchic' companies, as we proposed naming them (Arvanitis and Villavicencio, 1998), will develop most of their processes by themselves. The fragility of such a strategy appears clearly under financial pressure. None the less, most of these companies will avoid getting involved in publicly supported programmes.

Conclusions

We have shown that different patterns of technological learning in firms can be identified. These are based upon differences in the way companies obtain knowledge from the environment, the way this knowledge is managed and diffused into the organization, as well as the way knowledge coming from the suppliers or the clients is processed and transformed into new capabilities. It should be stressed that the economic behaviour of a company seems to be strongly linked to the rough changes in the economic environment experienced in Mexico. But instead of sweeping it away, one observes that the industry has shown a real capacity to anticipate these changes. This was possible because of the strong learning capabilities accumulated by their former experience in a rapidly changing economic environment. By developing R&D or getting tied to a foreign technology provider, Mexican chemical companies have been able to manage adequately the announced crisis that followed the NAFTA treaty.

At the same time, one can observe the lack of direct state intervention in the chemical industry (with the very notable exception of the state owned company, PEMEX). Companies have influenced the NAFTA negotiations, and have typically found resources for their projects outside the public sphere. Thus all the changes in the industry can be easily qualified as 'market-driven'. This is true not only when assuming that, in the absence of strong public policy, the market is dominant, but also by observing the fact that changes affecting the provision of raw material or of technical inputs have been dealt with quite efficiently by the chemical companies themselves. This ability to precede changes is a fundamental aspect of technological and organizational learning. It is the result of a constant effort to improve the technology, although the motives and the patterns might be different across different clusters of companies.

Most of the discussion in economics of innovation insists upon the importance of sectoral characteristics and the size of companies. These are quite easily observable dimensions, and can be examined at an aggregated or a firm level. We do believe these factors to be essential, but not unique. In this chapter we have defined three clusters of companies. Two clusters are groups of mainly large firms and the third one groups of SMEs. This third cluster could be divided into many sub-clusters, based upon the types of markets or the technical linkage patterns. The purpose of such an analysis would be to redefine the criteria that permit identification of a specific pattern of learning and a specific type of management of technology. But it would obscure the fact that these companies have had to deal with considerable financial pressure due to changes in the overall economic pattern of Mexico. Most of these companies are SMEs and the key to their resolution of difficulties has been their extremely strong links to their clients. This is not to say that larger companies have been less favourable to listening to client needs; instead it allows them to demonstrate that they are more committed to a type of market, and by way of consequence to a type of technology, than to a specific client. If our interpretation is correct then one would need to be cautious about the benefits of flexibility. Larger firms have been less flexible than knowledgeable; smaller firms have been less flexible than cautious. And all of them have devised adequate technological strategies that permitted them to face these changes.

Notes

1. All data on technological activities, R&D, engineering and technical linkages of the Mexican chemical companies are drawn from a representative survey in 142 companies that was done between October and November 1994 in a joint research project between IRD (formerly ORSTOM) and UAM-X. See main results in Villavicencio *et al.* (1995); elaboration on the technological behaviour of companies can be found in Arvanitis and Villavicencio (1998).

2. This *stricto sensu* corresponds to the definition managed by the large manufacturers' associations like the Chemical Manufacturing Association (CMA) in the USA or the *Asociación Nacional de la Industria Química* (ANIQ) in Mexico.

3. It should be kept in mind that we are talking of rather low figures of employment in absolute terms (around 150 thousand workers) as compared to employment in the chemical industry worldwide (for example, 1,045 thousands workers in the US chemical industry) (see Arvanitis and Villavicencio, 1998).

4. The degree of protection of national chemical production fell from 86.8 to 18 per cent between 1985 and 1987. This drastic lowering of barriers to imports went further: by 1988 domestic production protected by import permits was minimal (2.5 per cent) and the protection of local production by the regulation of import prices disappeared totally. In 1988, the average tariff level was almost 13 per cent. This change is very important and probably prepared the industry for the further abatement of legal protections. Furthermore, most of the suggestions made by the chemical trade association (ANIQ) have been included in the final agreements of the NAFTA. See CEPAL (1996). Additionally, 70 per cent of the clauses of the NAFTA that were negotiated concerned the exchange of products between Canada and the USA that are not produced in Mexico.

5. In 1996, exports were above US$4 thousand million, while imports were US$3 thousand million. But 1996 was a most exceptional year, since the previous year's exports were almost $6.7 thousand million in 1995. This diminution explains the positive trade balance of 1996, which is generally negative in this industry.

6. General data on patenting by Aboites and Soria (1997). We use a different definition of 'chemical fields' through the international patent classification from these authors, who are restricted to chemical processes in the chemical industries ('Core chemical fields') and extract a more limited database from the Aboites and Soria general patent database. Thanks to Manuel Soria for allowing the use of data.

7. See Mercado (1995) for a similar analysis for Brazil, and Mercado (1996) for Venezuela.

CHAPTER TWELVE

The Pharmaceutical Industry

R. Gonsen and J. Jasso

Introduction: characteristics and performance[1]

This chapter studies the pharmaceutical industry using the concepts of national innovation systems, where the pharmaceutical industry corresponds to a sector at a meso-economic level. The following sections present an economic characterization of this sector, the role of government as the new institutional framework and a characterization of technological capabilities of the pharmaceutical industry. It also presents the institutions that establish linkages with pharmaceutical firms and the knowledge flows that occur between them, together with a characterization of firms. Finally, this chapter concludes with a discussion of the factors that define the technological regime for the pharmaceutical sector, i.e. opportunity conditions, appropriability conditions, cumulativeness and knowledge base.

The pharmaceutical industry in Mexico consists of approximately 200 firms that manufacture pharmaceuticals (medicaments or finished drugs) and pharmochemicals (active ingredients). The gross value of total pharmaceutical production has been an approximate constant 1.6 per cent of the total Mexican manufacturing industry in the period from 1980 to 1993. In the last year of this period, employment in this sector represented 1.2 per cent of the total in the manufacturing industry, while labour productivity for 1993, a remarkable 0.84, was 2.6 times above the average labour productivity of the whole manufacturing industry. Investment in the pharmaceutical industry increased steadily throughout the second half of the past decade; moreover, new investment by foreign firms has grown to more than US$400 million for 1996–7, encouraged by NAFTA.

The market structure of pharmaceuticals in Mexico is neatly divided into two distinct groups: the first one is government-oriented and consists of mainly generic and mature products; the second, directed at the private sector, is characterized by the use of trade marks, differentiation of products and higher added values. The private market is the most dynamic since it has the largest profit margin (as opposed to the government market), due to aspects such as differentiation, use of trade marks and patent protection. In 1996, the private share in total value of the pharmaceutical market rose to 89 per cent, whereas its volume share was reduced to 54 per cent, owing to an enormous price increase of medicaments of 175 per cent.[2] Foreign firms dominate the total market, with 72 per cent of its value in 1996. Foreign companies also have the largest share of the private market, 82 per cent in the same year.[3] In the case of the government demand for more mature or generic products, this is satisfied by domestic companies: 83 per cent in value terms in 1996.

Industrial concentration in the private market is high. The 40 largest pharmaceutical firms have 68 per cent of total sales in 1996, with only five domestic firms in this group. As for geographical concentration, 92 per cent of plants are located in Mexico City, and México and Jalisco states.

While the average export/import ratio of the pharmaceutical industry in the OECD countries was 1.2 between 1990 and 1994, Mexico's was 0.3. However, exports increased by a yearly average of 29 per cent in the period 1990–6, whereas imports grew by 17 per cent yearly. Despite this favourable trend, the pharmaceutical industry had a trade deficit of $216 million in 1996, with the largest deficit for active substances. The country of destination of exports varies by sub-sector. From 1990 to 1996, 59 per cent of the exports of active ingredients were exported to developed countries, while 86 per cent of exports of finished drugs went to developing countries, mostly within Latin America. None the less, a large portion of these exports is made by foreign firms that have chosen Mexico as an export platform, since exports by foreign subsidiaries depend on the global commercialization strategy of their parent companies.

The new institutional framework and the macroeconomic setting

The pharmaceutical industry is subject to a number of government measures that affect its innovation activities. In developed countries an important action with an impact on innovation activity is that of control. Institutions such as the Food and Drug Administration (FDA) in the United States exert strict federal regulations on R&D, manufacturing, commercialization and utilization of drugs. Thus, firms' R&D activities have to comply with regulations even for products that do not reach the market, manufacturing plants are periodically inspected by FDA agents and the industry is required to prove the safety and effectiveness of the drugs it produces. Generics firms must also comply with FDA manufacturing regulations. Increasing stringency of the regulations in the past decades has meant an increase in both the period of time for completion and the costs of R&D, especially those involved in the development phase.

In Mexico, stringent regulations are also applied for the sake of consumer protection, but given that new drugs are not really developed in this country, the retarding impact of control measures on innovation is rather negligible. Even more so, regulatory controls imposed on the pharmaceutical industry in Mexico have promoted the upgrading of technological capabilities of manufacturing firms by ensuring the effective application of quality control systems as well as the implementation of good manufacturing practices (GMPs). Manufacturing plants are periodically visited by inspectors of the Ministry of Health as well as the Ministry of Trade and Industrial Promotion (SECOFI) to verify their compliance with prevailing regulations. Another public body that supervises compliance with drugs quality standards and manufacturing processes is the Mexican Institute of Social Security, the largest purchaser of drugs for the public sector, which keeps close contact with the FDA in the United States.

Another government action that has had an impact on the industry's technological performance in Mexico has been that on price controls. Traditionally, SECOFI has enforced a controlled price policy on medicaments. Medicines' average price in Mexico has been traditionally much lower than the international average. Even in spite of the recent relaxation of the price policy and the corresponding generalized rise in prices, domestic prices are still lower than international ones. To illustrate this point further, in 1995 the average price per medicine in Mexico and the rest of Latin America was $2.74 and $4.11 respectively.[4] This government policy generated higher efficiency levels in firms which needed to survive on smaller profit margins, but was also a deterrent to investment in R&D and growth.

Industrial government promotion is another aspect which did not have a major or direct impact on innovation activities, but did have an effect on local technological capabilities. Specifically in the sub-sector of pharmochemicals, the legal framework prevalent in the decades prior to commercial liberalization helped to create a mostly Mexican industrial sub-sector. Governmental industrial policies that led to the dominance of Mexican firms were mainly in the areas of commercial protection, foreign investment and intellectual property protection.[5] In relation to the last area, active ingredients and finished drugs were not subject to patenting under the Law of Inventions and Trademarks,[6] thus, Mexican firms that were established, as a result of the promotional government programmes, were able to produce foreign active ingredients that were copied under the protection of the law.

Peres (1990) concluded that this situation led to a general recognition that, although the Mexican pharmaceutical industry (referring to both finished drugs and pharmochemicals) was capable of producing high quality products, it did not have any technological capacity of its own. There are some divergences from this conclusion. It is true that this industry did not introduce any new products into the market; however, copying or reverse engineering is an activity that requires technological skills to discover how a product is made. Such activities give rise to the accumulation of certain technological capabilities that are not reflected in independent creation capacities, but do contribute to industrial development. From this perspective, the absence of patentability in this industrial area was a factor contributing to activities that implied a form of technological effort. It is not clear whether any form of local technological capability at all in this sector would have been developed if patent protection to foreign companies had been granted. It should none the less be acknowledged that accumulated technological capabilities during the period of protection were not developed enough to achieve international competitiveness and, consequently, commercial liberalization implied the disappearance of more than half the pharmochemical plants in Mexico.

With liberalization and the opening of the economy, Mexican laws and regulations concerning intellectual property rights were brought into conformity with international standards and agreements. However, patent protection has not encouraged local innovative activity as is usually the case in more developed economies. In the period 1992–6, 511 patents were granted to the pharmaceutical industry. Of these, only ten patents were granted to Mexicans. After 1991, patenting activity by Mexicans diminished even further in relation to that by foreigners (from 7.5 per cent in 1980–91 to 2 per cent in 1992–6).[7] Usually, innovative foreign companies have their new active ingredients, new medicaments, new formulations or new production processes already patented elsewhere before their application to the Mexican Patents Office. By patenting in Mexico, they extend the protection of their innovations to the Mexican market. It can be argued that the current patent system has been useful to foreign entities for commercial strategies and has not acted as an incentive for invention.

The pharmaceutical innovation system

Technological capabilities and institutional specificities

The pharmaceutical industry is described as a meso-system at the sectoral level by the nature of the innovative process that underlies the pharmaceutical sector as well as the specificities of the technological competencies required and the technological regime that characterizes it. The technological competencies of a typical pharmaceutical firm at the international level are mainly related to the capabilities of operating and adapting chemical or biochemical processes, conducting formal R&D and building up complex distribution networks and marketing operations. Technological competencies of firms based in Mexico are a subset of the above, given the low level of R&D and the existing gap in manufacturing active ingredients. Although all firms must comply with GMPs, most of them are experienced only in the final simpler steps. In turn, marketing may have a high level of competition mainly within the firms directed to the private market.

The *manufacturing* of medicaments has two phases: one dealing with the manufacture of the active ingredient, usually a technologically complex process, and one that brings together the active ingredient with a number of materials that constitute the excipient (formulation) and then processing into the final drug form (tablet, capsule, etc.). In Mexico, a clear distinction is made between the producers of the final product, usually called pharmaceutical industry *per se*, but referring to the production of finished drugs only, and the producers of the active ingredient, usually called the pharmochemical industry. The great majority of firms established in this country, both domestic and foreign subsidiaries, carry out only the second, less technologically complex, manufacturing stage of finished drugs, a situation that reflects a high degree of dependence on foreign technology, since the critical technological input has to be imported.

The *research* for a new drug is carried out in the R&D departments of pharmaceutical companies. At the start of the modern pharmaceutical industry, innovative firms followed trial-and-error methods to discover new products; such methods evolved into rational drug design by the 1970s and 1980s. In the 1990s, R&D activity was of a more 'basic research' nature, as deeper understanding of disease mechanisms at the molecular level has been gained, together with the incorporation of advanced research techniques. The increasingly complex nature of research activities in this industry has, as a consequence, brought a notable increase in the costs of R&D in developed countries. Compared to other industries, the pharmaceutical industry has the largest expenditure in R&D as a percentage of sales. By the end of the 1980s, the percentage for the pharmaceutical industry, at the international level, was already high, averaging above 15 per cent. In 1997, this figure rose to 19.4 per cent, well above any other industry, including telecommunications (5 per cent) and electronics (4.9 per cent).[8] Another consequence of the changes affecting research methods in the pharmaceutical industry is an increased emphasis on linkages between industry and research institutions, given the more basic nature of such research, as well as between pharmaceutical companies and highly innovative biotechnology companies (see Chapter 12).

The discovery phase usually takes from five to ten years. However, the development phase of a new product lasts approximately eleven years, including pre-clinical, clinical, efficacy and marketing studies.[9] The costs associated with this phase are generally far larger than the costs of the discovery; it is estimated that discovery accounts for 23 per cent of the total R&D spending, development 74 per cent and approval 3 per cent (SCRIP, 1991, p. 53). This implies that almost three-quarters of the R&D is dedicated to testing the safety and efficacy of the new medicament. Although clinical validation tests no longer relate to the activity of discovery and formulation of a new product, in the Schumpeterian sense, clinical studies are an indispensable part in the process of innovation, given that, without them, the invention, in this case a new medicament, could not reach the market.

Research activity is minimal in firms established in Mexico. It is estimated that the percentage of total revenue devoted to R&D within the industry during 1991 was between 1.2 and 1.6 per cent for large and medium companies, and from 0.2 to 0.4 per cent for small companies (INEGI/ST, 1992). The very different nature of innovative activity of the industry in Mexico in relation to the international industry explains the enormous difference in R&D expenditure. An assessment of these industries by Brodovsky (1987) indicated that companies in Mexico, both domestic and international, were competent copiers and manufacturers of existing pharmochemicals and finished drugs, but they develop neither new products nor novel pharmaceutical forms. A more recent assessment by CEPAL (1995) confirms this fact.

As for clinical research, some multinational subsidiaries subcontract clinical tests in Mexico. Clinical research in Mexico has a long tradition and it is usually carried out in well recognized public institutions like cardiology hospitals or nutrition hospitals. These institutions perform, on request, clinical studies for foreign firms and, exceptionally, for domestic ones. Clinical research activity in Mexico has increased in the past years. This is reflected in an increase in total expenditure in clinical research from US$4,200 in 1993 to almost US$8,700 in 1997.[10]

The functions of *marketing* (sales, distribution, advertising and promotion) constitute essential complementary assets in the pharmaceutical industry for introducing new drugs into the market. In particular, distribution may involve a complex network built up over time. Promotion may involve large numbers of firms' representatives that provide information concerning a medicament to physicians and pharmacists. Marketing in Mexico is an area where training receives special attention from the pharmaceutical industry. Three of the main competitive factors in the private market of the pharmaceutical industry are differentiation, medical visits and publicity.

The institutional framework and the pharmaceutical industry

As mentioned before, the tacit component of knowledge in the international pharmaceutical industries is complemented by relevant codified and generic parts, coming from developments in several scientific disciplines. The sources of such knowledge are placed outside the boundaries of the firm, so that it has to identify,

Table 12.1 Linkages and Institutional Framework in the Pharmaceutical Industry

Type of relationships	International	Mexico
Interfirm	Important: alliances, research contracts, joint agreements, joint ventures, acquisitions and mergers with other pharmaceutical firms and biotechnology companies, at the local and international levels.	Scarce: at the local level, some collaboration with other companies belonging to the same group. None with biotechnology companies. At the international level, technology licensing from foreign companies, conventional relationships between subsidiaries and parent companies.
University–industry	Growing formal linkages. Long term.	Weak and informal linkages. Short term.
Educational institutions	Adequate supply of human resources	Adequate supply of human resources.
Government control	Important (very strong FDA)	Important (Ministry of Health, Ministry of Trade and Industrial Promotion).
Government promotion	Public funds for basic and applied research. Explicit policies for biotechnology promotion.	Public funds for basic and applied research. No promotion of biotechnology.

select and acquire the former from different places through a number of mechanisms, such as licences, strategic alliances or research contracts (Table 12.1).

With regard to *interfirm relationships*, the complex nature of research in the pharmaceutical industry has enhanced the need to complement absent or poor research capabilities in the new scientific areas by means of linkages with other firms that may possess such capabilities. In consequence, established firms in the international pharmaceutical industry are signing a variety of contracts with small high-technology firms known as new biotechnology firms or dedicated biotechnology firms (DBFs). These firms carry out research activities at the frontier of the state-of-the-art, dominating a group of technologies generically known as new biotechnology. Whereas these firms have strong research capabilities, they usually lack manufacturing and commercialization ones, and therefore benefit from their linkages with established firms that do possess such capabilities. The number of alliances, joint agreements, research contracts, etc. between these two types of firms is notable, as well as the number of acquisitions and mergers. It is considered that cooperative alliances between large pharmaceutical firms and DBFs now constitute an international network of complex inter-organizational linkages worldwide (Bower and Whittaker, 1993).

In addition to the changing nature of research necessary for new drug development, other factors, such as increased costs and risks, and more stringent regulations, have contributed to increase the number of linkages between companies, not only of large established firms with DBFs, but also between competitors. A number of American and European firms established joint ventures with Japanese firms, and many brand name companies in the United States and Europe took over smaller generics manufacturers in the former (Silverman *et al.*, 1992). This situation has enhanced even more the global nature of the pharmaceutical industry, as well as its concentration.

Conversely, interfirm technological linkages in Mexico relate mainly to technology licensing. Between 1982 and 1989, 313 technology transfer agreements were registered in Mexico,[11] of which 51 per cent were signed between Mexican entities, while 49 per cent were with foreign institutions located mainly in the United States (62 contracts), Germany (23 contracts) and Switzerland (19 contracts). If only contracts with foreign entities are considered, the more frequent contractual objects are: *trade-name use* (89), *technical knowledge* (76) and *technical assistance* (59). In contrast, with regard to contracts with Mexican entities, the more frequent contractual objects are *software* (47), *technical assistance* (46) and *administration* (36). An interesting point to note is that all contracts on *patents and invention certificates*[12] were established with foreign firms. Moreover, of the total contracts that include *trade-name use* as a contractual object, 84 per cent correspond to foreign firms, as do 75 per cent of the contracts on *technical knowledge*. This distribution indicates that contracts with foreign entities have a larger technological content than local contracts, reflecting the technological dependency of the Mexican pharmaceutical industry on foreign licences in that period. Qualitative information supports the fact that this situation also prevailed during the 1990s.

Furthermore, research alliances and collaborations, which are currently the general trend on the international scene, are extremely scarce in Mexico. However, there is evidence of recent links of domestic firms with foreign ones that do take on some form of technological collaboration; although it should be stressed that these examples constitute the exception rather than the rule in the Mexican pharmaceutical industry. Regarding the particular case of linkages with DBFs, there were some attempts in this direction in the past, albeit with little success.[13]

Collaboration among Mexican firms is rather poor beyond those of their own group. From a sample of 30 pharmaceutical companies established in Mexico,[14] 23 reported introducing new or improved products or processes between 1994 and 1996. In all but two cases, these were the outcomes of in-house work and only six firms reported additional collaboration with other companies. Generally speaking, companies consider that collaboration with other companies of the same group is the most important source of information for innovation projects, as opposed to information from any source outside the group.

Another consequence of the changes affecting research methods in the world pharmaceutical industry is an increased emphasis on *linkages between industry and research institutions*, given the more 'basic' nature of such research. Even large firms, which perform basic research at their own R&D laboratories, have established a growing number of formal linkages with universities and other research institutes.

In Mexico, university–industry linkages are short term, specific and informal to the extent that some of them are mere casual approaches from scientists seeking private financing for their own projects. In some other cases, links are personal acquaintances (from college times or other) of university scientists and technical personnel of firms.

It is interesting to note here that the Institute of Biotechnology (formerly Centre for Genetic Engineering and Biotechnology) of the National University of Mexico conducts research relevant to the pharmaceutical industry (see Gonsen, 1998). An indication of the level of advanced research that this institute carries out is the establishment of research contracts with companies such as Schering in Germany, Ciba Geigy and Genencor (a DBF) in the United States, well known for their research activities in new biotechnology. The low impact that public research has in the pharmaceutical industry established in Mexico is an indication of the level of isolation of these research groups within the Mexican industrial environment.

Within the present context, it is expected that the four or five largest Mexican companies could establish links with academic institutions to validate new pharmaceutical presentations, but it is very unlikely, given the technical and financial resources required, that they could become involved in basic research activities. The extremely high costs involved in the development of new molecules (typically, more than US$200 million) make it unrealistic for even the five largest Mexican firms, with total annual sales of $24–65 million, to have the capital resources to compete with the levels of R&D investments of top international firms.

Type of firms

Concerning the pharmaceutical industry in Mexico, it should be considered, first, that there are two distinct classes of firms within this sector, in terms of their production processes: the first class elaborates the active ingredients (i.e. pharmochemicals) which are the main input for medicaments, whereas the second class formulates these pharmochemicals and mixes them with an excipient to obtain finished pharmaceuticals (i.e. finished drugs, medicines). Second, the majority of firms typically display a low degree of integration between the production of pharmochemicals and finished drugs. Hence, the technological complexity of production processes of pharmaceuticals in Mexico is low, for while the two phases of the pharmaceutical production chain (pharmochemicals and finished drugs) in more industrialized economies are usually integrated, few producers of finished drugs in Mexico actually manufacture active ingredients as well.

Third, prior to the 1991 changes in the Intellectual Property Protection Law, technological competencies of Mexican pharmaceutical firms were built mainly by imitating drugs produced elsewhere. Unfortunately, the capabilities thus far developed fell short of international competitiveness. When the markets opened up, a great number of firms producing pharmochemicals were shut down. Although new patenting rules, along with the rationalization of price controls, might ease the introduction on to the market of new products developed elsewhere, such rules do not offer enough incentives for domestic firms to develop new products, as these firms often lack the financial resources and accumulated R&D experience to carry out all the steps required in this innovative activity.

Fourth, it is clear that the pharmaceutical sector in Mexico cannot be considered as science-based. The institutional framework supporting this industry in Mexico, as compared with that of more developed economies, has not developed enough significant linkages with other actors of the NIS. The existing linkages with universities and public research organizations are not systematic nor institutional, and are more often than not confined to activities such as validation of clinical tests and seldom deal with basic research activities. The existence of some core scientific capabilities, like those related to the application of new scientific advancements in biotechnology within the public research domain, is rather isolated from the domestic industrial context. Moreover, it should be noted that perhaps the sole relevant linkages within the sector are those established between foreign subsidiaries and their parent companies, which are indeed developing complex networks of linkages with other pharmaceutical and biotechnology firms, and universities in a variety of countries.

The non-scientific nature of the pharmaceutical sector in Mexico can be further supported by the fact that R&D activities are concentrated at R&D departments of innovative firms abroad. Mexican companies with in-house R&D departments do not carry out the sort of activity which would lead to the discovery of new molecules for new active ingredients, concentrating instead on producing new formulations of already known medicaments, or cost reduction in the case of generic products.

Conclusions: technological regime

Four factors – opportunity conditions, appropriability conditions, cumulativeness and knowledge base – define the technological regime underlying each sectoral innovation system (Chapter 10). The following paragraphs characterize the pharmaceutical innovation system[15] according to these factors in the world leading firms and in Mexico (Table 12.2).

Opportunities for innovation

The pharmaceutical industry is characterized by high opportunity conditions. The sources of innovative opportunity are varied. First, the R&D departments of innovative firms have been able to incorporate increasingly complex research methods up to the latest research techniques of advanced scientific areas. Second, there are small high-tech companies dedicated specifically to the exploitation of such advanced techniques as recombinant DNA research, protein engineering and computer-aided design. Third, universities and public research organizations conduct scientific research, both basic and applied. Thus, the level and characteristics of technological opportunities depends on both research carried out by universities, other public research institutions and high-tech companies, and that carried out by firms' R&D departments.

In contrast, in Mexico opportunities to innovate are mainly related to technological effort that occurs within the firm or its suppliers; that is, on product differentiation through new materials for excipients or packaging or improvements with the introduction of new equipment. In the case of products directed at the public market, efforts to innovate focus on lower production costs, mainly through incremental changes in manufacturing processes. Advanced research relevant to pharmaceuticals conducted at universities and public research institutions in Mexico could represent another source of innovation but at the present time it only constitutes missed opportunities. However, investment in public research alone is not enough: the firm has to have the purpose of carrying out innovative activities and be able to attract highly qualified human resources, thus permitting and further encouraging communication with researchers at public institutions.

Table 12.2 Technological Regime: a Cluster of the Pharmaceutical Industry

Characteristics	International (leaders)	In Mexico
Opportunity conditions	*High* R&D departments of innovative firms. Small biotech companies. Universities and public research organizations.	*Low* In-house technological effort for product differentiation and/or decreasing production costs. Suppliers of equipment and materials for excipients and packaging.
Appropriability	*Strong* Patents. Vertical integration. Control of complementary assets (complex distribution networks, medical visits, advertising).	*Weak* Trade secrets. Complementary assets (distribution networks, medical visits, advertising for the private market).
Cumulativeness	*High* In-house production of advanced knowledge. Adoption of biotechnology in own R&D, by research agreements, by acquisition of biotech firms, etc.	*Medium* Incremental learning. No adoption of biotechnology (no in-house R&D, scarce links with research institutions or biotechnology companies).
Knowledge base	*High complexity* Tacit: firm's advanced competencies, including in-house R&D. Codified: coming from advances in several scientific disciplines.	

Appropriability conditions

The benefits from innovative activities in the pharmaceutical industry are appropriated by formal means of protection, namely patents, and informal means, such as vertical integration of in-house development and production of the critical technological substance, i.e. the active ingredient. In addition, the possession of essential complementary assets such as distribution networks plays a crucial role in strengthening such appropriability. The degree of technological appropriability differs notably within the institutional context in Mexico, where, up to 1991, it was not possible to patent pharmaceutical products.[16] Before 1991, a large proportion of the pharmochemical companies developed their own technologies for chemical synthesis of already known active ingredients. This implied greater research activity than is carried out today, whose results were appropriated by trade secret. With the new Law for the Promotion and Protection of Industrial Property, enacted in June 1991,[17] these types of products are now subject to protection under patenting. Thus the technological capacity to synthesize already known molecules is useful only in cases in which the product patent has, or will soon have, expired. This could mean for some companies an opportunity to specialize in generic products, although such specialization would mean a step away from innovative activity.

Cumulativeness

At the firm level cumulativeness is high in industries where a continuous source of innovation is R&D, together with the availability of major internal financial resources. Besides, strong appropriability conditions leads to high cumulativeness, which in turn reinforces a dominant position of few innovators. In addition, almost all the big pharmaceutical firms in the world have incorporated the scientific procedures of biotechnology as a standard part of their set of techniques in R&D. The adoption of biotechnology has been done in several ways, increasing, for instance, internal accumulation of technological capabilities by utilizing biotechnology's tools and techniques in their R&D departments, establishing their own biotechnology R&D centres and acquiring biotechnology firms.

These methods of accumulation do not occur in pharmaceutical companies based in Mexico. For these firms, the most important accumulation of knowledge takes place during manufacturing by incremental learning. In particular, the methods of incorporating biotechnology into pharmaceutical activities mentioned above are practically absent in Mexico. While international subsidiaries rely entirely on the biotechnological research that is conducted by their parent companies, domestic firms, as far as it is recorded, do not handle the new advanced techniques at their R&D departments, and are not actively involved in research agreements of this kind. The possibility of alliances with, or acquisitions of biotechnology-based firms also appears to be remote for several reasons: lack of financial resources, lack of perception by Mexican firms of the advantages and synergies that may be generated with this type of linkages and, probably most important of all, an absence of the objective of advancing the firm's technological capabilities by incorporating high-tech research in its activities.

Knowledge base

The nature of the relevant knowledge base of the pharmaceutical industry is of high complexity. The tacit component of knowledge relates to the firms' advanced idiosyncratic competencies, while the codifiable aspect of knowledge comes from advances in several scientific disciplines, such as molecular biology, cellular biology, molecular genetics, immunology and virology; hence its characterization as a science-based industry.

It is worth noting that the scientific areas quoted above have been critical to the development of corporate biotechnology-based R&D, particularly in the application of techniques such as recombinant DNA (genetic engineering) and hybridoma technology (monoclonal antibodies). Thus, scientific breakthroughs have allowed a molecular and cellular approach in research for the creation of proteins with therapeutic effects such as human insulin, human growth hormone, interferons and so on. More therapeutic proteins are expected in the market as more human genes are identified. Improvements in understanding of the human immune system have made possible safer, more effective replacements for existing vaccines as well as new vaccines. New techniques of mammalian cell culture have enabled humanized monoclonal antibodies to be developed that can be used in drug delivery and drug therapy. Monoclonal antibody-based kits have increased precision and specificity in diagnosis (NEDC, 1991; Sharp, 1995).

In Mexico, the nature of innovative activities and the absence of basic research in R&D departments largely diminishes the complementary role of the codified and generic part of knowledge emerging from scientific breakthroughs. Tacit and specific knowledge is transmitted largely by in-firm training. The required part of generic knowledge, which is simpler than in the international context and easily codifiable, is transmitted through formal education and off-the-job training.

Notes

1. Data in this section are based on Canifarma (1988), INEGI (1994a, 1994b), OECD (1997c) and estimations made from databases of INEGI (INEGI (1970–93), INEGI (1970–94), INEGI/ST (1992), SECOFI (1997a), Canifarma and CEPAL.
2. According to the National Index of Consumer Prices, *El Financiero*, 24 March 1997, p. 22.
3. See Chapter 5 on the role of foreign firms in Mexico.
4. Data provided by the Mexican Association of the Pharmaceutical Industry (AMIF).
5. For a description of such government policies and their role in supporting the pharmochemical sub-sector see Brodovsky (1987) and CEPAL (1995).
6. *Diario Oficial*, 10 February 1976, Mexico.
7. Data estimated from the database of the National Bank of Patents (IMPI, 1992). The international classifications included were: A61J3/00; A61K9/00; A61K31 to 49/00.
8. Data provided by AMIF.
9. These time periods correspond to those reported in the United Kingdom (*Financial Times*, 21 November 1990, p. 40). The mean development times reported in SCRIP (1991, p. 53), including review by the Food and Drug Administration of the United States, is 11 years and a half.
10. Data provided by AMIF.
11. The following is based on data from National Registry of Technology Transfer in Mexico (RNTT, 1982–9).
12. A certificate of invention was an instrument similar to a patent but without the granting of a monopoly of exploitation. Through the inventor certificate, the state acquired exclusive rights over the invention; the inventor, however, had the right to receive royalties if the invention was exploited. With the last change of patent law this legal figure was abolished.
13. See Gonsen (1998) for details on the cases of DBFs in the pharmaceutical area in Mexico.
14. National Innovation Survey, CONACYT (1997c).
15. See the definition of sectoral innovation system in Chapter 1.
16. Active ingredients and finished drugs were not subject to patenting under the Law of Inventions and Trademarks, *Diario Oficial*, 10 February 1976, Mexico.
17. *Diario Oficial*, 27 June 1991.

CHAPTER THIRTEEN

The Case of Biotechnology

R. Gonsen

Introduction

This chapter analyses the sectoral innovation system for the case of biotechnology. The term biotechnology has been used with varying meanings and a number of definitions can be found in the literature. The common interpretation is the one which associates biotechnology with the use of advanced techniques such as genetic engineering, cell fusion and protein engineering. In any case, biotechnology is not an industrial sector *per se*, but a set of advanced technologies which affect several industries. In some cases, the impact of biotechnology is already highly visible, as in the case of the pharmaceutical sector. To a lesser extent, but also affected by biotechnology, there are sectors such as the chemical industry, the food and feed industries, mining and oil recovery, agriculture and environmental issues, such as waste disposal and pollution control.

Because biotechnology is not a defined sector in the standard industrial classification but a group of techniques that are applicable to very different sectors of the economy, it is not possible to go through the usual economic characterization. In addition, the few companies that have been created in Mexico to exploit the advanced techniques of biotechnology at the industrial level have not succeeded (see Gonsen, 1998). An analysis of the sectoral innovation system (SIS) under this circumstance should be restricted to the potential of biotechnology in Mexico; thus, a stress on the human factor is necessary. The following sections analyse the institutions involved in the development of biotechnology, the situation of human resource formation and the technological regime that characterizes biotechnology.

Institutional framework and technological capabilities

According to Gonsen (1998), industrial biotechnological capabilities can be considered in three categories:

1. Core scientific capabilities, related mainly to novel techniques such as recombinant DNA and hybridoma. These capabilities refer to the manipulation, modification and transference of genetic materials. A high level of scientific skills is a necessary, but not sufficient, condition to achieve innovative performance in biotechnology.
2. Bioprocessing capabilities related to the manufacturing stage. These capabilities

are based on a knowledge of the characteristics and behaviour of micro-organisms and on the deliberate use of these characteristics to produce new products or processes.
3. Complementary capabilities related to those peripheral activities, such as marketing and distribution networks. These capabilities are indispensable to achieve the commercial phase.

The development of these capabilities has been carried out by institutions of a different nature. In developed countries, core scientific capabilities were initially developed at the universities and other public and private non-profit institutions that conduct scientific research, both basic and applied. As spin-offs of such research small firms were created to apply the advanced techniques of genetic engineering, cell fusion and so on, concentrating, thus, in the development of core scientific capabilities. These firms can be considered as R&D firms and they are usually known as new or dedicated biotechnology firms (DBFs), whereas bioprocessing and complementary capabilities have been mainly developed by large established firms or corporations, the most important of which are multinational corporations.

Given the history of formation of DBFs, these firms hold strong links with universities strengthening their core scientific capabilities. However, DBFs' nature as research firms forces them to complement their technological capabilities by means of different linkages with large established firms that transform the results of DBFs' research into industrial scale manufacture and also have the necessary capabilities to put biotechnological products into the market. Thus, DBFs have also established very strong links with the large established firms in order to complement the manufacturing and commercialization capabilities that, as research firms, they generally lack. Large established firms, in their turn, have increasingly acquired the skills and knowledge to conduct their own basic R&D, developing in this way their own biotechnology core scientific capabilities. However, the complexity of this type of knowledge is so high that they cannot cover all aspects required (for either technical or financial or both reasons). Therefore they keep a good number of linkages with universities and DBFs, in order to complement their capabilities. All this produces a complex network of linkages for research, manufacturing and commercialization of biotechnology-related products that has been established between universities, DBFs and large firms, particularly in developed countries.

The situation in Mexico is very different. In the industrial environment, there is no presence of DBFs working with the advanced tools of biotechnology. There were some attempts by scientists-industrialists, but unsuccessful.[1] Thus the important type of linkages formed between large established firms and DBFs or universities and DBFs is not found in the Mexican context. In their turn, linkages between universities and large established firms are rather weak and short term in nature. Despite the efforts of research institutions to establish linkages with industries, the collaboration level is extremely low. The most successful area of collaboration has been in traditional biotechnology. This does not mean that there is an absence of advanced core scientific capabilities at public research institutions in Mexico. There is a number of groups working on advanced techniques in different areas of application of biotechnology. The evaluation reported in Gonsen (1998) indicates that some of these groups possess the human and physical resources to conduct state-of-the-art biotechnology research.[2]

Another institution that should be considered as having a role in the development of biotechnology is the government. Particularly, the governments of several developed countries have played an important role in promoting and financing the development of this scientific field. Basic research has received a lot of governmental support in most industrialized countries. Given that basic research in biotechnology-related scientific areas such as molecular biology and protein engineering has a direct impact on the innovative process of industries affected by biotechnology, the government role in supporting such research becomes important for those industries. Beyond basic research, governments of both the more developed and some newly industrialized economies have designed explicit policies for supporting biotechnology development and its utilization in domestic industries. Priorities, policies and strategies for the absorption of advanced biotechnology by the industrial sector differ widely between governments, but the direct role of the public sector in promoting and financing the development of biotechnology in such countries has been very important. In contrast, in Mexico, despite the fact that biotechnology was recognized in government programmes as a priority area, there has not been an explicit policy of support for biotechnology, and efforts in this direction have been scarce and disperse (Gonsen, 1998).

Human resources for biotechnology

The development of advanced biotechnology and its commercial application require highly specialized human resources in several areas of the scientific domain. The type of technical expertise required includes specialists such as molecular biologists, immunologists, genetic engineers, microbiologists, cell culture specialists, electronic engineers and even sales personnel with technical expertise.

In Mexico, there are a number of institutions which offer postgraduate programmes in biotechnology as such. In addition, these institutions have long offered programmes in biotechnology-related areas such as biochemistry, cellular and molecular biology, genetics, microbiology and other relevant disciplines. Towards the end of the 1980s, there were about 50 master programmes and 22 doctoral programmes plus a number of specialization programmes.[3] More than 50 per cent of these programmes were created during the 1980s, which reflects the new and growing interest that was created in the formation of technical and scientific human resources in these areas in Mexico. Owing to the relatively recent creation of these programmes, a number of researchers are still obtaining degrees in foreign universities, particularly at the doctoral level.

The studies commissioned by CONACYT[4] to assess the quality of postgraduate programmes recognized that in biotechnology there were a few excellent programmes coexisting with a number of poor quality. According to Quintero (1985), academic excellence is considered to have been attained in the areas of genetic engineering, enzyme engineering, monoclonal antibodies, plant tissue culture, protein biotechnology and fermentation technology.

The existing postgraduate programmes in biotechnology-related areas provide the necessary base for a supply of qualified personnel. The potential is very high if one considers that there is great scope for increasing the proportion of enrolled students who actually graduate, enhancing the efficiency of completion. In the period 1985–8, 82 students per year obtained a biotechnology-related postgraduate degree (masters and doctorates) in Mexico.[5] While this could be considered a low number, it is difficult to determine the desired number. The demand for PhDs in Mexico is highly concentrated in public research and educational institutions. The demand increased dramatically in the past ten years with the creation of institutions dedicated exclusively to biotechnology research, such as the Centre for Genetic Engineering and Biotechnology Research (CEINGEBI), later transformed into the Institute of Biotechnology, and the Centre for Research and Advanced Studies of Mexico–Irapuato (CINVESTAV–Irapuato), dedicated to plant biotechnology. Thus, the demand for researchers in public and academic institutions may be considered to be increasing.

On the contrary, in the industrial environment, incentives in the labour market for obtaining a master's or doctoral degree are very low given that the low level of biotechnological activity in industry does not demand specialized skills at the postgraduate level. This is the case in the pharmaceutical industry, as discussed in Chapter 12.

Both the traditional and modern bioprocessing industries established in Mexico have demanded very few postgraduates. The new doctorates coming from bio-technology programmes often do not find a place in the Mexican industrial labour market.[6] This contrasts sharply with the situation in the United States where, according to the OTA's (1984) survey of firms in the United States using bio-technology, bioprocess engineers with PhDs were in such high demand from industry that there was a fear that a shortage would occur in universities' faculties in this field.

As for the stock of biotechnology researchers in Mexico in the public and private sectors, a rough estimate[7] indicates that there were 600–700 researchers (without considering technicians and students) in all biotechnology research areas (including plant biotechnology) towards the end of the 1980s. Comparisons with other coun-tries are inconclusive given the differences in economic size, the level of biotechnology R&D industrial activity and the level of basic and applied research. In addition, the definition of biotechnology varies across countries, and when statistics on personnel are available it is not clear exactly what they cover. Just to give an illustration of orders of magnitude, Brazil had 600 scientists in biotechnology-related activities in 1983 (Sercovich and Leopold, 1991, p. 79), and Korea had, in 1984, 220 workers in biotechnology R&D activities related to industry only (Yang, 1990, p. 177).

It should be noted that these national levels are of the same order as bio-technology R&D departments of single companies in developed countries. The Life Sciences Research Centre of Monsanto had 700–800 researchers (Medina, 1986, pp. 26–7) before it was transferred to another location with the aim of building an R&D team of about 1,300 (*Financial Times*, 17 April 1989, p. 12). ICI had 300 researchers investigating biotechnology in drugs and agrochemicals plus 310 employees in the biological products division entirely dedicated to biotechnology (*Financial Times*, 12 April 1989, p. 30). Ciba-Geigy had more than 150 researchers working on genetic engineering (*Fortune*, July 1983, p. 92). From Japan Tobacco's 700 R&D personnel,

Table 13.1 Technological Regime: Biotechnology

Characteristics	International	In Mexico
Opportunity for innovation	*Very high* Basic advanced research.	*Low* Advanced research not connected to industry.
Appropriability	Patents	Patents (since 1991)
Cumulativeness	*High* In-house production of advanced knowledge.	*Not applicable* Absence of DBFs or in-house advanced biotechnology research in large firms.
Knowledge base	*High complexity* Advanced frontier scientific research.	*Not applicable* Advanced biotechnology almost absent from Mexican industry.

100 used biotechnology techniques. Sumitomo had 80 researchers exclusively working on biotechnology. Biochemical companies such as Ajinomoto and Kyowa Hakko had R&D departments with 700 and 1,200 personnel respectively.[8]

Apart from other considerations, such as material and financial resources, competence of research and the conditions of R&D infrastructure, it is very difficult to determine whether the stock of biotechnology researchers estimated for Mexico is sufficient for biotechnological development. For public research biotechnology activity, it seems to be just below an acceptable level, while for existing industrial biotechnology R&D the number appears to be more than enough. Therefore, given the present conditions of industrial biotechnology activity in Mexico, characterized by a low degree of complexity with respect to the level of skills required and few or non-existent linkages between industry and basic research (Gonsen, 1998), a shortage of qualified manpower does not represent a serious bottleneck. In the present circumstances, it may be the case that the highly qualified personnel produced by Mexican biotechnology postgraduate programmes will find a place in industries abroad, particularly in the United States. Such personnel could have a more significant impact on the expansion of a local biotechnology-related industry if there were increased and more effective interaction between local industry and public research.

Technological regime of biotechnology

The technological regime of the biotechnological innovation system may be defined in the same manner as the other sectors considered in this book, i.e. based on the following four factors: opportunity conditions, appropriability, cumulativeness and knowledge base (Table 13.1).

Opportunities for innovation

The technological regime in the case of biotechnology is characterized by very high opportunity conditions and a wide variety of potential technological approaches and solutions (Breschi and Malerba, 1997). Even more, biotechnology is itself a source of innovation for other industrial sectors, such as pharmaceuticals, as shown in Chapter 12. The sources of innovative opportunity are clearly related to the applications of the latest scientific advancements in the research laboratories not only of universities, but also of DBFs and of large established firms.

For the case of Mexico, the situation in terms of innovative opportunities is similar to that pointed out for pharmaceuticals, i.e. the biotechnology-related scientific capabilities prevalent in some research centres in Mexico constitute missed opportunities as long as such research stays isolated from the industrial Mexican context. It is pertinent to recall here that, although there are some high quality postgraduate programmes in biotechnology, the demand for specialized skills at the postgraduate level by industry in Mexico is very low. Specialists in genetic manipulation, such as molecular biologists and immunologists, produced by the educational system in Mexico are concentrated in universities and public research institutions and at the moment there is very little demand for these types of specialists at the industrial level.

Appropriability conditions

According to Breschi and Malerba (1997), appropriability conditions may be very high when related to the appropriation of rents from the continuous introduction of streams of innovations generated by the firm. The benefits from innovative activity in biotechnology are mainly appropriated by formal means of protection, i.e. patents. In the institutional context of Mexico, as in the case of pharmaceuticals, up to 1991, it was not possible to patent biotechnology-related products.

The biotechnology-related products and processes that could not be patented in Mexico up to 1991 in accordance with the Law of Inventions and Trademarks covered the following:[9]

- plant and animal species and their varieties, and related biological processes;
- food and beverages for human consumption, and related biological processes;
- food and beverages for animal consumption, and related biotechnological processes;
- pharmaceutical products and medicines in general, and related biotechnological processes;
- fertilizers, insecticides, herbicides, fungicides and products with biological activity, and related biotechnological processes;
- genetic processes to obtain plant and animal species or their varieties.

All the items 'related to biotechnological processes', except for the ones related to plant and animal species, were eligible for inventor certificates.[10] In the period 1983–7, there were 2,299 inventor certificates granted, of which 122, that is to say 5.3 per cent, were related to biotechnology. Table 13.2 shows the distribution by area (according to the international patent classification) of the certificates granted in biotechnology in the period 1980–8 in Mexico. It can be noted that the majority (71 per cent) of certificates are related to pharmaceutical preparations. In this period, 46 per cent of the certificates in biotechnology were granted to United States citizens, while only 4 per cent (eight certificates) were held by Mexicans. There is no

Table 13.2 Inventors' Certificates in Biotechnology, Mexico, 1980–1988

Area	No. of certificates	Distribution (%)
Pharmaceutical preparations	132	71.4
Glucosides, nucleosides and nucleic acids	23	12.4
Fermentation processes	16	8.6
Micro-organisms, enzymes, mutation or genetic techniques	10	5.4
Research on or analysis of plant material	2	1.1
Plant novelties	2	1.1
Peptides and proteins	0	0
Micro-organisms	0	0
Research on and analysis of processes that use enzymes or micro-organisms	0	0
Total	185	100

Source: Biblioratos, Technology Development Office, Ministry of Commerce and Industrial Development (SECOFI), Mexico.

information available on the actual industrial use of the inventions covered by the certificates granted to nationals. Some experts, however, consider that the commercial value of such inventions was very limited. This evidence suggests that, for the case of biotechnology, the inventor certificate system did not have any significant effect on the promotion of local biotechnology inventiveness.

Cumulativeness

In the international context, biotechnology presents high cumulativeness conditions at the firm level. Innovative activities relate to understanding, acquiring and integrating new scientific knowledge, and continuously recombining such generic knowledge with the firms' advanced idiosyncratic competencies and specialized knowledge (Breschi and Malerba, 1997). This characterization of cumulativeness does not apply to the Mexican context given the absence of research firms dedicated to exploiting the advanced techniques of biotechnology in Mexico, and the case of large established firms located in Mexico, either local or multinational, which do not carry out advanced biotechnological research locally. As mentioned above, there are some excellent biotechnology research groups in Mexico, but in the most advanced scientific areas, like molecular biology, there is no transmission of generic knowledge to industry because of the lower level of research competencies possessed by firms established in Mexico.

Knowledge base

The relevant knowledge base for biotechnology, in the international context, involves tacit aspects related to firms' idiosyncratic capabilities and codified aspects related to frontier scientific knowledge. As in the case of pharmaceuticals, advances in several scientific disciplines, such as molecular biology, cellular biology and molecular genetics, provide the sources of knowledge that make biotechnology a highly science-based technology. Again, this characteristic will be missing in the

Mexican context as long as there is not an industry capable of incorporating advanced biotechnology into its operations, either by doing its own research or by complementing its capabilities through alliances with DBFs or university-based research.

Notes

1. See Gonsen (1998) for a detailed account.
2. This assessment was confirmed by a previous evaluation conducted by the Scientific Office of the US Embassy in Mexico and by experts' interviews.
3. The number of programmes was calculated based on the following sources: Robert (1985), Arechiga (1989) and Quintero (1989).
4. See 'Evolucion del Posgrado Nacional. Analisis y Perspectivas', *Ciencia y Desarrollo*, special issue, September 1989, Consejo Nacional de Ciencia y Tecnologia, Mexico.
5. Based on Arechiga (1989) and Quintero (1989).
6. Interview with Dr Casas-Campillo, founder of the first biotechnology department in Mexico.
7. Estimation based on interview with Dr Gustavo Viniegra, Senior Researcher at Metropolitan University, Iztapalapa, and on Medina (1989).
8. Interviews conducted in 1991 with each of these companies.
9. Based on information provided by the Technology Development Office of the Ministry of Commerce and Industrial Development (SECOFI), Mexico.
10. The inventor certificate was a legal figure that permitted the state to acquire exclusive rights over the invention, while the inventor had the right to receive royalties if the invention was exploited. This was applied until 1991, when the new patent law abolished this figure.

CHAPTER FOURTEEN

Strategies and Technological Capabilities in a Multinational Mexican Firm[1]

G. Dutrénit

Introduction

Recently academic researchers and management consultants have denoted an increased interest in understanding how firms can build, nurture and sustain strategic capabilities.[2] The strategic management literature considers that knowledge allows the creation of capabilities; therefore the process of building up the knowledge base is at the centre of attention. Through learning processes the firms build their knowledge base. There is increasing consensus that the capability building process takes time and is a costly process that requires a deliberate and sustained learning strategy.[3]

Strategic management literature assumes that firms have already accumulated the essential knowledge and the authors analyse how these firms can nurture, integrate, combine or fuse the knowledge that they already have to generate new knowledge at an international level. This literature presents two weaknesses. First, the evidence about how firms can build, nurture and sustain their strategic capabilities is still insufficient. Second, it has given little attention to how those capabilities were initially accumulated.

With regard to developing countries, the analysis of technological capability building has concentrated on the learning processes involved in building up a minimum base of essential knowledge to engage in innovative activity.[4] The idea is that firms are technologically immature, they learn over time and accumulate knowledge, so they can progressively develop new activities and acquire new capabilities. Technological development occurs over time and it is possible to identify stages.[5] However, this literature has hardly examined the later stage of accumulation (advanced innovative capabilities) as firms approach the international technological frontier and seek to build strategic capabilities.

The analysis of the success of the East Asian firms revealed that the consistent and persistent technology strategy pursued by the firms played an important role in catching up and acquiring competitive advantages.[6] Such a technology strategy was oriented to learning and progressively building technological capabilities. However, this analysis also showed that clear governmental support and a context that favoured innovation activities largely contributed to this success. In contrast, very limited evidence has been discussed about the characteristics of and restraints to the building up of strategic capabilities by Latin American firms. In addition, some descriptions of the capability building process show, on the one side, that there has not been a consistent and persistent innovation strategy,[7] and, on the other side, that the context has not contributed to a sustained accumulation of technological capabilities by industrial firms.[8]

This chapter analyses the characteristics of the technological capability building process of a Large Mexican firm and discusses the extent to which the dual and unstable technology strategy pursued by this firm contributes to explaining the weaknesses of that process.[9] The duality refers to the fact that two technology strategies have coexisted in parallel: one directed towards being a fast follower of the technology leader and the other directed to strengthening in-house developments in order to be 'technologically independent' in certain areas. The firm pursued these two technology strategies from the 1970s when it started a transition process from having the minimum essential knowledge base towards building strategic capabilities.[10] The instability of the technology strategy refers to the inconsistent organizational support to implement each strategy. This instability was greater at the end of the 1980s and 1990s due to major changes in the context – e.g. the change from a closed to an opened economy – and the macroeconomic turbulence that has characterized the Mexican economy in this period.

This chapter is based on a detailed case study of Vitro SA – an internationally competing and multinational Mexican group, with subsidiaries in the USA and Latin America – carried out in 1996.[11] This firm has a long tradition in the Mexican economy, occupying quasi-monopolistic positions in several industrial activities over the years. In the 1980s and 1990s this firm succeeded in a set of international markets. This paper concentrates on the case of the Glass Container division, Vitro Envases de Norteamérica, which represents 70 per cent of the domestic market and got to be the third player in the international market from 1989 to 1996. This case study reveals several problems that a Mexican firm competing behind but close to the international technological frontier should deal with to build primary strategic capabilities.

The chapter is organized in five sections. After this introduction, the next section presents a brief description of the industry. There follows an outline of the case study firm. Then there is a discussion of the characteristics of the capability building process and the dual and unstable technology strategy. The analysis is organized in three stages of the capability building process: the building of a minimum knowledge base (1909–70), the transition towards building strategic capabilities (1970–90) and the turbulence of the 1990s. The final section contains the conclusions.

The industry

Market trends

The glass container industry is composed of establishments primarily engaged in manufacturing glass containers for commercial packing and bottling and for home preserving (SIC code 3221 and SITC code 665). This industry produces inputs for the beverage, beer, food, cosmetic and pharmaceutical industries, using abundant raw materials. The production process is capital-intensive, but labour and materials represent a high percentage of the production cost. The industry is based on economies of scale and has high barriers to entry associated with high investment and high transportation costs. It is basically a local or regional business. The life cycle of the industry has reached a mature stage and from the 1980s there has been low or negative growth, except in emerging economies like Mexico.

The glass container industry throughout the world is highly concentrated. However, the structure of the industry worldwide is different. The European industry is composed of a few large groups and small and medium-size businesses, while in the USA there are only large firms. Markets are also different. The European market has traditionally required flexible production to supply a highly specialized demand. In contrast, the US market is very large and less diversified and thus has required long production runs. Latin American markets are smaller than the US one and have a diversified demand that requires small production runs. Oligopolies play at the international level. The main glass container producers at international level in 1995–6 were: first, Owens-Illinois (USA); second, Saint Gobain (France); and third Vitro (Mexico). These firms have subsidiaries in several other developed and developing countries.

The history of the industry in Mexico has its roots in 1909 with the creation of the first company of Vitro SA – Vidriera Monterrey at Monterrey – and it was associated with the evolution of the Mexican beer industry. From the 1940s to the 1960s the industry grew at high rates following the expansion of the domestic market favoured by the import substitution industrialization (ISI) model. Despite the anti-export bias of the first stages of the ISI, the glass container industry was exporting since the 1930s. The geographical and cultural closeness to the USA of the largest producer since the earliest days contributes to explaining this behaviour. However, exports were not significant in value until the 1970s.

The contraction of the domestic market in 1982 pulled down the demand for glass containers. The industry, but mainly the largest producer, looked more seriously into foreign markets to compensate for the contraction of the domestic demand. This business strategy was supported by a policy to stimulate export firms established by the government after the crisis, and by the export experience the largest producer already had in the US and Latin American markets. Glass container exports increased from US$9.4 million in 1975 to $127 million in 1992 and to $157 in 1995, and the export coefficient grew from 3 per cent in the 1970s to 7 per cent in 1985 and 14.6 per cent in 1992. The increase in exports partially explains the recuperation of sales since 1983.

The dynamics of the industry during the 1990s changed owing to a new economic, competitive and technological environment. The process of opening up the economy, which started in 1987, was furthered in the 1990s, and a regional market was established through the signing of the NAFTA agreement in 1993. At the same time there have been changes in the structure of demand; the glass container industry was threatened by containers made from other materials: plastic, aluminium and tetrapak. In addition, in December 1994 there was a new crisis in the Mexican economy, which reduced domestic demand. All these factors increased the level of competition and created pressure for higher efficiency, cost reduction, quality increase and product innovation.

The Mexican annual demand for glass containers grew from 4,300 million containers in 1987 to 4,900 million in 1994.[12] The value of the market between 1987 and 1994 did not change significantly due to the reduction in the price of the glass containers.

Price reduction and negative growth in the 1990s reveal the maturity of the Mexican market. The process of substituting cans and plastic bottles for glass, an international trend since the mid-1980s, has been slow in Mexico due to a consumption structure that is still highly focused on low-cost returnable glass bottles.[13] Glass still represented 78 per cent of the total containers of the soft drinks market in 1994, while in the USA it represented less than 10 per cent.

The main Mexican markets for glass containers are the food, beer, soft drink and wine industries. There have been some changes in the structure of the demand of glass containers. Beer was the most important market in the 1980s, while food and soft drink were the main markets in the 1990s.

The Mexican market structure is highly oligopolistic, as it is all over the world. There are six Mexican firms: (a) one large firm – Vitro Envases – which is the most diversified firm and dominates all the product markets except beer; (b) two medium-sized firms – Nueva Fanal and Sivesa – which were created as a result of the vertical integration of the two large Mexican brewers and control the beer market (Sivesa also supplies the soft drink market); and (c) three small firms. Historically, the largest producer has held a market share of 70–80 per cent. In recent years there has been an increase in the competition from small firms and the brewery-owned firms, which is associated with more client power, the importance of the client–producer interaction and the advantages of flexibility. The three larger firms held 93.8 per cent in 1996 and the small firms 6.2 per cent.[14]

Technological trends

The glass container industry is mature and equipment technology has been crucial for its path of technical change. Since the 1940s the 'IS machine' has dominated the equipment technology,[15] and determines all the complementary equipment to be used.[16] Several changes in complementary equipment and other stages of the glass container production process have followed the innovations in the IS machine. In general, innovation activity has been oriented to developing ways to increase speed, efficiency, machine throughput and machine coordination, and to reduce downtime and defects.[17]

Today competitiveness is largely based on control of the whole process of container production and the combination of different technologies to obtain better performance from the standard equipment. This latter is made effective by acquiring the mechanisms for one technology and coupling them with another technology. This makes knowledge in mechanical engineering essential. Glass composition and electronic control systems are also important knowledge bases.

There are two types of firms: vertically integrated firms which produce the equipment, such as Owens-Illinois and Heye Glas; and makers of glass containers only, such as Anchor Glass Containers Corporation, Saint Gobain and Bormioli. In each type some firms carry out R&D while others do not. The industry has followed the technological trajectory of a scale-intensive sector according to Pavitt's (1984) taxonomy. Suppliers of equipment and components (both independent firms and vertically integrated) and in-house technological activities carried out by design departments, production engineering departments and operating experience have been sources of innovation. However, many firms, apart from the largest players, can be considered to be supplier-dominated, following a strategy more dependent on innovations introduced by the equipment suppliers.

The three large Mexican firms use up-to-date technology but they have developed different types of technological capabilities. Vitro SA is a vertically integrated group in the case of glass containers – producing the raw materials, intermediate inputs and capital goods needed to manufacture the final products. Vitro Envases carries out R&D activities, has developed certain in-house technology and also uses Owens-Illinois technology. Sivesa and Nueva Fanal are purely glass container makers which acquire technology and equipment from the main suppliers at the international level. This industry was classified as a scale-intensive sector by Dutrénit and Capdevielle (1993), using Pavitt's taxonomy.[18]

The institutional framework

The Mexican glass container industry was favoured by the protection of the domestic market, the development of infrastructure and a set of general subsidies introduced during the ISI.

There is neither a glass research institute nor research groups on glass in Mexico. The only client for research on glass is Vitro SA – the largest player – which carries out R&D, but it has not generated sufficient demand for the university to be interested in the industry interests. Relationships have been mainly originated in the need to solve very specific and short-term problems. At times and related to its in-house R&D activities, when a problem of basic science or applied research emerges this firm contacts either Mexican or American research centres or universities. The Mexican universities have been more important as suppliers of graduates for the industry. Technical schools provide a general training so that the largest producer has interacted with local technical schools to redesign the curricula of the courses to be more oriented to the industry's needs. There have been some attempts to develop new programmes without much success. Due to the difficulties in getting agreements, it has developed its own technical training focused on the glass industry.[19]

The signing of the NAFTA and the setting of the regional market has had little impact on the industry. The reduction in tariffs has not affected significantly the industry products owing to the high barriers to entry. In contrast, the general tariff reduction has allowed costs to be reduced, through a reduction in the price of raw materials and other inputs, allowing producers to be more competitive.

To sum up, the glass container is a mature industry dominated by large oligopolies in most of the countries. Technological development is slow and largely follows a trajectory led by equipment technology. The Mexican industry follows international trends. The three large firms use up-to-date technology and have accompanied the technological frontier with some lag. The Mexican case is characterized by a lack of institutional framework to support the innovation activity. The change in the industrialization model from the ISI to an open economy has changed the conditions of competition. However, firms still benefit from high barriers to entry.

Profile of the case study

Vitro SA is an internationally competive and multinational Mexican group with subsidiaries in Latin America and the USA, which made half of its sales abroad in

1996.[20] It has its headquarters in Monterrey (Mexico) and came into being as a producer of bottles for the Cuauhtémoc brewery (now FEMSA). It was created in 1909 as a family-owned firm with Mexican capital and is now a publicly held company listed on the Mexican Stock Market (1976) and on the New York Stock Exchange (1991). It became a multinational firm in the 1960s with acquisitions in Latin America. In 1996 it was a US$2.2 billion sales Mexican group in glass-related activities. It was the second Mexican economic group by sales in 1994,[21] and ranked sixteenth in Latin America by sales in 1996.[22]

The company operated through six divisions in 1995: (a) glass containers; (b) flat glass; (c) packaging (plastic, can and machinery); (d) glassware; (e) home appliances; (f) chemicals, fibres and mining. Eighty-four per cent of total sales were glass-related products. The glass containers operations in Mexico and the USA generated 54 per cent of Vitro's sales in 1995. In 1996, with the divestment of Anchor Glass Container Corporation (AGCC)[23] and, after other investments in architectural and automotive glass, Flat Glass became the largest division in sales. Home Appliances is also increasing its contribution to the sales. Despite the changes, Vitro continues to be a glass group.

Vitro has traditionally used joint ventures as a core component of its strategy to develop new, fast-growing product lines, gain access to new markets, expand its distribution channels and acquire leading-edge technology. Vitro's major alliance in the glass containers business is with Owens-Illinois. The firm has always had a particular technological culture related to its own history. Its founders were strongly influenced by US entrepreneurs at the beginning of the 1900s. Since the earliest days they pushed the organization to introduce state-of-the-art technology, which behaviour has continued until today. On average, Vitro spends 1.2 per cent of the sales in technology-related activities. Additionally, it pays out around 0.6 per cent of sales to its technology licensor in the case of the glass container business.[24] In 1996, Vitro had 55 active patents and 19 applied for in the USA in 1995, and also had 53 active and 25 applied for in Mexico. Thirty of these patents are in glass container related fields.

Vitro Envases – the glass containers division – is the largest glass container manufacturer in Mexico. It has had a long experience of technology transfer to Latin American subsidiaries and other companies since 1964. With the purchase of AGCC in 1989, it became the second largest player in the US glass container market and the third largest in the world.[25]

In 1996 Vitro Envases consisted of eight plants in Mexico; 14 plants in the USA; one plant in Bolivia; two associated firms with three plants in Guatemala, Costa Rica and Peru; one distributor company in the USA; and two other minor companies. It had around 8,000 employees in Mexico and 5,000 in the USA. The Mexican plants were located strategically close to the largest towns, such as Mexico City, Monterrey, Guadalajara, Querétaro and Toluca. The Mexicali plant is located close to the US border.

Total sales in 1995 were around $1.6 billion, of which $0.6 billion were generated by the glass container activities in Mexico and $1.0 billion by activities in the USA. Sales in Latin America represent around 5 per cent of the sales in Mexico. In 1996 the total sales of VGC were reduced to $693 million, which included only the Mexican and Latin American operations. Exports have continually increased from

1981, following the reorientation of the industrial production towards the international market. By 1996, 70 per cent of the production of the Mexican subsidiaries was sold in the domestic market, 25 per cent in NAFTA markets and 5 per cent in Latin America.[26]

Vitro is one of the largest and most successful Mexican industrial groups that play at the international level. This group began at the beginning of the twentieth century and is related to the history of several Mexican industrial sectors. Vitro Envases is the largest glass container firm in Mexico and one of the main players in the industry at the international level.

The capability building process and the dual and unstable technology strategy

Vitro Envases has built innovative technological capabilities in several technical functions and has created different knowledge bases. It has been able to undertake activities in each technical function that match different stages of technological capability accumulation according to the taxonomies of Lall (1992) and Bell and Pavitt (1995).[27] Many activities needed to integrate knowledge bases located in different organizational units, as analysed by Prahalad and Hammel (1990), and Iansiti and Clark (1994) and Leonard-Barton (1995). Vitro Envases has also implemented several organizational arrangements to promote learning processes at individual and organizational levels, as analysed by Nonaka and Takeuchi (1995). However, nearly 100 years after start-up Vitro Envases is still missing strategic capabilities.

There was a long period from 1909 until 1970 spent building the minimum essential knowledge base.[28] In the 1970s the firm started shifting beyond that and began a transition process towards building strategic capabilities. However, even 25 years after starting that transition process, it has not been completed. Vitro Envases built advanced innovative technological capabilities in some technical functions and knowledge fields, and even embryonic strategic capabilities, but has failed to build the strategic capabilities to distinguish the firm competitively. The firm experienced difficulties in socializing the learning process at organizational level, coordinating different learning strategies pursued by different organizational units, and in integrating knowledge across organizational boundaries, which hampered the capability building process.[29] One of the main factors that contributed to explaining these difficulties that the firm confronted in building strategic capabilities is the duality and instability of its technology strategy.

Particularly since the 1970s, when Vitro Envases started the transition process, two technology strategies have coexisted in parallel: one directed towards being a fast follower of the technology leader, Owens-Illinois, and the other directed to strengthening in-house developments in order to be 'technologically independent' in certain areas.[30] The former course involved converting all the plants to the original Owens-Illinois technology, avoiding any in-house developments. It was conceived as a short-term version of the fast follower strategy without any R&D activities, even those oriented to quick assimilation of technology. The second strategy was based on the idea that Vitro Envases and the group (Vitro SA) had already created a body of knowledge, had built some embryonic strategic capabilities and therefore should continue undertaking R&D activities in those particular areas.[31] Each technology strategy required a different knowledge base, demanded the accumulation of different technological capabilities, required different types of linkages with the science and technology system and with other domestic and foreign firms, and in general determined a different path of accumulation.

While both strategies coexisted in parallel, they were neither consistent nor articulated. Top management was taking simultaneous decisions related to each of these strategies, sometimes in relation to the same areas. Therefore, there was not a clear decision about the direction of knowledge accumulation in the long-term. Additionally, and even more importantly, the support for each technology strategy was not stable and at some stages one was more supported than the other, and vice versa. The duality is related to the situation of a firm in a transition process from having the minimum essential knowledge to building strategic capabilities.[32] The instability of the technology strategy and the fact that from 1970 there were periods of more support to one or the other technology strategy was related to changes in the macroeconomics context. Power conflict inside the group also affected the instability of the technology strategy. A more detailed description of the capability building process and the technology strategy pursued by the firm in different periods is presented below.

Building a minimum knowledge base, 1909–70

From its creation in 1909 until 1970 Vitro Envases built the minimum essential knowledge base. From building routine production capabilities, it was able gradually to build innovative technological capabilities and so undertake a few innovation activities. External sources of knowledge were very important from the earliest days, but the firm was able to build up internal innovative technological capabilities and then combine external and internal sources of knowledge. The history of the creation of Vitro Envases reveals a concern for introducing state-of-the-art technology to solve technical problems. The firm was concerned with the most relevant innovations introduced by the technology leaders at a quicker pace than would be expected from the weak industrial development in Mexico at that time.

During the ISI period Vitro Envases built internal innovative capabilities. This was based on a technology strategy of being 'technologically independent'. This strategy has its roots in the 1940s, when Fama – the machine manufacturer firm – was created.[33] Initially the strategy had a broad focus, without defining areas of specialization, and coexisted with a sort of followership strategy to introduce the new equipment launched on the international market by the technology leaders. Even though the ISI promoted little attention to competitiveness, efficiency, technological upgrading and export activity (Pérez, 1996), as in the early days the firm continued to believe that 'technology matters'.

During the whole of this period, the depth of the knowledge accumulated by technical function was uneven. Basic innovative technological capabilities were essentially reached in production activities – product-centred – as well as in linkage activities with suppliers. The type of investment activities and process-centred activities undertaken corresponded to an intermediate stage in the process of building up technological capabilities. The development of a few original designs of plant and equipment by Fama reveals an intermediate level in capital goods activities too. The experience in technology transfer to Latin American countries since 1964 reveals more advanced capabilities in linkages with other glass container firms. However, some other technical functions were very weak, such as the linkages with customers and with the science and technology system.

Starting a transition process towards building strategic capabilities, 1970–90

The 1970s was a period of economic growth. Vitro Envases had already built the minimum essential knowledge base and, following the technology strategy of being 'technologically independent', it started a transition process towards building strategic capabilities. The 1970s was a period of flourishing in-house innovative technological capabilities, looking for different sources of knowledge, undertaking more technologically complex activities, implementing new ways of doing things and raising some areas of knowledge specialization.

However, the transition process has evolved in the context of a redefinition of the company's business strategy. After several decades of intense expansion of production capacities, the growth of the domestic market in the 1970s was insufficient to keep up with the rate of the firm's growth. The firm started looking to the US market to further its expansion plans. This strategy was reconfirmed in the 1980s with the contraction of the domestic market associated with the economic crisis of 1982, and the change towards an open and competitive market in Mexico from the end of the 1980s. A market-oriented strategy was directed to increasing exports and specifically to penetrating the US market. Such a strategy brought pressure to upgrade and improve equipment technology and increase operational efficiency (Nichols, 1993).

During this period the company pursued more clearly two distinctive parallel technology strategies. One was to continue aiming to be 'technologically independent', and the main event in this strategy was the organization of the technology function at the group level and the creation of Vitro-Tec, an R&D unit. The second strategy was to be a fast follower of the technology leaders, and the central event that supported this strategy was the signing of a technical agreement with Owens-Illinois, one of the technology leaders.

The technologically independent strategy

In 1977 Vitro decided to create a new organizational structure that was more explicitly committed to innovation. This decision was based on the capabilities already accumulated and the strategy of 'technological independence' conceived in the 1940s. This involved two related steps of organizational restructuring of the technological activities. On the one hand, incipient R&D activities were brought together in Vitro-Tec, a central unit serving the whole group. This unit specialized in basic and applied research and development activities and was oriented to strategic projects. At the same time, divisional technology centres were set up to work more closely with the production function, like Dirtec for Vitro Envases. They were more oriented towards minor improvements and adaptations. This organization of the technology function received organizational support.

The knowledge specialization process, the creation of a central R&D unit and the strengthening of the R&D activities at group and divisional levels increased the knowledge of process technology and allowed the firm to develop more complex innovation projects.

The accumulation in glass container related areas was directed, explicitly and implicitly, towards two main knowledge fields: electronic control systems and glass composition. A significant effort was put into developing knowledge in electronic control systems by Vitro-Tec and Fama and in glass composition by Dirtec. The R&D activities were supported with formal activities of literature search and experimentation. Domestic and foreign links were established with American and Mexican universities. As a result of the crisis of 1982 some projects were affected, but eventually the dynamic of accumulation continued. The result was the building up of embryonic strategic capabilities in these fields.[34]

At the same time, the innovative technological capabilities in investment project management and process engineering built before the 1970s were strengthened in this period and also became embryonic strategic capabilities. These capabilities were an important part of the knowledge base for increasing operational efficiency and expanding the investment in Mexico and Central America. The knowledge base in these areas was based more on the empirical experience in operating and adapting the equipment and undertaking investment projects than in formal R&D activities.

As a result of the establishment of Vitro-Tec, a quite systematic patenting activity was developed in the 1980s. In 1995 Vitro had 55 active patents in the USA and 19 applied for.[35] Most of the company's patents protected developments made during the late 1970s and the 1980s. Thirty-four of the 55 active patents were related to the glass container area.[36] Vitro had at least one patent in most of the knowledge areas in glass containers, which reveals a certain knowledge base.

The followership strategy

At the same time that the 'technologically independent' strategy was being supported, in 1974 the firm decided to sign a technical agreement with Owens-Illinois. The firm had begun to export to the USA and was under pressure to solve certain technical problems. The technology strategy was supposed to be unique but with different goals being articulated. On the one hand the goal was to solve some of the technical problems with the technical agreement and catch up with Owens-Illinois, while on the other hand the aim was to maintain in-house developments for the long term with Vitro-Tec.[37] In fact, this was the origin of a fast follower technology strategy, that coexisted with the 'technologically independent' strategy and produced pressure for a deviation of the development activities promoted by this strategy.

There were three types of problem related to the introduction of the Owens-Illinois technology. First, there was an important stock of equipment in operation that had been acquired from other technology sources, so the introduction was paced by the timing of the effective life of that equipment. Therefore, it was necessary to couple Owens-Illinois technology with the equipment technologies already in operation. Second, Owens-Illinois technology had to be adapted to Vitro

Envases-specific conditions. These two factors demanded the development of internal innovative technological capabilities to carry out successful operation of the Owens-Illinois technology. Third, the firm had already accumulated knowledge and a routine for carrying out adaptations, so Owens-Illinois technology was combined with already developed adaptations and improvements. Therefore, the technology transferred from Owens-Illinois to Vitro Envases promptly became an idiosyncratic Vitro/Owens-Illinois technology, which continually demanded in-house innovative technological capabilities to keep it in operation. These capabilities were of a different nature from those required for the 'technologically independent' strategy.

From 1970 to 1990 the target of technological development was relatively more favoured and the firm progressed towards completion of the transition process. According to the taxonomy of technological capability building, intermediate technological capabilities were built in product-related activities, and were maintained and also strengthened in the case of investment activities. Linkage with suppliers combined very basic activities of searching information with some attempts to undertake collaborative research. Linkages with customers and the science and technology system remained weak. The creation of knowledge and the building of an embryonic strategic capability in glass composition reveals advanced technological capabilities in this process-related activity, as the electronic control systems do in the case of the capital goods supply.

The turbulence of the 1990s

The 1990s was a period of turbulence in the businesses associated with changes in the economic environment and competition conditions. The process of opening up the economy was furthered and the regional market was established through the signing of the NAFTA agreement in 1993. At the same time, the industry was being threatened by containers made from other materials, which generated increasing pressures to look for cost reduction, quality improvement and product innovation. In addition, new entrants in the US market set up a change in the competitive conditions. The result of this was an increase in the level of competition in both Mexico and the USA. In addition, the Mexican crisis of 1994 again reduced domestic demand.

By 1990 Vitro Envases was also faced with two other pressures: (a) the need to update the facilities of AGCC, which was acquired in December 1989; and (b) changes in the power inside Vitro SA, which favoured the promoters of a fast follower technology strategy. Vitro Envases's business strategy, technology strategy and organizational structure were being continually adjusted to meet all these changing conditions. The firm was still undergoing a transition process, was under a lot of pressure and took business- and technology-related decisions that altered the direction of the knowledge accumulation process described above.

Strengthening the fast follower strategy and changing the direction of accumulation

Under those conditions described above, the firm reduced its R&D activities in this period and an important effort was put into assimilating Owens-Illinois technology and increasing the operational efficiency and product quality. The technology strategy of being a fast follower of Owens-Illinois was strongly supported, but this combination of events resulted in a particularly short-term version of the fast follower strategy and not the knowledge building version based on a defensive R&D strategy (Freeman, 1982). Two main facts supported that strategy. One was the introduction of the new 'narrow neck press blow' triple cavity technology of Owens-Illinois with the explicit prohibition of adapting it with any in-house improvements, and the other was the decentralization of Vitro-Tec towards divisions and the discouragement of the development and improvement activities.

Despite the signing of the technical agreement with Owens-Illinois in 1974, VGC had continued to use different technology sources and was aware of the latest technology in the market. At the end of the 1980s the 'narrow neck press blow' technology was a novelty in the international glass container market and Vitro Envases decided to acquire the triple cavity technology from Owens-Illinois. This decision was accompanied by the management's order to replicate Owens-Illinois technology and not introduce any in-house improvements into those machines.[38] The 1990s has been a period of learning about the routine operation and basic maintenance of this new complex process to ensure a high operational efficiency. The main concern was catching up with the present technology. The introduction of the Owens-Illinois technology had two main impacts. First, the process was accompanied by a change in the behaviour towards learning to be fast followers and quickly increasing operational efficiency instead of learning to undertake in-house developments. Second, the introduction of this technology concentrated a great effort on manufacturing and machine operation, and that effort affected the time assigned by Dirtec and Fama to more formal technology development activities oriented to different purposes.

In 1989 there was a change in the organization of the technology function of Vitro, and Vitro-Tec was decentralized into divisional technology centres. Dirtec – as the technology centre of Vitro Envases – assumed an even more important role in all the technological activities related to glass containers. This change was justified by the intention of closing the gap between the business functions of technology and production.[39] However, the characteristics of the decentralization reveal that it was seen primarily as a way of reducing the scale of R&D activities and changing the direction of accumulation, rather than as a measure to locate R&D capabilities closer to production. The following three facts illustrate this point. First, even though several Vitro-Tec personnel were relocated to the divisions, the criterion was not to move whole teams. Second, the technology centres, such as Dirtec, were explicitly oriented to giving technical assistance to plants and supporting their search for continuous improvements, while R&D activities were explicitly discouraged. Third, even though the patent department was kept at the group level, it was more oriented to supervising Vitro patenting interests than to supporting the use of patents as a source of information about competitors.

These two events affected the direction of accumulation, the target of knowledge management, the type of existing knowledge that needed to be shared and codified, the need for creating knowledge and the type of links with other sources of knowledge. In particular, those links related to nurturing R&D activities were reduced. In contrast, the firm prioritized links that could help to solve day-to-day problems. In the 1990s the knowledge bases built up earlier received differing attention and were managed in different ways according to changes in technology strategy. This was evident in the main areas of accumulation during the 1970s and 1980s. The capabilities for managing investment projects and process engineering were directly related to the focus on increasing operational efficiency and the target of transferring technology to Latin America. Therefore, in the 1980s there was a special concern to strengthen the knowledge bases that support these capabilities. In contrast, in the 1990s the development projects in glass composition and electronic control systems were stopped. The knowledge had been based on R&D activities, which were run down during this period. Vitro Envases continued to rely on the knowledge base built up much earlier. The knowledge creation process was replaced by activities directed just to avoiding obsolescence of existing knowledge. Hence, these embryonic strategic capabilities were not strengthened.

There were two basic new areas of knowledge accumulation, one concerned with improving job changes[40] activity and the other with increasing the linkages with customers and suppliers. Instead of focusing on knowledge fields, such as glass composition or electronic control systems, the new areas of accumulation had a more practical focus. They were oriented to increasing operational efficiency and product quality according to the new emphasis of the technology strategy. The building of capabilities in these areas required knowledge in mechanical engineering, glass composition and electronics to control the whole production process, as well as capabilities in process engineering. This knowledge had been built up earlier and was used to support these areas under the new strategic emphasis in this period.

The renaissance of the 'technologically independent' strategy

From 1994 there was a new emphasis on the 'technologically independent' strategy and some attempts were made: (a) to define strategically 'what to buy and what to develop', based on the knowledge base already built, and specifically to define the areas in which they wanted to develop technology; and (b) to change the way of doing things by promoting the sharing of existing knowledge, increasing knowledge codification and integrating knowledge across organizational boundaries, or, in other words, looking for more consistent knowledge management. The main event incorporated in this strategy was the identification of areas of strength and potential synergy at the group level.

However, this strategy did not go very far. While in the 1970s and 1980s the two technology strategies had moved in parallel, at this time the strategy of being a fast follower with the focus on operational efficiency and quality led all the technology-related activities. The 'technologically independent' strategy only received intermittent support from the top management, and had to evolve in the turbulent context of the 1990s. The main impact of the renaissance of this strategy was on the strengthening of knowledge management, oriented to using and integrating existing knowledge and facilitating the creation of new knowledge in certain areas. The setting up from 1994 of a number of organizational arrangements explicitly oriented to managing knowledge was the main contribution to that target. However, it is still very early to evaluate the scope of these changes.

Therefore, in the 1990s there was a change in the direction of knowledge accumulation which affected the level of innovative technological capabilities already built. In terms of the most advanced innovative technological capabilities revealed in the earlier period, such as the R&D activities related to production, Vitro Envases seems to have reduced its level of accumulation. The decentralization of Vitro-Tec towards the divisions was in fact a contraction of the company's R&D activities. In addition, the content of the technology-related activities changed towards more continuous improvement. The process of creation of new knowledge in the embryonic strategic capabilities in electronics or glass composition was halted, and these embryonic strategic capabilities were kept at the same level. The advanced innovative technological capabilities in investment activities were maintained. However, they were still based largely on experience. Even with no R&D activities, the transfer of technology to Latin America reveals the level of expertise reached in this technical function. New types of linkages were established with foreign suppliers based on collaboration in technology development and transfer of technology. However, these activities were still incipient until 1996. Although linkages with customers were strengthened, this remains a relatively weak activity. Even weaker have been linkages with the science and technology system in a context of contraction of R&D activities. The focus on continuous improvement and day-to-day running allowed the development of other capabilities related to the operation, such as job changes, besides the strengthening of process engineering. They were the focus of some development activity over this period.

In the 1990s, some attempts were made to develop a more explicit knowledge management in two dimensions: sharing knowledge at the organizational level, and integrating knowledge across organizational units. These attempts sought to use, adapt, integrate and change existing knowledge and also contributed to creating new knowledge in certain areas. However, the instability of the dual technology strategy in the 1990s made success difficult.

Conclusions

The capability building process described by the strategic management literature stresses the characteristics of the nurturing, rebuilding or renewing strategic capabilities or competencies. This is a long-term process that requires continuous improvement. The literature about the successful catch-up of a set of East Asian firms focuses on the articulation between different agents of the national innovation system and the gradual accumulation of technological capabilities pursued by firms for the development of competitive advantages. In both cases a deliberate and sustained technology strategy, which included a learning strategy and a consistent management of knowledge, played an important role in the explanation of these processes.

In contrast, the Vitro Envases case reveals that even though it was able to build up innovative technological capabilities in several technical functions and has created different knowledge bases, it has denoted difficulties to build the strategic capabilities to distinguish the firm competitively. The analysis shows that Vitro Envases pursued two technology strategies in parallel. It sought to rely on its innovative technological capabilities to be at the international technological frontier in certain areas and, at the same time, pursued a fast follower strategy. Both strategies were supported by decisions taken by the top management and received organizational support. However, the organizational support for each strategy was unstable over the whole period. The firm did not pursue a consistent or stable technology strategy. This affected the projects ongoing, the knowledge creation process and knowledge accumulation, and the aims and efforts to manage the company's knowledge. The instability of the technology strategy limited the building up of strategic capabilities.

Even though the duality of the technology strategy is associated with the condition of being a firm in a transition process from building a minimum essential knowledge to surviving in the market to building strategic capabilities, the instability of the technology strategy is a feature based on other issues. Changes in the context and macroeconomic instability are factors that contribute to explaining the instability of the technology strategy pursued by the firm. Power conflicts inside the group is another factor lying behind the instability, but this issue has been hardly touched in this chapter.

The analysis also reveals that the firm has built limited and sporadic linkages with other agents of the national innovation system, such as universities and technical schools. More linkages were established when the technology strategy of being 'technologically independent' was favoured. Therefore, the instability of the technology strategy also affected the building and reinforcement of domestic linkages. However, from the earliest days, the firm was able to establish strong linkages with different technology suppliers and with foreign universities when necessary. This suggests that it did not build more domestic linkages because they were not indispensable for the capability building process. What is intriguing is the fact that the firm carried out more R&D activities and built more research linkages at the time of the closed economy. In the context of an opened economy, pressures were greater for solving day-to-day problems, which reduced the efforts on R&D activities.

This analysis shows that this Mexican 'star group' has built innovative technological capabilities and has the potential to remain a world leader. But it also faces some risks of eroding its position. In order to strengthen its business and technological positions at world level, the problems related to the instability of its technology strategy need to be addressed. The unstable macroeconomic context put noise in the decision-making process.

Notes

1. I wish to thank Vitro SA for being willing to open their doors to me. Any inaccuracies or errors in the text are, however, my own responsibility.
2. See, for instance, Prahalad and Hamel (1990), Pavitt (1991), Teece and Pisano (1994) and Leonard-Barton (1992, 1995).
3. See, for instance, Bell (1984) and Dodgson (1993).
4. See, for instance, Katz (1986, 1987) and Lall (1987).
5. Based on Lall (1992), Bell and Pavitt (1995) identify four levels of technological capabilities, one of basic operating capabilities and three levels of innovative technological capabilities: basic, intermediate and advanced.
6. See, for instance, Hobday (1995) and Kim (1995).

7. See, for instance, Dutrénit (2000).

8. See, for instance, Katz (1985, 1995) and Vera-Cruz (1999).

9. Following Kim (1997b, p. 86), technological capabilities are defined as 'the ability to make effective use of technological knowledge to assimilate, use, adapt, and change existing technologies. It also enables one to create new technologies and to develop new products and processes in response to the changing economic environment.'

10. This is a stage of accumulation where the firm has built technological capabilities to reduce costs, improve quality and upgrade equipment to achieve parity with competitors. It corresponds to basic–intermediate innovative technological capabilities according to Bell and Pavitt's taxonomy.

11. This case study was carried out as part of a PhD thesis at SPRU (Sussex University). A full description of the case is presented in Dutrénit (2000).

12. Grupo Financiero Bancomer (1995, p. 45), based on INEGI.

13. This substitution process has accelerated in the second half of the 1990s and there has been an absolute reduction in the demand for glass containers.

14. Interview with managers of Vitro Envases' Technology Direction.

15. The IS machine is the most diffused machine used to form the glass container. It was launched on the market in 1925. The name refers to the operation of individual sections, each of which constitutes a complete machine unit and can be operated independently.

16. There are two main 'IS machines' technologies: Owens-Illinois and Emhart Glass. Owens-Illinois – with its more robust machines that allow high productivity – dominates the US market and several developing countries, such as Mexico. Emhart Glass – with its more flexible equipment – dominates the European market.

17. In the most recent decades there has been little research into glass container production. R&D activities are concentrated on ultra-lightweight, increased container strength (e.g. coatings), processing and batch melting technology improvements (USITC, 1993). A common view in the industry is that more strategic research should be oriented to changing the glass forming process and the 'IS machine' rooted in 1925.

18. Dutrénit and Capdevielle (1993) contains a technological profile of the whole Mexican industry based on Pavitt's (1984) taxonomy.

19. Interview with managers of Vitro Envases' Technology Direction.

20. Vitro SA (1996). This percentage excludes Anchor Glass Container Corporation's discontinued operations.

21. Based on Garrido (1998a, pp. 407–10, Table 4).

22. Based on Garrido and Péres (1998, pp. 34–7, Table 2).

23. AGCC is a large American corporation which was acquired by Vitro in 1989 and sold at the end of 1996.

24. Interview with the Corporate Director of the Technology Division.

25. This ranking changed in 1997 after the divestment of AGCC.

26. Interview with a manager of Vitro Envases's Marketing Division.

27. As described in note 5, Bell and Pavitt (1995) identify four levels of technological capabilities: basic operating capabilities and basic, intermediate and advanced innovative technological capabilities. They analyse those levels by technical function, which cover the main technological activities of the firm, such as investment, production, linkage activities.

28. This is a stage of accumulation where the firm has built technological capabilities to reduce costs, improve quality and upgrade the equipment to achieve parity with competitors. It corresponds to basic–intermediate innovative technological capabilities according to Bell and Pavitt's taxonomy.

29. Dutrénit (2000) contains a detailed description of these characteristics of the knowledge management.

30. A number of managers used the phrase 'technologically independent', which meant trying

to innovate and develop technology in certain areas, leading them to the international technological frontier, while continuing to purchase equipment and technology in other areas.

31. During the stage of building up the minimum essential knowledge base to survive in the market firms largely pursue a technology strategy of slow followers. After this they can pursue a fast follower strategy and remain as close seconds or look to building strategic capabilities by following a leadership technology strategy in selected areas. Taking the transition process up to the point of being an active learning fast follower can be a rational place to be for a firm from a developing country, and also for many firms from the advanced economies. However, the firm has enunciated a strategy of technological leadership and at times has tried to build strategic capabilities, which means that the idea of the pole of the transition process was to build strategic capabilities.

32. Dutrénit (2000) discusses the characteristics of the transition process.

33. Fama is a machine manufacturer company created by Vitro Envases as a result of a backward integration towards the production of capital goods.

34. There were several difficulties in this process, three of which were especially important. First, there were differences in the learning strategies pursued by the organizational units related to the development of knowledge in these fields, and they devoted different resources to this activity and learned in different directions. As a result, they accumulated different types and depths of knowledge by knowledge field and by technical area. Second, there were changes in the organizational support for R&D projects over this period that reduced the effort on creating knowledge and building up innovative technological capabilities in one direction. Third, a sort of internal benchmark with the Owens-Illinois technology was established in such a way that it reduced the credibility of in-house developments, mainly while they were still at an experimental stage. These difficulties reveal some of the types of problems encountered by a firm passing through the transition process from building the minimum essential knowledge base to building strategic capabilities.

35. Vitro's patents represent 10 per cent of the patents of the technology leaders. This number is significant because Mexican firms actually neglect this activity.

36. Patents in glass container areas were granted to Vitro-Tec, Fama and 'Vidriera Monterrey'. Following Ditac (1995), the analysis refers to all of them as Vitro's patents.

37. Interviews with technical staff and managers of Vitro-Tec during 1987–9.

38. Interviews with technical staff and managers of Dirtec and Vitro-Tec.

39. Interviews with the technical staff and managers of Vitro-Tec during 1987–9.

40. Job changes are the activity of changing the variable equipment of the IS machine.

CHAPTER FIFTEEN

The Automobile Sector

R. Constantino and A. Lara

Introduction

The automobile sector is very important for the Mexican economy. At the international level, Mexico is currently considered one of the twelve biggest automobile production centres in the world, but also one of the three countries with the greatest rates of growth in the automobile sector. At the national level the importance of this sector grows, not only because of its impacts on the structure of direct employment, foreign trade and added value statistics, but also because of the extended networking linkages established by this sector with others like the steel and metal, chemical, non-metallic products, selected textiles, electric and electronic sectors.

The Mexican automobile sector is formed by two different subsets of complex industrial classes. The first one is '*manufacturing and assembly of motor vehicles*' (MAMV), which shows a rapid specialization effort in design, assembly and marketing activities for final demand products as a response to the globalization production path (see Table 15.1). The second industrial class in the Mexican automobile sector is the '*auto parts and components*' class (APC). This is oriented towards the manufacture and assembly of a growing number of components for motor vehicles: from vehicle bodies, trailers and motors to chips. The economic importance of this activity relies on the scale economies associated with the specialization process, which, in the case of an average 3,000 components for a motor vehicle, means an increase in the size of the suppliers' market but also in the velocity of know-how diffusion, due to linkages with other sectors.

The industrial structure of the Mexican automobile sector is highly concentrated. The MAMV possesses an oligopolic shape. In 1999 there were 17 assembling firms, but 97 per cent of the cars produced came from only five corporations.[1] Of those, the US companies maintain up to 65 per cent of total production. Something similar occurs in the APC. While the number of companies in the APC is much greater than in the MAMV, the scale of the plants plays an important role in defining market concentration. In this case, in 1999 there were 1,401 companies specializing in the assembly and production of auto parts and components. Of those, only 9 per cent can be considered large-scale plants, and these represent 90 per cent of the total added value produced, 90 per cent of the stock of physical assets and almost 80 per cent of labour employed.

Traditionally the Mexican automobile sector has been dynamic. From the beginning of assembly operations in the country in the mid-1920s to the mid-1980s the sector was oriented to satisfying the domestic demand for vehicles. The performance

Table 15.1 Composition of the Mexican Automobile Sector

Manufacturing and assembly of motor vehicles	Dominated by five large assembly plants (Chrysler, Ford, General Motors [GM], Nissan and Volkswagen [VW]). Concentrate on automobile assembly and represent 95 per cent of sales in 1993; light trucks are 3 per cent. The big three US companies in 1995 represent 61 per cent of automobile assembly in Mexico. 49 per cent of the gross domestic product is located in the State of Mexico and the Federal District; and 24 per cent in the northern states of Coahuila, Sonora, Chihuahua, Nuevo León, Sinaloa, Durango and Aguascalientes (INEGI, annual: 1996).
The auto parts industry	Specializing in the manufacture and assembly of motors, vehicle bodies and trailers. 25 companies, which represent 5 per cent of the total companies, have 70 per cent of the sector's total sales (NAFIN, 1995, p. 178). This sector is made up of between 500 and 600 companies, 90 per cent of which are formed by Mexican capital; most of these have obsolete technology, produce mature components with low added value. This sector is also formed by the *maquiladoras* (twin plants), most of which are of US origin. A total of 93 per cent of their raw materials are imported, and 90 per cent of the industry's production is destined to exports (NAFIN, 1995, p. 179).
Suppliers of raw materials to the assembly and auto parts sectors	Supply steel, aluminium, cast iron, lead, glass, tool machines, chemical products, synthetic rubber, natural rubber, selected textiles, metal products and electric and electronic components. The production of steel in Mexico is in the hands of six companies: AHMSA, HYLSA, IMEXSA, SICARTSA, TAMSA and ACERIAS.

of the sector during this period shows a slow but continuous long-run growth path, mainly induced by a steady macroeconomic environment. The economic instability associated with the globalization of the Mexican economy in the mid-1980s decreased the size of the internal market for vehicles, and, together with the reform of the enactment framework to promote the efficiency in this sector, generated a new productive trajectory sustained by exports.

The exports are the current axis in the path of growth of the Mexican automobile sector. According to official data available for up to 1999, 73 per cent of the total production of vehicles is designated to export and the other 27 per cent is directed towards the domestic market. While the export model has become the new strategy for growth in the automobile sector, both MAMV and APC classes have enlarged their importance in industrial statistics, essentialy due to an increase in labour productivity. However, from the point of view of its economic importance, the MAMV is more significant than APC.

The pattern of growth based in the increasing intensity of foreign trade has produced two different economic outcomes in the Mexican automobile sector. On one side, it has facilitated the constitution of a new geographical arrangement of the productive activities. In a sense, the export strategy has built a geographical cluster for the automobile sector as long as the key activities are extended to the central and northern parts of the territory. While a model of a closed economy promotes the concentration of the MAMV and APC in the metropolitan area of Mexico City to capture the benefits of scale and scope economies due to the size of the domestic market, the open economy model has induced a rearrangement of the productive operations of this sector along a territorial promenade that goes from the Mexico City metropolitan area to the north of the country and the border with the United States of America. The second outcome is related to the evident globalization process of the Mexican automobile sector. According with the current structure of foreign trade, almost 90 per cent of total exports from this sector are directed to the member economies of the NAFTA. This fact tends to strengthen the idea that, more than a globalization process, the automobile sector follows a regionalization trajectory.

Because of the geo-economic importance of the automobile sector for the Mexican economy, in this chapter we present an inquiry into the structure and nature of the linkages established by the automobile sector. In the first section of the chapter we identify some of the key issues related to the current performance of the automobile sector. The second section is concerned with some historical characteristics, like the Mexican institutional and macroeconomic environment, that are essential to an understanding of the evolutionary path of the sector. The third part of this chapter relates to the accumulative attributes that have been important in inducing an improving performance in the Mexican automobile sector. In the fourth section there is an analysis of the automobile innovation system. The sources of innovation are examined with reference to the internal technical efforts of the Mexican automobile sector. The final section of this chapter deals with the key elements that characterize the cluster of the sector in terms of the variables defined in Chapter 10.

The path of the Mexican automobile sector

The history of the automobile sector in Mexico can be summarized in four periods. The first epoch goes from 1925 to 1962. Before 1925 the automobile sector was composed of only motor vehicle importers. In 1925 the first assembly plant was established in Mexican territory and in 1962 the Mexican Congress approved the first Act referring to this sector. During this period the assembly operations of motor vehicles used only imported parts and components. In this sense, the Mexican APC industrial class was practically non-existent.

The second age considered is 1962–76. Formerly the Mexican autoparts and components class appeared during the import substitution model (ISM). The Mexican macroeconomic policy guided by the ISM promoted the emergence in the 1960s of the Mexican APC. Between 1962 and 1976 the automobile sector showed vertical integration among the manufacture and assembly activities with the auto parts and components suppliers. In fact, most of the auto part and components enterprises installed between those years were subsidiaries of MAMV companies and large multinational firms specializing in motor vehicle components. During this phase the Mexican producers of auto parts were incipient, except for those linked to large-scale producers.

The third phase in the evolution of the Mexican automobile sector corresponds to the period of an increasing number of independent and reduced scale producers of auto parts. Between 1977 and 1982, several changes occurred in the sector and in the Mexican economy. First, while at the beginning of the 1960s European corporations such as Renault and Volkswagen controlled up to 50 per cent of the Mexican domestic market of cars, this changed. From the beginning of the 1970s American corporations controlled the majority of the internal market. Second, the size of the domestic market for durable goods increased, mainly because of the financial flows due to the oil boom. Finally, the increasing competence of Asian automobile producers' corporations such as Nissan forced the American producers to promote different strategies of production. In a sense, it is possible to consider this period of time as the consolidation age of the APC suppliers structure. While the MAMV producers still maintain their respective APC subsidiaries, new medium- and small-scale Mexican suppliers were added to the sector. However, this implies a fundamental differentiation in the APC suppliers into first level and second level suppliers (Laming, 1989).

The fourth phase corresponds to the open economy model or the globalization process in the Mexican economy. This period (1982–99) is characterized by the ineffectiveness shown by the closed economy model, throughout the imports substitution policy, to promote economic growth coupled with the balance of payments instability after the oil boom. It can be subdivided into two different segments: first from 1982 to the end of 1980s, in which the size of the Mexican domestic market reduced its size because of the financial and debt crisis. In the second period, from the end of the 1980s to 1999, the structural change of the Mexican economy took place. To this fourth phase corresponds the openness strategy in the automobile sector. The current international model observed in the Mexican automobile sector has two causes: first, the macroeconomic crisis of the Mexican economy, which reduced the size of the internal market for durable goods; second, the nature of the worldwide automobile sector restructuring when the Toyota management model proved successful.

Cumulativeness and improving performance

In a comprehensive way, the historical performance of the Mexican automobile sector demonstrates that the current path of economic success in world markets is the result of synergies between corporate decisions of allocation within the firms, the fiscal supporting conditions established by the Mexican government and the expanded capability of human capital to dominate production routines (Brown, 1998). It is possible to argue that the specialization path observed in the Mexican automobile sector is due to the exploitation of the comparative advantages of the Mexican economy, based on a low direct cost of production. While this is true in a static model, it is not satisfactory in a dynamic sense to explain the trajectory adopted in this sector to enter a new world economy. The cost of production, and hence the comparative advantages, are formed not only by the price of basic inputs and wages, but also by the intangible abilities developed by firms to reduce the transaction costs among the members in the cluster.[2]

A clarifying example is the linkages between the steel and automobile sectors. Very important components of any vehicle are made up of steel and smelted metals. According to some international sources of data, Mexico possesses a comparative advantage compared with Brazil, Taiwan and Korea because the price of those raw materials is 15–30 per cent lower in Mexico than in those countries. The convergence of the technological trajectories across industries is crucial. The technological convergence can be found between the suppliers of raw material (steel, aluminium and plastics) and autoparts (abilities in forging and manufacturing which have been accumulated and adapted since the beginning of the 1930s), and the automobile industry's own ability to organize, coordinate and guarantee the quality of the manufacturing processes as a whole. The technological and organizational convergence between the automobile sector and the steel industry also results from the modernization processes of the firms within the steel industry.[3]

The importance of the technological convergence among different sectors is well perceived throughout the analysis of the different activities related to the production of vehicles. The steel and alloy sectors are crucial in the performance of the automobile sector. The four basic activity groups involved in the production of a vehicle are: raw material and initial processing; manufacture of components and subassembly; manufacture of accessories and auxiliary pieces; and final assembly. The co-evolution of the steel and alloy sectors with automobile manufacturing firms is readily seen in a world-class industry which produces engines, parts for the suspension system, parts and accessories for the brakes system and chassis, among other parts and accessories. The steel and automobile industries share a common path characterized by an interactive convergence process in which the imbalances, improvements or technological innovations that take place in one sector affect the path of the other.

The technological convergence between different sectors is very important, not only because of the observed tendency to diminish the production costs, but for building technical and innovative capabilities throughout interdependent networks of users and producers, as in the instance of the steel and smelted metals sectors and the automobile sector. In the case of the Mexican automobile sector this has been seen since the early 1960s, when General Motors and Ford started the production of cylinder blocks and motor heads. Thus smelting technology, of US origin, was later widely disseminated within the industry. In 1997, large assembly firms were quite familiar with the manufacturing processes of most critical steel and aluminium parts (Moreno, 1994; IMEF, 1995). Large corporate groups are responsible for an important share of the manufacture of steel- and aluminium-intensive autoparts and produce parts for engines and suspension systems. Additionally, a substantial proportion of engine parts and brake systems are domestically produced. Throughout the latest example, it is possible to see that Mexico has succeeded in accumulating over the time a set of technical abilities regarding the treatment of steel and aluminium to be employed in the automobile sector.

According to the latest example of technical convergence among different sectors, Mexico has shown that in the automobile cluster there is the ability to learn. And this becomes a key issue as we introduce the analysis of the innovative responses from the sectors to changes in the economic environment. In a sense, the innovation cannot be achieved if there is no learning capabilities available at the sector.

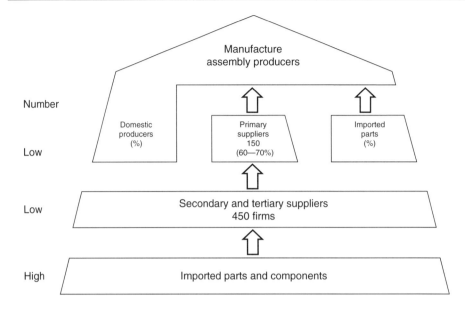

Figure 15.1 User–Producer Linkages in the Mexican Automobile Cluster.
Source. SECOFI, *Diagnóstico y desarrollo del plan estratégico y de acción para la promoción de agrupamiento industriales,* 1999.

However, the existence of the learning ability in itself does not ensure that innovation processes can be successful.

The automobile innovation system

The changes in the organizational structure of the Mexican automobile sector over the time show an accumulative trend in innovative capabilities. This can be illustrated with the evolution from a first phase in which the production of vehicles was concentrated in the car corporations, with no interaction with domestic producers, to a fourth phase during the 1980s, in which there are highly differentiated and deeply specialized relationships between the vehicles assemblers and skilled producers of auto parts and other intermediate inputs.

The current structure of the Mexican automobile sector can be described as a semi-linked umbrella (Figure 15.1). At the top of the structure appears the pool of manufacturers and assemblers of motor vehicles and below them a completely dissimilar set of auto parts and components producers. In this same level of the structure it is feasible to find three different kinds of auto parts and components suppliers. The first is formed by the pool of subsidiaries of the automobile assemblers. The second constitutes Mexican and foreign conglomerates of specialized auto parts and components suppliers. This segment of firms are large enterprises and world-class companies. The third variety is shaped by foreign-made components producers. All these three different types of components suppliers correspond to the category of first-level auto parts and components agents or primary agents.

In the Mexican automobile sector, the most important networks identified are those linking the terminal car industry or the set of manufacturers and assemblers of motor vehicles with the pool of primary agents. This is because of the intensity in the exchange of information between users and producers. In a sense those enterprises constitute the linked and integrated cluster of the Mexican automobile sector.

According to the description of the Mexican automobile sector as a semi-linked umbrella, there is a secondary level of auto parts and components suppliers. This is formed basically by Mexican medium and small companies. Those firms act like suppliers of the primary agents and maintain limited linkages with the rest of the cluster. Finally, at the bottom of the structure is the imported parts segment. This provides inputs to the secondary and tertiary producers. In a precise sense, this fragment of the automobile sector is completely detached from the Mexican cluster structure.

The Mexican automobile sector presents two different levels of interaction. The first, or hard nucleus, is built through bidirectional and regular exchanges of information and knowledge between the manufacturers and assemblers of automobiles and the pool of primary suppliers. Naturally, this is not the more extended form of cooperation and the share of enterprises in this set is small. The second kind of interaction, or soft outline, is constructed around the limited exchanges among the pool of secondary suppliers and the hard nucleus. The number of enterprises in this segment is the largest. According to the statement above, the Mexican automobile sector presents a dual path over the time. In the hard nucleus there is intense cohesion. Nevertheless, in the soft outline there is growing gap from the technical frontier.[4]

Research and development in the automobile sector

Empirical studies developed for the Mexican case (Brown, 1998) have revealed that there are some attributes intrinsic to the primary and secondary producers at the automobile sector. To be selected as an auto parts and components supplier, the firm must be a world-class company. This means that the producers must possess a sufficient plant capacity to satisfy the demand from the assemblers' plants. Normally the world-class companies in the automobile sector maintain growing levels of productivity, offer international prices, have an increasing automatization in the production process, produce with zero defects and are characterized by a labour organization in groups (Potshuma, 1997).

In contrast, the secondary suppliers in the Mexican automobile sector are characterized by high price levels, inadequate quality products and low liability (Brown, 1998). Consequently, the primary auto parts and components suppliers use an increasing amount of imports for inputs. The requirements to be fulfilled by the secondary producers in providing car components to the primary companies are price, quality and time or volume for delivery.[5]

The Mexican enterprises have increased their technical capabilities because some of them have participated in linked projects with final assembler corporations. Others have designed specific components for the vehicles produced for the internal market. In contraposition to this, the auto parts and components subsidiaries have little participation in R&D activities. This is because the parent corporations of car components producers participate directly in the vehicle manufacturers' plants in the design for cars and vehicles, and then send to their subsidiaries based in Mexico the design, machinery and technical support if needed. Even when some change in design is required this is performed at the parent corporation and not in the subsidiary.

Despite the fact that R&D activities are acknowledged as crucial in the development of the industry's competitive capacity, in 1991 only 45 per cent of firms in the automobile sector were engaged in any kind of R&D activities. In the auto parts industry, 33 per cent of all firms performed some R&D activities. A significant percentage of the firms developed R&D activities within the central plant, while 7 per cent relied on R&D performed in other establishments of the firm. It should be noted that only 1.5 per cent of firms hired R&D services from universities and 0.7 per cent from public and private technology centres. Nevertheless, this highly skewed distribution pattern is congruent with what is visible in more advanced economies and it seems that given the highly specific nature of the technology in the sector, the primary source of new knowledge and experiences for improving technological and organizational processes is the company itself.

The R&D activities performed in the automobile sector are also differentiated by the type of product and productive process of each sub-sector. A total of 70 per cent of the plants in the sector produce mature products. This might partially explain why firms within the sector allocated in 1991 only 0.4 per cent of their sales to R&D (STPS, 1992, p. 99) and, in particular, why they seem to concentrate their efforts on improving production processes rather than designing new products. In the whole manufacturing sector, R&D activities are concentrated in 8 per cent of the firms. This modern elite group backed the growth of business R&D expenditure from 1991 to 1995.[6]

It should be noted that R&D activities within the automobile sector are increasingly assuming an important role; as competencies evolve over time, different specificities are developed. R&D activities are becoming more integrated in operational, organizational and administrative activities, such as the improvement and design of new processes, improvement and adaptation of equipment and organization of work groups to test out new developments and production techniques. Moreover, the role of R&D in firms is outstanding with regard to communication, exchange of information and experience among different departments of a firm, like production, engineering, quality control, maintenance and marketing (Zapata, 1994; Valdespino and Vázquez-Mellado, 1995; Domínguez and Brown, 1996).

The acquisition of technology and equipment

In this sector, the flows of technological knowledge from abroad are extremely important. Certainly knowledge, and its corresponding externalities, are the main important assets in a dynamic economy. But the sources of the knowledge can vary. It is possible to find it in a codified form or even incorporated into machinery and equipment. The most important sources of knowledge in the Mexican automobile sector are shown in Table 15.2. As can be observed, 65 per cent of knowledge flows are explained by codified knowledge and knowledge incorporated in machinery and equipment.

The first options chosen by firms in the automobile sector are external sources of information: specialized literature and attendance at fairs and exhibitions. Nineteen

Table 15.2 Sources of Knowledge in the Automobile Sector

Source	Percentage
Literature, advice and specialist events	28
Purchase of new machinery or equipment	19
Design/manufacture of own equipment	18
Technological transfer from parent company	14
Purchase of technological packages	11
Purchase of used machinery	2
Other sources	5
Do not know	2
None	1

Source: Maestría en Economía y Cambio Tecnológico Database, Mexico, 1997.

per cent of the firms rely on the acquisition of new machinery or equipment, which is a strikingly similar proportion to those that design and manufacture their own (18 per cent).

Another important indicator of how this industry incorporates new technologies in production processes relates to the scrapping of machinery and equipment. At the end of 1990s, the average age of machinery and equipment in the final automobile sub-sector was greater than that in the auto parts sub-sector; the average of the former varies within a range of five and seven years, while for almost half the firms in the latter, it varies between three and five years.[7]

Two important reasons could be given to explain the difference between these two sub-sectors. On the one hand, it is more difficult to discard old equipment when it is still involved in the production processes of complex assembly plants, since doing so requires a substantial rearrangement of different production phases. Achieving perfect complementarity between different machinery involved in complex assembly is not trivial because of the organization required in large establishments. On the other hand, this difference in complexity implies a different way of acquiring information with respect to plants that produce auto parts.

As far as we know, the nature and structure of the automobile clusters in the United States, Europe and Japan are different from the Mexican. Nevertheless, the distribution of the age of the machinery is similar. From the beginning of the 1970s, when the competence of Asian car producers using the 'Toyota paradigm' impacted the world automobile production, a new form of cooperation between users and producers was raised in this sector (Humprey, 1995; OECD, 1996a). Here the producers of auto parts were responsible for a very active role in the development of new ideas and the design of auto integrated systems, not only through the emergence of a flexible production scheme, but also by supporting a growing velocity of change to enhance product differentiation. The Mexican cluster is now not far from the international trend of production.

Training, skills and characteristics of human capital

The kind of equipment utilized in the assembly and auto part firms is positively correlated with the professional profile and level of skill of the personnel hired to operate them. It follows that older firms, mostly in the assembly sector, having usually achieved a higher organizational efficiency, enjoy better channels for accumulating, processing and distributing information, thus enhancing the learning opportunities of their personnel over those at newly established firms. Moreover, the greater complexity in the assembly sector requires personnel with higher skills. This is true not only with regard to formal education, but also in terms of training in job activities.

In the two industrial classes the structure of the personnel hired is similar. The greater proportion of employees in the terminal car industry and the vehicles components class are qualified workers. The main difference between the two industrial classes is the percentage of professional staff. While the proportions of managerial, supervisory and non-qualified workers are similar, the dissimilarities in the age of the machinery and equipment implies the need to employ more skilled workers in the engineering field in those classes which own new equipment in order to uncodify the knowledge embodied in the machinery.

In a sense, it can be said that blue collar personnel in assembly plants are an important element in achieving organizational efficiency, whereas this capability in the auto part industry seems to be lesser and more within the scope of management and professionals. Furthermore, the average age of personnel in the finished vehicles industry is greater than the corresponding average in the auto part industry. The assembly sub-sector, in accordance, places greater emphasis on training programmes.

The organization of the plant and the need for more training programmes are the most important preconditions for globalization of the Mexican plants (Carrillo, 1993; Micheli, 1995; Vargas, 1995; Cressan, 1997; García and Lara, 1997; Pereira, 1997; Juárez, 1997). Nevertheless, this is not an exclusive difference in the Mexican industrial structure. In a knowledge-based economy, the current nature of international exchanges requires a growing amount of knowledge for production to assure the possibility of developing complex tasks (OECD, 1997e).

Technological learning strategies, intra- and inter-company

The international assembly corporations operate according to a globalized strategy. As such, the most sophisticated components are produced in the more developed countries. Their subsidiaries in Mexico fall into either of the following two groups: *assembly of critical components*[8] which are produced elsewhere, and *processing of critical materials*[9] related to the performance of the automobiles. Within this strategy, firms endeavour to guarantee exclusive supply, through firms regularly located close to the assembly plant (Ramírez, 1994; Buendía, 1998). In particular, as much as 20 per cent of all auto part plants in Mexico have an exclusivity arrangement with a single assembly plant (UAM-X, 1997).

The results of a 1997 survey on user–producer relationships and their impact on the generation of technological capacity in Mexico show that scale-intensive firms in both the autopart and assembly sectors relate almost exclusively with firms that belong to the same technological sector (UAM-X, 1997). Not surprisingly, their linkages with firms in other sectors, such as the science-based, are considerably scarcer and weaker, which is a major difference from what is observed in more industrialized economies, where most firms within the automobile sector are very up-to-date on new discoveries in products (think of electronics, new materials and so on), thus constantly benefiting from new technological knowledge.[10]

According to the above-mentioned survey, it can be said that most user–producer relationships in Mexico are about improving quality, design and timing in production. On a second level, users and producers work jointly to improve and adapt equipment and test new equipment, while the simple exchange of technological information and related experiences between users and producers seems to be less frequent.

Despite the above, it should be noted that one of the most significant efforts of Mexican firms – which is undoubtedly a result of international competition – is their attempt to structure dense organizational and technological information networks especially aimed at adopting more rigorous forms of statistical quality control (Bueno, 1996). Both the automobile and auto part sectors are going through a transitional stage, which requires time and which results, above all, in an unequal learning capacity in the firms and, consequently, in a non-uniform rate of creation of new forms of cooperation among firms (Lara and Corona, 1997a). While approximately 26 per cent of the firms in the automobile industry have introduced just-in-time (JIT) systems, only slightly more than 1 per cent of those that manufacture, repair and transport equipment have followed suit, which should prove useful in illustrating the above statement. Nevertheless, it can be claimed that small portions of the Mexican enterprises in this sector are absorbing new forms of inter-firm cooperation.

Regional competence and technological convergence

It is not surprising that most of the firms within the automobile sector are concentrated in two industrial districts: central and northern Mexico. The central district is relatively larger, since out of a total of sixteen final assembly plants, eleven are located in central Mexico, within a 650-kilometre radius and with a population in excess of fifty million people. These plants specialize in manufacturing engines, critical body and suspension parts. The industrial district in northern Mexico consists of five firms that came into existence towards the end of the 1970s. Firms in this second conglomerate cater essentially to export markets, manufacturing engines, engine parts and electric/electronic sub-systems. With regard to auto part plants, they seem to be concentrated in northern Mexico, for 40 of the total of 55 plants are located in this region. Most of these plants seem to be highly specialized in technology, since 31 of them work exclusively in electric/electronic activities. Of these 22 deal mainly with the assembly of the wiring harnesses of automobiles. Chihuahua concentrates most of the latter plants: of the 20 plants within this state, 16 are closely linked with these electric/electronic assembly activities.

The effects of the geographical concentration of the firms within this sector is illustrated in the following case. As a result of the concentration and moreover, the specialization in Ciudad Juárez (northern Mexico) of General Motors' electric/electronic activity, in 1995 the Delphi-Juárez auto parts engineering centre was opened. This centre is a subsidiary of the US-based Delphi-E group, which, for the first time in its history, decided to open a research and development centre outside the United States. With an investment of US$150 million and employing 860 workers, the centre designs, tests and produces solenoids and sensors.[11] This centre was opened for a variety of reasons, but mainly to reduce the distance from the then closest centre, Anderson, located 2900 kilometres from the GM plants in Mexico, thus reducing transportation costs, improving communication and adaptation, and covering a wider range of quantity, design and new materials. The volume and quality of information, knowledge and know-how that flows among the personnel of these plants has also improved, up to the point where this centre is functioning as a platform for distributing components not only throughout Mexico but within the United States as well. The Juárez centre is profiting from the external economies built up in Mexico during more than 15 years of industrialization, and, in particular, from the availability of low-cost skilled personnel, specifically the very competent Mexican engineers, who are sometimes complemented with engineering graduates from the University of Texas, El Paso, the University of New Mexico and the University of Texas, Austin (Carrillo and Hualde, 1996). Hence it follows that, from this perspective, the technological cluster located on the northern border is closely linked to the existing technological cluster in the United States.

The institutional framework

After several decades of steady economic growth, the Mexican economy entered a period of relative instability during the 1970s. That era was characterized by imbalances in the current account balance and a growing fiscal deficit. Until the beginning of the 1980s, the demand in the automobile industry had been fuelled by the domestic market, solidly supported by strong protectionist trade policies, which were essential to the development of this industry. Such development cannot be understood without the industrial policy decrees for the automobile sector of 1962, 1972, 1977, 1983 and 1989. The first four aimed at replacing imported auto parts with Mexican parts, while the last was specifically designed to stimulate technological specialization and international trade. There are three outstanding features of the regulatory framework within which the automobile industry was embedded during the import substitution phase: strict requirements for minimum local content, limited production of autoparts by assembly firms and heavily restricted imports of finished vehicles.

During the years that followed, the import substitution model gave way to a more open one, owing to, first, Mexico's insertion into international trade through the GATT and second, the signing of the NAFTA. Consequently, nowadays the industry's geographical and commercial orientation is towards the export of finished vehicles to the United States and Canada. It should be noted that one of Mexico's goals through the NAFTA is to modify the trade specialization of the automobile industry. Hence Mexico is interested in the proposition regarding the rules of origin on the composing parts of a motor vehicle, which aims to stimulate foreign assembly firms to establish auto part plants in the region. Rules of origin will also be enforced in *maquiladora* auto part plants, thus improving their supply chains within the region.[12] None the less, these requirements must be gradually waived in order to foster modernization among domestic firms and the restructuring of foreign ones (e.g. Japanese and German) located in Mexico.

Diminishing trade barriers and new horizontal industrial policies within the NAFTA have stimulated automobile and auto part firms within the region to specialize on the manufacture of specific components and vehicles, profiting from economies of scale and dynamic learning curves.[13] This specialization process has placed increasing pressure on, on the one hand, free trade, and, on the other, modification of foreign direct investment laws in Mexico, rapidly forcing the disappearance of several domestic auto part firms which have been replaced by foreign suppliers of the assembly sector.

At the beginning of the 1990s, a more precise relationship arose between the automobile industry – particularly the auto parts sector – and metrology centres, in an attempt to achieve improved quality of products and processes. Likewise, based on the certification demands that are placed on auto part firms, there was a significant rapprochement between them and quality certification organizations. Statistical control techniques, together with private sector and government quantification instruments, helped firms to assess their own routines and to refine their cognitive processes, to reflect on their problems and to improve their interactive learning. These quantification and observation techniques and instruments used by firms are among the most powerful tools in the exchange of technological information within the sector. Increasingly, the development path of firms, as well as the kind of relationships between them, depends not only on the strength of the firms' own quantification centres but on the available services of metrology and standardization laboratories as well.

The institutional segment of the Mexican automobile cluster is made up, in the first instance, by test and certification laboratories. The former are linked to electric/electronic fields, metallurgy and manufacture of auto parts; the latter revolve around the National Metrology Centre or CENAM (*Centro Nacional de Metrología*), which is in turn subdivided into several departments: electrical, metrology, physical, material, mechanical and technical support. On a second level, there is another important group of certification laboratories for the electrical and automobile industries which operate more like a network of test and certification laboratories and whose existence is the result of the cooperative efforts of public and private institutions, government, research institutions, industrial, trade and service associations, etc. These laboratories are united in the National Organization for Standardization and the National Commission for Normalization (Figure 15.2). The proper functioning of this network requires mutual recognition, cooperation and, above all, elaboration of strategies aimed at fortifying the competitiveness of the sector, because increasing the quality of the processes and the products within any industry supposes an equivalent increase in the instruments and methods of observation, quantification and certification, and this is, in essence, a social convention that demands communication between firms and institutions.

Globalization of the automobile sector

At the beginning of the 1980s, the automobile firms located in Mexico began to support a strategy addressed towards the increasing of their exports, particularly engines. Nowadays the Mexican automobile industry has a large proportion of the

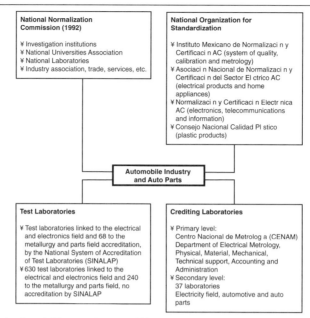

Figure 15.2 Institutional Cluster: Automobile Industry and Auto Parts.

world production market. For example, in 1995, 83.5 per cent of the automobiles produced in Mexico were exported; this process has to be explained considering not only the current trade framework but the macroeconomic setting as well, where the diminution of domestic demand plays an important role.

It is known that producing for export requires high quality in auto parts, something that has been achieved through the replacement of local producers by either imports of auto parts or the localization within the country of foreign producers. Between 1992 and 1995, 155 high technology firms were established, the vast majority of them foreign firms nested within a globalized network that maintain close linkages with the parent firm in terms of production strategy and R&D. However, a small group of local producers can be identified that hold certain competitive advantages.

It could be said that the automobile sector is pushing towards globalization of Mexican manufacturing industry, but while there are increasing interchanges in terms of commodities, intermediate and capital goods, there is not a corresponding process in local R&D and technological activities. From 1,290 patents registered in the Mexican sector between 1980 and 1992, only 123 were registered as 'without priority', for the first time in Mexico. Of these, 48 belong to Mexican firms and 75 to foreign ones. This clearly highlights the fact that the purpose of R&D activities within the sector is not the creation of new products and components, but an improvement of the production processes, a fact that provides evidence in support of the idea that the strategy of Mexican firms is to appropriate innovation by means of industrial secrets and not through patents.

The nationalities of the 21 companies with the largest number of patents registered in the automotive field in the USA between 1986 and 1990 were 12 Japanese companies, five Western European and four US. (Patel and Pavitt, 1995a). These 20 companies held 50.06 per cent of all patents in this technological field. The strength of these large companies is expressed in the technological advantage shown: 2.21 for Japan, 1.02 for Western Europe and 0.55 for the USA in this field. Patenting activity takes place primarily within each country: only 4.4 per cent of patents in the automotive technology field are produced outside the country of origin, 3.2 per cent for Europe, 0.9 per cent for the USA and 0.1 per cent for Japan (Patel and Pavitt, 1995a, 1995b). The process of technological decentralization is taking place within Japan, the USA and Europe.

The process of technological and organizational renewal means that each company works out strategies for *transition* from the old technologies to the new technologies *on a global scale*. Companies in the sector are working out strategies that allow them to compete by developing and appropriating from their technological nucleus, creating new processes and products in the R&D centres located in the most developed countries. They also efficiently utilize their networks of knowledge and technological experience throughout their value chains distributed *on a global scale*. When it is to their advantage, the large companies in the automobile sector create new R&D centres in less industrialized countries, where mature components are produced or where manufacturing activities were formerly reduced to simple labour-intensive assembly.

This perspective helps us to understand the increasing innovation and development activity observed in Mexico: for example, the creation of an R&D centre by Delphi-General Motors, described above; or the growing R&D efforts by Mexican companies, in particular those related to the steel/aluminium–automotive parts manufacturing–final assembly value chain. The technological changes occurring within the sector that are characteristic of the globalization process in the automobile sector are not just the substitution of obsolete materials and components by new.[14] Improving competitiveness requires that companies efficiently manage the specific technological transitions occurring in each of the manufacturing plants distributed throughout both industrialized and developing countries.

The substantive question about the globalization process that a company asks is: what components or sub-systems are needed to produce on a national or global scale? The answer must be sought not only in technology or in the difference between internal and external transaction costs or in the differences in international productivity levels. Japanese and US automobile companies produce 30 per cent and 60 per cent respectively of their parts in their own facilities (in-house parts production) (Lara and Corona, 1998). These various supply strategies express, in addition to the factors noted with respect to costs and technology, the strength of national institutions to create solid technological and economic bases that encourage cooperation.

Technological cooperation and integration among the companies depend on a series of factors: the structuring of intellectual property; the nature of incentives; the trust needed to exchange technological information; and how companies manage and control their technological training processes (Buckley and Casson, 1997). The nature of the knowledge exchanges and the institutional environment in which they occur in the developed economies show that the Mexican automobile semi-linked cluster is closer to the case of an assembler structure than an innovative producer one.

Conclusions

The Mexican automobile sector presents a double structure and differentiated flows of knowledge exchange. On one side, there is a primary set of producers formed by the manufacturers of vehicles and a pool of auto parts and components suppliers. In both cases, these enterprises are world-class companies and the linkages between them are close. Some of the suppliers for the vehicle manufacturers participate directly in the design and development of new products in the parent plants and laboratories of the manufacturers.

The linkages between the enterprises forming the primary level of producers in the Mexican automobile sector shape the nature and intensity of the innovative efforts. Due to the fact that most of the companies classified as primary producers are subsidiaries of parent companies based in developed economies, the technical capabilities presented by those in the country are exogenous and take the form of technical transfer through the dispersal of machinery and equipment, technical support and managerial techniques. A small number of the Mexican enterprises classified as primary producers develop some R&D activities and become the central repositories of Mexican knowledge in the automobile sector. The other side of the Mexican automobile sector is formed by the set of secondary and tertiary producers. Typically these enterprises confront obstacles to establishing linkages with the set of primary producers. The empirical studies developed for the Mexican case have demonstrated, in a wide sense, that the difficulties faced by this pool of producers are not necessarily technical, but organizational and cultural.

In the Mexican automobile sector there are two technical trajectories that are not necessarily convergent. On one side there is a cohesive network with strong linkages and exchange of information. This set of producers has facilitated the successful integration of the Mexican automobile sector in the international markets. The technical performance of this producer segment is at the world frontier but the diffusion of knowledge is limited. On the other side, there is an ample set of producers of auto parts and components which shows a gap from the performance of the primary producers. In this sense the Mexican automobile cluster is semi-linked. This can be considered the most important difference between Mexico and the automobile clusters in Europe, the United States and Japan.

The Mexican automobile sector has been successful at the international level. In a strict sense, more than a globalization of the Mexican industry, we see a regional or hemispherical expansion strategy. The incursion of the Mexican automobile sector in the international markets is strongly defined by the nature of the restructuration at the world level of this industry. In this sense, the performance of the geographical cluster in Mexico shows the reorganization of the Mexican industry from a model of production for domestic consumption to another directed towards integration of the markets of the economies in the NAFTA.

Technological convergence in this sector occurs with the convergence of suppliers of raw materials (steel, aluminium, etc.) and foundry and plot centres with firms producing terminal goods. This convergence may lead to the idea that adjustment and selection mechanisms within the sector express not only internal pricing mechanisms, but also the learning process that happens inside firms. The evolution of the automobile sector seems to imply the existence of a co-evolutionary path shared by

Table 15.3 Technological Regime: a Cluster of the Automobile Sector

Characteristics	International (leaders)	In Mexico
Opportunity for innovation	Dynamic evolutionary path stimulated by the convergence in this sector of different technological fields. Technological convergence of the scale-intensive sector with the science-based sector (electronics, national production engineering). Interfirm relationships with science-based and scale-intensive firms.	Evolutionary path inhibited by the weak existence of science-based sectors. Convergence of electric/electronics sector harnesses opportunity window for the Mexican automotive and electronic sector. Interfirm relationships with scale-intensive firms. Endogamic relationships (steel, iron, glass, aluminium and electric sectors).
Appropriability	Patents and dynamic economic learning. Technological gaps. Process and know-how secret.	Weak patent level. Dynamic economic learning. Technological and wage gaps.
Cumulativeness	Great internal, private and public R&D laboratories. Experimental and highly qualified personnel in point technology fields (electronics, new materials).	Few, small, internal R&D laboratories. Virtual non-existence of experimental and highly qualified personnel in point technology fields. Experimental and highly qualified personnel in mature technology fields.
Knowledge base	Production engineering national suppliers. Strong R&D activity. Internal R&D bound to private and public R&D. R&D whose purpose is the creation of new processes and products.	Foreign suppliers of production engineering. Weak R&D activity.

markets and institutions. Along this path, the new institutional scenario within the NAFTA and the globalization of this portion of the domestic industry are crucial. In fact, from the beginning of the 1990s, with the combination of the NAFTA and the sluggish behaviour of the domestic market, the automobile and auto part firms were forced to approach the international market for the commercialization of their products and components. Globalization, however, means quality, and quality cannot be achieved without cooperation between the big, medium and small enterprises that constitute the automobile and auto part industries. To gain international competitiveness, cooperation strategies between firms within the automobile sector, aimed at establishing logistic and quality programmes and fostering the flow of information, knowledge and experience, must be developed. The case of the Mexican automobile sector shows the importance of the interaction between firms and a specific pool in institutions (certification, metrology, test centres) whose common purpose is to work (directly or indirectly) towards the improvement of quality in product and process.

On the basis of the above analysis and the synthesis method, Table 15.3 compares the main specificities in Mexico with those in industrialized economies. From Table 15.3 the following observations can be made regarding technological sources, appropriability, opportunities and cumulativeness (see Chapter 10). Technological sources of Mexican automobile industry are mainly concerned with imported capital goods, intermediate commodities and foreign consultants. R&D activities are rather weak, mostly dealing with improving processes and products. Technological activity is appropriated through industrial secrecy and not via patents. Furthermore, this process, which guarantees the competitiveness of the automobile industry, is also supported by salary gaps. While cumulativeness in Mexico is often achieved through human capital skills, the country is still lagging behind more advanced countries, in particular in the utilization of new technologies.

In more industrialized economies there is a high degree of technological convergence between the automobile industry and certain science-based sectors, such as electronics and new materials; in Mexico a similar degree of technological convergence is found with more traditional industries like steel and aluminium. Technological changes in the automobile sector located in the industrialized countries are not reduced to changes in the electrical-mechanical technological field: this sector includes new technological fields (microelectronics, software, new materials, etc.).[15] This diversification in sources of technological change leads companies to establish cooperative alliances with public and private institutions, for the purpose of creating and/or strengthening the multitechnological nucleus of companies in the sector; achieving this is viable only within specific *national technological clusters*.

The evolving performance of the sector from the beginning of the industry in Mexico to the end of the 1990s shows the importance of institutional change to promote integration in the industry. Currently, a misappropriate integration between primary and secondary producers in the automobile sector has provoked the growing weight of imports to maintain the competitive position of the sector at international levels. But imports do not facilitate the advance of local knowledge to improve innovative activities.

Notes

1. The largest automobile corporations in Mexico are General Motors (USA), Ford Motor Company (USA), Chrysler (USA), Volkswagen (Germany) and Nissan (Japan). These are not only the largest, but also the oldest firms in the Mexican market. The three American firms were established in the period 1925–38, Volkswagen in 1954 and Nissan in 1962.
2. The globalization path in the automobile sector has induced the emergence of specialization strategies, developed by individual car manufacturers and national automobile clusters to enhance market competitiveness. Those strategies rely upon the idea that marginal production costs are U-shaped and the minimization of the cost function can be reached through specialization. But the nature and structure of the production costs are not enough to understand the dynamic behaviour of the Mexican automobile industry. In a broad sense, the minimization of the cost function is not the cause but the result of the specialization process.
3. Modernization in terms of replacement of the old technology, the construction of mini-steel mills, production through the process of continuous tapping, the establishment of tension-levelling, high technology machines for cutting, machines for longitudinal cuts, as well as press cutters, etc., which at the same time permitted a reduction in costs, an increase in flexibility and expansion of the lines of products destined for the automobile sector, such as sheet steel (up to 1 mm thickness) for the automobile industry, springs, hot and cold rolled sheet steel, galvanized steel, fine plate steel that is cold laminated to the 05 quality level, required for the exterior coating of the auto body, fine plate steel that is submitted to electrolytical galvaniza-

tion, fine plate steel covered with a zinc–iron anti-rust protective coating and products with a greater added value.

4. These considerations shape the differences between the MAMV and APC classes in the innovative efforts of the Mexican automobile sector, as does the nature of the dynamic externalities observed in the knowledge exchanges of the automobile innovation system.

5. The latest characteristics pointed out fix the boundaries for innovative activities. Those activities elected to improve the economic efficiency, such as R&D or the acquisition of knowledge by different means, present some degree of heterogeneity due to the nature of the two different subsets of enterprises. In a broad sense, it is possible to affirm that the innovative capabilities of the Mexican primary suppliers of auto parts are growing. But the innovation gap between primary and secondary suppliers will possibly grow in the short run, if there are no positive incentives from industrial policy to activate cooperation between these two different segments of the cluster.

6. In 1994, the average percentage of revenue allotted to technological R&D by companies in the automobile sector was 2.1 per cent. It is one of the five sub-sectors with the most intense R&D activity. The average percentage of revenue allotted to R&D in the manufacturing sector is 1.0 per cent (STPS, 1995, pp. 140–1).

7. Innovation is a process by which the groups solve problems. In a broad sense innovation represents the ability to enhance the performance of any organization through the different kinds of knowledge available (know-what, know-who, know-how) to do things. As we perceive, the knowledge embodied in new equipment and machinery is a pool of new abilities accessible to strengthen the efficiency of firms in productive operations. In an extensive sense, new equipment possesses new and better knowledge to do things. In the Mexican automobile sector before 1995 the auto parts industrial class owned the newest machinery and equipment applied to production on average, while the final automobile class held the old.

8. Manual transmission, propeller shaft, wire harness, drive axle, clutch, brake hose, brake master cylinder, alternator, steering unit.

9. Cast parts (piston, disc brake, piston ring, drum brake), forged parts (gear blank, front axle, knuckle joint), stamped parts (exhaust system, oil pan, body parts, plastic parts).

10. Ninety-one per cent of companies associated with the intensive-scale automotive parts sector are also intensive-scale companies (UAM-X, 1997).

11. Delphi-Juárez's principal client is GM (67 per cent of sales), and to take advantage of the economies to scale that are essential for this activity it also supplies Toyota, Honda, Ford, Isuzu, Mercedes and BMW.

12. Through the year 2001, the *maquiladora* regime will be maintained for those companies that meet the rules of origin.

13. From the point of view of dissemination of knowledge and technological experience, one of NAFTA's objectives is to improve the defence of copyright law and through this means the conditions for appropriateness of innovative activities in the sector we are studying.

14. Some of the routes taken in the process of technological renewal in the automobile sector are the following: (a) process and mature components improvement (e.g. replacement of steel by aluminium or new materials); (b) development of hybrid components incorporating the old and the new (e.g. automatic transmissions incorporating electronic sensors); (c) replacement of old technologies (e.g. transistors) by new technology (e.g. integrated circuits); (d) changes in components that in turn require modifications in automobile design (e.g. the diffusion of integrated circuits requires adaptation in the generator and energy distribution system, as well as an increase in functions performed by harnesses, etc.).

15. General Motors, to mention only one case, registers patents in various technological fields: non-electrical machinery, electrical machinery, electronic capital goods and components, telecommunications and defence-related technologies, to mention some of the most important technological fields.

CHAPTER SIXTEEN

Regional and Local Systems of Innovation in Aguascalientes

G. Abdel Musik

Introduction

Innovation activities can be studied at a variety of conceptual levels. Until the early 1980s, innovation studies had concentrated almost exclusively on analysing the firm level. The Schumpeterian and evolutionary economic traditions, for example, assume that innovation activities within firms are the motor of economic change. A new approach, which considers the national level as critical, emerged in the late 1980s. This approach considers a wide range of factors and institutions which enable a particular country to generate and diffuse technology, acknowledging the systemic nature of innovation. Its efforts have crystallized in the national innovation system (NIS) approach, as presented by Lundvall (1993), Nelson (1993) and Edquist (1997).

Between the firm (micro) level, which uses technology, and the national (highly aggregated) level exists an intermediate regional level. It is at this level that firms carry out most of their day-to-day interactions. Even though the importance of the region in innovative activities has long been recognized by historians and geographers as critical (Storper, 1997), it is only in the past few years that regions have been analysed from a systems of innovation perspective (Cooke *et al.*, 1998; de la Mothe and Paquet, 1998).

The objective of the present chapter is to analyse how institutions and firms can interact at the regional level to enhance the competitiveness of the region. In order to illustrate these interactions, the chapter focuses on the case of Aguascalientes, a Mexican state which has been able to upgrade its industrial and technological capabilities in the past twenty years. This particular region presents an interesting case study because, despite having no natural resource base and being one of the smallest states in the country (0.9 per cent of the population and 0.3 per cent of the national territory),[1] its economy has consistently outperformed the national average. In the past twenty years, the state[2] received 4.5 per cent of total FDI in Mexico; its rates of growth in both manufacturing and exports far exceeded the national average; its exports accounted for 2.2 per cent of total national manufacturing exports, despite its location nine hours away from the border (CEDECE, 1998).

The region cannot be considered a 'high technology' cluster, in the traditional sense of regions with high concentrations of electronics or biotechnology firms. In terms of traditional R&D indicators, Aguascalientes is below the national average.[3]

However, within the broader Schumpeterian definition of innovation, which includes managerial and organizational improvements, the region has developed a very competent manufacturing base where even small firms have adopted world-class management practices. This is reflected by the following achievements: the first small firm in Mexico with ISO 9000 certification, an exporting base of over 200 firms and domestic firms with extensive process design capabilities.[4]

The rest of this chapter recounts the evolution of the Aguascalientes cluster, describing the elements which have contributed to upgrading the region's capabilities. The following section presents the framework used to analyse the cluster. The evolution of the region's competencies during the ISI period, the transition period and the new regulatory framework are described. This structure is consistent with the rest of the book, allowing comparisons between the evolution of specific elements within the national system, and the evolution of this particular region. Each section concentrates on certain events which provided critical contributions to the state's capacities for technological innovation and/or diffusion. The final section provides some conclusions and policy recommendations on the observed interactions which fostered regional technological improvement. This research is based on over 70 interviews, including 42 firm surveys in three independent but related sectors: automotive, metal mechanics and electric and electronics.

Framework: regional clusters in the national system

The role of regions as centres of innovative activity has been studied extensively during the past decade. Studies concerning regional innovation have centred on the concepts of regional networks (De Bresson and Amesse, 1991; Freeman, 1991) and regional clusters (Porter, 1990; Enright 1997), and tend to emphasize examples such as Silicon Valley (Saxenian, 1991), Northern Italy (Pyke *et al.*, 1990) or Baden-Württemberg (Cooke and Morgan, 1994), which empirically show that industrial development is more of a regional phenomenon than a national phenomenon, and that competitive industries tend to concentrate in very localized regions.

As described by Cimoli in Chapter 10, the concept of cluster is very useful for studying regional and sectoral innovation systems. A particular regional cluster will contain a variety of institutions and organizations, including firms, government organizations, higher education institutions and research centres. A well developed regional innovation system (RIS) might in some ways be richer than the NIS. In addition to the organization and institutions developed by the national government, which can operate in any particular national location, regions will generate institutions that will be expressly designed to satisfy its specific requirements.

The presence of a variety of firms, higher education organizations and supporting government institutions appears to be a necessary condition for having an innovative region. However, it is not a sufficient condition; even this high agglomeration of organizations and institutions does not guarantee the presence of innovation within a region or rapid economic growth dynamic. Many countries and regions have tried to reproduce the experience of successful clusters, trying to create their own Silicon Valleys. Even though some of these regions have developed a certain critical mass of industry, they have not been particularly innovative.

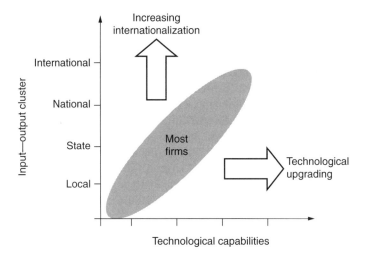

Figure 16.1 Technological Capabilities and Degree of Internationalization.

For a region to operate as a well articulated cluster, rather than just a set of firms, agents need to interact with each other constantly, not only through formal commercial transactions, but also through informal meetings which provide a wide variety of information including technical, marketing, labour market and private–public interactions (Saxenian, 1999; Voyer, 1999). These strong interactions will result in certain patterns of similarity and non-similarity of behaviour, in terms of types of technologies exploited.

However, the interactions will not be limited to inside the regional cluster. Nelson and Rosenberg (1993) argue that using a national approach will have limitations, as the overlap between institutions supporting different sectors might be small, while other organizations will act globally. This statement is equally true for regions. For example, a large multinational plant (Xerox, Nissan) will have access to practically any product and process technology available in the world. By contrast, a small local workshop will usually have most interactions within a small geographic region, reflected in a limited variety of available technology. Agents (whether firms, government institutions or research centres) located within the regional cluster have different degrees and reach of interaction with agents outside the cluster, consequently having different possibilities of adapting new technologies.

Figure 16.1 illustrates this relationship between geographic reach and technological capabilities. The vertical axis shows the agent's degree of internationalization; by such degree we refer to the intensity to which the agent interacts outside the region. In the case of a firm, this refers to the destination of its output, and the sources of its inputs and its knowledge. The horizontal axis shows the degree of technological sophistication. The shaded area shows that we would expect a greater concentration of agents; that is, agents with higher technological capabilities will tend to be more internationalized, while less sophisticated firms will tend to buy, sell and interact locally. Agents, and firms in particular, will be able to move along this space; in general, firms that want to export need to upgrade their technological capabilities to become competitive at an international level. We can expect that firms will tend to cluster with other firms which have similar technological capabilities.[5] This graph provides a framework to analyse the region.

The next three sections describe eight events that can be considered critical contributions to Aguascalientes's industrial competencies. These events include both new elements which in some way complemented the previously existing structure and new ways in which firms started operating as a cluster, and not merely a set of firms. In order to be consistent with the rest of the book, these eight events are arranged chronologically under the headings of import substitution, transition period and trade liberalization (see Chapter 10). The end of each section describes the significance of these events in terms of the framework presented by Figure 16.1.

ISI period: creation of basic infrastructure

Consensus of locals on the industrial project

For most of the history of Aguascalientes, and until the early 1970s, manufacturing activities were very limited.[6] In 1970, only 15 per cent of the state's GDP came from manufacturing activities, compared to the national average of 24 per cent. Most of the state's manufacturing was in the food and garment sectors,[7] and took place in small family workshops which used very traditional production techniques (Cruz, 1974). Accordingly, the state government's economic development programmes were targeted towards the agricultural sector, where they could benefit a larger percentage of the population.

In 1974, the Governor decided to pursue a radically different development strategy, to shift regional development efforts from agriculture to manufacturing and to make an effort to attract outside investment to the region. Given the government's limited experience in industrial promotion,[8] government officials first tried to determine industry requirements by asking the different agents involved, namely the owners of the larger manufacturing firms in the region[9] and the unions. The initial survey showed that the state lacked infrastructure and access to markets, the basic conditions for attracting investment.

The state government was able to create consensus among the local managers and labour leaders that the limited land availability of the state would limit an agricultural development strategy and that it was necessary to pursue an industrialization project strongly. With this in mind, managers started attending meetings regularly in local industry chambers. Similarly, the local delegate of the CTM (the federal confederation of unions in Mexico) approached managers, and offered support to attract outside investment.[10]

Developing the basic infrastructure

With this support from both management and labour, the government developed the following infrastructure and service projects:

- *Industrial park.* Perhaps the most important project during the 1970s was the creation of an industrial park. In 1973, Nacional Financiera (NAFIN, the federal industrial development bank) decided to support the development of medium-sized cities in 23 states as part of the national decentralization programme. This programme included the development of industrial parks which provided physical infrastructure, services, plus a wide array of support mechanisms such as fiscal incentives and project evaluation assistance. The state government created a trust for the Aguascalientes industrial park. The project was so successful in attracting industries that profits from the first industrial park have financed three more.
- *Commercial infrastructure development.* Aguascalientes garment manufacturers were famous for their detailed embroidery products. There were literally hundreds of garment workshops, most of them small, whose sales depended on San Juan de los Lagos, Jalisco, a nearby town visited seasonally by pilgrims from the neighbouring states. The government, together with the garment manufacturers, developed Plaza Vestir, a still-active shopping centre which provided a yearlong outlet. Another commercial bottleneck was the local market for grains and agricultural inputs, which supplied not only Aguascalientes, but also people from the neighbouring states of San Luis Potosí, Durango and Jalisco. The government built an agricultural market, and moved commercial activities outside of downtown Aguascalientes.
- *Industry financing institutions.* In 1978, NAFIN responded to a state government request to open a local representation, when none had been opened in eight years. This provided financing for industrial development projects at very favourable conditions. This financing for general manufacturing industry was complemented by sector-specific support, such as a credit union for the garment industry.[11]
- *Educational institutions.* Taking advantage of federal programmes aimed at decentralizing higher education, the state attracted or developed during the late 1970s a variety of higher and technical education institutions, including the Tecnológico de Aguascalientes, CONALEP and CEVETIS. These institutes supply qualified plant workers, production supervisors and engineers to the growing industries.

This effort to fortify the underlying support services soon resulted in new investment for the state and a broadening of the local manufacturing base. During the late 1970s three metal mechanics firms and two auto part firms built plants in Aguascalientes.[12] In the more traditional sectors, new firms were also established, such as Frigorizados La Huerta in the agro-industrial sector and Hilaturas San Marcos, manufacturing synthetic fibre. All these firms built large-scale plants with a high degree of technological sophistication, and they are still some of the most important firms in the state.

Attraction of large foreign firms and the need for specialized infrastructure (1981–4)

Even though there was a change of state government in 1980, the newly elected governor decided to continue with a strong push towards industrialization. However, the emphasis during his six-year term shifted from building infrastructure to

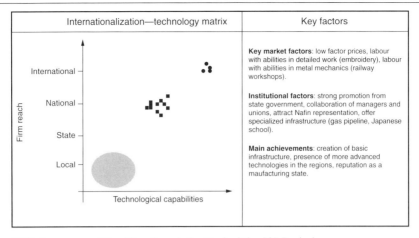

Internationalization—technology matrix	Key factors

Key market factors: low factor prices, labour with abilities in detailed work (embroidery), labour with abilities in metal mechanics (railway workshops).

Institutional factors: strong promotion from state government, collaboration of managers and unions, attract Nafin representation, offer specialized infrastructure (gas pipeline, Japanese school).

Main achievements: creation of basic infrastructure, presence of more advanced technologies in the regions, reputation as a maufacturing state.

Figure 16.2 Summary of the Situation at the End of the ISI Period.

bringing in foreign investment to complement existing industries. It is between 1980 and 1983 that three major multinational corporations, Nissan, Texas Instruments (TI) and Xerox, decided to establish plants in Aguascalientes. These three plants currently employ over 7,000 employees and are still perceived as the 'crown jewels' of the region's industry.

Multinational corporations usually consider a variety of locations before choosing a plant site and, in order to attract these firms, local governments need to play a very active role. This includes both promoting the state with potential firms and awarding special incentives as a way of improving the state's attractiveness. In the case of Aguascalientes, the key aspects promoted to attract MNEs to the state were stability of the labour force, high quality workers to perform very detailed work, resulting from the embroidery tradition, and high participation of women in the labour force, particularly important for the electronics industry. From these different advantages, the state emphasized particular ones, depending on each firms' specific needs.[13] In addition to promoting already existing advantages, the government actively assisted them in every possible way. This support included obtaining a waiver on the limitations of foreign ownership, specialized infrastructure and specialized services for foreign executive families.[14]

The three events described above – creating consensus, developing infrastructure and attracting large firms – gave Aguascalientes the necessary base to take off as an industrial state. These past ten years of the ISI period were extremely successful in at least three aspects: first, the creation of important parts of the necessary underlying infrastructure, preparing the bases for coming investment; second, the creation of important networking institutions, such as chambers, where managers gather to exchange points of view; third, a change in the image of the state, since Aguascalientes was no longer perceived by the rest of the country as an agricultural state, but started building its reputation as an industrial state. Once the critical mass was present, it was easier to attract service firms which would create better local conditions for more firms.

Figure 16.2 summarizes the state of Aguascalientes industry at the end of the ISI period. On the lower left, we can observe a tight cluster of small enterprises with low technical capabilities. These are local firms which have long-term ties, from having operated in the region for decades, plus increased involvement in the state's industrial development programme. By contrast, we can observe the recently arrived medium and large firms in the centre and upper right of the graph. These firms have higher technological capabilities and a higher degree of internationalization; however, given their recent arrival and lack of previous mutual knowledge, they operate quite isolated from each other. The list to the right of the graph shows the critical market and institutional factors which created the environment for innovation (Dosi, 1988a, 1988b), and the main accomplishments during this period.

Transition period: close contact between large firms

Development of collaboration: large firm and transplant associations

Mexico has a long tradition of industrial corporatism, and until 1994 every manufacturing firm had by law to belong to the national industrial chamber CANACINTRA. Even though these institutions played an important role as industry lobbying groups, they were not useful forums for information exchange. As an alternative to chamber meetings, firms in different regions created alternative associations in the 1980s.

The most influential one is the Grupo de Industriales de Aguascalientes AC, where top managers of the 16 largest firms meet every month to discuss issues of common concern. The group started holding informal meetings in the mid-1980s and, given its success, soon became a legal association. Its members include MNEs, domestic and local companies. As a way of developing mutual trust, the first meetings took place within the plants, and were followed by plant tours. As a result of this initial move, members have developed a 'complete openness' policy, where other firms in the group have access to the plants, certain documents and training courses of the other members. The result is a system of extensive formal and informal information trading.

In order to be more efficient, the group is divided into work committees, headed by one firm which might have special knowledge of or interest in a particular issue. These issues include best practice, safety, transport, natural resources and education; each one of these committees is headed by a different firm.[15] In the best practice committee, for example, each firm submits topics[16] where they require knowledge from other firms, and others where they can offer expertise.

In addition to the Grupo de Industriales de Aguascalientes, other firms have created groups to facilitate knowledge flows. One interesting case is the *kaizen* (continuous improvement) meetings of Japanese transplants. Since Nissan started assembling automobiles in 1982, ten additional Japanese auto part suppliers have set up shop in Aguascalientes, partly as the result of strong government promotion efforts.[17] In accordance with the Japanese philosophy of continuous improvement, all these firms use *kaizen* methodologies to upgrade their production processes. Every month, employees from all plants get together to present the best cases of

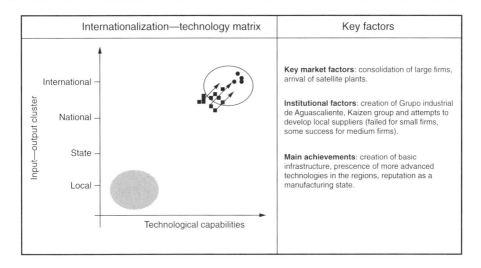

Figure 16.3 Summary of the Situation at the End of the Transition Period.

kaizen improvement in different areas of the plant. These *kaizen* meetings effectively diffuse process improvements across all the other plants.

As with the Grupo de Industriales de Aguascalientes, *kaizen* meetings have helped to diffuse knowledge generated in each plant to all other Japanese plants; however, smaller firms receive no information through these channels. In order to facilitate the flow between larger and smaller firms, both government and large firms designed supplier development programmes to increase the linkages between them and local suppliers. After all, one intended objective of attracting foreign investment was for them to develop local suppliers and increase local content rules. Since the mid-1980s most of the larger firms have had vendor development programmes where they supply financing, machinery and know-how.[18] Similarly, the government has programmes of supply chain integration.

Despite these efforts, programmes have had at best mixed results. Only some medium-sized firms have developed the necessary quality or capacity to supply top-tier firms. From a regional innovation system, this means a huge gap between the firms which have access to technologies and less sophisticated local firms.

Figure 16.3 offers a summary of the industrialization–technology matrix at the end of the transition period. On the lower left, we can still observe the cluster of local low technology firms, which as a group stayed in the same place where it originally started; firms kept close to other local firms, but were slow to recognize the need to increase their technological capabilities and international orientation. On the upper right, we can observe that the larger firms, which were originally operating as individuals, were slowly evolving into a cluster, mostly as a result of the Grupo de Industriales de Aguascalientes. At this point, information began to flow freely among them, and they were able to benefit mutually from the information exchange. We can also observe, in the centre of the graph, that some medium-sized, medium technology firms are moving towards the upper right corner by selling to the larger firms, which provide them with world-class assistance to manage their own firms.

New regulatory framework: upgrading of technological capabilities

State policy for technology development (1992 to the present)

In 1992, Aguascalientes had one of the most solid manufacturing bases in the country relative to its size. However, it was also evident that the capabilities to generate and diffuse knowledge, particularly when compared with the amount of industry present in the region, were extremely limited. Just like twenty years earlier, when the state implemented a very active policy to attract industry, the new government set as its priority attracting institutions with technological capabilities.

One particular concern was the lack of independent research centres. The state government wanted to be sure of the short-term impact of the centres in the regional economy, yet realized that it takes many years to establish and stabilize a research centre. In order to reconcile these opposite objectives, the state's strategy was to attract subsidiaries of successful centres from other states, rather than creating new ones. In order to achieve this goal, the government started a very active campaign to attract existing research centres which offered free land, construction subsidies and housing finance to centres willing to settle in Aguascalientes. In exchange, the government requested that centres should develop joint projects with local industry and should concentrate on applied, rather than basic, research.

In the initial prospecting, the state approached several SEP-CONACYT centres, a network of federally supported centres dealing with specialized topics (see Chapter 7 of this volume). A variety of centres were approached, including some dealing with material science and biodegradability. At the end, these efforts were successful in attracting three centres.

CIATEC, the first research centre to establish in Aguascalientes,[19] started operations in October 1994. Its mission is to establish joint projects with industry to improve their productivity, quality and competitiveness. Given its objectives, the researchers asked to be located in the middle of a modern industrial park, rather than next to other research centres. They work on three different schemes: consulting (brief interventions), technological development (usually including developing some machinery) and research projects (which are medium-term technology projects with a basic research component). The majority of projects with industry are to develop machinery, and all project-related expenses are paid by the contracting firm.

Researchers in CIATEC keep a wide network of contacts with the research community, in both Mexico and the rest of the world. In order to stay at the technological frontier, researchers update their knowledge base through projects, 6 per cent salary bonus for 'personal improvement', tri-annual training and congresses. When the project deals more with basic research, they usually create alliances with national and/or foreign institutions.[20] Even with this wide network of alliances, the positive effects of the network are regionally bounded: over half the projects were contracted by firms in Aguascalientes, and the rest are from neighbouring states.[21]

The second centre to come to Aguascalientes was the Centro de Investigaciones Opticas (CIO, Centre for Optics Research), a branch of one working in León[22] since 1980. The state government was interested in its capabilities of offering graduate degrees, plus its wide applicability to local industries. Before deciding on which areas to concentrate on, a group of researchers visited around 40 firms to identify industry needs. As a result of the industry meetings they currently focus on two research areas: colorimetry and material characterization.

CIO can sell products or projects, or just provide services to industry. The colorimetry lab is already working on the formulation of new colours for textile dying and automotive painting; another project is developing mirrors for photocopying machines.[23] Additionally, it provides education programmes, both graduate degrees and certificate courses. Besides their clear benefits to industry, CIO personnel regard certification courses[24] as a vital ingredient in creating a common language between the firms and the scientists, and thus allowing further collaboration.

Both CIATEC and CIO report that managers still do not see technology as a priority, and most prefer purchasing, copying or reverse engineering, partly because of lack of financing. This creates a situation where the centres have to promote their services actively, by 'selling' the benefits of technology projects. Initially, they tried to work through chambers or government institutions, but this approach did not generate many projects. Currently, each centre has a full-time staff member in charge of pursuing individual relationships and finding out exactly which problems they can solve.

Bridging institutions

Comisión Estatal de Desarrollo Económico y Comercio Exterior (CEDECE), the state's agency in charge of economic development,[25] has played a key role recently. The role of CEDECE has been evolving: from 1992 to 1994, its top priority was attracting foreign direct investment. Since 1995, in addition to its FDI attraction efforts, the state has implemented support programmes for small and medium local enterprises. The importance of the small and medium enterprises as a sector with great job-creating potential had been practically ignored in its first years, and in fact the two divisions in charge of this support were created recently. Currently, they have an employment programme which has given scholarships for self-employment and to increase labour skills.

Even though the CEDECE programmes described above have helped the local economy, its most important contribution has been in its role as information broker. As pointed out by Casalet (Chapter 7 of this volume), there is no coordination between different federal, state and local organizations in charge of supporting technological innovation; firms that want access to these services have to figure out what each one is offering, and how they can best benefit from them. In the case of Aguascalientes, CEDECE has developed a wider perspective of the support programmes and the firm's needs, and helps firms to understand how best to take advantage of the available services. In other words, CEDECE has acted as a catalyser of all the other institutions, acting as a 'meta-bridge' between firms, government institutions, labour, bridging institutions and research centres. Its relationships with firms are in fact so close that CEDECE has an honorary seat with the Grupo de Industriales de Aguascalientes.

Among the institutions that CEDECE is looking for more interaction in are higher education institutions (HEIs) and firms. In order to coordinate these efforts, the state is trying to reconfigure the Comité Estatal de Vinculación to work with new styles of linkages. One model is Programa de capacitación para y en el trabajo (Probecap) from CONALEP, which gives on-the-job training.[26]

Transfer of technology: CIMO and consultants

As previously mentioned, large firms developed in the mid-1980s mechanisms by which technology could flow between them, particularly the Grupo Industrial Aguascalientes. However, this knowledge was not flowing to medium and small firms. Ever since trade liberalization, these firms have faced a particularly hard situation where they need to compete at international standards, but in many cases lack the resources to develop their own technology.

In recent years, new institutions and organizations have evolved which have permitted technology to flow from large to small firms. The key organization in Aguascalientes is Calidad Integral y Modernización (CIMO), a federal programme financed by the Ministry of Labour. CIMO's main objective is to support the micro, small and medium enterprises, by paying 35–70 per cent of eligible training and consulting projects. Its philosophy is identifying individual demand within the sectors and regions, rather than offering pre-structured programmes.

This support has resulted in a growth in the number of consultants, including academics and researchers, offering their services to the local economy. CIMO has 180 registered consultants in areas ranging from accounting to production, from human resources to quality certification; very few of them are qualified to design machinery or processes. Given this rapid growth, CIMO controls consultant quality not through an official certification process,[27] but by keeping a record by firm and consultant to track historic results. To assure consistent quality in each project, consultants do not get paid until the client firm signs a letter of satisfaction with the consulting firm. Despite the relatively small size of the state, Aguascalientes had in 1997 the largest number of CIMO projects in the whole country,[28] showing an increasing awareness by the firms that needed to improve their processes and the vitality of the consultants' market.

This new group of consultants has played an important role in enhancing the competitiveness of the small and medium enterprises,[29] particularly by defusing top management practices from large firms to smaller ones. This is particularly true for consultants who were previously employed by major MNEs,[30] and who currently run their private consulting practices. These former employees were trained within their respective firms on top-of-the-line managerial practices, which could later be transferred to the smaller firms.

One example of a successful firm is Cadea Consultores, a consulting firm which currently employs 38 people. The firm was started by the former director of operations, the director of quality assurance and the plant manager of the Texas Instruments plant.[31] Given their experience, they currently offer services on ISO 9000, just-in-time, and preventive maintenance. In two years they worked with 28 small[32] and medium companies, of which ten have already received their ISO 9000 certification. Their practice has expanded beyond the local economy: they currently have offices in León, San Luis Potosí, Querétaro and Mexico City; they want to

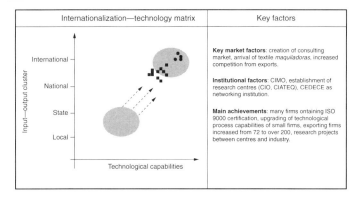

Figure 16.4 Summary of the Situation after the NAFTA.

represent a firm from the USA; and they are starting their first international projects in Costa Rica and Bolivia.

Widening the export base

Perhaps the best indicator of the increasing competitiveness of the state is its export performance. Aguascalientes's share of total Mexican manufacturing exports has been increasing steadily, from 0.9 per cent in 1992 to 2.2 per cent in 1997. This is particularly surprising for a state not on the Mexico–USA border. The 1997 exports reached US$1.7 billion, of which Japanese automobile firms exported US$1,138 million, 65 per cent of the state total.[33]

Even though exports are highly concentrated in the Japanese automobile sector, the number of exporting firms increased from 72 in 1992 to 221 by December 1997. The growth rate of exports for different sized firms shows that that quarterly growth rate for medium firms has exceeded growth in large firms in three of the last five quarters. These figures reflect the growth of exports across a wide variety of sectors. Despite its growth of almost 80 per cent in two years, automobiles' and auto parts' share of total exports has decreased from 70.5 to 66.7 per cent. This reflects the extraordinary growth rates in other sectors, such as metal mechanics, garments and other manufacturing, which have trebled their exports in the same period.

The growth of textiles and garments is due to the conversion of many medium textile and garment firms to *maquiladoras*; currently there are about 67 *maquiladoras*, which sub-contract up to 250 workshops in sub-*maquila*. These *maquiladoras* receive technology from garment manufacturers, and they transfer the technology to the sub-*maquilas*.

Figure 16.4 presents the current situation in Aguascalientes graphically. Large firms are working in a very coordinated manner and constitute a tight network. Many medium and small firms have been able to improve their process quality. Overall, the figure shows that firms are moving from the lower left to the upper right, and though they are generally still far from international best practices, they have reached a level of competencies that allows them to export. Additionally, some medium firms are taking advantage of the research centres in the state, and are generating some technology. The fact that the economy is so balanced and that exports represent such a high proportion of total production has made Aguascalientes less vulnerable to the economic crisis which has hit the country in the past few years; in fact, the state was the first one to recover employment growth after the 1994 peso crisis.

Conclusions

Aguascalientes is currently one of the most industrially dynamic regions in Mexico, and is experiencing greater technological dynamism than most of the country. When comparing the statistics of patents per capita and formal R&D to similar statistics in other OECD countries, these levels are quite low for the state, even in relation to other places in Mexico. Most firms do not have an R&D department, show no patenting activity and rarely work together with other firms or research centres in joint research activities. However, other indicators of performance, such as manufacturing growth, number of exporting firms and ISO 9000 certification, reflect important advances in technological capabilities. Both statistics and the empirical observation show that most innovative activity is taking place at a plant level in an informal way, rather than through formal collaborations.

Innovation at the regional level results from the interaction of very diverse institutions, ranging from micro-enterprises to federal government institutions. There are a variety of government, private, and research institutions trying to enhance the region's technological capabilities. All these agents play different roles as generators, brokers or diffusers of information, and it is through complex interaction networks that innovation is possible. Figures 16.2, 16.3 and 16.4 summarize the process Aguascalientes has gone through in the past two decades, including what seems to be the critical market and institutional factors permitting this process. Again, they seem to point at the importance of clusters rather than individual organizations.

Knowledge seems to be flowing among certain subsets of firms, through the creation of organizations created specially to comment on problems of mutual concern. There exist large information and technological asymmetries between firms of different sizes. Two groups of firms have developed particularly effective knowledge diffusion mechanisms: very large firms, through the Grupo de Industriales de Aguascalientes; and Japanese firms, which have monthly *kaizen* groups to communicate process and administrative improvements among them. Effective means of communication have not evolved for smaller, domestic firms, which have to rely on informal contacts for this effect. For these firms, the imitation effect seems to be critical. We can observe this, for example, in the adoption of the ISO 9000.

The right-hand side of Figures 16.2, 16.3 and 16.4 illustrate the complementary role of markets and institutions in technological development, and we can observe that some of these agents play the role of (or create) institutions, while others will interact with the region mostly in market transactions. This seems to agree with Dosi's (1988a) and Cimoli and Dosi's (1995) emphasis that upgrading (or downgrading) of the technological capabilities in the region is a result of a positive interaction between some existing market factors and some institutions which were able to take the available opportunities. As shown in the previous chapters, distrust between managers and government officials and researchers seems to be the status quo in Mexico. In the absence of an already operating market, an institution that builds credibility and confidence is necessary to bridge the different agents in this region (CEDECE in the case of Aguascalientes).

The presence of specialized research centres which supply very qualified researchers, such as the SEP-CONACYT centres, has proven an effective way of stimulating research and development in several firms. Two characteristics seem to be apparent in the Aguascalientes experience: First, firms perceived quite a low need for innovation projects (in fact, most projects involving both firms and research centres have evolved from a strong marketing effort from the centre). Second, researchers' areas of work are in fact an important part of the region's technological competences, and will determine which technological trajectories it will undertake. Thus, for example, establishing the Centre for Optical Research has meant an increasing interest by firms in applying laser or colorimetry technologies, which would surely have not been the case if centres dealing with, for example, materials or acoustics had been established.

The region might have the necessary elements to promote technological development, yet have difficulty in matching the supply and demand for technological assistance. In this respect, CIMO seems to have been an exemplar of effective institutions. Its operation combines elements of institutional intervention with elements of market creation, by allowing firms to choose the type of services they will require from consultants. Perhaps, one of its greatest advantages has been to allow great flexibility for each region to establish the characteristics of its programme according to both technological competences and industry needs.

A final conclusion is the need to look beyond the firm and national levels when analysing a system of innovation. The regional perspective allows us truly to integrate the different elements present in the systems of innovation perspective.

Notes

1. The population and industrial activity is quite concentrated, for two-thirds of its inhabitants live in its capital city, also called Aguascalientes, while the state's other ten municipalities each have fewer than 60,000 inhabitants, working mostly in agricultural activities. The state has a privileged location with respect to the domestic market, relatively close to the three largest cities in the country (Mexico City, Guadalajara and Monterrey).
2. The terms region and state are not necessarily equivalent. In some cases, an economic region (defined by the intensity of economic transactions) will be only part of the state, while in others, a region will be composed of several states. Given the high degree of interaction that has evolved between the different state agents, it makes sense in this case to use the state as the relevent region of analysis.
3. In terms of traditional R&D indicators, there were only two patent applications filed for all of 1997, both of them requested by individual researchers. Similarly, though there are some high-tech firms, most of them are involved in labour-intensive processes, and lack any R&D departments.
4. We can find firms doing process innovation in a variety of industries, such as Fomasa (automotive products), De todo en Alambre (metal working), Ordemex (agro-industrial equipment).
5. Firms with less capability might be interested in meeting firms with higher capability; however, more often than not, the more advanced firms will not reciprocate.

6. The state had an early start in manufacturing when the Guggenheim family established the Grand Central Foundry of Aguascalientes in 1901, yet had a major setback when this plant closed in the early 1940s, greatly reducing manufacturing output.

7. Over 80 per cent of production was concentrated in two sub-sectors: food and beverages accounted for 66.4 per cent of total production, while textiles and garments represented an additional 14.8 per cent.

8. In that same year he asked Carlos Lozano, then 24 years old, and head of CEDECE (see below) until 1998, to design an industrialization programme.

9. In 1974 the main sectors were agriculture, wine-making, textiles, garments, railway repair and some metal-working.

10. The closure of the Central Foundry had greatly reduced union activism. The foundry stopped operating partly because of labour problems, creating unemployment, so that leaders became more moderate in their positions.

11. Fifteen years before credit unions became popular in the rest of Mexico.

12. Imhasa, Raleigh, Hecort, Fomasa and Motodiesel Mexicana.

13. For Xerox, they talked about the female garment workers, used to doing very detailed work. In the case of Nissan, the main sales argument was the state's experience in the metal mechanics sector, largely resulting from the railway repair shop.

14. During the import substitution era, firms had to have a majority of Mexican participation. In order to waive this requirement, it was necessary to get direct approval from president Jose Lopez Portillo. Nissan asked the government for a gas pipeline. TI and Xerox decided to establish on the condition they would attract an American school. Similarly, Nissan demanded a Japanese school.

15. Best Practice (headed by Siemens), Safety (Xerox), Transport (Spimex), Natural Resources (Nissan), Education (Texas Instruments).

16. These topics range from supplier management, organization, time management, productivity to continuous improvement.

17. Comisión Estatal de Desarrollo Económico y Comercio Exterior, whose main objective was attracting investment from the outside, both foreign and from large domestic firms. This has been done through a serious marketing effort, which includes videos in Spanish, English and Japanese promoting the state and showing top managers relating their experiences in the state. In order to have even more direct contact, the governor and director of CEDECE make a yearly trip to Japan to try to attract more of Nissan's suppliers to establish satellite plants in the state.

18. Nissan is fairly closed to local suppliers, but a few of the Japanese transplants have made an effort and achieved some degree of local integration, developing a tiered system of suppliers, similar to the one in Japan.

19. The original CIATEC is located in Queretaro, and currently has 125 people, compared to only 15 working in Aguascalientes. The current workforce allows the new CIATEC to work simultaneously with one large project and several small ones.

20. With national universities such as UNAM or IPN. They also have an association with Southwest Research Institute, and work with schools such as Texas A&M and the University of Virginia. They also work with and for other SEP-CONACYT centres such as CISESE where they have joint control projects, and are building a robot for CINVESTAV.

21. The actual distribution of projects is 54 per cent in Aguascalientes, 23 per cent in Querétaro, 15 per cent in Jalisco and 8 per cent in San Luis Potosí.

22. Government gave 25,000 square metres of land, and they want 200 people in the centre; currently it has one researcher and 9 support people. The Guanajuato centre currently has 35 researchers and 100 support personnel (including technicians).

23. Xerox is considering a joint venture to produce high refraction mirrors, currently sourced

from Germany. This joint venture would supply photocopier glass and mirrors, to be jointly developed by Xerox and the centre, and then sell the technology to a possible supplier.

24. They have taught three certification courses in colorimetry: one for Xerox, one for INEGI (cartographers) and one open to the public. They want to offer a new certificate in textile finishing.

25. CEDECE operated previously as a Secretariate of Economic Development. However, it has become a commission in order to work more independently of the state government and closer to firms.

26. The Porbecap (programa de becas de capacitación) gave in four years a total of 31,504 scholarships. Another state programme, the Servicio Estatal de Empleo, acts as a brokerage service between the unemployed and firms looking for employees: in 1996, one of every four people found a job through this service (Indicadores Económicos de Aguascalientes).

27. Currently CEDECE-CIMO-UNITEC-Bonaterra are working towards creating a certificate for local experts in process consulting, and another certificate for consultants in ISO 9000. Given the large number of consultants, and their respective specialities, CIMO and ASOCEA have developed a programme on process consulting which will allow a more global view of the firm, particularly necessary when dealing with small firms.

28. With 2,800 actions, affecting an average of nine workers each. Regional CIMO does not have a financial limit, but depends on the demands by firms.

29. Consulting markets are clearly segmented depending on the size of the firm: larger firms will usually approach more established national or international consulting firms, while many of the medium firms access technology through chambers; this leaves the micro and small enterprises as the main customers for local consultants.

30. Throughout the interviews, it was possible to identify six consultants that originally worked in Xerox, three more from Texas Instruments and at least one from Nissan.

31. Currently, about 75 per cent of CADEA workers formerly worked at Texas Instruments, Xerox or Ford.

32. One of them has 40 employees, and is the first small firm in Mexico to complete the certification process.

33. Exports from Japanese firms have been growing very rapidly, from US$410 million in 1993 to over $1 billion in 1996, representing an annual growth rate of 29 per cent.

CHAPTER SEVENTEEN

Conclusions: An Appreciative Pattern of the Mexican Innovation System

M. Cimoli

Stylized fact: towards a modernized assembly plant

This chapter sketches a brief outline of an appreciative pattern of the Mexican NIS, which should describe and generalize some of the ideas proposed in this book. Specific conclusions are presented in each of the 16 chapters. It should, however, be borne in mind that the purpose of this chapter is to present the main stylized fact that should serve as a basis for discussion and support an appreciative pattern of the Mexican NIS. In brief, the main stylized facts that emerge are:

Macro instability

The Mexican economy is very unstable, compared to other OECD countries. GDP growth is more variable, the real exchange rate is more volatile and inflation is higher. This instability spreads to almost all key variables that affect the innovation process. Hence, it is of the utmost importance to stabilize the nation's economy. However, macro stability, credibility and reduction of uncertainty are objectives that have been only partially achieved. In this context, entrepreneurs and, particularly, small and medium-sized firms adopt a defensive behaviour that implies that they do not assume long-term risks for investment in innovation. Conversely, subsidiaries of MNEs and large domestic firms take financial risks in international markets through their financial divisions and controlled banks.

Low technological opportunities

After the trade reform, Mexico has substantially increased its participation in the world arena, in terms of exports as well as imports. Most of the surviving and efficient firms (both MNEs and large domestic firms) have increased their exports (components for automobiles, chemicals, plastic products, glass, beer, electronics, steel, cement, etc.) and imports of intermediate and capital goods. The image that we have is that Mexico is a country in which production activities are highly globalized and that a new specialization in the global chain of production is emerging. The analysis of the composition of technological sectors and their evolution over time permits observation of a high level of stability in the technological specialization oriented towards traditional activities that are characterized by a mature technology.

On the one side, this specialization of the production system limits its own techno-logical opportunities. On the other, low technological opportunity is the main element that explains the reduced efforts and lower quasi-rents. Thus, a 'vicious circle' is established.

Poor R&D efforts

Mexico's R&D efforts are rather poor in comparison to those at the technological frontier. Moreover, R&D is highly concentrated in the export sectors (automobiles, glass, cement, office machinery and computers, electronic equipment, etc.). R&D effort principally focused on addressing the modernization of production processes and improvements in production organization and product quality.

As for sources of new technological knowledge, the vast majority of firms rely almost exclusively on their internal sources. Regardless of the sectors in which firms operate, they have not developed cooperative R&D efforts with other firms and institutions. Furthermore, in none of the technological sectors have firms made significant expenditures on R&D, except for those that are export-oriented, and these firms have principally invested in improving processes, organization or quality. As a matter of fact, the pattern of R&D efforts – which have been scarce and scattered – and other modes of technology transfer has been mainly dominated by a higher integration of imported inputs in most competitive sectors.

Globalization of production and low contribution to local R&D efforts

The pattern of how Mexican industry has been globalized could be viewed by an incomplete web of domestic interactions between competencies and technological flows through the four types of sectors: science-based, specialized suppliers, scale-intensive and natural resource/traditional supplier-dominated sectors. For the most part, the supply of goods for the science-based and specialized suppliers sectors are imports, while the exports from these sectors, as well as goods from the scale-intensive sector, include a large proportion of *maquiladora*-type exports. The interaction of the four types of sectors in Mexico is highly oriented towards external linkages with the globalized world economy. Our analysis of Mexican globalization involves both foreign and domestic firms. First, we examine the firms and industries dominated by foreign firms (FF, subsidiaries and joint ventures); second, we study the firms and industries under the control of domestic firms (NF, including conglom-erates and minority foreign participation). The FF are the most dynamic agents in terms of their response to the international competitive pressures during the past decade. However, both the FF and NF are more significant exporters, activating different channels to incorporate foreign technology and remaining an important source of technology and production inputs. The FF and the larger NF rely extensively on foreign sources of advanced technology, though in doing this they spread the effects of globalization through the more competitive parts of Mexican industry. None the less, all types of firms have some integration with countries that lead in international trade and technological innovations, thus becoming dependent on imported technology, as well as on imports of the most technologically dynamic products and intermediates. In fact, the main changes are observed in the modes of how sectors and the type of firms (considering FF and NF) are inter-linked with foreign production networks and sources of technology. In particular, the pattern of R&D efforts and other modes of technology transfer have been mainly dominated by a greater integration of imported inputs in the most competitive sectors. The evidence shows that their local contribution to R&D efforts and interactions with local institutions are scarce and scattered.

Low contribution of FDI to local technological activities

Foreign direct investment (FDI) refers to activities and decisions taken by MNEs. These activities and decisions, developed in consideration of international production, exert a strong influence on the direction of trade flows, scale and content, as well as on trade specialization, competitiveness and foreign trade balances of both the host and home countries. This is the case of a host country like Mexico. In fact, in large part, the Mexican patterns of trade specialization and performance (for example, international competitiveness) can then be analysed as the outcome of the processes that result from MNEs' decisions on the localization and quality of FDI. In this context, regional integration through the NAFTA has played a crucial role as an institutional regime or framework that supported the incentives for the MNEs. Today, technological developments occur mainly in the home bases of MNEs and only a small portion is transferred to countries like Mexico. This process ensures, on the one hand, that Mexico participates actively in the globalization of production and, on the other hand, that its participation in the globalization of scientific and technological activities is very poor. As companies transfer only some of their R&D activities to Mexico, we can expect that the present concentration of corporate R&D will by and large lead to an even stronger international divergence of technological development. Internationalization of R&D is developed within developed economies and regions with revealed technological advantages. Technological cooperation between firms seems, in practice, to exclude firms that do not already have an established reputation within the developed economies. This view supports results obtained by empirical research on the organization of research activities in multinational firms, where it is noted that even multinational companies perform most of their innovative activities in the home country (Patel and Pavitt, 1991; Cantwell, 1989, 1997; Chenais, 1995; Freeman and Hagedoorn, 1995).

Non-optimality of institutional response

The development literature introduces approaches and models in which the variables are mainly quantitative. Examples include per capita income, capital intensity indices, manufacturing labour share, rate of return of capital and their changes over time. However, as has been shown by the Mexican case, the analysis of a development process requires the analysis of the qualitative dimension, such as changes in the regulatory framework, changes in the political regime, regional agreements such as the NAFTA and the emergence of new institutions. Thus, if we accept this view, the background of the national innovation system is a useful toolbox for the analysis of the non-random distribution of competencies, capabilities and revealed performance of a country (Acs and de la Mothe, 2000).

According to this view, the Mexican case – like other detailed historical case studies – shows that institutional structures tend to adapt and change in response to pushes and pulls exerted by the production system and structural reforms, mainly regarding the process of liberalization and privatization. This adaptive path is not exclusively a market process where incentives from relative prices determine the behaviour of agents. Indeed, qualitative changes involve another set of incentives provided by the historical path and specificity of each organization, the decisions of policy-makers and the political 'cycle' from one sexenio to the other.

The evolution of institutions may be a very complex process, involving the actions not only of private firms, but also of such organizations as the government, universities, private non-profit and new technologies. Our analysis of the Mexican innovation system shows that institutions do not change optimally in response to changes in normative rules and the incentives from liberalization policies. Instead, the assumption of non-optimality of institutional response is generally observed across the different types of institutions and historical phases.

Low interaction of science sectors with local institutions

The interaction between firms and the local institutions that produce knowledge is very poor, a fact which is most keenly felt by those companies belonging to the science-based sector. The results show that domestic firms consider internal sources of knowledge as more important for their innovative activities than external sources. Within the production system the activities of engineers and technicians and the experience of the labour force constitute the most relevant sources of knowledge, particularly for firms within the scale-intensive and science-based sectors. According to firms, users are also an important source of technological knowledge, especially in the specialized suppliers and supplier-dominated sectors. Public sector or university research centres are not a relevant source of information for Mexican firms. This is a rather remarkable fact in the case of firms within the science-based sector, since this sector is strongly linked with such centres in the more developed countries.

Low technological opportunity and organizational rigidity of university

It is a well-known fact that technological capabilities are greatly strengthened through the development of institutions fostering innovation, either public or private, intermediate organizations and specialized service firms, and institutions belonging to the scientific and technological infrastructure of the country (in the Mexican case, it is interesting to consider the role played by the specialized institutions, bridging institutions and SEP-CONACYT system, in particular that of those centres linked to technological development).

A key element in the development of technological capabilities is the existence of close linkages between the production system and the institutional infrastructure. Presently, regardless of the existing efforts towards creating institutions that develop and strengthen technological capabilities, fragmented structures prevail, which are rather alien to the needs of the productive sector. Moreover, a little explored characteristic in the trajectory of the institutions analysed so far refers to the evaluation of the assessment and the results achieved by them.

Throughout our historical phases, government and educational organizations have devoted special attention to policies whose implementation was mainly oriented to fostering enrolments at different levels in the educational system. Although efforts have been made, Mexico's stock of technicians, engineers and scientists is still insufficient, as is enrolment at the secondary and tertiary levels, in particular when compared with the enrolment rates for the typical age groups at each level in other OECD countries. Another important issue is the low number of personnel employed in R&D in public centres and universities.

In general terms, it can be said that Mexico is considerably behind the international level of knowledge production. When compared to countries such as the United States, Japan and the United Kingdom, Mexico shows a pattern of generation of knowledge in which government encouragement is weak, there is little support from the business sector and HEIs carry out most of the R&D activities. Universities and research centres concentrate the greater part of science competencies – funding, personnel and infrastructure – within the country. Research capabilities are still weak if compared internationally. University–industry relationships based on research activities, are still weak, showing a trend to increase from the early 1990s. The main causes are: the lack of an innovative culture and recognition of the value of knowledge on the part of firms; incipient institutional strategies for linkage activities in HEI and a lack of consideration of those institutions regarding their role in technological development; and inadequately defined technological and industrial policies on the part of government.

The degree of intensity of firms in the use of knowledge produced by HEI is low in different industrial sectors. Despite this low intensity, university–industry collaborations in Mexico are taking place on a regional basis, given geographic proximity between research institutions and specific problems related to local natural resources and industrial activities. This has been possible due to a set of policies applied by different sectors towards decentralization and the establishment of formal linkages.

Inhibition of local networking activities

A substantial and widespread perception is that networks are a powerful engine for innovation systems. Information and knowledge networks, much like the interstate motorways in the 1950s or the steam machines of the early industrial revolution, provide the basic infrastructure of the modern economic system. But whereas earlier infrastructures were very physical in nature, today's new infrastructures are typified as being intangible or 'smart'. The static and dynamic efficiencies of economic systems (i.e. both the allocation of given resources to given economic functions and the development and diffusion of technical and organizational innovations) depend increasingly on the degree of access to advanced linkages between firms and knowledge flows in a particular institutional environment (De Bresson and Amesse, 1991; Freeman, 1991).

From the theory of development economics in the 1960s and 1970s, it is well known that the trade and internationalization of production were not necessarily neutral to the growth path of different countries. Thus, some countries have selected a road that is characterized by increasing gaps or immiserizing growth. Trade liberalization and foreign investment flows are not the only elements that help to create a prosperous development path. The firms' and sectoral learning patterns, as well as overall national capabilities, are dynamically coupled via input–output flows, knowledge-spillovers, backward and forward linkages, complementarities and context-specific externalities. Together, they contribute to shaping the organizational and technological context within which each economic activity takes place. In a sense, they set the opportunities and constraints that each individual production and innovation process faces – including the availability of complementary skills, information on intermediate inputs and capital goods – and demand stimuli to improve particular products. This has a direct link with the analyses that focuses on structural change and development (here, within a vast literature, contributions include Hirschman, Rosenstein Rodan, Gerschenkron, Chenery and Sirquin). A traditional statement of that rationale is as follows:

> One suggestion along this line was that development is accelerated through investment in projects and industries with strong forward or backward linkage effects. I argued that entrepreneurial decision making in both the private and public sectors is not uniquely determined by the pull of incomes and demand, but is responsive to special push factors, such as the linkages, emanating from the product side. ... By now, the various linkages and their interaction have taken on a new character and importance. They appear to constitute a structure that is capable of generating an alternative path toward development or underdevelopment for the different staple exporters. In other words, some of the principal features of a country's development in the period of export-led growth can be described in terms of linkages deriving from its staple. (Hirschman, 1977–70 and 80)

Regarding recent parables of globalization and liberalization, it could be conjectured that the benefits generated by knowledge-intensive networks are not equally distributed. Moreover, the specialization of production supports a system of networks where the demand for knowledge and innovation is continuously addressed towards advanced economies. This increases their capabilities of capturing the benefit and advantages. At first sight there thus appears a contradiction between the 'new age vision' that supports the idea that countries capture equally the benefits of globalization and most empirical evidences that demonstrate the increasing gaps in the capabilities of capturing the benefit of networking and innovative activities (Cimoli, 2000; Cimoli and de la Mothe, 2000).

In a sense, networks represent a socio-institutional response that is developed and deployed in order to address the increasing complexities of economic interdependence. Economies of scale and increasing returns, both characteristics of economic systems at the beginning of the new millennium, are strongly conditioned by the availability of a strategic infrastructure, such as human and physical channels for information flows. The building and provision of those services are essential, not only to fuel the process of introduction and diffusion of incremental technical and organizational innovations, but also to develop new economic responses to environmental, social and economical constraints or targets.

In addition to the above, the analysis of the effectiveness of the linkages supporting both knowledge flows and, hence, innovation processes is complicated by the presence of all those informal types of relationships between firms and institutions (and among them) that in the standard literature fall under the heading of 'externalities' Clearly, further investigations are required to provide a more solid basis for this representation of our structure. None the less, we believe that such a structure would be helpful in understanding the mechanisms by which networks determine the success and failure of innovation. However, recent advances in the economics of innovation have highlighted the powerful role of externalities in the generation of new technologies and a virtuous development path.

Accordingly, the economic mechanism that permits firms to capture the benefits of networks and innovation is cooperation.[1] Experience tells us that cooperation is the key issue to understand the diffusion of innovations. All processes of change require high levels of both cooperation and competition among firms and other actors. In addition to this, it also needs responsive and strategic regulation to obtain the required mix of static and dynamic efficiencies. Any kind of economic change needs proper compatibility and coordination to manage the system, as well as the timely introduction and diffusion of innovations in order to enhance its efficiency.

These new globalized scenarios increasingly modify the competitiveness of nations and their integration in terms of production capacities across firms, industries and nations. Industries and firms are now integrated in an international network according to different types of linkages designed as networks of contractors or more coordinated, integrated and organized production chains in different sites around the world. Many other factors give specific shape to these networks, such as the proximity to trade against concentration, or scale gains that act as trade-off rules of action for MNEs deciding to invest locally against exporting.

Most of the production activities in Mexico have increased their demand for knowledge and technology provided by foreign sources. Our evidence indicates that firms have modernized their exporting plants, which suggests that industrial adjustment has occurred preferentially through process innovation, such as the improvement of production organization, the improvement of skills and the adaptation of machinery and equipment – not the renewal of fixed capital – which would permit MNEs and large domestic groups to achieve a higher competitiveness performance. Moreover, there are three main reasons why the dynamics of inter-industry flows is not functioning to improve R&D efforts and linkages with the local institutional framework. For example, *maquiladora* operations dominate the production of science-based components, thus allowing for very limited links with and flows to other domestic suppliers of intermediates. Particularly, when the analysis is developed for the most recent years, it seems to confirm how the *maquila* industry is one of the leading actors in industrial modernization. The diffusion of this type of industry introduces only very weak connections with the domestic productive firms and institutions. The '*maquila* innovation system' mainly supports and stimulates networking activities in foreign firms and institutions, reinforcing knowledge and technological advantages in developed economies.

The imported equipment used throughout the industrial system replaces (and is a surrogate for) the learning capability that could accumulate in specialized domestic suppliers of equipment in a well integrated industrial system. The main changes could be observed in the way in which sectors and firms (considering foreign firms and non-foreign firms) are interlinked with foreign production networks and sources of technology. In particular, the pattern related to R&D efforts and other modes of technology transfer has been mainly replaced by a greater integration with imported inputs, stronger linkages with foreign engineering services and institutions (as universities and other research institutes) for the most successful exporting sectors.

Their direct contribution to R&D and technology transfer is not substantial. The evidence on R&D activities and technical collaboration (technology transfers) shows that efforts and local interactions of this kind are scarce and scattered.

The personnel employed in R&D activities, quality control and local adaptation of design mainly interact within multinational firms where they work and, furthermore, those firms are characterized by reduced linkages with the domestic higher education institutions, local research centres and laboratories. In this context, for example, universities show an increasing effort to improve and create linkages with the production system. But those efforts are inhibited by two principal factors. On the one side, we have the bureaucratic organization of most public universities and, on the other, we see a lack of demand from the industrial sector – the modernized one and the more science-based – which demand 'knowledge' from institutions and research centres abroad. In the long term, these ideas are consistent with a depreciation of competencies of local human capital and adverse incentives to develop linkages with local research centres.

These points have all inhibited local networking activities. The conclusion to be drawn from this section is that the effects of the stimuli generated by the openness of the economy are starting to wear off and, furthermore, local networking activities do not have sufficient support, in terms of linkages between the different agents in most of the innovation system in Mexico. In others words, the production system has modernized a small part of the economy, due to the effects derived from the opening up of the economy. However, this process has not been accompanied by an increased effort to stimulate the creation of local networks, such as the non-market system of linkages, a business culture and institutions that enable firms to interact with each other.

Production system and technological capabilities

Figure 17.1 presents a combination of stylized patterns, through which we can see the behaviour of production capacities, competitiveness and sectoral linkages, on the one hand, and the path of technological capabilities, on the other, throughout the three different industrial development stages considered in this book (see Figure 10.1).

Regarding the production side, we can see that during the ISI period, Mexico's production capacity and sectoral linkages enjoyed considerable growth, to enter later into a transition phase where there is no clear trend regarding these indicators, although the linkages do start to decrease. Well into the third phase (new regulatory framework), competitiveness and production capacity follow a trend of growth. The linkages between domestic firms, however, continue to decrease. Nevertheless, the fact is that it is precisely in the large firms that are focused towards the export market that both competitiveness and production capacities are growing. This growth should not be overlooked. Furthermore, the decrease in domestic intra- and inter-sectoral linkages among firms shows that these are increasingly replaced by an international integration process (e.g. globalization). In fact, together with this process, we can see a dramatic loss of articulation in the existing linkages between those firms producing export goods and their domestic suppliers of inputs (which

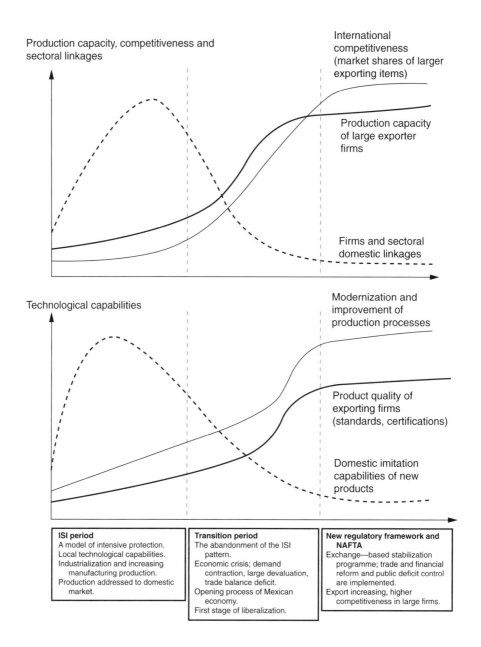

Figure 17.1 Mexican Technological Capabilities.

represents a much lower degree of knowledge and technology diffusion).[2] We should not forget that several of these firms' comparative advantages are owing to the particular allocation of production factors, such as the low cost of labour.

On the other hand, technological capabilities grew principally in the process of improving and increasing product quality, during the last phase considered. However, this growth was based on imported technology, embedded in machinery and equipment. In other words, a process of technological modernization has been taking place. Although direct imitation of imported goods has gradually decreased, during the ISI period these goods registered a considerable increase, which meant that during that period domestic development in the creation of either new products or exogenous technology has increasingly less opportunities.

There are two implications based on the above-mentioned concept: the first one, which has already been referred to, is the intense dependence on foreign technology in the development of new products and processes; the second is that firms have gained competitiveness through activities targeted at (existing) products and not at creating new ones. This pattern indicates that firms have modified their efforts and competencies. In the broadest sense, most firms have redirected their efforts and competencies from an orientation towards new product imitation to the modernization and improvement of production processes.

We should take into consideration that the trends presented in these stylized facts are not found throughout the whole Mexican industrial structure, but only in some of its parts, and, in some instances, in specific economic agents. There is, within the domestic manufacturing industry, a dichotomy: on the one hand, there is a small group of modernized firms; on the other, there is a much larger grouping of companies that is much less efficient. Furthermore, the modernized group, as mentioned previously, is becoming increasingly globalized with regard to the orientation of its production capabilities, as well as its capacity to acquire foreign technology.

The Mexican NIS: consequences of forging ahead, catching up and falling behind

The model presented hereafter is not intended to be a rigorous analytical analysis of the Mexican NIS; rather, what we do attempt is to present a loose description of the general pattern which emerged while this work was in process. By referring to the analysis of Mexico introduced above, it is possible to make an interpretation and representation of the principal exchanges between the NIS and growth performances (Fagerberg, 1988, 1995; Dosi *et al.*, 1990; Cimoli and Soete, 1992; Soete and Verspagen, 1992; Cimoli, 1998). In Figure 17.2, the interplay between NIS and the process of catching up is graphically represented.

Looking at the left side, think of an 'NIS effort and competencies frontier' (NIS(E-C) frontier) which could be identified as the actual created assets that each economy has built on in order to support innovation and the diffusion of this innovation. Each π–y schedule, where π is approximate labour productivity and y the GDP per capita as a proxy to the scope of catch-up, is built on a given NIS(E-C) frontier.

Each schedule π–y tells us that an increase in domestic productivity will lead to a higher domestic income (with respect to the world economy). In other words, a 'trade growth approach' based on the stimulus that provides the international

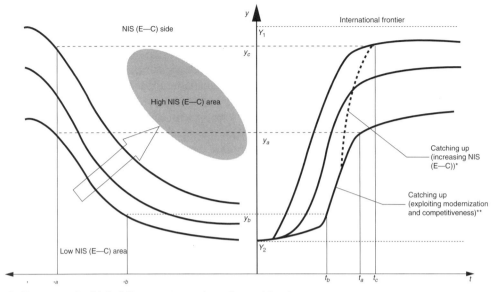

* Catching up opportunity of Mexico if efforts, competences and networking are reinforced.
** The actual Mexico pattern of catching up based on modernization of production system.

Figure 17.2 NIS, Trade Growth Performances and Catching Up.

demand is assumed here.[3] Mexico gains, in terms of dynamic comparative advantages, when a path of productivity growth is taking place. General support could be found, among other elements, in the learning mechanisms, production organization and improvements in product quality.

Within the learning economics, the mechanisms of adoption and learning substantially modify – and add new interpretations to – the cost functions faced by the sectoral country productivity. The description of the process proposed here explains how unit costs decrease in accordance to a technologically determined learning curve, with competencies clearly possessing a cumulative character. This process has been adapted in the evolutionary-structuralist models which introduced some sort of Verdoorn-Kaldor law for the explanation of the interplay between learning, dynamics of productivity and trade specialization.

The introduction of endogenous dynamics increasing return is displayed by a mechanism which explanation is based on an increase of exports and higher international market shares (see Cimoli, Dosi and Soete, 1986, Krugman, 1987).

By referring to these relationships, different schedules can be obtained. An increase in domestic efforts and competencies (literacy rate, secondary and tertiary enrolment ratios, third level students in maths, science and engineering, scientists and engineers in R&D, R&D in GNP, private and public sector R&D, direct FDI stock, capital goods imports, etc.) moves the function to the right. In the same direction, all effort addressed to improve the functionality of the NIS competencies – related to both institutions and resources – will move the π–y schedule to the high NIS (E-C) area. In the high NIS(E-C) area, the number of commodities produced and exported will increase (new international markets could be gained for 'new' commodities that have already been imported or produced only for the local market). Thus, domestic efforts to increase the participation of 'new' commodities in the world market are mainly embodied in the changes of NIS(E-C) addressed to support innovation and diffusion of innovation.

An important conclusion can readily be seen in this work: the Mexican NIS has exploited – based on international demand and the opening of the economy to increased foreign competition – the potential to develop technological capabilities within the industrial sector. What, unfortunately, is not happening is the movement towards a higher NIS(E-C) area, a movement which would allow Mexico to reach the international frontier. This idea is further explained in the paragraphs that follow.

On the right side of the figure, the growth trajectories are displayed. The trade that leads the growth process is taking place on a single schedule that relates how y changes over time. Thus, if our country is behind the international frontier, a process of catch-up is taking place when its productivity increases and learning mechanisms (associated with organizational changes, improved adaptation of imported capital goods and quality improvements, etc.) are obtained in production activities (see * in Figure 17.2). Two limits are represented, when the catching-up path takes place: (Y_1) and (Y_2) could be considered as physiological bottom-up relative growth possibilities. Specifically, Y_1 represents the 'international frontier', which captures the performance attained by the developed economies.

In fact, we can imagine that the Mexican innovation system is positioned in the lowest of the schedules pictured on both sides of Figure 17.2. Over time, it has moved along these same schedules (the increase in income from Y_b to Y_a), but it has not been able to climb up to the one immediately above. In other words, this movement has, in the case of Mexico, constituted the entirety of the modernization process without improving either efforts or competencies.

Again, on the left side, a successful effort to increase this NIS(E-C) asset would cause an upward shift in the schedule π–y. The same could be obtained when the set of institutions, which jointly and individually contribute to the development and diffusion of new technologies, improves the capacity to transfer and absorb knowledge flow and, consequently, the diffusion of the innovation process. Thus, an effort to increase NIS competencies and improve how it functions would permit Mexico to climb to the next level of the schedule y–t, thus reducing the gap from the international frontier. In other words, a stronger effort to obtain a functional (well organized) NIS and higher competencies will lead to an upward shift in the schedules π–y and y (the increase in income from y_a to y_c). A higher participation and higher income with respect to the world economy could be reached; thus, a process of catch-up would be taking place and would reduce the gap to reach the growth required at the international frontier.

Most of the effects described above can be neutralized by a greater effort to increase the NIS competencies asset and improve how it is organized by advanced countries. In this case, an increase in the international frontier (Y_1) and an increase in the gap from other nation's growth trajectories could be obtained. A scenario with a stable gap in the growth trajectories in terms of the international frontier could be viewed as the result of similar efforts in NIS competencies.

The catch-up process introduced here places emphasis on the differences in the scope of growth led by exports and a nation's potential to support an innovation system. In this sense, two mechanisms are introduced and described in Figure 17.2. First, a country could exploit productivity growth on the basis of improved competitiveness and increased exports. This process is built on a given NIS(E-C) framework. Thus, learning mechanisms, organizational changes and improvements in the quality of production activities are important sources for catch-up. Second, we can say that since the catch-up process is shaped by the actual NIS(E-C) frontier, an effort to increase this asset and an improvement in how it functions would increase the country's growth trajectory to near the international frontier.

The model outlined above accounts, in a relatively straightforward manner, for the following general property: all effort that a nation makes to improve the functionality of the NIS competencies – related to both institutions and resources – could be viewed as a necessary condition to improve its economic performance. In this same sense, one can see that a growth trajectory involving catching up (or forging ahead) is taking place. Conversely, a trajectory involving falling behind is associated with poorly organized NIS competencies and lower efforts to increase this asset.

Final remarks

Most policy-makers view the Mexican trade liberalization processes as a sufficient condition to support the acquisition of foreign technology and to capture and absorb locally the benefits from the internationalization of trade, investment and technology flows. In fact, policy-makers point out that the openness of the economy expanded the nation's technological opportunities, thus improving its technological efforts. In other words, up to now, policy-makers have played a passive role, expecting the market to perform miracles due to the openness of the economy.

In contrast, the chief idea behind our appreciative model is that the effects from the stimuli that international demand generates are starting to wear off and, furthermore, the domestic networks between local firms and institutions are increasingly eroded. From the stylized facts described above, we can detect a structural dichotomy in the domestic manufacturing industry: on the one hand, there is a small group of modernized export firms; on the other, there is a much larger group of companies that are much less competitive and not as successful in the modernization process. Furthermore, the modernized group, as mentioned previously, is becoming increasingly globalized in terms of the orientation of its production and its capacity to acquire foreign technology. More important, the liberalization process has mainly provided incentives to develop networks with firms and institutions that are located in the developed economies.

The inhibitions in local networks and interaction with high knowledge contents do not stimulate one of the most important source for growth: positive external factors and increasing returns. In fact, the pre-competitive system was not sufficiently supported in terms of the efforts and competencies that finally would allow the Mexican economy to engage fully in the process of catching up. In others words, the Mexican production system has modernized part of the economy by capturing the effects of opening up the economy; however, this process needs to continue with an increasing effort to improve competencies (training in complex skills, experience and conscious effort that enable a country's enterprises efficiently to buy, use, adapt, improve and create technologies), non-market systems of linkages, local networks, business culture and institutions that enable firms to interact with each other.

A few examples of how technological capabilities can upgrade are provided by historical case studies, which show the mechanisms through which the NIS, by fostering R&D and knowledge production flows, has been enhancing the firms and industries' capabilities, by finally inducing an improvement in performances. The same type of relationship is confirmed by other recent case studies, which reveal the extent and types of collaborations between enterprises and the public sector research base (formal collaborations, such as commissioned research, joint R&D projects, co-patenting and co-publications; informal transactions, such as informal contacts and use of published scientific knowledge; and other areas, such as spin-offs from universities, technology transfer to enterprises, patents and product developments). At a more specific level, and in particular by focusing on education policy, analysis of the Taiwan experience will provide another example of the relationship running from the NIS to enhanced competence and better performance. In Germany, Japan and Sweden, we can see that, at least in most of the post-war period, education and training systems have been particularly efficient in providing people with the required standards in terms of knowledge and skills. University and government laboratories can therefore be considered an important source for companies' technological capabilities. These include not only knowledge production but also knowledge identification, application, absorption and diffusion. In this respect, 'education-led' and 'local networking-led' growth patterns can contribute to a shift towards international specialization, from standard products to much more sophisticated and specific products. This process has been characterized by a gradual movement towards products that are more technologically complex. Moreover, a specialization that is increasingly oriented towards innovative commodities has often been supported and associated, particularly in the cases of an economic success story, with long-term planning initiatives and public sector investments in the pre-competitive systems and network incentives.

Notes

1. Cooperation does not mean the abandonment of markets. As far as we know, in all economies the relationships between individuals, firms and organizations of all kinds occurs in a context of bounded rationality. Consequently, while the trade-off can be modelled as a zero-sum game, cooperation and trust are key factors in understanding the existence of solid continuous linkages between economic actors. Cooperation is a portrait of the learning ability of organizations in an economy. The objective of cooperation in economics is to diminish the effects of uncertainty produced by market failures and evolution of societies through time. In a sense, cooperation across networks enhances the capability of firms for economic competition, since it has a positive effect on their abilities to increase the stock of useful knowledge applied to production (Cimoli and de la Mothe, 2000).
2. There is a large literature on production linkages in the Mexican economy. Two forms of approach can be identified. Sectoral studies rest on field work, identifying the particular relationships between producers and suppliers, building up the net of interdependence and chains of activities. For example, studies of the motor car industry can be found in Lifschitz (1985) and Lifschitz and Zottele (1985), and for the whole economy in Cervini (1993). Using

input–output studies, linkage indexes can be constructed that order the extent of interdependence between producers. Generally these sort of indexes were constructed for sales (forward) or for supplies (backward), as in Ortiz (1990) and Capdevielle and Hernández Laos (1999). The observed trend shows a reduction of intra- and intersectoral linkages. See Chapters 4 and 5.

3. It has to be noted that here some assumptions are introduced in order to focus our attention on the interplay between NIS and performance; particularly, a given level of both employment and demand absorption of domestic market.

Bibliography

Aboites, J. and Soria M. (1997) *Innovacion, patentamiento y estrategias tecnologicas. El caso de México* (Mexico City: Ed. Porrua).

Abramovitz, M. (1989) *Thinking About Growth* (Cambridge: Cambridge University Press).

Abramovitz, M. (1994) 'The Origins of the Postwar Catch-up and Covergence Boom', in J. Fagerberg, N. von Tunzelman and B. Verspagen (eds), *The Dynamics of Technology, Trade and Growth* (Aldershot: Edward Elgar).

ACS (1996) *Technology Vision 2020: The US Chemical Industry* (Washington, DC: American Chemical Association).

Acs, Z. and de la Mothe, J. (2000) 'Knowledge and Smart Holes', in Z. Acs (ed.), *Regional Innovation and Global Change* (London: Pinter).

Aghion, P. and Howitt, P. (1989) 'A Model of Growth through Creative Destruction', mimeo, Massachusetts Institute of Technology.

Amsden, A. (1989) *Asia's Next Giant: South Korea and the Last Industrialization* (Oxford: Oxford University Press).

ANUIES (1996) *Vinculación entre los sectores académico y productivo en México y Estados Unidos. Católogo de casos* (Mexico City: Asociación Nacional de Universidades e Instituciones de Educación Superior).

ANUIES (1997) *Vinculación academia-empresa* (Mexico City: Asociación Nacional de Universidades e Instituciones de Educación Superior).

ANUIES (n.d.) *Anuarios estadísticos de licenciatura y posgrado 1985 a 1995* (Mexico City: Asociación Nacional de Universidades e Instituciones de Educación Superior).

Arechiga, H. (1989) 'Evaluación del posgrado en biotecnología', in CONACYT, *Evolución del Posgrado Nacional. Análisis y Perspectivas*, Special Issue of *Ciencia y Desarrollo* (Mexico: Consejo Nacional de Ciencia y Tecnología).

Arteaga, A. and Micheli, J. (1997) 'Trabajo y Tecnologia en Mexico: Indicadores de la Restructuracion del Aparato Manufacturero', mimeo, UAM, Mexico City.

Arvanitis, R. (1998) 'The Chemical Industry: Learning and Competitiveness', in S. Lall (ed.), *Science and Technology Policies in Developing and Transition Countries: Reform and Technological Co-operation with Europe* (Brussels: DG-XII, European Union).

Arvanitis, R. and Mercado, A. (1996) 'Los retos para la I&D en la industria química de América Latina', in A. Pirela (ed.), *Cultura empresarial en Venezuela: la industria química y petroquímica*, (Caracas, Fundación Polar/CENDES).

Arvanitis, R., Russell, J. and Rosas, A. (1995) 'La producción científica de México en química vista a través de la literatura internacional', paper presented to the conference 'La química desde Lavoisier', Universidad Autónoma Metropolitana.

Arvanitis, R., Russell, J. and Rosas, A. (1996) 'Experiences with the National Citation Reports Database for Measuring National Performance: The Case of Mexico', *Scientometrics*, **35** (2), pp. 247–55.

Arvanitis, R. and Villavicencio, D. (1998) 'Technological Learning and Innovation in the Mexican Chemical Industry: An Exercise in Taxonomy', *Science, Technology, and Society*, **3** (2), pp. 153–80.

Aspe, Armella P. (1993) 'El camino mexicano de la transformación económica', Fondo de Cultura Economica, Mexico.

Baily, M. and Chakrabarti, A. (1985) 'Innovation and Productivity in US Industry', *Brookings Papers on Economic Activity*, **2**, pp. 609–32.

Bancomext (1997a) *Catálogo de productos y servicios 1997*, (Mexico City: Banco de Comercio Exterior).

Bancomext (1997b) *Programa de Apoyo Integral 1997*, (Mexico City: Banco de Comercio Exterior).

Bardhan, P. (1996) 'The Political Economy of Development Policy: An Asian Perspective', Paper presented to the 'Development Thinking and Practice' conference, 3–5 September, Washington, DC.

Barro, R. (1989) 'A Cross-country Study of Growth, Saving, and Government', NBER working paper 2855.

Basberg, B. (1987) 'Patents and the Measurement of Technological Change: A Survey of the Literature', *Research Policy*, **12** (2), pp. 131–43.

Baudry, B. (1995) *L'économie des relations interentreprises*. (Paris: La Decouvertex).

Bazúa, F. (1997) 'Estado, mercado e interés público en la educación superior', in A. Mungaray and G. Valenti (eds), *Politicas Públicas y Educación Superior* (Mexico City: ANUIES).

Bazúa, F. and Valenti, G. (1991) 'La educación superior en el México de fin de siglo: cinco problemas y una política estratégica', *Argumentos*, December, pp. 51–71.

Bell, M. (1984) 'Learning and the Accumulation of Industrial Technological Capacity in Developing Countries', in K. King and M. Fransman (eds), *Technological Capacity in the Third World* (London: Macmillan).

Bell, M. and Pavitt, K. (1993a) 'Accumulating Technological Capability in Developing Countries', in L. H. Summers and S. Sahan (eds), *Proceedings of the World Bank Annual Conference on Development Economics*, supplement to the *World Bank Economic Review* and the *World Bank Research Observer* (Washington, DC: World Bank).

Bell, M. and Pavitt, K. (1993b) 'Technological Accumulation and Industrial Growth: Contrasts between Developed and Developing Countries', mimeo, SPRU, Sussex University.

Bell, M. and Pavitt, K. (1995) 'The Development of Technological Capabilities', in I. Haque (ed.), *Trade, Technology and International Competitiveness* (Washington, DC: The World Bank).

Bellardi, M. (1989) 'The Industrial District in Marshall', in E. Bamford (ed.), *Small Firms and Industrial Districts in Italy*, (London: Routledge).

Bianchi, P. (1997) *Construir el mercado, lecciones de la Unión Europea: el desarrollo de las instituciones y las politicos de competitividad*, (Buenos Aires: Universidad Nacional de Quilmes).

Blomstrom, M. (1991) 'Host Country Benefits of Foreign Investment', in D. McFetridge (ed.), *Foreign Investment, Technology and Economic Growth* (Calgary: University of Calgary Press).

Blomstrom, M. and Wolf E. (1989) 'Multinational Corporations and Productivity Convergence in Mexico', NBER working paper 3141.

Bosworth, D. (1981) 'Technological Manpower', in R. Lindley (ed.), *Higher Education and the Labour Market* (London: Direct Printers).

Bower and Whittaker (1993) 'Global R&D Networks: The Case of the Pharmaceutical Industry', *Journal of Industry Studies*, **1** (1), pp. 50–64.

Bracho, T. (1990) 'La concepción del nivel medio superior en la política educativa: problemas organizacionales y filosofía políticas del sistema', in T. Bracho (ed.), *La modernización educativa en perspectiva. Análisis del programa para la modernización educativa* (Mexico City: FLACSO).

Brainard, L. S. (1997) 'An Empirical Assessment of the Proximity–Concentration Trade-off between Multinational Sales and Trade', *American Economic Review*, **87** (4), pp. 520–44.

Brennan, J. *et al.* (1996) 'Students, Courses and Jobs: The Relationship between Higher Education and the Labour Market', Jessica Kingsley.

Breschi, S. and Malerba F. (1997), 'Sectoral Innovation Systems: Technological Regimes, Schumpeterian Dynamics, and Spatial Boundaries', in Ch. Edquist (ed.), *Systems of Innovation* (London and Washington, DC: Pinter).

Brodovsky, J. (1987) 'The Mexican Pharmochemical and Pharmaceutical Industries', in F. Thorup (ed.), *The United States and Mexico: Face to Face with New Technology*, US Third World Policy Perspectives no. 8, Overseas Development Council (Washington, DC: Transaction Books).

Brown, F. (1998) 'La producción de autopartes ante la restructuración de la industria automotriz', mimeo, Mexico City.

Brown, F. and Dominguez, L. (1999) 'Productividad: el desafío de la industria mexicana', mimeo, Mexico City.

Bruno, M. (1995). *Gestão da cooperação técnica entre empresas e estratégia empresarial: Estudos de caso no setor química*, (São Paulo: Universidad de São Paulo, Faculade de Economía, Adminstração e Contabilidade, Departamento de Administração).

Brusco, S. (1982) 'The Emilian Model: Productive Descentralization and Social Integration', *Cambridge Journal of Economics*, **6** (2) pp. 167–84.

Buckley, P. and Casson, M. (1997) 'An Economic Model of International Joint Venture Strategy', in P. Beamish and P. Killing (eds), *Cooperative Strategies* (Lexington, MA: Lexington Press).

Buendia, E. (1998) 'La relacion Proveedor – Ensamblador en la Indistria Automotriz en Mexico', thesis, UAM, Mexico City.

Bueno, C. (1996) 'Relaciones estrategicas comprador-abastecedor in la industria automotriz: una comparacion entre México y Japón', in J. Micheli (ed.), *Japan Inc. en México: Las empresas y modelos laborales japoneses* (Mexico City: UAM/Migel Angel Porrúa/ Universidad de Colima).

Buesa, M. and Molero, J. (1992) *Patrones del cambio tecnológico y politica industrial* (Madrid: Editorial Civitas).

Buffie, E. F. (1990) 'Economic Policy and Foreign Debt in Mexico', in J. Sachs (ed.), *Developing Country Debt and Economic Performance* (Chicago: University of Chicago Press).

Calvo, G. (1987) 'On the Costs of Temporary Policy', *Journal of Development Economics*, **27** (1–2), pp. 245–67.

Canifarma (1988) *La industria farmacéutica en Cifras 1978–1987* (Mexico City: Cámara Nacional de la Industria Farmacéutica).

Cantwell, J. (1989) *Technological Innovation and Multinational Corporations* (Oxford: Basil Blackwell).

Cantwell, J. (1991) 'The Theory of Technological Competence and Its Application to International Production', in D. G. McFetridge (ed.). *Foreign Investment, Technology and Growth* (Calgary: University of Calgary Press).

Cantwell, J. (1992) 'The Internalisation of Technological Activity and Its Implications for Competitiveness', in O. Granstrand, L. Hakanson and S. Sjolander (eds.), *Technology Management and International Business*, (Chichester: Wiley).

Cantwell, J. (1997) 'The Globalization of Technology: What Remains of the Product Cycle Model?', in D. Archibugi and J. Michie (eds), *Technology Globalization and Economic Performance* (Cambridge: Cambridge University Press).

Capdevielle, M. Cimoli, M. and Dutrénit, G. (1997) 'Specialisation and Technology in Mexico: A Virtual Pattern of Specialisation', 1R 97–016, IIASA, working paper.

Capdevielle, M. and Dutrénit, G. (1995) 'Competitividad, dinamismo y patrón tecnológico de las exportaciones manufactureras mexicanas en los ochenta', in E. Soto (ed.), *Globalización, economía y proyecto neoliberal en México* (Mexico City: UAM-GRESAL).

Capdevielle, M. and Hernandez Láos, E. (1999) *Patrones de especialización, el comportamiento de los agentes. El desarrollo de capacidades tecno-productivas; Una evaluación desde la perspectiva evolutiva de los efectos de la apertura en la industrialización Latinoaméricana. El caso de México* (Mexico City: Cap. 6).

Capdevielle, M., Molina, T. and Rosado, G. (1999) 'Especialización productiva y comercio internacional en la industria manufacturera mexicana', in J. Flores (ed.), *Globalización, estado y actores sociales en México*, (Mexico City: UAM-Xochimilco).

Carlsson, B. and Stankiewicz, R. (1995), 'On the Nature, Function and Composition of Technological Systems', in B. Carlson (ed.), *Technological Systems and Economic Performance: The Case of Factory Automation* (Dordrecht: Kluwer).

Carrillo, J. (1993) *La Ford en México: Restructuración Industrial y Cambio en las Relaciones Sociales*, thesis, El Colegio de México, Mexico.

Carrillo, J. (1995) *La Ford en México: Reestructuración Industrial y Cambio en las Relaciones Sociales*, thesis, El Colegio de México, Mexico.

Carrillo, J. and Hualde, A. (1996) 'Maquiladoras de Tercera Generación: El caso de Delphi-General Motors', *Espacios: Revista Venezolana de Gestión Tecnológica*, **17** (3), pp. 111–34.

Casalet, M. (1995) *Red de Apoyos públicos y privados hacia la competitividad de las Pymes* (Mexico City: Convenio NAFIN/Flacso).

Casar, J. (1993) 'Competitividad de la industria manufacturera mexicana 1980–1990', *El Trimestre Económico*, **60** (237), pp. 113–83.

Casar, J. (1994) 'El sector manifacturero y la cuenta corriente: evolucion reciente y perspectivas', in F. Clavijo and J. Casar (eds), *La industria mexicana en el mercado mundial. Elementos para una politica industrial* (Mexico City: Fondo de Cultura Economica).

Casar, J. (1996) 'Un balance de la transformación industrial en México', in J. Katz (ed.), *Estabilizacón macroeconómica, reforma estructural y comportamiento industrial* (Santiago de Chile and Buenos Aires: CEPAL/ADRC and Alianza Editorial).

Casar, J., Padilla, C., Marvan, S., Rodriguez, G. and Ros, J. (1990) *La organización industrial en Mexico* (Mexico City: Siglo XXI).

Casas, R. and De Gortari, R. (1997) La vinculación en la UNAM: Hacia una nueva cultura académica basada en la empresarialidad', in R. Casas and M. Luna (eds), *Gobierno, academia y empresas en México. Hacia una nueva configuración de relaciones* (Mexico City: IIS-UNAM/Plaza y Valdés).

Casas, R. and Luna, M. (1997a) 'Government, Academy and the Private Sector. Towards a New Configuration', *Science and Public Policy*, **24** (1), pp. 7–14.

Casas, R. and Luna, M. (eds) (1997b) *Gobierno, academia y empresas en México. Hacia una nueva configuración de relaciones*, (Mexico City: IIS-UNAM/Plaza y Valdés).

CEDECE (1998) 'La inversion extranjera en Aguascalientes 1980–1998', mimeo.

CEPAL (1995) *La industria farmacéutica y farmoquimica mexicana en el marco regulatorio de los años 1990* (Santiago de Chile: Comision Economica para America Latina y el Caribe).

CEPAL (1996) *Impacto del TLCAN en la pequeña y mediana empresa de la industria quimica en México* (Mexico City: Comisión Económica para America Latina y el Caribe, ONU).

Cervini, H. (1993) 'Cambios de las transacciones interindustriales en la economía de Mexico para el perfodo 1980–1990', *Análisis Económico*, **11** Enero–Junio, pp. 3–46.

Chakrabarti, A. K. (1990) 'Innovation and Productivity: An Analysis of the Chemical, Textiles and Machine Tool Industries in the US', *Research Policy* **19** (3), pp. 257–69.

Chesnais, F. (1988) 'Multinational Enterprises and the International Diffusion of Technology', in G. Dosi, C. Freeman, R. Nelson, G. Silberberg and L. Soete (eds), *Technical Change and Economic Theory* (London: Pinter).

Chesnais, F. (1995) 'Some Relationships Between Foreign Direct Investment, Technology, Trade and Competitiveness', in J. Hageddoorn (ed.), *Technical Change and the World Economy*, (London: Edward Elgar).

Chi-Ming Hou and San Gee (1993) 'National Systems Supporting Technical Advance in Industry: The Case of Taiwan', in R. Nelson (ed.), *National Innovation Systems. A Comparative Analysis* (New York: Oxford University Press).

Ciborra, C. (1991) 'Alliances as Learning Experiments: Cooperation and Change in High Tech Industries', in J. M. Mytelka (ed.), *Strategic Partnerships: States, Firms and International Competition* (London: Pinter).

Cimoli, M. (1988) 'Industrial Structures, Technical Change and the Modes of Regulation in the Labour Market', DRC discussion paper 60, SPRU, University of Sussex.

Cimoli, M. (1998) 'National Systems of Innovation: A Note on Technological Asymmetries and Catching-up Perspective', IR 98–030, ITASA, working paper.

Cimoli, M. (2000) 'Liberalisation Policies and Competitiveness in Mexico: Are Technological Capabilities Upgraded or Downgraded?' in M. Puchet and L. Punzo (eds), *Mexico beyond NAFTA Perspectives by the European Debates'* (London: Routledge).

Cimoli, M., Cingano, F. and della Giusta, M. (1998) 'Modes of Industrial Development, S&T Policies and Competitiveness in Mexico', in S. Lall (eds), *Science and Technology Policies in Developing and Transition Countries: Reform and Technological Co-operation with Europe* (Brussels: DG-XII, European Union).

Cimoli, M. and de la Mothe, J. (2000) 'The Governance of Technology and Development', in J. de la Mothe (ed.), *Science Technology and Governance* (London: Pinter).

Cimoli, M. and della Giusta, M. (2000) 'The Nature of Technical Change and Its Main Implication on National and Local Systems of Innovation', in D. Batten, C. S. Bertuglia, D. Martellato and S. Occelli (eds), *Learning, Innovation and Urban Development* (Boston: Kluwer).

Cimoli, M. and Dosi, G. (1995) 'Technological Paradigms, Patterns of Learning and Development: An Introductory Roadmap', *Journal of Evolutionary Economics*, **5** (3), pp. 242–68.

Cimoli, M., Dosi, G. and Soete, L. (1986) 'Innovation Diffusion Institutional Differences and Patterns of Trade: a North–South Model', DRC Paper no. 36 – SPRU, University of Sussex.

Cimoli, M. and Soete, L. (1992) 'A Generalized Technological Gap Trade Model', *Economie Appliquée*, **45**, pp. 33–54.

CIT-UNAM (1997) *Proyectos atendidos y convenios firinados por la Secretaría de Desarrollo Tecnológico y la Red de Nacleos de Innovación Tecnológica, 1983–1996*, February, Mexico.

Claessens, S., Oks, D. and van Wijnbergen, S. (1993) 'Interest Rates, Growth, and External Debate: The Macroeconomic Impact of Mexico's Brady Deal', World Bank Policy Research Working Papers 1147, Washington, DC.

Clavijo, F. (1980) 'Reflexiones en torno a la inflación mexicana, 1960–1980', *El Trimestre Económico*, **47** (188), pp. 1023–54.

Cline, D. (1995) *International Debt Reexamined* (Washington, DC: Institute for International Studies).

Coe, D. and Helpman, E. (1995) 'International R&D Spillovers', *European Economic Review*, **39** (5), pp. 859–87.

Coe, D., Helpman, E. and Hoffmaister, A. (1997) 'North–South R&D Spillovers', *Economic Journal*, **107** (440), pp. 134–49.

Cohen, D. (1993) 'Low Investment and Large LDC Debt in the 1980s', *American Economic Review*, **83** (3), pp. 437–49.

CONACYT web site: http://www.conacyt.main.conacyt.mx

CONACYT (1976) *Plan nacional indicativo de ciencia y tecnología* (Mexico City: Consejo Nacional de Ciencia y Tecnología).

CONACYT (1987/8) *Diagnóstico del posgrado, en ciencia y desarrollo* (Mexico City: Consejo Nacional de Ciencia y Tecnología).

CONACYT (1989) *Ciencia y Desarrollo*, Consejo Nacional de Ciencia y Tecnología, Mexico.

CONACYT (1994) *Programa de Apoyo a la Ciencia en México*, Consejo Nacional de Ciencia y Tecnología, Mexico.

CONACYT (1995) *Indicadores de actividades científicas y tecnológicas* (Mexico City: Consejo Nacional de Ciencia y Tecnología).

CONACYT (1996a) *Resumen de actividades 1991–1996* (Mexico City: Consejo Nacional de Ciencia y Tecnología).

CONACYT (1996b) *Indicadores de actividades cientificas y tecnológicas* (Mexico City: Consejo Nacional de Ciencia y Tecnología).

CONACYT (1997a) *Encuesta de cambio organizacional* (Mexico City: Consejo Nacional de Ciencia y Tecnología).

CONACYT (1997b) 'Encuesta de intercambio tecnológico', mimeo, Consejo Nacional de Ciencia y Tecnología, Mexico City.

CONACYT (1997c) *Indicadores de actividades cientificas y tecnológicas, México* (Mexico City: Consejo Nacional de Ciencia y Tecnología).

CONACYT (1997d) *Trabajos Publicados por Científicos e Ingenieros Mexicanos*. Internal Document, Dirección Adjunta de Política Científica y Tecnológica, CONACYT.

CONACYT, SECOFI and Banco de México (1997) 'Comercio de Bienes de Alta Tecnología', mimeo.

CONALEP (1994) *Comparación de oferta educativa tecnológica del nivel medio superior (resultados nacionales)* (Mexico City: CONALEP).

Cooke, P. and Morgan, K. (1994) 'The Regional Innovation System of Baden Württemberg', *International Jornal of Technology Management*, **9** (3–4), pp. 90–112.

Cooke, P., Uranga, M. and Etxebarria, G. (1998) 'Regional Systems of Innovation: An Evolutionary Perspective', *Environment and Planning*, **30**, pp. 1563–84.

Coriat, B. and Dosi, G. (1998) 'Learning How to Govern and Learning How to Solve Problems', in A. Chandler, P. Hagström and Ö. Sölvell (eds), *The Dynamic Firm* (Oxford: Oxford University Press).

Coriat, B. and Taddei, D. (1994) *Made in France* (Paris: Livre de Poche).

Corona, J. M. (1998) 'Competitiveness and Dynamics of the Textile Sector', in S. Lall (ed.), *Science and Technology Policies in Developing and Transition Countries: Reform and Technological Cooperation with Europe* (Brussels: DG-XII, European Union).

Corona, L. (ed.) (1997) *Cien Empresas Innovadoras en Mexico* (Mexico City: Porijia Ed./ UNAM).

Cressan, G. (1997) *Evaluation d'un investtissement dans un environnement incertain. Etude d'un project industriel au Mexique* (Rennes: University of Rennes).

Cruz, J. G. (1974) 'Industrializacion y desarrollo economico del estado de Aguascalientes', thesis, Universidad Nacional Autonoma de Mexico, Mexico City.

Dahmen, E. (1989) 'Development Blocks in Industrial Economics', in B. Carlson (ed.), *Industrial Dynamics*, (The Netherlands: Kluwer Academic Publishers).

David, P. (1994) 'Why Are Institutions the Carriers of History? Path Dependence and the

Evolution of Conventions, Organizations and Institutions', *Structural Change and Economic Dynamics*, **5** (2), pp. 207–20.

De Bresson, C. and Amesse, F. (1991) 'Networks of Innovation: A Review and Introduction to the Issues', *Research Policy*, **20**.

De la Garza, M. (1994) 'El problema de integración y eslabonamientos de la industria mexicana', in A. Argtiello and J. A. Gómez (eds), *La competitividad de la industria mexicana frente a la concurrencia internacional* (Mexico City: FCE-NAFIN).

de la Mothe, J. and Paquet, G. (1996) *Evolutionary Economics and the New International Political Economy* (London: Pinter).

de la Mothe, J. and Paquet, G. (1998) *Local and Regional Systems of Innovation* (Boston: Kluwer).

De Maria y Campos, M. and Sercovich, S. (1998) 'Hacia una nueva visión de la politica de desarrollo industrial y competitividad', *El Mercado de Valores*, Enero, pp. 3–21.

Dini, M. and Katz, J. (1997) 'Nuevas formas de encarar la politica tecnológica: el caso de Chile', *Comercio Exterior*, **47** (8) pp. 607–25.

Ditac (1995) *Compendia de Tecnología sobre Fabricación de Envases de Vidrio a Través de Patentes Norteamericanas, 1970–1995* (Monterrey: Vitro SA).

Dodgson, M. (1993) 'Organizational Learning: A Review of Some Literatures', *Organizational Studies*, **14** (3), pp. 375–94.

Doern, G. B. (1999) *Global Change and Intellectual Property Agencies* (London: Pinter).

Domínguez, L. and Brown, F. (1996) *La naturaleza micro y macroeconómica del cambio técnico: El caso de la industria de autopartes* (Mexico City: UNAM).

Dosi, G. (1984) *Technical Change and Industrial Transformation* (London: Macmillan).

Dosi, G. (1988a) 'Sources, Procedures, and Microeconomic Effects of Innovation', *Journal of Economic Literature*, **6**, pp. 1120–71.

Dosi, G. (1988b) 'The Nature of the Innovative Process', in G. Dosi, C. Freeman, R. Nelson, G. Silverberg and L. Soete (eds), *Technical Change and Economic Theory* (London: Pinter).

Dosi, G., Freeman, C., Nelson, R., Silverberg, G. and Soete, L. (eds) (1988) *Technical Change and Economic Theory* (London: Pinter).

Dosi, G., Marsili, O., Orsenigo, L. and Salvatore, R. (1993) 'Learning, Market Selection and the Evolution of Industrial Structures', HASA working paper.

Dosi, G. and Nelson, R. (1993) 'Evolutionary Theories in Economics: Assessment and Prospects', in *Market and Organisation: The Competitive Firm and Its Environment* (Nice: LATAPSES).

Dosi, G., Nelson, R. and Winter, S. (eds) (2000) *The Nature and Dynamics of Organizational Capabilities* (Oxford and New York: Oxford University Press).

Dosi, G., Pavitt, K. and Soete, L. (1990) *The Economics of Technical Change and International Trade* (London: Harvester Wheatsheaf).

Dosi, G., Teece, D. and Winter, S. (1992) 'Toward a Theory of Corporate Coherence: Preliminary Remarks', in G. Dosi, R. Giannetti and P. A. Toninelli (eds), *Technology and Enterprise in a Historical Perspective* (Oxford: Clarendon Press).

Dunning, J. H. (1981) *International Production and the Multinational Enterprise* (London: George Allen & Unwin).

Dussel, P. (1996) 'La industrializacion orientada hacia las importaciones. Teoria y evolucion del cambio estructural de la manifactura mexicana', unpublished, UNAM, Mexico.

Dutrénit, G. (1998) 'The Glass Container Industry', in S. Lall (ed.), *Science and Technology Policies in Developing and Transition Countries: Reform and Technological Cooperation with Europe* (Brussels: DG-XII, European Union).

Dutrénit, G. (2000), *Learning and Knowledge Management in the Firm: From Knowledge Accumulation to Strategic Capabilities* (Aldershot: Edward Elgar).

Dutrénit, G. and Capdevielle, M. (1993) 'El perfil tecnológico de la industria mexicana y su dinámica innovativa en la década de los ochentas, *El Trimestre Económico*, **239**, pp. 643–64.

Eaton, B. C., Lipsey, R. and Safarian, A. E. (1994) 'The Theory of Multinational Plant Location: Agglomerations and Disagglomerations', in L. Eden (ed.), *Multinationals in North America* (Calgary: University of Calgary Press).

Edquist, Ch. (ed.) (1997) *Systems of Innovation: Technologies, Institutions and Organizations* (London: Pinter).

Edquist, Ch. and Lundvall, B. (1993) 'Comparing the Danish and Swedish Systems of Innovation', in R. Nelson (ed.), *National Innovation Systems. A Comparative Analysis* (Oxford: Oxford University Press).

Edwards, S. (1997) 'Productivity and Growth: What Do We Really Know?', NBER working paper 5978.

ENESTYC (1992) *Encuesta Nacional de Empleo, Salarios, Tecnología y Capacitación en el Sector Manufacturero*, Instituto nacional de Estadística, Geografía e Informática, Secretaría del Trabajo, INEGI, Mexico.

Enright, M. (1997) 'Regional Clusters and Firm Strategy', in A. Chandler *et al.* (eds), *The Dynamic Firm* (Oxford: Oxford University Press).

Etzkowitz, H. and Leydesdorff, L. (1997) *University and the Global Knowledge Economy* (London: Pinter).

Fagerberg, J. (1988) 'International Competitiveness', *Economic Journal*, **98**, pp. 355–74.

Fagerberg, J. (1995) 'Convergence or Divergence? The Impact of Technology on "Why Growth Rates Differ" ', *Journal of Evolutionary Economics*, **5** (3), pp. 269–84.

Feder, G. (1988) 'On Exports and Economic Growth', *Journal of Development Economics*, **12** (1–2), pp. 59–73.

Fernández, A. (1995) 'Deregulation as a Source of Growth in Mexico', in R. Dornbusch and S. Edwards (eds), *Reform, Recovery and Growth* (Chicago: University of Chicago Press).

Fernández, J. (1998) 'Macroeconomic Environment for Innovation', mimeo, CONACYT.

Ferraz, J., Kupfer, D. and Haguenauer, L. (1996) *Made in Brazil* (Rio de Janeiro: Editoria Campus).

Freeman, C. (1982) *The Economics of Industrial Innovation*, 2nd edn (London: Pinter).

Freeman, C. (1987) *Technology Policy and Economic Performance: Lessons from Japan* (London: Pinter).

Freeman, C. (1991) 'Networks of Innovation: a Review and Introduction to the Issues', *Research Policy*, **20** (5), pp. 499–514.

Freeman, C. and Hagedoorn, J. (1995) 'Convergence and Divergence in the Internalization', in J. Hageddoorn (ed.), *Technical Change and the World Economy* (Cheltenham: Edward Elgar).

García, A. and Lara, A. (1997). 'Cambio tecnológico y aprendizaje laboral en General Motors', paper presented to international research conference 'Working Lean: Labor in the North American Auto Industry', Puebla, Mexico, 28–30 April.

Garrido, C. (1995) *Historia evolutiva y estrategias de siete grupos economicos en Mexico, documento de investigacion, Unidad de Desarrollo Industrial y Tecnologico* (Santiago de Chile: CEPAL).

Garrido, C. (1998a) *El liderazgo de los grupos industriales en Mexico en grandes empresas y grupos industriales latinoamericanos* (Santiago de Chile: CEPAL-Siglo XXI).

Garrido, C. (1998b) 'Ajuste estructural y cambio emresarial en Mexico. Configuracion, desempeiio y tendencias del liderazgo de los grupos economicos nacionales', mimeo, UAM-A.

Garrido, C. and Péres, W. (1998) 'Las grandes empresas y grupos industriales latinoamericanos en los años noventa', in W. Péres (ed.), *Grandes empresas y grupos industriales latinoamericanos* (Mexico City: Siglo XXI).

GATT (1994) *Acuerdo sobre Aspectos de los Derechos de Propiedad Intelectual Relacionados con el Comercio*, Acuerdos Sobre Comercio y mercancia del GATT, Ronda de Uruguay.

Gibbons, M., Limoges, C., Nowotny, H., Schwartzman, S., Scott, P. and Trow, M. (1994) *The New Production of Knowledge. The Dynamics of Science and Research in Contemporary Societies* (Thousand Oaks, CA: Sage).

Gomulka, S. (1971), *Inventive Activity, Diffusion and the Stages of Economic Growth* (Aarhus: Skrifter fra Aarthus Universtets Ökonomisske Institut 24).

Gonsen, R. (1998) *Technological Capabilities in Developing Countries. Industrial Biotechnology in Mexico* (London: Macmillan).

Gould, B. G. (1997) *Una reflexión sobre la planeación y operación de programas de vinculación* (Mexico City: UABH/ANUIES, Colección Biblioteca de la Educación Superior).

Granovetter, M. (1985) 'Economic Action and Social Structure: The Problem of Embeddedness', *American Journal of Sociology*, **91**, pp. 481–510.

Greenaway, D., Morgan, W. and Wright, P. (1988) 'Trade Reform, Adjustment and Growth: What Does the Evidence Tell Us?', *Economic Journal*, **108** (450), pp. 1547–61.

Grossman, G. and Helpman, E. (1989) 'Product Development and International Trade', *Journal of Political Economy*, **97** (6), pp. 1261–83.

Grupo Financiero Bancomer (1995) 'La industria Mexicana de Envases de Vidrio,' Analisis Sectorial, Mexico City.

Guerrieri, P. (1993) 'International Competitiveness, Trade Integration and Technological Interdependence in Major L.A. Countries', presented at the 9th Scientific Conference, 30 Sept.–1 Oct., Milan.

Guevara Niebla, G. (1992) 'México: ¿Un pais de reprobados?', *Nexos*, **162**, pp. 33–44.

Harrison, A. and Hanson, G. (1999) 'Who Gains from Trade Reform? Some Remaining Puzzles', NBER working paper 6915.

Hayward, S. (1997) 'A Political Economy Approach to Labour Markets in Knowledge-intensive Industries. The Case of Biotechnology', in M. Talay *et al.* (eds), *Technology, Culture and Competitiveness. Change and the World Political Economy* (London: Routledge).

Helpman, E. (1997) 'R&D and Productivity: The International Connection', NBER working paper 6101.

Hernández Laos, E. (1994a) *Diferenciales de productividad entre México, Canada y Estados Unidos* (Mexico City: Cuadernos del Trabajo 5, Secretaria de Trabajo y Previsión Social).

Hernández Laos, E. (1994b) *Tendencias de la productividad en México (1970–1991)* (Mexico City: Cuadernos del Trabajo 8, Secretaria de Trabajo y Previsión Social).

Hernández Laos, E. (1998) *Fuentes de las ventajas competitivas en la industria mexicana* (Bogotá: Colciencias).

Hernández Laos, E. and Ten Kate, A. (1998) 'México, fuentes de las ventajas competitivas en la industria', in *La industria de América Latina ante la globalización económica* (Bogotá: Colciencias).

Hernández Laos, E. and Velasco, R. (1990) 'Productividad y competitividad de las manufacturas mexicanas, 1960–1985', *Comercio Exterior*, **40** (6), pp. 658–66.

Hertog, P., Roelandt, T., Boekholt, P. and Van Der Gang, H. (1995) *Assessing the Distribution Power of National Innovation Systems* (Amsterdam: Apeldoorn).

Hilebrand, W., Messner, D. and Meyer-Stainer, J. (1994) *Fortalecimiento de la capacidad tecnológica en los paises de desarrollo* (Berlin: Instituto Alemán de Desarrollo).

Hirschman, A. (1977) 'Generalized Linkage Approach to Development, with Special Reference to Staples', in M. Nash (ed.), *Essays on Economic Development and Cultural Change in Honor of B. F. Hoselitz*, (Chicago: University of Chicago Press).

Hobday, M. (1995) *Innovation in East Asia. The Challenge to Japan* (Aldershot: Edward Elgar).

Hodgson, G. (1988) *Economics and Institutions* (Cambridge: Polity Press).

Hounshell, D. A. and Smith, P. A. (1988) *Science and Corporate Strategy: Du Pont R&D 1902–1980* (Cambridge: Cambridge University Press).

Humprey, J. (1995) 'Industrial Reorganization in Developing Countries: From Models to Trajectories', *World Development*, **23**, pp. 149–162.

Hunter, L. (1981) 'Employers' Perceptions of Demand', in R. Lindley (ed.), *Higher Education and the Labour Market* (London: Direct Printers).

Iansiti, M. and Clark, K. (1994) 'Integration and Dynamic Capability: Evidence from Product Development in Automobiles and Mainframe Computers', *Industrial and Corporate Change*, **3** (3), pp. 557–605.

Ibarra, L. A. (1995) 'Credibility of Trade Policy Reform and Investment: The Mexican Experience', *Journal of Development Economics*, **47** (1), pp. 39–60.

IIS-UNAM (1985–94) *Base de datos de empresas vinculadas con la UNAM, la UAU y otros* (Mexico City: Instituto de Investigaciones Sociales, UNAM).

IMPI (1992) *Banco de datos de patentes 1980–1992 (BANAPA)* (Mexico City: Instituto Mexicano de Propiedad industrial (IMPI), CD-ROM).

INEGI (1970–93) *Sistema de cuentas nacionales* (Mexico City: Instituto Nacional de Estadística, Geografía e Informática).

INEGI (1970–94) *Censos industriales* (Mexico City: Instituto Nacional de Estadística, Geografía e Informática).

INEGI (1989) *XIII censo industrial 1988* (Mexico City: Instituto Nacional de Estadística, Geografía e Informática).

INEGI (1993) *Los profesionistas en México. XI censo general de población y vivienda* (Mexico City: Instituto Nacional de Estadística, Geografía e Informática).

INEGI (1994a) *La industria química en México* (Mexico City: Instituto Nacional de Estadística, Geografía e Informática).

INEGI (1994b) *XIV censo industrial 1993* (Mexico City: Instituto Nacional de Estadística, Geografía e Informática).

INEGI (annual) *National Accounts System* (Mexico City: Instituto Nacional de Estadística, Geografía e Informática).

INEGI/ST (1992) *Encuesta nacional de empleo, salarios, tecnología y capacitación en el sector manufacturero* (ENESTYC) (Mexico City: Instituto Nacional de Estadística, Geografía e Informática, Secretaria del Trabajo).

Instituto Mexicano de Ejecutivos en Finanzas (1995) *La competitividad de la empresa mexicana* (Mexico City: NAFIN).

IPN (1996a) *Oferta institucional sobre servicios externos y desarrollos tecnológicos (Preliminary Results)*. Dirección de Vinculación Académica y Tecnológica, IPN, April.

IPN (1996b) *Encuesta para determinar la oferta de servicios tecnologicos efectuada a instituciones de educación superior y centros de servicios e investigación tecnológica del pais*. Dirección de Estudios de Posgrado e Investigación, IPN, November.

ITESM (1993) *El cumplimiento de la misión del ITESM a través de sus egresados* (Monterrey: Instituto Tecnológico de Estudios Superiores de Monterrey).

Johnson, B. and Lundvall, B. (1994) 'Sistemas nacionales de innovación y aprendizaje institucional', *Comercio Exterior*, **44** (8), pp. 695–704.

Jones, D. and Womack, J. (1985) 'Developing Countries and the Future of the Automobile Industry', *World Development*, **13** (3), pp. 393–407.

Juárez, N. (1997) 'La productividad y el trabajo en el contexto de la producción esbelta en VW de México', paper presented to the international research conference 'Working Lean: Labor in the North American Auto Industry', Puebla, México, 28–30 April.

Katz, J. (1984) 'Latin American Metalworking Industries', in M. Fransman and K. King (eds), *Technological Capability in the Third World* (London: Macmillan).

Katz, J. (ed.) (1986) *Desarrollo y crisis de la capacidad tecnológica latinoamericana* (Buenos Aires: BID-CEPAL-CIID-PNUD).

Katz, J. (ed.) (1987) *Technology Generation in Latin American Manufacturing Industries* (London: Macmillan).

Katz, J. (1995) 'Technology and Industrial Restructuring in Latin America: The New Evidence', paper presented at the conference 'Transfer of Technology: Trade and Development', University of Venice.

Katz, J. (1997a) 'Structural Reforms, the Sources and Nature of Technical Change and the Functioning of the National Systems of Innovation: The Case of Latin America', paper presented at the international symposium 'On Innovation and Competitiveness in NIEs', Seoul, May.

Katz, J. (1997b) *The Dynamics of Technological Learning During the ISI Period and Recent Structural Changes in the Industrial Sector of Argentina, Brazil and Mexico* (Santiago de Chile: CEPAL).

Katz, J. (2000) 'Structural Reforms, the Sources and Nature of Technical Change and the Functioning of the National Systems of Innovation: The Case of Latin America', in D. Nelson and L. Kim (eds), *Systems of Innovation* (Oxford: Oxford University Press).

Keller, W. (1997) 'Trade and the Transmission of Technology', NBER working paper 6113.

Kent, R. (1998) 'El financiamiento público de la educación superior en México: la evolución de los modelos de asignación financiera en una generación', in *Tres décadas de politicas de estado en la educación superior* (Mexico City: ANUIES).

Kessel, G. and Samaniego, R. (1995) 'Apertura comercial, productividad y desarrollo tecnológico. El caso de México', BID, Serie de Documents de Trabajo, no. 112, Washington, DC.

Kim, L. (1993) 'National System of Industrial Innovation: Dynamics of Capability Building in Korea', in R. Nelson (ed.), *National Innovation System* (Oxford: Oxford University Press).

Kim, L. (1995) 'Crisis Construction and Organizational Learning: Capability Building in Catching-up at Hyundai Motor', report, October, College of Business Administration, Korea University, Seoul.

Kim, L. (1997a) 'Korea's National Innovation System in Transition', paper presented at the international symposium 'On Innovation and Competitiveness in NIEs', Seoul, May.

Kim, L. (1997b) *From Imitation to Innovation. The Dynamics of Korea's Technological Learning* (Cambridge, MA: Harvard Business School Press).

Kim, L. (1999) *Learning and Innovation in Economic Development* (Cheltenham: Edward Elgar).

Kluth, M. and Andersen, J. (1995) 'Pooling the Technology Base: The Globalisation of European Research and Technology Organisations (RTOs)', paper presented to the 'Euroconference on the Globalisation of Technology', Cambridge.

Krugman, P. (1987) 'The Narrow Moving Band, the Dutch Disease and the Competitive Consequences of Mrs Thatcher', *Journal of Development Economics*, **27**, pp. 41–55.

Krugman, P. (1988) Financing vs. Forgiving a Debt Overhang', *Journal of Development Economics*, **29** (31), pp. 253–68.

Lall, S. (1987) *Learning to Industrialize: The Acquisition of Technological Capability by India* (London: Macmillan Press).

Lall, S. (1992) 'Technological Capabilities and Industrialisation', *World Development*, **20** (2), pp. 165–86.

Lall, S. (1996) 'Las capacidaes tecnológicas', in J. J. Salomn *et al.* (eds), *Una búsqueda incierta. Ciencia, tecnología y desarrollo* (Mexico City: FCE-CIDE-LTNU).

Lall, S. (1997) 'Technological Change and Industrialisation in the Asian NIBs: Achivements and Challenges', paper presented at the international symposium 'On Innovation and Competitiveness in NIEs', Seoul, May.

Laming, R. (1989) 'Research and Development in the Automotive Components Suppliers of New Entrant Countries: The Prospects for Mexico', Acapulco, IMVP International Policy Forum, mimeo.

Landes, D. (1970) *The Unbound Prometheus* (Cambridge: Cambridge University Press).

Lara, A. (1998) 'NAFTA, Technological Regionalisation and Specialisation in the Consumer Electronics-TV Sector', in S. Lall (ed.), *Science and Technology Policies in Developing and Transition Countries: Reform and Technological Co-operation with Europe* (Brussels: DG-XII, European Union).

Lara, A. and Corona, J. M. (1997a) 'Intercambio de información tecnológica entre industrias de automotores y autopartes', *Comercio Exterior*, **47** (2), pp. 90–103.

Lara, A. and Corona, J. M. (1997b) 'The Car Industry, NAFTA and Technological Specialisation', in *Science and Technology Polices in Developing Countries: The Case of Mexico* (Venice: University of Venice and Universidad Autónoma Metropolitana-Xochimilco).

Lara, A. and Corona, J. M. (1998) 'Automotive Industry, NAFTA and Technological Specialisation', in S. Lall (ed.), *Science and Technology Policies in Developing and Transition Countries: Reform and Technological Co-operation with Europe* (Brussels: DG-XII, European Union).

Laursen, K. and Lindgaard, Ch. (1996) *The Creation, Distribution and Use of Knowledge. A Pilot Study of the Danish Innovation System* (Copenhagen: Danish Agency for Trade and Industry, Ministry of Business and Industry).

Lee Young Won (1997) 'The Role of Science and Technology Policy in Korea's Industrial Development', paper presented at Science and Technology Policy Institute, international symposium on 'Innovation and Competitiveness in Newly Industrializing Economies'.

Leonard-Barton, D. (1992) 'Core Capabilities and Core Rigidities: A Paradox in Managing New Product Development', *Strategic Management Journal*, **13**, pp. 111–25.

Leonard-Barton, D. (1995) *Wellsprings of Knowledge* (Cambridge, MA: Harvard Business School Press).

Levine, R. and Renelt, D. (1992) 'A Sensitivity Analysis of Cross-country Growth Regressions', *American Economic Review*, **82** (4), pp. 942–63.

Lifschitz, E. (1985) *El complejo automotor en México y America Latina* (Mexico City: Universidad Autónoma-México).

Lifschitz, E. and Zottele, A. (1985) *Eslabonamientos productivos y mercados oligopólicos* (Mexico City: Universidad Autónoma Metropolitana-Azcapotzalco).

Luna, M. and Valdivieso, S. (n.d.) 'La eficiencia productiva del sector manufacturero', mimeo.

Lundvall, B.-A. (1988) 'Innovation as an interactive process: from user–producer interaction to the national system of innovation', in G. Dosi *et al.* (eds), *Technical Change and Economic Theory* (New York: Columbia University Press).

Lundvall, B.-A. (ed.) (1993) *National Systems of Innovation: Towards a Theory of Innovation and Interactive Learning* (London: Pinter).

Lustig, N. (1992) *Mexico. The Remaking of an Economy* (Washington, DC: The Brookings Institution).

Lustig, N., del Rio, F., Franco, O. and Martina, E. (1989) *Evolución del gasto pablico en ciencia y tecnología 1980–1987* (Mexico City: Academia de la Investigación Científica).

Maddison, A. (1991) *Dynamics Forces in Capitalist Development* (New York: Oxford University Press).

Maklund Gorran TekPol Analys Nutek (1997) *A Quantitative Study of the Swedish Innovation System*, Preliminary Outline, Stockholm.

Malerba, F. and Orsenigo, L. (1996) 'The Dynamics and Evolution of Industries', *Industrial and Corporate Change*, **5** (1), pp. 51–88.

Mansfield, E. (1991) 'Academic Research and Industrial Innovation', *Research Policy*, **20**, pp. 1–12.

Marquez, T. (1982) *10 Años del Consejo Nacional de Ciencia y Tecnología* (Mexico City: CONACYT).

Mattar, J. (1996) 'Desempeño exportador y competitividad internacional: algunos ejercicios para Mexico', *Comercio Exterior*, **46** (3), pp. 193–202.

Mattar, J. and Schatan, C. (1993) 'El comercio intraindustrial e intrafirma México–Estados Unidos', *Comercio Exterior*, **43** (2), pp. 103–20.

Medina, F. (1986) *La propiedad industrial en la biotecnología y sus consecuencias para México. Un punto de vista independiente desde la perspectiva de la industria mexicana* (Mexico City: Estudio para la Organización Mundial de la Propiedad Intelectual (OMPI-ONU)).

Medina, F. (1989) 'Oportunidades de desarrollo en biotecnología', paper presented to the 'XXIV Convención Nacional: Contribución del Ingeniero Químico a la Reactivación del País', Instituto Mexicano de Ingenieros Químicos, Morelia, Michoacan, Mexico, 18–20 October.

Mercado, A. (1995) *Desarrollo tecnológico en la industria química fina del Brasil: Clasificación taxonómica y determinación de una secuencia evolutiva de su capacitación tecnológica* (Caracas: Fondo Editorial FINTEC).

Mercado, A. (1996) *Particularidades innovativas de los segmentos productivos. Cultura empresarial en Venezuela: la industria química y petroquímica* (Caracas: Fundación Polar/CENDES).

Metcalfe, S. (1995) 'The Economic Foundations of Technology Policy', in P. Stoneman (ed.), *Handbook of the Economics of Innovation and Technical Change* (Oxford: Blackwell).

Mexico businessline web site *http://mexico.businessline.gob.mex*

Micheli, J. (1995) *Nueva manufactura, globalización y producción de automóbiles en México* (Mexico City: FE-UNAM).

Misa, T. (1991) 'Constructive Technology Assessment: Cases, Concepts, Conceptualization', paper presented at the 'Conference on Constructive Technology Assessment', Enschede, The Netherlands, September.

Mogaud, J. (1968) 'L'équivalent travail d'une production', *Population*, **43**.

Moreno, B. (1994) 'La competitividad de la industria automotriz', in F. Clavijo and J. Casar (ed.), *La Industria Mexicana en el Mercado Mundial* (Mexico City: Fondo de Cultura Económica).

Muñoz Izquierdo, C. (1990) 'Relaciones entre la educación superior y el sistema productivo', *Revista de la Educación Superior*, **76**, pp. 193–230.

Muñoz Izquierdo, C. (1996) *Diferenciación institucional de la educación superior y mercados de trabajo* (Mexico City: ANUIES).

NAFIN web site *http://www.nafin.gob.mx*

NAFIN (1995) *Informe de actividades 1995* (Mexico City: NAFIN).

NAFIN (1996) *El mercado de valores, nos 5 and 6* (Mexico City: NAFIN).

NAFIN (1997) *Catálogo de productos y servicios 1997* (Mexico City: NAFIN).

NAFIN (1998a) *Desarrollo industrial y descentralización en el norte de México, no. 3* (Mexico City: NAFIN).

NAFIN (1998b) *Hacia una politica industrial de largo plazo, no. 1* (Mexico City: NAFIN).

NAFINSA-ONUDI (1985) *México: Los bienes de capital en la situación económica presente* (Mexico City: NAFINSA).

NEDC (1991) *New Life for Industry. Biotechnology, Industry and the Community in the 1990s and Beyond* (London: National Economic Development Council (NEDC)).

Nelson, R. (ed.) (1993) *National Innovation Systems. A Comparative Analysis* (Oxford: Oxford University Press).

Nelson, R. (1994) 'Economic Growth via the Coevolution of Technology and Institutions', in L. Leydesdorff and P. van den Besselaar (eds), *Evolutionary Economics and Chaos Theory* (London: Pinter).

Nelson, R. (1996) 'The Concept of Institution as an Attractor, Snare and Challenge', HASA, mimeo.

Nelson, R. (1998) 'The Agenda for Growth Theory: A Different Point of View', *Cambridge Journal of Economics*, **22**, pp. 497–520.

Nelson, R. and Pack, H. (1999) 'The Asian Miracle and Modern Growth Theory', *Economic Journal*, **109**, (457), pp. 416–36.

Nelson, R. and Rosenberg, N. (1993) 'Technical Innovation and National Systems', in R. Nelson (ed.), *National Innovation Systems. A Comparative Analysis* (Oxford: Oxford University Press).

Nelson, R. and Winter, S. G. (1982) *An Evolutionary Theory of Economic Change* (Cambridge, MA: Harvard University Press).

Nelson, R. and Wright, G. (1992) 'The Rise and Fall of American Technological Leadership: The Postwar Era in Historical Perspective', *Journal of Economic Lilterature*, **30** (4), pp. 1931–64.

Nichols, N. A. (1993) 'From Complacency to Competitiveness: An Interview with Vitro's Ernesto Martens', *Harvard Business Review*, **71** (5), pp. 163–8.

Nonaka, I. and Takeuchi, H. (1995) *The Knowledge-creating Company* (New York: Oxford University Press).

OECD (1992a) *La mondialisation industrielle. Quatre études de cas* (Paris: OECD).

OECD (1992b) *La technologie et l'économie. Les relations déterminantes* (Paris: OECD).

OECD (1994) *Reviews of National Science and Technology Policy. Mexico* (Paris: OECD).

OECD (1996a) *Natinal Innovation Systems: Report on Pilot Case Studies* (Paris: OECD).

OECD (1996b) *Technology and Industrial Performance* (Paris: OECD).

OECD (1996c) *Wheels of Change: The Automobile Industry* (Paris: OECD).

OECD (1997a) *Basic Indicators for Describing the Flow of Human Resources in Science and Technology (HRST)* (Paris: OECD).

OECD (1997b) *National Innovation Systems* (Paris: OECD).

OECD (1997c) *Main Science and Technology Indicators* (Paris: OECD).

OECD (1997d) *The Knowledge Based Economy* (Paris: OECD).

OECD (1997e) *Exámenes de las politicas nacionales de educación. México educación superior* (Paris: OECD).

Ornelas, C. (1995) *El sistema educativo mexicano. La transición de fin de siglo* (Mexico City: CIDE, NAFINsa and FCE).

Ortiz, E. (1990) 'Cambio estructural y coeficientes de eslabonamiento. El caso de la economia mexicana', *Economia: Teoria y Práctica*, **14** Invierno–Primavera, pp. 107–16.

Ortiz, E. (1994) *Competencia y crisis* (Mexico City: Siglo XXII).

Ortiz, E. (1998) 'Successful Integration and Economic Distress', in C. Paraskevopoulos (ed.), *Global Trading in Transition* (Aldershot: Edward Elgar).

Ortiz, E. and Sima, M. (1999) 'Successful Integration and Economic Distress: The New Dual Economy. The Case of Mexico in NAFTA', in K. Appendini and S. Bislev (eds), *Economic Integration in NAFTA and the EU* (Basingstoke: Macmillan).

OTA (1984) *Commercial Biotechnology: An International Analysis* (Washington, DC: US Congress, Office of Technology Assessment, OTA-BA-218).

Paredes Lopez, O., Gonzalez de Mejia, E. and Lecona, S. (1996) 'La importancia de la colaboración científica regional: el caso de PROPAC', *Boletin de la Academia de la Investigación Científica*, **30** (May/June).

Patel, P. and Pavitt, K. (1991) 'Large Firms in the Production of the World Technology: An Important Case of Non-globalization', *Journal of International Business Studies*, **22**, pp. 1–22.

Patel, P. and Pavitt, K. (1995a) 'Divergence in Technological Development among Countries and Firms', in J. Hagedoorn (ed.), *Technical Change and the World Economy: Convergence and Divergence in Technology Strategies* (Aldershot: Edward Elgar).

Patel, P. and Pavitt, K. (1995b) 'Patterns of Technological Activity: Their Measurement and Interpretation', in P. Stoneman (ed.), *Handbook of the Economics of Innovation and Technological Change* (Oxford: Blackwell).

Pavitt, K. (1984) 'Sectoral Patterns of Technical Change: Towards a Taxonomy and a Theory', *Research Policy*, **13**, pp. 343–75.

Pavitt, K. (1991) 'Key Characteristics of the Large Innovating Firms', *British Journal of Management*, **2**, pp. 41–50.

Peraso, F. (1992) 'Debt Reduction Versus "Appropriate" Domestic Policies', *Kyklos*, **45** (5), pp. 457–67.

Pereira, A. F. (1997) 'Improving Working Conditions in the Mexican Maquiladoras: The Role of Regional Economic Integration, Labour Standards and Industrial Relations', paper presented to the international research conference 'Working Lean: Labor in the North American Auto Industry', Puebla, Mexico, 28–30 April.

Péres, W. (1990) *Foreign Direct Investment and Industrial Development in Mexico* (Paris: OECD).

Péres, W. (ed.) (1997) *Políticas de Competitividad Industrial* (Mexico City: Siglo XXI).

Pérez, C. (1983) 'On the Nature of Technology', lecture given at the University of Sussex, 23 June.

Pérez, C. (1992) 'Cambio técnico, restructuración competitiva y reforma institucional en los paises en desarrollo', *El Trimestre Económico*, **59** (233), pp. 23–65.

Pérez, C. (1996) 'La modernización industrial en América Latina y la herencia de la sustitución de importaciones', *Comercio Exterior*, **46** (5), pp. 347–63.

PETAL (1990) *Preliminary Version of the Final Report* (Campinas, Brazil: Prospectiva Tecnológica para América Latina).

Planque, B. (1990) *Note sur la notion de réseau d'innovation* (Saint-Etienne: Colloque ASRDLF).

Porter, M. (1990) *The Competitive Advantage of Nations* (London: Macmillan).

Potshuma, A. (1997) 'The Brazilian Auto Components Industry at the Crossroads: Restructuring and De-nationalization of a Domestic Industry', mimeo.

Prahalad, C. K. and Hamel, G. (1990) 'The Core Competencies of the Corporation', *Harvard Business Review*, **68** (3), pp. 79–91.

Pyke, F., Becattini, G. and Sengenberger, W. (1990) *Industrial Districts and Inter-firm Co-operation in Italy* (Geneva: ILLS).

Quintero, R. (1985) 'Prospectiva de la Biotecnología en México', in R. Quintero (ed.), *Prospectiva de la Biotecnología en México* (Mexico City: Fundación Javier Barros Sierra AC, Consejo Nacional de Ciencia y Tecnología).

Quintero, R. (ed.) (1989) 'El programa de posgrado en alimentos', in *Evolución del Posgrado Nacional. Análisis y Perspectivas* (Mexico City: CONACYT).

Raghavan, C. (1990) *GATT, the Uruguay Round and the Third World* (London: Zed Books).

Ramirez, M. (1994) 'Public and Private Investment in Mexico, 1959–1990: An Empirical Analysis', *Southern Economic Journal*, July, pp. 1–17.

Ramírez-Sanchez, J. (1994) 'The New Location and Interaction Patterns of the Mexican Motor Industry', thesis, University of Sussex.

Reséndiz Núñez, D. (1998) 'Agenda mexicana para la educación superior', *Este Pais: Tendencias y Opciones*, **84**, pp. 16–21.

Richardson, G. B. (1972) 'The Organization of Industry', *Economic Journal*, **82** (327), pp. 883–97.

Rivera-Bátiz, L. A. and Romer, P. (1991) 'Economic Integration and Endogenous Growth', *Quarterly Journal of Economics*, **106** (2), pp. 531–55.

RNTT (1982–9) *Registro de contratos de transferencia tecnológica*, (Mexico City: Registro Nacional de Transferencia Tecnológica (RNTT), Dirección de Transferencia Tecnológica, Secretaría de Comercio y Fomento Industrial).

Robert, M. (1985) 'El cultivo de tejidos vegetales en México', in R. Quintero (ed.), *Prospectiva de la biotecnología en México*, (Mexico City: Fundación Javier Barros Sierra, AC, Consejo Nacional de Ciencia y Tecnología).

Rodrik, D. (1991) 'Policy Uncertainty and Private Investment in Development Countries', *Journal of Development Economics*, **36** (2), pp. 229–42.

Romer, P. (1993) 'Implementing a National Technology Strategy with Self-Organizing Industry Investment Boards', *Brooking Papers on Economic Activity*, **2**, pp. 345–90.

Rosenberg, N. and Nelson, R. R. (1994) 'American Universities and Technical Advance in Industry', *Research Policy*, **23**, pp. 323–48.

Ross, J. (1993) 'Mexico's Trade and Industrialization Experience since 1960: A Reconsideration of Past Policies and Assessment of Current Reforms', working paper, University of Notre Dame.

Sachs, J. (1988) 'Conditionality, Debt Relief, and the Developing Country Debt Crisis', NBER working paper 2644.

Samaniego, R. (1984) *The Evolution of Total Factor Productivity in the Manufacturing Sector in Mexico, 1963–1981*, (Mexico City: Serie Documentos de Trabajo, El Colegio de México).

Santos, A. (1999) 'La secundaria: perspectivas de su demanda', doctoral thesis, Mexico.

Saxenian, A. (1991) 'The Origins and Dynamics of Production Networks in Silicon Valley', *Research Policy*, **20** (5), pp. 423–38.

Saxenian, A. (1999) 'Regional Systems of Innovation and the Blurred Firm', in J. de la Motte and G. Pacquet (eds), *Local and Regional Systems of Innovation* (Boston: Kluwer).

Scherer, F. M. (1983) 'R&D and Declining Productivity', *American Economic Review*, **73** (2), 515–18.

Schmelkes, S. (1996). *La calidad de la educación primaria. El caso de puebla*, mimeo, Mexico City.

Scott, P. (1995) *The Meanings of Mass Higher Education* (Windsor: Society for Research into Higher Education and Open University Press).

SCRLP (1991) *Yearbook 1991* (London: PIB Publications).

SECOFI web site: *http:/www.secofi.gob.mx*

SECOFI (1993) 'Capitulo XVII sobre propiedad intelectual', *Tratado de libre comercio para America del Norte* (Mexico City: SECOFI).

SECOFI (1997a) 'Reforma de la lay de propiedad industrial', *Diario Oficial* (Mexico City: SECOFI).

SECOFI (1997b) *Boletín informativo de la red CETRO*, (Mexico City: SECOFI).

SECOFI (1997c), *Estadísticas de comercio exterior* (Mexico City: SECOFI).

SECOFI (1997d) *Empresas integradoras, fortaleza para competir* (Mexico City: SECOFI).

SEP (1989) *Programa de modernización educativa 1989–1994* (Mexico City: SEP).

SEP (1992) *Evaluación de la educación superior tecnológica. Informe de resultados*. (Mexico City: SEP).

Sercovich, F. and Leopold, M. (1991) *Developing Countries and the New Biotechnology. Market Entry and Industrial Policy*, IDRC-MR279e (International Development Research Centre), Ottawa.

Sharp, M. (1996) 'The Science of Nations: European Multinationals and American Biotechnology', STEEP discussion paper 28, SPRU, February.

Sharp, M. (1991) 'Pharmaceutical and Biotechnology: Perspectives for the European Industry', in Ch. Freeman, M. Sharp and W. Walker (eds), *Technology and the Future of Europe. Global Competition and the Environment in the 1990s*, (London: Pinter).

Silverman, M., Lydecker, M. and Lee, P. (1992) *Bad Medicine: The Prescription Drug Industry in the Third World* (Stanford, CA: Stanford University Press).

Sobarzo Fimbres, H.E. (1997) 'Cambio tecnológico y perfil de la mano de obra en el sector manufacturero en México', in *Cuadernos del trabajo 11* (Mexico City: Secretaria de Trabajo y Previsión Social).

Soete, L. and Verspagen, B. (1992) 'Competing for Growth: The Dynamics of Technology Gaps. Convergence and Innovation', paper presented at the Conference on 'Economic Growth and the Structure of Long-term Development', Varenna, 1–3 October.

Solis, L. (1981) *Economic Policy Reform in Mexico: A Case Study for Developing Countries*, (New York: Pergamon Press).

Solow, R. M. (1956) 'A Contribution to the Theory of Economic Growth', *Quarterly Journal of Economics*, **70** (1), pp. 65–94.

SPRU (1996) *The Relationship between Publicly Funded Basic Research and Economic Performance*, Report prepared for HM Treasury, SPRU, University of Sussex.

Storper, M. (1997) *The Regional World: Territorial Development in a Global Economy* (New York: Guilford Press).

STPS (1992) *Encuesta nacional de empleo, salarios, tecnologia y capacitación en el sector manufacturero* (Mexico City: Secretaria del Trabajo y Prevision Social/INEGI).

STPS (1995) *Encuesta nacional de empleo, salarios, tecnologia y capacitacion en el sector manufacturero* (Mexico City: Secretaria del Trabajo y Prevision Social/INEGI).

Teece, D. and Pisano, G. (1994), 'The Dynamic Capabilities of Firms: an Introduction', *Industrial and Corporate Change*, Vol. **3** (3), pp. 537–56.

Teece, J. and Bennet, Z. (1997), 'Contracts, Firm Capabilities, and Economic Development: Implications for NIEs', presented at the seminar: *Innovation and Competitiveness in Newly Industrializing Economies* Seoul, 26 May.

Teitel, S. (1984) 'Technology Creation in Semi-industrial Economies', *Journal of Development Economics*, **16**, pp. 39–61.

Ten Kate, A. and De Mateo, F. (1989) 'Apertura comercial y estructura de la protección en México: Estimaciones cuantitativas de los ochenta', *Comercio Exterior*, **39** (6), pp. 497–512.

Ten Kate, A. and Wallace, R. B. (1980) *Protection and Economic Development in Mexico* (Westmead: Gower).

Teubal, M. (1984) 'The Role of Technological Learning in the Exports of Manufactured Goods: The Case of Selected Capital Goods in Brazil', *World Development*, **12**, pp. 349–65.

Tybout, J. and Westbrook, D. (1995) 'Trade Liberalization and the Dimensions of Efficiency Change in Mexican Manufacturing Industries', *Journal of Internation Economics* **39** (1–2), pp. 53–79.

UAM-X (1997) *Survey: Relación proveedor – usuario y su impacto en la generación de capacidad tecnológica en México* (Mexico City: Universidad Autónoma Metropolitina-X).

Unger, K. (1985) *Competencia monopólica y tecnología en la industria mexicana* (Mexico City: El Colegio de México).

Unger, K. (1993) 'Productividad, desarrollo tecnológico y competitividad exportadora en la industria mexicana', in *Economía mexicana nueva epoca*, (Mexico City: CIDE).

Unger, K. (1994) *Ajuste estructural y estrategias empresariales en México. Las industrias petroquímica y de máquinas herramientas*, (Mexico City: CIDE).

USITC (1993) *Industry and Trade Summary: Glass Containers* (Washington, DC: US International Trade Commission).

Valdespino, G. and Vázquez-Mellado, O. (1995) *Diagnóstico de la cultura organizacional y la administración de la Tecnología: MACIMEX-Planta I* (Mexico City: CIT).

Valenti, G. and del Castillo, O. (1997) 'Interés público y educación superior: un enfoque de políticas públicas, in A. Mungaray and G. Valenti (eds), *Politicas públicas y educación superior* (Mexico City: ANUIES).

Valenti G. and Bazúa, F. (1993) 'Hacia un modelo alternativo de evaluación de los programas de posgrado en México', *Universidad Futura*, **4** (13), pp. 60–74.

Valenti, G., Varela, G. and Gonzales, R. (1996) *Los egresados de la UAM; una formación laboral de gran aceptación laboral*, (Mexico City: UAM).

Valenti G., Varela, G. and Gonzales, R. (1997) *Los egresados de la UAM en el mercado de trabajo. Investigación evaluativa sobre la calidad de la oferta de servicios educativos* (Mexico City: UAM).

Valenti, G. and Varela, G. (1997) 'Sistema de evaluación de las IES en México', *Revista Política y Cultura de la UAM-X*, **9**, pp. 131–47.

Varela, G. (1993) *Después del 68. Respuesta de la política educativa a la crisis universitaria*, (Mexico City: UNAM-Miguel Angel Porrima).

Vargas, N. (1995) *Diagnóstico de tecnología y cultura organizacional: Rines de Acero Kelsey Hayes* (Mexico City: CIT/CIESAS).

Velho, L. M. (1985) 'Science on the Periphery: A Study of the Agricultural Scientific Community in Brazilian Universities', doctoral thesis, SPRU, University of Sussex.

Vera-Cruz, A. (1998) 'The Brewing Industry', in S. Lall (ed.), *Science and Technology Policies in Developing and Transition Countries: Reform and Technological Co-operation with Europe*, (Brussels: DG-XII, European Union).

Vera-Cruz, J. A. (1999) 'The Impact of Changes in the Economic and Policy Context on Firms' Technological Behaviour: The Mexican Breweries', DPhil thesis, SPRU, University of Sussex.

Vessuri, H. (1993) 'Higher Education, Science and Engineering in Late 20th Century Latin America: Needs and Opportunities for Co-operation', *European Journal of Education*, **28** (1), pp. 49–59.

Villar Lever, L. (1996) 'Del aprendizaje escolar al ejercicio de la profesión. El caso de la Universidad Tecnológica de Aguascalientes', paper presented at the 'Congreso Latinoamericano de Sociología del Trabajo, São Paulo.

Villavicencio, D., Arvanitis, R. and Minsberg, L. (1995) 'Aprendizaje tecnológico en la industria quimica Mexicana', *Perfiles Latinamericanos* **4** (7), pp. 121–48.

Vithlani, H. (1996) *An Empirical Study of the UK Innovation System* (London: Department of Trade and Industry).

Vitro S. A. (1981–98) *Annual Report* (Monterrey: Vitro SA).

Von Hippel, E. (1988) *The Sources of Innovation*, (Oxford: Oxford University Press).

Voyer, R. (1998) 'Knowledge-Based Industrial Clustering: International Comparisons', in J. de la Mothe and G. Pacquet (eds), *Local and Regional Systems of Innovation* (Boston: Kluwer Publishers).

Wade, R. (1990) *Governing the Market: Economic Theory and the Role of Government in East Asian Industrialisation*, (Princeton, NJ: Princeton University Press).

Walker, W. (1993) 'National Innovation Systems: Britain', in R. Nelson (ed.), *National Innovation Systems. A Comparative Analysis*, (Oxford: Oxford University Press).

Walsh, V. (1984) 'Invention and Innovation in the Chemical Industry: Demand Pull or Discovery Push?', *Research Policy*, **13**, pp. 211–34.

Warman, F. and Thirlwall, P. (1994) 'Interest Rates, Saying, Investment and Growth in Mexico 1960–90? Test of the Financial Liberalization Hypothesis', *Journal of Development Studies*, **30** (3) pp. 629–49.

Winter, S. (1984) 'Shumpeterian Competition under Alternative Technological Regimes', *Journal of Economic Behaviour of Organizations*, **5**, pp. 287–320.

WIPO (1970) *Patent Cooperation Treaty* (Washington DC: WIPO).

World Bank (1986) *Mexico: Trade Policy, Industrial Performance and Adjustment* (Washington, DC: World Bank).

Yang, H. (1990) 'Survey Report: Republic of Korea', in *Biotechnology in Asia. Development Strategies and Potentials* (Tokyo: Asian Productivity Organization).

Zapata, F. (1994) *La Reestructuración industrial en México: El caso de la industria de las autopartes* (Mexico City: El Colegio de México).

Zysman, J. (1994) 'How Institutions Create Historically Rooted Trajectories of Growth', *Industrial and Corporate Change*, **3**, pp. 243–83.

Index

added value 58–60, 59, 63, 71
  sectoral patterns 60–1, 62
ADIAT AC 131
Aeronaves de México 43
Agrícola Batiz 184
agriculture 165
Aguascalientes 175, 262–75
  achievements 263
  advances in technological
      capabilities 274
  attraction of large foreign firms and need
      for specialized infrastructure 266–8
  attractions for MNEs 267
  and bridging institutions 271–2
  collaboration between large firms during
      transition period 268–9
  creation of basic infrastructure during ISI
      period 265–8
  creation of industrial park 266
  economy 262
  establishment of research centres 270–1,
      275
  and HEIs 271–2
  kaizen methodologies 268–9, 274
  and R&D 274
  state policy for technology
      development 270–1
  summary of situation after NAFTA 273
  transfer of technology through CIMO
      and consultants 272–3
  widening of export base 273–4
Argentina 38
Arteaga, A. and Micheli, J. 180
Arvanitis, R. and Villavicencio, D. 162
Asian NIEs 7–8, 9
automated machinery
  introduction of 180
automobile sector 162, 175, 182, 243–60
  acquisition of technology and
      equipment 250–1
  cluster of 259
  composition 243, 244

cumulativeness and improving
    performance 246–8, 260
current structure of Mexican 248–9
during ISI period 178–9, 254
exports 256
globalization of 245, 255–7, 258, 259
historical phases of Mexican 245–6
importance 243
institutional framework 254–5
linkages between steel and alloy sectors
    and 247, 260
and patenting 256–7
performance 244
and R&D 71, 249–50, 256, 257, 258, 260
regional competence and technological
    convergence 253–4
relationship with metrology centres 255
sources of knowledge 250–1, 260
specialization path 246, 255
structure of Mexican 248–9
technological learning strategies 252–3
training, skills and characteristics of
    human capital 251–2
user–producer relationships 248t–9,
    252–3
Autonomous Metropolitan University
    (UAM) 157

Baily, M. and Chakrabarti, A. 29
Bajío region 165
balance of payments 39, 42
Bancomext (Banco de Comercio
    Exterior) 112, 114, 115–16, 122, 127
banking system: nationalization 43
Bardhan, P. 8
Barro, R. 36
best practice technique 65
Bimbo 182, 183
biotechnology 210, 218–25
  appropriability conditions 222, 223–4
  categories of capabilities 218–19
  and cumulativeness 222, 224

and DBFs   211, 212, 223
and government   220
human resources for   220–2
impact   218
institutional framework and technological
    capabilities   218–22
knowledge base   222, 224–5
opportunities for innovation   222–3
and patenting   223
postgraduate programme for   220–1, 222
and universities   219
Blomstrom, M. and Wolf, E.   35
Brady, Nicholas J.   42
'brain drain phenomenon'   138
Brazil   36, 38
brewing industry   179
bridging institutions   113, 117–19, 122–3,
    185
and Aguascalientes   271–2
clients of   119
difficulty in evaluating performance
    of   118
and financial autonomy   118–19
functions   118
origins   109, 111
personnel employed by   119
private consultants as   119–20
Britain: education policies   138
Brodovsky, J.   210

Cadea Consultores   272–3
Calidad Integral y Modernización *see*
    CIMO
Calmecac   133
Calvo, G.   46
CANACINTRRA   268
Cananea   43
Capdevielle, M. *et al.*   27, 68
capital goods   64, 70
    increase in imports of after trade
        liberalization   50
capital intensity   90
Casar, J.   13
Casar, J. *et al.*   66
CCTC   132
CDIDT   131
CEDECE (Comisión Estatal de Desarrollo
    Económico y Comercio
    Exterior)   271, 275
CelQuim   199–201
Cementos Mexicanos (CEMEX)   183
Cemtec   183
CENAM (National Centre of
    Metrology)   118, 133
Centre for Optical Research *see* CIO

Centre for Research and Advanced Studies
    (CINVESTAV)   157
Centre for Technological Innovation
    (CIT)   164
Centro de Investigaciones Opticas *see* CIO
CEPAL   210
Certificados de Devolución de Impuestos
    (CEDIS)   37
Cetindustria   131
CFE   43
chemical industry   60, 175, 179, 182,
    189–205
    appropriability conditions   202
    cluster of companies in Mexican   198–
        204
    cumulativeness   202–3
    during ISI period   179
    and exports   194
    external linkages   197, 198, 203
    general characteristics of Mexican   192–
        5, 192
    lack of state intervention in   204
    learning capabilities in Mexican
        firms   195–7
    links with universities   162, 197
    and new products   195–6
    opportunity conditions   202
    overview of trends worldwide   190–2,
        193
    and patenting   195, 202, 215
    and R&D   179, 191, 193, 194–5, 196–7,
        202, 204
    share of GDP   192
    technology in   191
Chile   38
CIATEC   270, 271
Ciba-Geigy   221
CIEES   147, 148
CIMO (Calidad Integral y
    Modernización)   132, 272, 275
Cimoli, M. and Dosi, G.   9
CIO (Centro de Investigaciones
    Opticas)   270–1, 275
citation analysis   158
Claessens, S. *et al.*   42
Clavijo, F.   35
clinical medicine   158
Coe, D. *et al.*   52
Cohen, D.   38, 41
competitiveness, international   68–70
computer manufacturing firms   62
CONACYT (National Council for Science
    and Technology)   121, 125, 139, 147,
    158, 220
    see also SEP-CONACYT system centres
Conasupo   43

CONOCER (Council for Standardization and Certification of Labour Skills) 118, 120, 132
consultants
  and Aguascalientes 272–3
  private consultants as bridging institutions 119–20
corporate income tax 34
Council for Standardization and Certification of Labour Skills *see* CONOCER
cyber-networks 7

DBFs (dedicated biotechnology firms) 211, 212, 219, 223
debt crisis (1982) 32, 40, 41, 42, 53, 57
dedicated biotechnology firms *see* DBFs
Delphi–Juárez auto parts engineering centre 253–4, 257
Denmark 74
deregulation 32, 41, 43–5, 57, 83, 178
DINA 183
DNAP (DNA Plant technology Co.) 184
domestic capital goods industry 36, 37
Dosi, G. 23, 274
Dussel, P. 13

East Asia 3, 52, 226
economic growth, and productivity growth 23
economic performance
  and NIS 15–16
  and research 106
economy, Mexican 26–31, 32
  changes in production structure 26–7
  and debt crisis (1982) 32, 40, 41, 42, 53, 57
  growth 33, 57
  increase in openness 31, 62, 68, 83, 105, 110, 111, 278, 290
  instability of 26, 278
  macroeconomic indicators 27
economy, world 6–7
education 106, 142–4, 282
  enrolment 142–5, 150
  government expenditure on 140–1
  learning problems 143
  main objective 106
  policies in Britain 138
  and sectoral learning patterns 5
  weakness in ties between production system and 14
  see also HEIs; universities
Edwards, S. 51
Electrical Research Institute *see* IIE
electronics industry 3, 179

employment 60, 61, 63
  characteristics of 147–8
  sectoral patterns 62
Empresas La Moderna 183–4
engineering/engineers 146, 147, 148, 151, 157
Entrepreneurial Development Programme 116
Excellent Graduate Programmes Register 139–40
exchange rate 16, 33, 39
exports 45, 68
  and FF and NF 84, 85
  growth in 13, 31
  measures taken to remove anti-export bias 37–8

FDA (Food and Drug Administration) 207
FDI (foreign direct investment) 14, 18, 31, 89
  and chemistry industry 192–3
  importance of 86–8
  low contribution of to local technological activities 280
Federal Law of Metrology and Normalization (1992) 117
feedback mechanisms 10, 14
Ferronales 43
FF (foreign firm) 81, 83–8, 279
  examples of 81
  and fixed capital investment 89–91
  importance of 86
  international and domestic linkages 83–6
  and patenting 66, 93
  R&D activities and technology transfer 82, 88–9, 91–3
  sectoral analysis of global and localized technological flows 95–8
  technology embodied in equipment and intermediates 94–5
firms
  active role in innovation process 29
  disappearance of after trade liberalization 48, 177
  repositories for knowledge 29
  training profile 148–9
  types of and their historical paths 181–5
  see also individual firms
fishing, deregulation of 44
fixed capital investment 89–91
FOGAIN 126
Fondo de Equipamiento Industrial (FONEI) 37
Food and Drug Administration *see* FDA

food industry   182
footwear sector   180
Ford   247
foreign direct investment *see* FDI
foreign firms *see* FF
foreign technology   88–9, 287
FUNDAMECA   133
FUNDEC   131

gas industry   87
GATT   45, 124, 254
GDP   15, 39, 57, 83
General Import Tariff: Rule XIV   34, 37
General Motors   247
glass container industry   175
  exports   228
  history of Mexican   228
  institutional framework   230
  market trends   227–9
  and R&D   230, 234–5
  technological trends   229–30
  see also Vitro Envases
globalization   12, 18–19, 31, 81–98, 278,
    279–80, 283, 285, 290
  and ascent of knowledge-based
      economies   6
  and FDI *see* FDI
  growth in   13–14
  'optimal cycle' of   28
  of research   7, 28
  see also FF
Gonsen, R.   218–19, 219–20
Gould, B.G.   160
Greenaway, D. *et al*   51
Grupo Bimbo *see* Bimbo
Grupo de Industriales de
    Aguascalientes   268, 269, 271, 272, 274
Grupo Maseca *see* Maseca
Grupo Pulsar *see* Pulsar

Harrison, A. and Hanson, G.   51
HEIs (higher education institutions)   137,
    138, 139, 149, 150
  and Aguascalientes   271–2
  characteristics of   140
  collaboration with industry *see*
      university–industry collaboration
  completion rates   145–6
  enrolment   142, 144–5, 150
  evaluation mechanisms   147
  financing of by government   139–40,
    140–1
  number of graduates   146
  problems of   147
  and R&D   156–7, 282
Helpman, E.   52

Hertog, P. *et al.*   118
high-tech goods   95
higher education institutions *see* HEIs
Higher Education Modernization
    Fund   140
Hirschman, A.   283
HRST (human resources in science and
    technology)   106, 137–51, 285
  educational enrolment   142–5, 150
  employment conditions and
      salaries   147–8
  firms' training profile   148–9
  government expenditure on
      education   140–1
  and governmental policies   139–40
  indicators   143
  linkages with NIS   138–9
  main actors in development of
      competencies   137, 149
  stock between 1985 and 1995   146–7
human resources
  and biotechnology   220–2
  and science and technology *see* HRST
Hylsa   182, 183

Ibarra, L.A.   36, 38–9
ICI   221
IIE (Electrical Research Institute)   110,
    128
IMDT   132
IMF: implementation of stabilization
    programme   39–40
Immediate Programme for Economic
    Reorganization (PIRE)   42
IMNC   132
IMP (Mexican Institute for
    Petroleum)   110, 129
IMPI (Mexican Institute of Intellectual
    Property Rights)   118, 133
import substitution industrialization *see* ISI
imports   13, 31, 40–1, 45, 50, 68, 94
  criteria for permission for   33
  growth of intermediate and capital goods
      after liberalization   50
  of machinery   50
  and NF and FF   84–5
IMTA (Mexican Institute on Water
    Technology)   110, 128
incentives   104, 114
  provision of by institutions   114–16, 121
income, unequal distribution of   37
Index of Modernization Efforts   180–1
industrial sectors *see* sectoral patterns
industrialization
  instruments to promote   33–4
  and technological capabilities   176–8

industry: collaboration with universities *see*
    university–industry collaboration
inflation
    control of by trade liberalization 45
    rise in 39, 40, 41, 53
information
    provision of by institutions 117, 131–3
ININ (National Institute for Nuclear
    Research) 110, 129
Institute for Scientific Information
    (ISI) 157
institutions 8–9, 16–17, 19, 77, 103–7,
    280–1
    bridging *see* bridging institutions
    concept of and role in NIS 103–5
    functional matrix of institutions
        supporting innovation 114–16
    historical evolution of supporting
        innovation 110–11
    and modernization 111–13, 122
    and production system 175–85
    providing of incentives 114–16, 121
    specialized 116–20, 123, 128–9
    supporting human resources 106
    supporting innovations 105–6, 109–35,
        125–7
    supporting knowledge production 106–7
    types of in Mexico 17
Instituto Mexicano de Comercio Exterior
    (IMCE) 37
Instituto Technológico de Celaya 164
Intellectual Property Protection Law 213
intellectual property rights *see* IPRs
Interinstitutional Committees for
    Evaluating Higher Education 147
Interministrial Committee for Public Sector
    Imports 34
internationalization 1, 6, 68–70
inventor certificate programme and
    biotechnology 223–4
investment 24, 26, 28–30, 38–9, 49, 53
    and abundance of financial
        resources 38, 39
    contrast between 1970s and 1980s 38
    decrease in 70
    effect of trade liberalization on 45–7
    enhancement of private by public 35–6
    fixed capital 89–91
    foreign direct *see* FDI
    reduction in new capital assets 57
    stimulation of by ISI period 35–6
IPN (National Polytechnic Institute) 157,
    160, 162
IPRs (intellectual property rights) 124,
    134–5
ISI (import substitution industrialization)

period 33–7, 43, 52–3, 57, 88, 109, 176,
    228, 285, 287
abandonment of 37–40
advantages and disadvantages 36–7
Aguascalientes 265–8
characteristics 32
and innovation process 35–7
and institutions 111
instruments in promoting 33–5
and productivity 35
sectoral patterns 70
stimulation of investment 35–6
technological capabilities during 176–7
Italy 119

just-in-time systems 253

Keller, W. 51
Kessel, G. and Samaniego, R. 47, 48
knowledge 29
    importance of to economic
        development 6–7
    institutions supporting production
        of 106–7
    internal and external sources 73–4, 76
    use of university by firms 162–3
    utilization of 31
knowledge-based economies 6–7
knowledge flows 74–5, 75–6, 76, 88, 118,
    283
Korea 36, 138

labour productivity 35, 63–4, 91
large domestic firms 181–3
Latin America 7, 9, 16, 38
Law of Foreign Investments 111
Law of Inventions and Trademarks 208
Law of Promotion of New and Necessary
    Industries 34
Law for the Promotion and Protection of
    Industrial Property (1991) 215
Life Sciences Research Centre of
    Monsanto 221
Luna, M. and Valdivieso, S. 47, 48

Madrid, Miguel de la 43
maquiladora industry 27, 68, 70, 95, 97,
    180, 181, 254, 273, 284
Maseca 182, 183
Metcalfe, S. 8
Mexican innovation system *see* Mexican
    NIS
Mexican Institute of Intellectual Property
    Rights *see* IMPI
Mexican Institute for Petroleum *see* IMP
Mexican Institute of Social Security 207–8

Mexican Institute on Water Technology *see*
  IMTA
Mexican Investment Council   111
Mexican NIS   12–20
  consequences of forging ahead, catching
    up and falling behind   287–90
  and institutional dimension   16–17
  integrative model   15
  levels of analysis and main building
    blocks in   17–20
  technological capabilities   15–16
  temporal dimension and phases of
    history   13–15
Mexicana de Aviación   43
mining, and deregulation   44
MNEs (multinational enterprises)   13, 26,
  28, 31, 72, 278
  and FDI   86, 280
  historical technological pattern   181
  and research   88
  Southeast Asian   7
  subsidiaries of   27, 28, 177
  technological alliances with large local
    firms   182, 183
Modelo Brewery   182
modernization process
  main characteristics   181
  and technological capabilities   178–81
Monsanto   184
Monterrey Technological Institute   160
multinational enterprises *see* MNEs

NAFIN (Nacional Financiera)   111–12,
  114–15, 122, 266
NAFTA (North American Free Trade
    Agreement)   1, 105, 110, 134, 135, 159,
    178, 181, 194, 228, 236, 254
National Autonomous University of Mexico
    see UNAM
National Commission for Higher
    Education   147
National Commission for
    Normalization   255
National Council for Science and
    Technology *see* CONACYT
national firms *see* NF
national innovation system *see* NIS
National Institute for Nuclear Research *see*
    ININ
National Organization for
    Standardization   255
National Plan for Modernization and
    Foreign Trade (1990–94)   112
National Polytechnic Institute *see* IPN
National Research System   139
National System of Researchers *see* SNI

National University of Mexico   213
nationalization   43
Nelson, R.   11, 53, 105
Nelson, R. and Rosenberg, N.   264
networks   7, 282–5
new industrialized economies (NIEs)   2–3,
  7, 9
NF (national firm)   81, 279
  and fixed capital investment   89–91
  international and domestic linkages   83–
    6
  R&D activities and technology
    transfer   89, 91–3
  sectoral analysis of global and localized
    technological flows   95–8
  technology embodied in equipment and
    intermediates   94–5
NIS (national innovation system)   11
  concept of   2
  and economic performance   15–16
  main building blocks and linkages   7–12
  policy-oriented definition   8
  suppositions required for analysis of
    performance   23–5
Nissan   268
non-oil exports   116, 122
NORMEX   132
North American Free Trade Agreement *see*
    NAFTA
Nueva Fanal   229, 230

OECD   134
oil prices
  fall in   42, 45
  increase in   38
oil reserves   39–40
organizations   17, 104, 111, 112
Owens-Illinois   232, 234, 235–6, 237

Pacific Rim NIEs   7, 8
PACIME (Program to Support
    Science)   158
PACTOS   45
patenting   66–8, 92–3, 134, 166
  and automobile sector   256–7
  and biotechnology   223
  and chemical industry   195, 202, 215
  and foreign firms   66, 93
  growth of non-resident   67, 134–5
  international   65
  and IPRs   134, 135
  and pharmaceutical industry   136, 208–9
  sectors for   135
  and Vitro Envases   235
Pavitt taxonomy   4, 25, 30, 58, 62, 82
Pegado   201

PEMEX   43, 135, 192, 204
Peres   208
peso   43, 43
petrochemical industry   44, 87, 135, 192
PETROPROD   201–2
pharmaceutical industry 178, 206–17, 221
   appropriability conditions   215–16
   characteristics and performance   206–7
   contracts with foreign firms   212
   cumulativeness   216
   external linkages   210, 211
   government measures affecting
      innovation activities   207–8
   and institutional framework   211–13
   interfirm relationships   211–12
   knowledge base   216–17
   links with universities   162, 212–13, 214
   manufacturing of medicaments   209
   and marketing   210
   non-scientific nature of   214
   opportunities for innovation   214–15
   and patenting   136, 208–9
   and R&D   209–10, 214, 216, 217
   technological capabilities and
      institutional specificities   209–10
   types of firms   213–14
PIEBT   125
Portillo, López   40
PREAEM   126–7
privatization   32, 43, 105, 109, 110
producer–user relationships *see* user-
      producer relationships
productivity   23–5, 28–9
   and economic growth   23
   and foreign R&D   52
   growth in   23, 35
   impact of trade liberalization on   47–52
   and innovation   29, 32
   inter-industry gaps in   66, 77
   international gaps in   64–6
   and ISI period   35
   labour   63–4
   link with innovation   23–4
   reasons for fostering of by increased
      openness of economy   49–51
   and sectoral patterns   149
Promotional Centre for Design   131
PRONAFICE   45
public expenditure   33, 53
   growth in   38, 39, 40
Pulsar   183, 184

quality control   180
Quintero, R.   220

R&D (research and development)   5, 28,
      284, 285

and Aguascalientes   274
and automobile sector   71, 249–50, 256,
      257, 258, 260
and chemical industry   179, 191, 193,
      194–5, 196–7, 202, 204
foreign   47, 51–2
and foreign and national firms   82, 88–9,
      91–3, 96, 97
and glass container industry   230, 234–5
globalization of   7, 28
government expenditure on   141, 142,
      156
and HEIs   156–7, 282
and innovative output   6
internationalization of   280
and large local firms   182
and patenting   67
personnel employed in   142, 143, 150,
      157
and pharmaceutical industry   209–10,
      214, 216, 217
poorness of Mexican efforts   279
relationship between research and
      economic performance   106–7
sectoral expenditure on   67, 71–3
and SEP-CONACYT *see* SEP-
      CONACYT system centres
spillovers of investment from one country
      to another   51–2
and university–industry
      collaboration   159–60, 161, 162, 164,
      165
Ramirez, M.   35, 38–9
regional clusters   263–5
regional innovation system (RIS)   263
regions
   importance of in innovation
      activities   262
   role of in innovation   263–4
   see also Aguascalientes
Registry of Excellent Graduate
      Programmes   147
relative wages   70–1
research and development *see* R&D
road transport: effect of deregulation
      on   43–4
Rodrik, D.   46
Ross   35
Rule XIV *see* General Import Tariff

Salinas, Carlos   43
Samaniego, R.   35
SB (science-based) sector   30, 77, 82, 279,
      281
   added value and employment   60–1
   characteristics of   4, 5, 25

and FF and NF 83–6
growth of productivity in United
    States 65
and knowledge flows 74
labour and total factor productivity 63,
    64
and patents 67
production structure 62
and productivity 149
and R&D 5, 71
and R&D activities in NF and FF 91–3
and technological flows 97
scale-intensive sector *see* SI sector
science competencies evolution and trends
    of 155–8
science graduates 151
science and technology (S&T) 155–6, 178,
    185
    and chemical industry 191
    evolution and current trends 155–6
    government expenditure 142, 155, 156
science-based sector *see* SB sector
scientific journals 158
scientists 148
SD (supplier-dominated) sector 4, 5, 30,
    63, 77, 82
    added value and employment 60, 61
    characteristics 25
    and FF and NF 83–6
    and fixed capital investment 89
    and knowledge flows 74–5
    and patenting 67
    productivity 65
    and technological flows 97
    and wages 70–1
SECOFI Fideicomisos Privados 125
SECOFI (Ministry of Trade and Industrial
    Promotion) 122, 125, 207
sectoral innovation system (SIS) 19
sectoral patterns 60–1, 70–5, 279
    analysis of global and localized
        technological flows 95–8
    education profiles of employees 149
    and educaton system 5
    embodied technology 70
    and employment 62
    expenditure on R&D 67, 71–3
    international and domestic linkages in FF
        and NF 83–6
    knowledge sources 73–4
    and Pavitt's taxonomy 4, 25, 30, 58, 82
    and production structure 61–3
    and production system 30–1
    and productivity 149
    R&D activities and technology transfer in
        NF and FF 91–4

and relative wages 70–1
user–producer relationships 74–5
Seminis 184
SEP-CONACYT system centres 109, 117,
    124, 120–2, 130, 158, 270, 275
SI (scale-intensive) sector 4, 5, 25, 77, 82,
    279
    added value and employment 60, 61, 64
    and capital intensity 90
    and FF and NF 83–6
    and fixed capital investment 89
    high capital intensity 70
    and knowledge flows 74–5
    labour productivity 63
    and patenting 67
    and productivity 65, 149
    R&D activities and technology transfer in
        NF and FF 91–3
    and technological flows 97
Sivesa 229, 230
small firms, and productivity 48–9
SMEs 17, 111, 112, 114–15, 116, 117, 122,
    194, 198, 204
SNI (National System of
    Researchers) 156, 157
Solow, R.M. 23
specialization 14, 76–7, 97, 180
SS (specialized supplier) sector 4, 5, 25,
    30, 82, 279
    added value and employment 60, 61, 62,
        77
    and capital intensity 90
    and FF and NF 83–6
    and knowledge flows 74
    and R&D 71
    R&D activities and technology transfer in
        NF and FF 91–3
    and technological flows 97
    and technological knowledge 75
Stabilization Programme (1985) 42, 45
supplier-dominated sector *see* SD sector
Survey on Employment, Salaries,
    Technologies and Training in the
    Manufacturing Sector
    (ENESTYC) 148–9

Taiwan 291
tax system 34, 35, 39
technological capabilities 11, 15–16, 24–5,
    75
    and development process 2–7
    distinction between production capacity
        and 3
    and industrialization 176–8
    institutions supporting 185

knowledge accessibility and local
    absorption   6–7
and modernization process   178–81
and NIEs   2–3
and performances   10–11
and production system   285–7
and productivity   24
reasons for gaps between countries   11–
    12
technological information, transfer of   25–6
Technological and Organizational Change
    Survey (ENACTO)   148
technological universities   140, 145
technology
    embodied in equipment and
        intermediates   94–5
    expenditure on   49
    foreign sources   88–9
    transfer of   31, 91–3, 96, 285
telecommunications, deregulation of   44
Telmex   43, 44
Ten Kate, A. and De Mateo, F.   49
tequila crisis (1994)   73
textile industry   180
total factor productivity (TFP)   63
trade
    intra-industry   68, 72
    table of international   69
trade liberalization   13–14, 41, 45–7, 83, 88,
    105, 110, 282–3, 290
    benefits to innovation   53–4
    impact on productivity   47–52
    and investment   45–7
trucking industry   44
Turkey   142
Tybout, J. and Westbrook, D.   47–8, 49

UNAM (National Autonomous University
    of Mexico)   155, 157, 158, 160, 162,
    164
United States   62, 65
    and added value   59–60, 61
    automobile industry   257
    and biotechnology   221
    chemical industry   190
    and FDA   207, 208
    and FDI   87
    and glass container industry   228
    and patenting   68
    R&D expenditure   71, 72
    wages   70
universities   285, 291
    and biotechnology   219
    collaboration with industry *see*

university–industry collaboration
and DFBs   219
enrolment   144, 145
and glass container industry   230
impact of financial restrictions   139
importance to innovation process   154
personnel devoted to R&D in   143
and research   106
and science and technology   155
source of technological knowledge   74
see also HEIs
University of Guadalajara   160, 166
university–industry collaboration   107, 145,
    148, 154–5, 159–70, 282
building of networks   165, 167
chemical industry   162, 197
diversity of initiatives and variety of
    objectives   164
factors contributing to growth of   159
financial resources   160–1
formal and informal   163
funding for   167
intensity of use of university knowledge
    by firms   162–3
obstacles to and problems   166, 170
organizational structures   160
and pharmaceutical industry   162,
    212–13, 214
quantity of projects   161
and R&D   159–60, 161, 162, 164, 165
regional dimension   163, 165, 169
taxonomy and characteristics of   166–9,
    170
transfer of knowledge   164–5, 169–70
user–producer relationships   74–5, 94
    and automobile sector   248–9, 252–3
UTT   131

Visa-Femsa   182, 183
Vitro Envases   227, 229, 230, 231–9
agreement with Owens-Illinois   235–6,
    237
building of minimum knowledge base
    (1909–70)   233–4
linkages   240
and patenting   235
profile   231–2
and R&D   237, 238, 239, 240
sales and exports   231–2
strategic capabilities difficulties   232–3,
    240
strengthening fast follower strategy and
    changing the direction of
    accumulation   237–8

technologically independent
    strategy   234–5, 238–9
transition process towards building
    strategic capabilities   234
and turbulence of (1990s)   236

Vitro SA   182, 227, 228, 230, 231, 236

wages, relative   70–1
Walsh, V.   4
Warman, F. and Thirlwall, P.   38